National Geographic
ATLAS OF
WORLD HISTORY

The compass rose, used to indicate direction
on navigation charts and maps for earth, sea, and sky, evokes
the age of exploration and the spirit of discovery.

National Geographic
ATLAS OF
WORLD

Noel Grove

Prepared by
The Book Division
National Geographic Society
Washington, D.C.

HISTORY

Broken skull from South Africa and a lightning bolt *(preceding pages)* suggest the spark of intelligence that would someday create such cities as Hong Kong *(above)*.

Contents

Foreword

This *Atlas of World History,* by describing the intersection of Time and Space, the two dimensions of history, helps give us the bearings we most need today. Technology and culture in many parts of the modern world have led us to underestimate, or discount, the significance of chronology and geography. Our accelerated economy of constant invention, seasonal models, fast foods, and instant communications, with atomic subdivisions of time into the nano-second (one-billionth of a second), has dulled our sense of how long epochs, centuries, and millennia have shaped human experience. And the wholesale grouping of historical events by sociologists and ideologues has blurred our sense of the power of individuals and events. Meanwhile, the airplane and electronic communications have dimmed our vision of the shaping power of continents, mountains, oceans, and climates. This book, we hope, will help reawaken us to the significance of all these dimensions in our long human past.

Here, also, is an invitation to discover both the mystery and the miracle of human experience on our planet. "Atlas," as a word for a collection of maps, entered the English language in 1636 with the publication of Mercator's epoch-making *Geographic Description of the World* (by Gerard Mercator and John Hondt). On the frontispiece of that book the strong man Atlas is shown supporting the heavens. The Greeks imagined that Atlas, one of the primeval Titans, was sentenced, as punishment for his part in a revolt against the gods, to support the heavens with his head and his hands. So he became a favorite folk explanation of why the sky does not fall. Once, when Atlas was not hospitable to Perseus, son of Zeus, Perseus used the Gorgon's head to turn Atlas into stone. Incidentally, this explained the origin of the Atlas Mountains in North Africa.

Whenever we consult an atlas, then, we should be wary of seeming too wise about the large causes in history and geography. If we no longer need Atlas to help us understand how the heavens are supported, we still need the Greek sense of wonder to grasp the mystery of time and space, of history and geography, in the human chronicle. If we sharpen our senses of chronology and geography, we will be reawakened, also, to the uncanny power of the human race to overcome these limits. And so be cautious of prediction.

One chastening lesson of this atlas is that there is no proportion in history. We cannot measure or predict the significance of places or peoples by the dimensions of space or time. We dare not underestimate the power of an individual or of a tiny community. This enticing mystery is dramatized for us by the human miracles recounted and depicted in the *Atlas of World History.* The Athenian polis in some two centuries of the classical age of Socrates (b. 469 B.C.), Plato, and Aristotle (d. 322 B.C.) probably held less than 100,000 people but would provide the vocabulary of philosophy for the Western millennia. The life and teachings of a Galilean Jew who died before the age of 35 and left no writing would dominate Western history. Then the visions and prophecies of an orphaned inspired camel-driver would compete for the loyalties of peoples of the Middle East and Asia into modern times. And the ideology of a 19th-century

Temple at Segesta, in Sicily, stands as testimony to the spread of Hellenism when the Greeks traveled westward, taking with them high standards of art and architecture.

German philosopher-journalist in three ponderous volumes would incite and justify revolutions across Europe and Asia.

We find no hint of the destined roles of Portugal and the Netherlands in the chronicle of empires and of science when we look at their narrow dimensions on the map of Europe. The flourishing culture of a vast and ancient China long remained a world to itself. Yet the outreaching power of Jerusalem and Rome, of Paris and New York City attest the power of urban institutions to reach out to the world.

And the power of large ideas—of a Ptolemy, a Copernicus, a Newton, an Einstein—over continents and generations has been beyond imagining.

The moon landing and explorations of space in the 20th century reveal that the Age of Discovery, which opened in the West in the late 15th century, had no end. Yet some world-transforming events have been sparked in surprisingly brief compass. Two centuries of Italian culture in the Renaissance left a legacy to the West hardly equaled by all the earlier millennia of North American culture. And the Protestant Reformation in the West delivered its impact within two centuries.

Just as there is no proportion in history, no usual relation between the size of communities and their impact on the world, so there is no "normal" pace of change in human experience. Every event and every technology carries its own rate and reach of influence. While movable type and the printing press quickly facilitated the spread of information and misinformation and brought the world together, they also fostered national languages that separated some people from others, feeding the forces of chauvinism and belligerence.

Even today, after centuries of the printed word, much of the world remains inaccessible to books, and the people of some advanced countries remain semi-literate. The great transformation in human economy, the industrial revolution that shook western Europe within two centuries, still leaves much of the world untouched. The unpredictable influence of the world's great religions is revealed in this *Atlas,* but their permeating influence on politics, culture, and the arts remains immeasurable.

This *Atlas* is a story, then, not only of the accelerating power of science and technology and progress, but also of the influence of ignorance on cultures and the relations between them. Why did the American continents remain so long unknown and "undiscovered" by the peoples of Europe? And what were the consequences of

European merchants and explorers Marco Polo and his family traversed the East with a caravan of trade goods. Their caravan, painted on the wooden panels of a 14th-century atlas, is shown crossing the Asian mountains *(below).* Today 20th-century humans explore regions as exotic to them as China was to the Polos. Russian space station *Mir (opposite),* whose name means "peace," has been a laboratory not only for joint scientific advances but also for peace between spacefaring Russia and the United States.

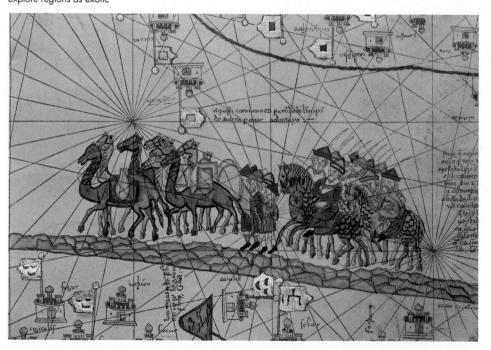

this ignorance? And of its epochal removal after the 15th century? What were the consequences for the Chinese people of their long isolation from the West? And the consequences for the West of its long-delayed discovery of Asian cultures? And what does all this tell us of the inquiring human spirit? This *Atlas* gives us some basis for reflection.

To encompass world history here has, of course, required selection, compression, and abridgment—the human experience painted with a broad brush. This in turn invites our caution and our awakened curiosity. For each of us, this *Atlas* should be only a prologue to further exploration in maps, and in our rich literature of geography, history, and biography. So, our reach for history can help prepare us too for the unexpected.

Daniel J. Boorstin

Librarian of Congress Emeritus
Former Director of the National Museum of History and
Technology, and Senior Historian of the Smithsonian
Institution, Washington, D.C.

About This Book

The story lines of history, like the warp and woof of an intricately woven tapestry, intertwine with a multiplicity of colors and textures, in designs that only a master weaver could have created. This *Atlas of World History* clearly portrays these interwoven threads of the human story, the layers upon layers of life, beginning even before hominids became fully human. The tapestry grows more complex with the rise and development of many civilizations, civilizations that often came into being simultaneously around the world. Ultimately, this compilation of history shows the growing interdependence of the human community as a global village.

Because so much of history was occurring at the same time, a strictly chronological presentation would have appeared to be a jumble of information. In this book, therefore, you will find layerings, overlappings, interweavings; but always the carefully crafted text ties the facts and interrelationships of simultaneous events together.

The book is divided into six chapters, each focusing on a separate era, beginning with a map of the world that highlights selected historical events; the map for Chapter Six is the only one in this series that shows present-day boundaries of nations. Additional maps in each chapter amplify the text visually and give more information on such subjects as early settlements, the spread of empires, major battles and wars, and routes of global exploration.

For each chapter, an introductory essay brings synthesis to the seemingly loose threads of the era, giving the reader a framework for the diversity of information in the fact-filled text. Moving on into the heart of a chapter, each section focuses on a time period, a civilization, or a theme.

Certain thematic or universal subjects that did not fit neatly into a time period have been treated separately. For example, Chapter Five, covering a two-hundred-year period of ever quickening change, contains several theme sections, including "Revolutions in the Arts" and "New Weapons and Strategies of War." Providing an overview of history, time lines run throughout the book to highlight some of the salient personages, events, and historical movements of the period treated in the text. Fact boxes bring various subjects, such as capsule biographies and fascinating historical tidbits, into tighter focus.

The abundant illustrations, photographs, and artwork of rare clarity and depth are designed to enhance the reader's understanding and aesthetic enjoyment of history. As such, they are essential components of this illustrated history of the world. Ready-reference materials make up the Appendix, which includes charts of emperors, kings, popes, presidents, and prime ministers. The additional reading list and comprehensive index round out the *National Geographic Atlas of World History*, a work that weaves the fabric of human history into one life-enriching volume.

Martha Crawford Christian

Editor, *Atlas of World History*

Lorenzo the Magnificent leads mounted kinfolk of the Medici family, patrons of Florentine art, in a 15th-century fresco.

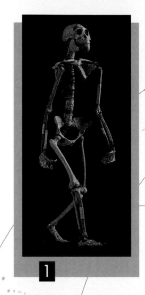

1

7

4

2

ca 1200 B.C.
The Olmec culture emerges in Mexico.

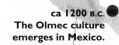

6

10

AROUND THE WORLD

1 Africa: Striding toward humanity, *A. afarensis* walked upright, according to the silent testimony of skeletal remains. Later hominids wandered far, peopling the earth.

2 Australia: This ancient art was found at an Aboriginal sacred site in Australia's northern Kimberley region.

3 Asia: At Ur a 70-foot-high three-tiered temple called a ziggurat was built of sun-baked bricks. At its summit was a statue of the moon god, Nanna, which was washed, fed, and clothed by priests.

4 Europe: The most famous megalith, Stonehenge in southern England, started as a circular ditch, its stone arrangements evolving over 1,500 years to have both solar and lunar alignments.

The Ancient World

ca 3000 B.C.
**Building of
Stonehenge begins.**

ca 1450 B.C.
**Mycenaeans dominate
sea trade routes.**

ca 2000 B.C.
**In Crete, Minoans erect
a palace at Knossos.**

ca 5000 B.C.
**The Sumerian civilization
forms in Mesopotamia.**

ca 2550 B.C.
**Construction of
the Great Pyramid
is completed in Egypt.**

ca 1270 B.C.
**Moses leads Israelites from
Egypt to Canaan.**

ca 6000 B.C.
**Farming develops in the
fertile Indus Valley.**

ca 1500 B.C.
**Bronze and jade objects
are created during
the Shang dynasty.**

ca 750 B.C.
**The African Kingdom
of Kush conquers
Egypt.**

5 Africa: Pharaoh Ramses II's wife Nefertari lives immortalized in art. A tomb inscription praised the graceful queen: "Possessor of charm, sweetness, and love."

6 North America: A stone head weighing several tons perhaps represents an honored leader of the ancient Olmec civilization.

7 North America: The Olmec planted corn as early as 2250 B.C. Women stripped away the dry kernels by rubbing the cobs together and then ground them on a stone grinder. Dough was moistened and flattened into thin disks, then baked over a fire.

8 Asia: In this Hindu painting cowherds and maidens cheer their hero, Lord Krishna, from the banks, as serpent nymphs plead for mercy. Krishna is punishing a many-headed serpent king for poisoning a river.

9 Asia: Deadly rendering, a fierce face glares from an ax blade found in a Shang tomb along with 48 victims. Its fine bronze craftsmanship serves as a reminder of the Shang practice of human sacrifice.

10 Europe: From the Minoans, Europe's first advanced civilization, has come the legend of Theseus defeating the bull-man, Minotaur, depicted here on a vase dating to the sixth century B.C.

The Emergence of Culture: Early Man to 500 B.C.

To someone who has grown up with computers and space travel, the dawn of humanity might seem to yawn across an unfathomable gap. Yet the distance between walking upright and walking on the moon is not as far as it might seem. If the entire history of the earth—some 4.6 billion years—were represented by an average-size man stretching his arms overhead, the length of time that humans have lived on the planet would occupy the outer edge of a fingernail. Within that short space, the portion marking the years in which they have had significantly different lives from those of the animals around them would be even smaller.

For millions of years humans and their primitive predecessors were concerned with little more than survival, taking food and shelter where they could, constructing only the most basic tools. The challenges of an ever changing environment might have been the spark that ignited intellect. For two million years the Ice Age gripped the earth, and the expanding and contracting ice caps affected weather. Glaciers more than a mile thick at times covered much of the Northern Hemisphere and made rain forests drier in the tropics. In warmer periods additional rainfall made arid savannas flourish. These variations demanded resourcefulness.

People near the ice could survive only by using fire and extra covering. Wearing the skins of animals to keep warm required being able to sew. Sewing meant fashioning bone needles to poke holes in the hides through which threads could be passed. The spear-thrower was developed so that the spear could be thrown a longer distance. The bow and arrow appeared in southern and eastern Africa some 20,000 years ago. Caves sometimes were not available in areas of ample food supply, so shelters had to be constructed. Huts built from the bones of elephantlike mammoths and covered with animal skins may have lasted for years.

As their cleverness made them more comfortable, people began turning to diversions such as art and music. Both a flute made of bird bone and the head of a woman carved in ivory have been dated back 25,000 years. Carvings, more decorative than functional, began appearing on weapons and tools. Cave paintings proliferated on rock walls as hunters described their relationships with animals and perhaps tried to ensure their success in capturing them. People buried useful objects with their dead, suggesting the growth of religion and belief in an afterlife.

Gradually, a great scattering of humanity took place. The lowering of the seas during the Ice Age may have opened land bridges to continents now separated by oceans, and migrants drifted into North America and Australia. By 10,000 B.C. people lived on every continent except Antarctica. As the Ice Age diminished and the glaciers melted, vast forests grew over previously open spaces, making game more difficult to find. The large herbivores, such as mastodons, that could feed a group of people for weeks began to disappear. Instead of following roving herds, people began settling in one place and exploiting the food around them. By creating crude boats, nets, and hooks, they took food from the water, which meant using repeatedly those harbors that were safe from storms. More permanent homes were built there, and communities took shape.

The growth of communities accelerated when the first farmers began growing their own food instead of simply gathering produce from wild plants. Domestication of animals probably began with dogs but later included herbivores, which released people from hunting wild game. The extra time at home allowed them to turn their energies toward creating more things. Houses became more permanent and more comfortable. Monuments to gods were built even more substantially than houses, and many endure today as windows on that dim past. Communities became larger and the first towns appeared, then grew into cities.

Citizens in clustered dwellings needed such goods as baskets and clothing, so specialized tradesmen learned skills they could barter for food; later they would sell their skills for money to buy food. Life in permanent communities seems to have led to an explosion of technology. Plows, spun pottery, sailing vessels, and the first metal instruments appeared almost simultaneously. The wheel allowed the quick movement of heavy burdens. Planning became important for successful harvests, which gave rise to calendars. Communities needed organization, so governments and leaders gained importance by making rules and settling disputes.

Actual history—as opposed to prehistory—starts with the first system of writing, which began in the Middle East about 5,000 years ago. Trade may have sparked the need for lettering, to keep track of who made transactions and in what amounts. So important was writing to civilizations that it appeared independently at far-flung locations in ancient Mesopotamia, China, and Central America.

Historians can be grateful that the first writing was done on materials durable through the ages—baked clay, bone, and stone. Thousands of texts still readable give modern scholars glimpses into life in those earliest settlements. Deciphering them can be difficult, especially if the method of writing is no longer used. The ability to read ancient Egyptian hieroglyphics was given a huge boost with the discovery of the Rosetta Stone, found when Napoleon's army invaded Egypt. The key to reading the hieroglyphics on the stone lay in the other two languages the text was also rendered in: an early Egyptian script and Greek.

The ability to provide ample food caused an increase in the population of humans. Allegiances broadened. Humans found their loyalties extending beyond family and tribe to entire communities that commanded surrounding countryside. Conflicts sprang up as ownership of the most productive areas and the treasures accumulated within them were coveted. Strong rulers raised armies and made conquests that were often devastating, but through the conflicts ideas and customs also spread to areas beyond their origins.

Not everyone became a part of what we call civilization. The nomadic way of life continued in many parts of the world and still exists in scattered pockets today. But during the Ice Age and for long periods afterward, civilization took root. Humans, who had long lived at the mercy of the elements and powerful carnivores, had set themselves on an inventive path that has continued for centuries. ■

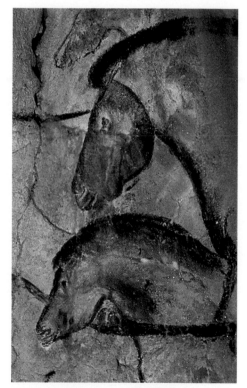

Art rears its head from the dim past at Chauvet cave in southeastern France, where horses painted on the walls were radiocarbon-dated as being more than 30,000 years old. Sophisticated depictions of predators and prey in the earliest known art here startle researchers.

Overleaf:
A mixed herd adorns the Reindeer Panel in Chauvet cave. Amid reindeer can be seen a long-horned aurochs—an extinct wild ox and ancestor to modern-day cattle—and the crude head of a horse.

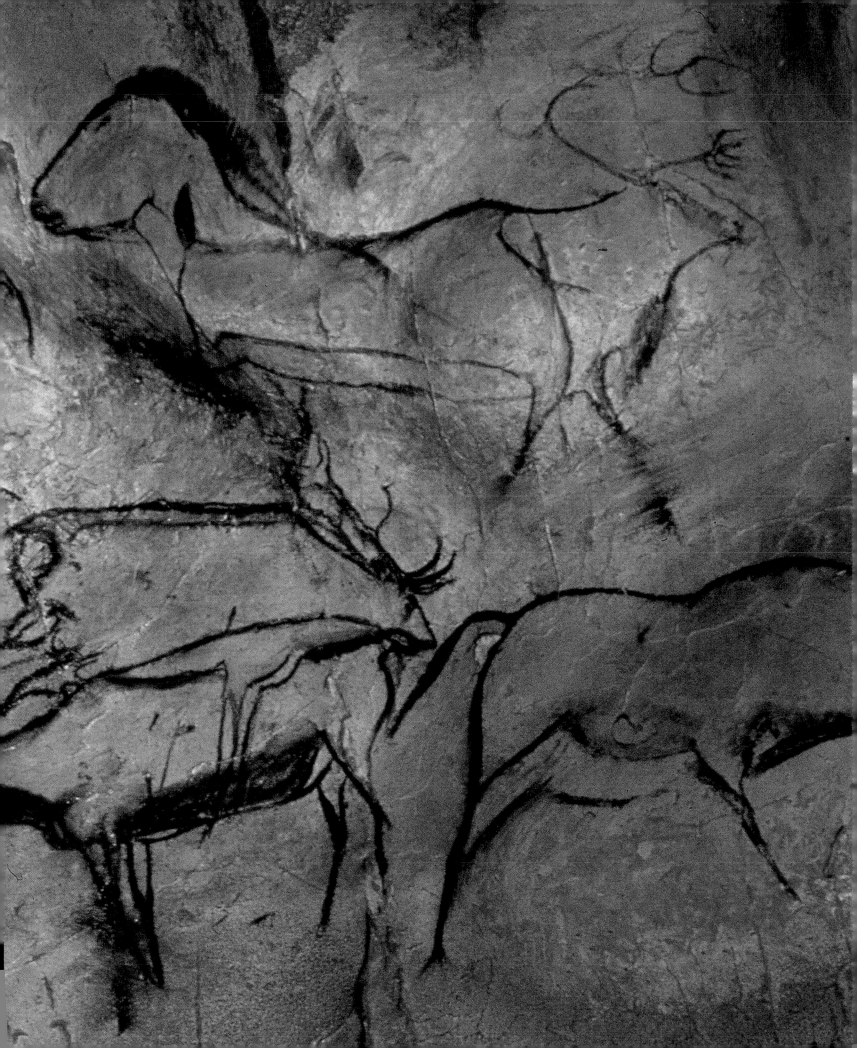

ca **3,400,000** BP* | Isthmus of Panama develops as land bridge linking the Americas.

ca **2,000,000-1,500,000** BP | Oldest hominid, *Australopithecus afarensis*, disappears from fossil record.

ca **2,000,000** BP | Most recent great Ice Age begins.

ca **1,800,000** BP | End of Pliocene epoch. *Homo erectus* begins to migrate from Africa.

BP*—used for dates farther back than 20,000 years before present, with 1950 as benchmark

A Complex Family Tree

Solving the puzzle of human origins requires the assembly of scattered bone fragments that have rested in the earth for thousands, sometimes millions, of years. From those pieces has emerged a long line of bipedal creatures known as hominids, a line that begins with divergence from the apes and ends at our own species, *Homo sapiens.*

From the study of bones and the way they were once positioned in the living body, scientists can determine whether an animal spent most of its time standing upright on two legs or down on all fours—the main difference between early hominids and apes. The oldest of the upright walkers, a hominid known as *Australopithecus afarensis,* dates

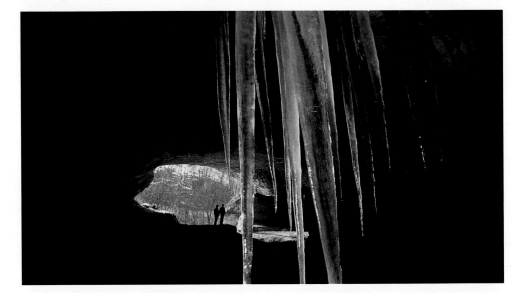

back more than four million years.

A gradual cooling in Africa may have shrunk woodlands so that some forest dwellers sought food on open savanna, where an upright stance offered a better view of enemies or a meal. Humanlike in posture, *A. afarensis* remained somewhat apelike

ca 950,000 BP   First evidence of hominids in Europe.

ca 460,000 BP   World's earliest definite use of fire, in China.

ca 100,000 BP   Neandertals appear, last of the more primitive upright walkers. First known burials, in the Middle East.

in appearance, having had a sloping forehead, flat nose, and large teeth. Its brain was only about a third the size of a modern human brain, and it probably lacked development in areas that allow speech. Long arms and curved hands indicate that the hominid remained a tree climber.

Although it may have been ancestral to all hominids that followed, *A. afarensis* disappeared from the fossil record 1.5 to 2 million years ago. Meanwhile, other hominids were emerging on the scene.

Larger, more powerfully built *Australopithecus robustus* and *boisei* had more sizable brains but still were unable to articulate speech. They probably used very simple tools such as digging sticks, but even modern

chimpanzees have been seen adapting small grass stems to fish termites out of holes.

Like *afarensis*, *robustus* and *boisei* eventually hit evolutionary dead ends, but before they did, an even more advanced group, the first of our genus *Homo*, made its appearance.

Homo habilis, or "handy man," had a brain half the size of ours but one capable of supporting speech. As its name implies, it managed to shape stone tools. A descendant, *Homo erectus*, made even more advanced tools and controlled fire.

Another early version of the genus *Homo* appeared about 100,000 years ago, a muscular human with a broad face and projecting brow. The last of these primitive people, the

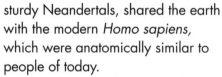

EARLY CAVE ART

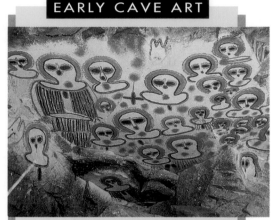

For millennia, artists used rocks as a medium for depicting their people, their myths, and the creatures they knew. These figures (above), found at an Aboriginal sacred site in Australia's northern Kimberley region, show ancestral beings known as *wandjina*. The stripes hanging from their shoulders represent rainfall. Over the years this art has been reverently repainted by Aborigines.

sturdy Neandertals, shared the earth with the modern *Homo sapiens*, which were anatomically similar to people of today.

Then the Neandertals may have died out and been replaced by the more advanced *H. sapiens*, leaving modern humans as the only survivors of a complex family tree. ■

Icicles in Vindija Cave in Croatia *(opposite)* testify to the extreme cold endured by cave-dwelling Neandertals some 50 millennia ago. Climatic changes forced early people to become more resourceful. Remains of early hominids indicate that bipeds such as *afarensis*, **far left**, progressively grew more similar to modern *Homo sapiens*. By fleshing out bone fragments, the artist depicted a slow sprint toward today's physique.

● People first settle
in Australia.

ca 55,000 BP

● First known rock art,
in Australia.

ca 45,000 BP

● Small stone tools
made in Israel.

ca 40,000 BP

● Cro-Magnons move into
Europe from Africa.

ca 38,000 BP

● Neandertals disappear,
and *Homo sapiens*
continues to people
the earth. Simple
counting device used
in South Africa.

ca 35,000 BP

Peopling of the Continents

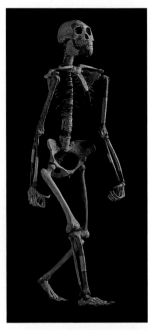

Africa is recognized as the cradle of humanity, and the first world traveler, *Homo erectus*, is believed to have left there 1.8 million years ago. The reasons are not clear; but *H. erectus* had a brain large enough for intellectual curiosity, meaning that this primitive person may have simply wondered what lay beyond the horizon. Remains have shown up in China, India, and Southeast Asia, and this early human may have reached southern Europe. A later version of *H. erectus*, Neandertal man, was resourceful enough to survive the Ice Age at northern latitudes.

Homo sapiens, the modern humans, either branched off from those earlier species or originated on their own in Africa some 100,000 years ago. Whatever their origins, they began a second great migration

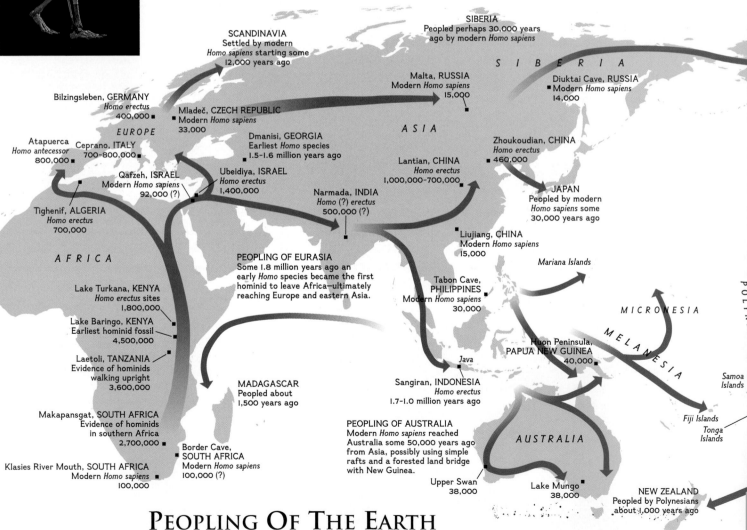

SIBERIA
Peopled perhaps 30,000 years
ago by modern *Homo sapiens*

SCANDINAVIA
Settled by modern
Homo sapiens starting some
12,000 years ago

Malta, RUSSIA
Modern *Homo sapiens*
15,000

Diuktai Cave, RUSSIA
■ Modern *Homo sapiens*
14,000

Bilzingsleben, GERMANY
Homo erectus
400,000 ■

Mladeč, CZECH REPUBLIC
■ Modern *Homo sapiens*
33,000

Dmanisi, GEORGIA
Earliest *Homo* species
1.5-1.6 million years ago

Zhoukoudian, CHINA
Homo erectus
■ 460,000

Atapuerca
Homo antecessor
800,000 ■

Ceprano, ITALY
700-800,000 ■

Qafzeh, ISRAEL
Modern *Homo sapiens*
92,000 (?)

Ubeidiya, ISRAEL
Homo erectus
1,400,000

Lantian, CHINA
Homo erectus
1,000,000-700,000

Narmada, INDIA
Homo (?) *erectus*
500,000 (?)

JAPAN
Peopled by modern
Homo sapiens some
30,000 years ago

Tighenif, ALGERIA
Homo erectus
700,000

Liujiang, CHINA
Modern *Homo sapiens*
15,000

Mariana Islands

AFRICA

PEOPLING OF EURASIA
Some 1.8 million years ago an
early *Homo* species became the first
hominid to leave Africa—ultimately
reaching Europe and eastern Asia.

**Tabon Cave,
PHILIPPINES**
Modern *Homo sapiens*
30,000

MICRONESIA

Lake Turkana, KENYA
Homo erectus sites
1,800,000

Lake Baringo, KENYA
Earliest hominid fossil
4,500,000

Laetoli, TANZANIA
Evidence of hominids
walking upright
3,600,000

**Huon Peninsula,
PAPUA NEW GUINEA**
40,000

Java

MELANESIA

*Samoa
Islands*

MADAGASCAR
Peopled about
1,500 years ago

Sangiran, INDONESIA
Homo erectus
1.7-1.0 million years ago

Fiji Islands

Makapansgat, SOUTH AFRICA
Evidence of hominids
in southern Africa
2,700,000

PEOPLING OF AUSTRALIA
Modern *Homo sapiens* reached
Australia some 50,000 years ago
from Asia, possibly using simple
rafts and a forested land bridge
with New Guinea.

AUSTRALIA

*Tonga
Islands*

**Border Cave,
SOUTH AFRICA**
Modern *Homo sapiens*
100,000 (?)

Klasies River Mouth, SOUTH AFRICA
Modern *Homo sapiens* ■
100,000

Upper Swan
38,000

Lake Mungo
38,000

NEW ZEALAND
Peopled by Polynesians
about 1,000 years ago

POLYNESIA

PEOPLING OF THE EARTH

ca **26,000** BP — Hunter-gatherers in Europe construct houses with roofs of clay.

ca **25,000-20,000** BP — Cave art flourishes in southern Europe.

ca **25,000** BP — People live in caves in Brazil. Clay used by hunter-gatherers to make statuettes.

ca **24,000** BP — First rock paintings in Africa.

ca **23,000** BP — In Poland, ivory boomerang made.

Striding toward humanity, *A. afarensis* (**opposite**) walked upright, according to skeletal testimony. Later larger hominids wandered far, peopling the earth. A carving of an Ice Age bison licking its back has surfaced in France. Early ivory carvings found in Siberia (**bottom, right**) were probably fertility symbols.

when the Ice Age locked up huge quantities of water in ice packs, lowering the seas by hundreds of feet. The English Channel became dry, then flooded again when temperatures rose, temporarily isolating people who had wandered across it. Land bridges opened between Siberia and North America, and hunters following game walked from one continent to the other. They certainly entered the Americas when land was exposed 14,000 years ago, and some sites far away in South America hint that crossings may have been made even earlier, 20,000 years ago or more. Australia was probably colonized before that by people arriving from New Guinea. A complete land bridge may have existed, or narrowed channels of seawater could have been crossed on simple rafts. Sites in Australia date back some 40,000 years.

The last large frontier to receive people was the South Pacific, where island-hopping settlers ventured forth on rafts. Humans made their first appearance in Hawaii about 400 years after the birth of Christ, and Easter Island and New Zealand were peopled within the last 1,600 years. ■

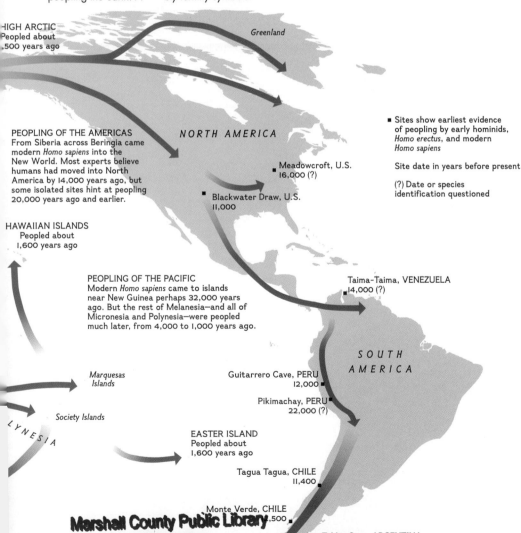

HIGH ARCTIC
Peopled about
,500 years ago

Greenland

NORTH AMERICA

PEOPLING OF THE AMERICAS
From Siberia across Beringia came modern *Homo sapiens* into the New World. Most experts believe humans had moved into North America by 14,000 years ago, but some isolated sites hint at peopling 20,000 years ago and earlier.

■ Sites show earliest evidence of peopling by early hominids, *Homo erectus*, and modern *Homo sapiens*

Site date in years before present

(?) Date or species identification questioned

Meadowcroft, U.S.
16,000 (?)

■ Blackwater Draw, U.S.
11,000

HAWAIIAN ISLANDS
Peopled about
1,600 years ago

PEOPLING OF THE PACIFIC
Modern *Homo sapiens* came to islands near New Guinea perhaps 32,000 years ago. But the rest of Melanesia—and all of Micronesia and Polynesia—were peopled much later, from 4,000 to 1,000 years ago.

Taima-Taima, VENEZUELA
14,000 (?)

SOUTH AMERICA

Marquesas Islands

Guitarrero Cave, PERU
12,000 ■

Pikimachay, PERU
22,000 (?) ■

Society Islands

OLYNESIA

EASTER ISLAND
Peopled about
1,600 years ago

Tagua Tagua, CHILE
11,400

Monte Verde, CHILE
,500 ■

Los Toldos Cave, ARGENTINA
■ 12,000

Fell's Cave, CHILE
11,000

Wherever people wandered, over time they evolved slightly to adjust to new environments, but the basic anatomy of modern humans has not changed for 100,000 years. ■

21

ca 18,000 B.C. Hunter-gatherers settle in Zaire. Earliest known human sculpture made in Asia. Coldest point of most recent Ice Age.

ca 17,000 B.C. Wild cereal gathered near Sea of Galilee.

The Ice Age

ce ages are believed to be caused by slight changes in the earth's orbit around the sun and by very slow wobbles as the planet spins on its axis, altering its attitude toward the source of heat. As the earth cools, snow falling in northern latitudes fails to melt and is compressed into ice so thick that its own weight causes it to spread, inching outward.

Numerous ice ages have occurred, but the great Ice Age began about two million years ago and reached its peak perhaps a mere 20,000 years ago. Between those two dates the average annual temperature rose and fell over the centuries, causing glaciers sometimes two miles thick to advance across the northern parts of the planet and then retreat as warming trends melted them.

Some climatologists say this most recent ice age is not completely over. Glaciers in the far north continue to

EARLY TOOLS

Until metal tools appeared some 5,000 years ago, early humans relied on stone for durable, long-lasting implements. Using one rock as a hammer, the "knapper" struck downward on another rock, causing flakes to peel off and leaving a cutting edge for a chopper or hand ax. The best-shaped flakes could also be used for lighter tools such as awls or missile points. A stone ax, shown here, dates back 1.6 million years.

ca **16,000** B.C. Kutikina Cave occupied in Tasmania by tool-users. Mammoth bones used in Europe for roofs of huts, especially in western Russia.

ca **15,000** B.C. Paleolithic artists paint and engrave hundreds of images in Lascaux Cave, in France. Northern Africa experiences last rainy period.

creep forward, but because we are in a warmer phase, they eventually calve into the sea. A tenth of the earth's surface is still covered in ice.

At the height of this ice age, the earth's land was covered with a frigid cap that stretched from Arctic islands south to areas now called the Ohio and Missouri River Valleys, below today's city of Chicago. In Europe ice covered the Scandinavian Peninsula, parts of the British Isles, northern Germany, and Poland.

Reshaping much of the earth's surface, glaciers bulldozed debris ahead of them, gouging lake basins. When the glaciers melted, they scoured the land with river torrents that flowed for centuries like many Amazons. Miles-wide floodplains, still detectable on the landscape, were probably carved in that massive melting. According to measurements of continental shelves and coral islands, sea levels rose as much as 360 feet.

Glaciers reshaped history as well, making human lives more difficult but forcing adaptations and creativity. ■

Mammoth bones and hides housed humans living on the East European plain 15,000 years ago. To keep themselves warm, adaptive humans learned to sew animal skins together with bone needles, shown here up to four inches long *(above)*.

ca **9000** B.C. Hunter-gatherers camp on the east side of what will become Jericho. Arrowheads first made in America.

ca **8500** B.C. Jericho founded, first walled town in world.

ca **8000** B.C. Hunter-gatherers begin to establish settlements in both Old and New Worlds. For Europeans living on coasts, shellfish becomes an important source of protein.

7500 B.C. Earliest known cemetery in North America.

Beginnings of Agriculture in Southern Asia

The end of the Ice Age watered much of the world with glacial melt and increased rainfall, stimulating prolific plant growth. Humans had long been gathering nuts, berries, and the seeds of wild grains to eat. Perhaps 10,000 years ago they found that by planting seeds they could gather food without wandering to find it. Einkorn, a predecessor of wheat, made an early transition from wild, seedy grass to domesticated grain.

Fertile, moist valleys of the Indus River in what is now Pakistan held some of the first agricultural settlements, where wheat and barley were grown in fields. Date palms were among the first tree crops, followed

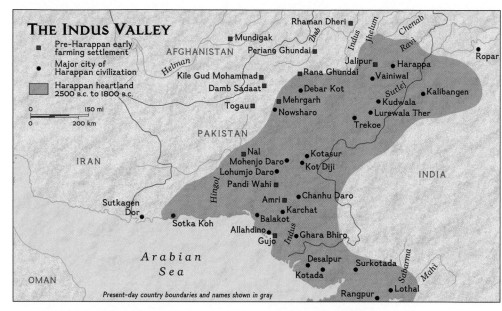

THE INDUS VALLEY

■ Pre-Harappan early farming settlement
● Major city of Harappan civilization
▨ Harappan heartland 2500 B.C. to 1800 B.C.

0 ——— 150 mi
0 ——— 200 km

Present-day country boundaries and names shown in gray

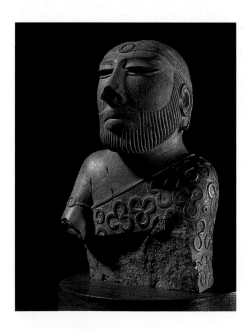

by figs and olives.

Domestication of cattle, along with goats and sheep, has been documented as taking place 8,000 years ago. And the construction of houses advanced from building with earthen walls to using sturdier mud bricks, sometimes with stone foundations.

With stability came better tools and implements. Pottery appeared about 6,000 years ago, decorated with stylized images of cattle and other farm animals. Agricultural productivity and trade with other communities escalated substantially with the discovery that cattle could be used to pull plows and wheeled vehicles.

An abundance of copper ore allowed the Indus region to become the first known center for metallurgy in South Asia, giving rise to more durable chisels, axes, spear points, and knives. Metal sickles replaced those made of flint and eased the work of harvesting grain. Even harder metals were made later by combining copper with tin, creating bronze.

In the third and second millennia B.C., the first full-blown urban culture in southern Asia developed in the Indus Valley. Named for Harappa, a major settlement, the Harappan civilization flourished for about 700 years, its success based on agriculture, manufacturing, and trade. ■

Seven-inch steatite bust **(left)**, found at ancient Mohenjo Daro along the Indus River, hints at an increasing urbanity in the Harappan culture. Growth of early cities spurred the development of commercial farming to feed clustered populations.

DOMESTICATION OF ANIMALS

The dog, originating from the wolf, was the first animal to be tamed. Sheep and goats probably preceded cattle on farmsteads. Domesticated pigs first appeared in today's Turkey some 9,000 years ago. The horse, probably first domesticated in north-central Asia and from there migrating into the rest of the world, proved to be invaluable in the forward movements of civilizations.

ca **7000** B.C. Early farmers settle at Çatal Hüyük, in the fertile grasslands of Anatolia, herding cattle and cultivating various crops.

6500 B.C. Earliest known metallurgy, in Middle East.

ca **6000** B.C. Rice cultivation in Thailand.

ca **5000** B.C. First metal tools appear.

ca **4000** B.C. First use of plow.

ca **3500** B.C. Invention of the wheel in Mesopotamia.

ca **3000** B.C. First construction at Stonehenge begins.

25

ca **6500** B.C.   First farming in Greece and the Aegean.

ca **5200** B.C.   Early agriculturalists experiment with barley and seed grasses in the Nile Valley.

ca **5000** B.C.   Yangshao culture in China produces painted pottery. People in Mexico begin to cultivate maize. Land bridge disappears between England and France. In Nubia, civilization takes hold. Rice cultivated in China. Copper first used in Mesopotamia. Chumash Indians fish from plank canoes off the coast of Peru.

The Life-Giving Nile

For thousands of years hunters and gatherers had wandered across the lower Nile Valley in the Middle East, taking advantage of the rich plant and animal life alongside earth's longest river.

Tools found at campsites of some 15,000 years ago include sickles for harvesting wild grains and grinding stones for making flour. Around 7000 B.C. many of these wanderers adopted a more settled style of life and agriculture took root.

Fertile soils and easily navigable waters made the Nile River Valley and the nearly 10,000-square-mile Nile Delta popular areas for settlement. Although ample rains fell over much of the upper Sahara at that time, annual flooding spread a coat of rich silt over the land near the river, making it especially fertile.

The first small, insular communities gradually became larger and eventually united into one kingdom. Egyptians developed engineering skills by which they built a network of irrigation canals and sluice gates on either side of the great river, nurturing crops. Workers grew wheat to make bread, barley to brew beer, and flax to weave linen for clothes.

Sometime before 2000 B.C. a change in climate dried the Sahara, but civilization along the Nile continued to thrive in its well-watered valley. The surrounding desert formed a barrier against invaders, allowing Egyptian empires to grow and develop, uninterrupted, for centuries.

At the edge of plenty, desert sands and an ancient pharaoh's unfinished pyramid border lush farmland near the Nile River, now as in the past. Hand-dug canals watered crops and carried materials for erecting monuments to the first nation-state.

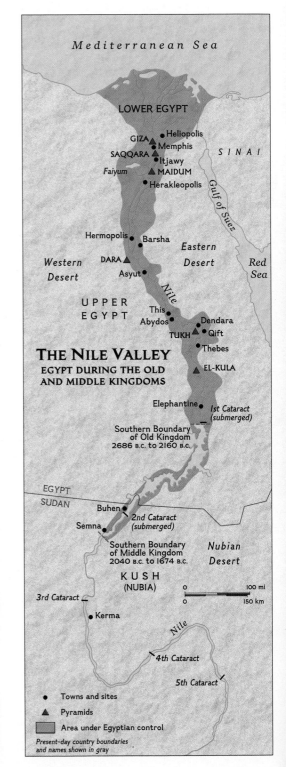

THE NILE VALLEY
EGYPT DURING THE OLD AND MIDDLE KINGDOMS

Mediterranean Sea

LOWER EGYPT

GIZA ▲ ● Heliopolis
SAQQARA ▲ ● Memphis
● Itjawy
Faiyum   ▲ MAIDUM
● Herakleopolis

SINAI

Gulf of Suez

Hermopolis ● ● Barsha
Western Desert
DARA ▲
● Asyut

Eastern Desert

Red Sea

UPPER EGYPT
This ●
Abydos ●   ● Dendara
TUKH ▲ ● Qift
● Thebes
▲ EL-KULA

Nile

Elephantine ● ● 1st Cataract (submerged)

Southern Boundary of Old Kingdom 2686 B.C. to 2160 B.C.

EGYPT
SUDAN
Buhen ●
● 2nd Cataract (submerged)
Semna ●

Southern Boundary of Middle Kingdom 2040 B.C. to 1674 B.C.

Nubian Desert

KUSH (NUBIA)
3rd Cataract

● Kerma

0   100 mi
0   150 km

Nile

4th Cataract

5th Cataract

● Towns and sites
▲ Pyramids
▮ Area under Egyptian control

Present-day country boundaries and names shown in gray

4236 B.C. First date in the ancient Egyptian calendar.

ca 4000 B.C. First farmers in Britain. Farmers in the Sahara domesticate animals.

ca 3500 B.C. Copper in use in Thailand. Sumer, world's first ancient civilization, emerges in the lower reaches of Iraq's Tigris and Euphrates Rivers. Sumerians succeed in producing the first food surplus in history; they invent cuneiform script. Llama used as pack animal in Peru.

3372 B.C. First date in Maya calendar.

Continued prosperity depended on the skills necessary to control and harness the annual river floods for maximum crop benefit. Canals were built, not only for watering the crops but also for transporting their yields for distribution within the kingdom and beyond.

Food surpluses were kept in the pharaoh's household, requiring record-keeping, so the Egyptians devised their own form of writing. For agricultural success the Egyptians also held their rulers responsible for interceding with the gods to guarantee satisfactory harvests. Dynasties could topple when insufficient flooding resulted in widespread famine. ■

Carrying offerings from distant provinces to the center of power, a procession of bearers crosses the wall of Ptahhotep's tomb, dating to some 4,400 years ago *(above)*.

Tomb-building along the Nile River perhaps spurred the first gathering of separate communities under a central government.

○ **ca 3300** B.C. Sumerians start to use clay tokens in exchange for goods.

○ **ca 3050** B.C. Unification of the Egyptian kingdom.

○ **ca 3000** B.C. Weights and measures standardized in Mesopotamia and Egypt. First stone temples erected in Malta. First pottery in the Americas created in

Ecuador and Colombia. Plow first used in China. Wheel used on chariots in Mesopotamia. Bronze Age begins in Crete.

○ **ca 2800** B.C. Village societies based on horticulture are becoming established in the Amazon region.

Mesopotamia and Babylonia

Climate was often the engine that drove human development. As the Ice Age had stimulated resourcefulness, summer drought in the Middle East sparked cooperation and gave birth to one of the first-known civilizations, Sumer.

Previously, cities had sprung up because some valuable commodity for trade—salt at Jericho or obsidian at Çatal Hüyük in today's Turkey —simply resulted in clustered living. Each family in the confined space provided for its own food, by garden or barter. Establishment of a widespread community required a broader resource base, with fertile soils for growing extensive crops. Such a waiting cornucopia existed near the Tigris and Euphrates Rivers in what is now Iraq, then called Mesopotamia, "land between the rivers."

Fertile though the soil was, it received little rain during the summer. Growing crops required the building of canals to bring water from the rivers, and their construction and maintenance required the work of many people. Around 7,000 years ago a group known as Sumerians settled on the Tigris and Euphrates alluvial plains and consolidated their efforts to make the land bloom, producing the world's first food surplus.

Mask from more than 20 centuries B.C. *(above)* reflects the power of the Akkadian rulers, who carved out Mesopotamia's first empire in the region of the Tigris and Euphrates.

The success of their agriculture freed some members of the population to focus on other pursuits; thus, artisans, teachers, and a religious elite came into being. Storing the extra food required a system for recording who had deposited and who had withdrawn items, so the first-known writing was invented. Sumerians had wheeled vehicles, important in trade and chariot warfare, and were among the first metallurgists. Their metals included materials not found in their home territory, which suggests trade with faraway groups.

With the flowering of Sumerian culture a number of cities arose in Mesopotamia. Each became its own independent power, a city-state commanding the land around it. Quarrels between cities became part of Sumerian life. The cities' wealth and success also invited attacks from less-developed cultures in hills above the fertile valley.

Around 2300 B.C. King Sargon united Sumeria to end the disputes and to defend against outsiders. He also extended his military control beyond Sumer's borders to secure trade routes. Both trade and conquest helped spread Sumerian ideas and may account for the rapid growth of cities that took place outside Mesopotamia for centuries.

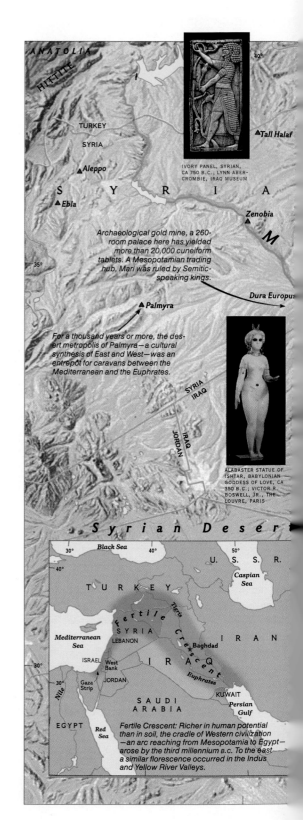

IVORY PANEL, SYRIAN, CA 750 B.C.; LYNN ABERCROMBIE, IRAQ MUSEUM

Archaeological gold mine, a 260-room palace here has yielded more than 20,000 cuneiform tablets. A Mesopotamian trading hub, Mari was ruled by Semitic-speaking kings.

For a thousand years or more, the desert metropolis of Palmyra—a cultural synthesis of East and West—was an entrepôt for caravans between the Mediterranean and the Euphrates.

ALABASTER STATUE OF ISHTAR, BABYLONIAN GODDESS OF LOVE, CA 350 B.C.; VICTOR R. BOSWELL, JR., THE LOUVRE, PARIS

Fertile Crescent: Richer in human potential than in soil, the cradle of Western civilization —an arc reaching from Mesopotamia to Egypt— arose by the third millennium B.C. To the east a similar florescence occurred in the Indus and Yellow River Valleys.

● ca 2700 B.C. Chinese start making bronze and weaving silk.

ca 2500 B.C. ● People begin to build the Sphinx at Giza to guard the pyramid of the pharaoh Khafre. The horse is domesticated in central Asia. Corn becomes the staple diet throughout Central America.

ca 2300 B.C. ● King Sargon unites Sumeria.

ca 2200 B.C. ● Middle Jōman period in Japan. Beginning of the Bronze Age in Ireland.

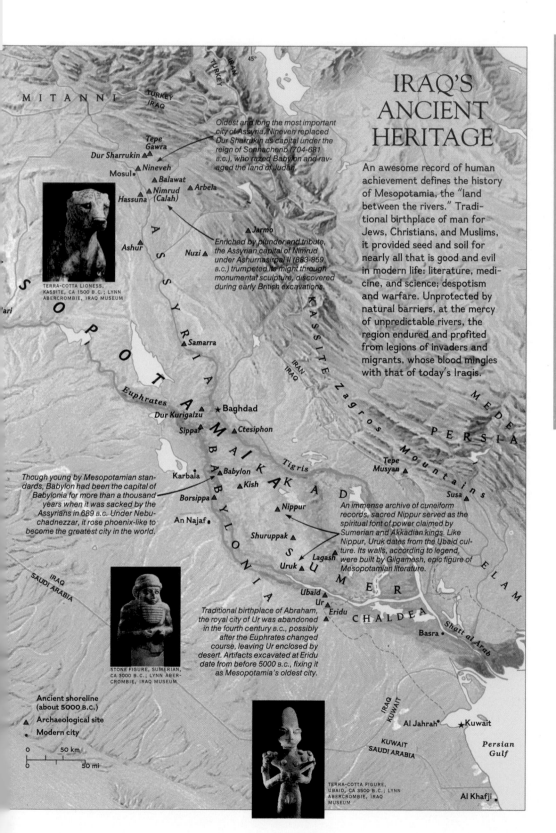

IRAQ'S ANCIENT HERITAGE

An awesome record of human achievement defines the history of Mesopotamia, the "land between the rivers." Traditional birthplace of man for Jews, Christians, and Muslims, it provided seed and soil for nearly all that is good and evil in modern life: literature, medicine, and science; despotism and warfare. Unprotected by natural barriers, at the mercy of unpredictable rivers, the region endured and profited from legions of invaders and migrants, whose blood mingles with that of today's Iraqis.

Oldest and long the most important city of Assyria, Nineveh replaced Dur Sharrukin as capital under the reign of Sennacherib (704-681 B.C.), who razed Babylon and ravaged the land of Judah.

Enriched by plunder and tribute, the Assyrian capital of Nimrud under Ashurnasirpal II (883-859 B.C.) trumpeted its might through monumental sculpture, discovered during early British excavations.

TERRA-COTTA LIONESS, KASSITE, CA 1500 B.C.; LYNN ABERCROMBIE, IRAQ MUSEUM

An immense archive of cuneiform records, sacred Nippur served as the spiritual font of power claimed by Sumerian and Akkadian kings. Like Nippur, Uruk dates from the Ubaid culture. Its walls, according to legend, were built by Gilgamesh, epic figure of Mesopotamian literature.

Though young by Mesopotamian standards, Babylon had been the capital of Babylonia for more than a thousand years when it was sacked by the Assyrians in 689 B.C. Under Nebuchadnezzar, it rose phoenix-like to become the greatest city in the world.

STONE FIGURE, SUMERIAN, CA 3000 B.C.; LYNN ABERCROMBIE, IRAQ MUSEUM

Traditional birthplace of Abraham, the royal city of Ur was abandoned in the fourth century B.C., possibly after the Euphrates changed course, leaving Ur enclosed by desert. Artifacts excavated at Eridu date from before 5000 B.C., fixing it as Mesopotamia's oldest city.

Ancient shoreline (about 5000 B.C.)
▲ Archaeological site
● Modern city

0 — 50 km
0 — 50 mi

TERRA-COTTA FIGURE, UBAID, CA 3500 B.C.; LYNN ABERCROMBIE, IRAQ MUSEUM

THE ZIGGURAT AT UR

The Sumerians believed gods lived in houses and inhabited statues just as persons inhabit bodies. At the city of Ur a 70-foot-high, three-tiered temple called a ziggurat was built of sunbaked bricks (above). It was viewed as the link between earth and the heavens. At its summit was a statue of the moon god, Nanna, which was washed, fed, and clothed by priests devoted to its keeping.

Eventually, constant attacks by outsiders brought chaos to Sumer. In 1792 B.C. the strong leader Hammurapi came to power and consolidated the warring groups into a unity now known as the Old Babylonian Empire, with an enlarged Babylon as its capital. Babylon had been an undistinguished village in Mesopotamia during the heyday of the Sumerian civilization.

Although Babylonia held shorter tenure as a predominant power than some other ancient empires, its cultural potency extended over many centuries and still affects life today.

Little is known of Babylon physically because that early city's ruins are buried below the water table, making them inaccessible. Clay

ca 2000-700 B.C. Bronze Age in Scotland.

ca 2000 B.C. Inuit live in the Arctic, hunting caribou and seals for food. In southern Siberia, Neolithic culture begins. Minoan civilization produces painted pottery.

ca 1800 B.C. Ceremonial centers are established in Peru.

ca 1786 B.C. The Hyksos, from Palestine, rule Egypt.

ca 1620 B.C. Indo-Europeans known as the Hittites become a strong force in Anatolia.

ca 1500 B.C. Collapse of Minoan civilization in Crete.

● **ca 1400** B.C. First alphabet-type script devised by the Phoenicians. Development of farming and village life in Copan, Honduras.

● **ca 1200** B.C. Yams are grown in West Africa. Greeks destroy city of Troy on coast of western Turkey after ten-year war.

ca 1182-51 B.C. ● Reign of Pharaoh Ramses III of Egypt.

● **ca 1120** B.C. City of Mycenae destroyed; Mycenaean civilization comes to an end.

ca 1045 B.C. ● Kingdom of Zhou established in China.

● **ca 1000** B.C. Early Iron Age begins in Italy.

753 B.C. ● Rome founded on Tiber River in Italy.

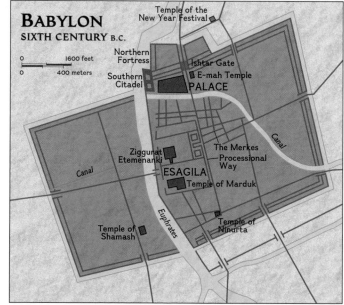

tablets that survive from that period tell of achievements in mathematics, astronomy, literature, and law.

Hammurapi set forth a code of ethics aimed at preventing the mighty from oppressing the weak—282 laws covering such matters as property, rent, and medical treatment. The most famous passage in this oldest surviving law code concerns the "eye for an eye, tooth for a tooth" principle of punishment that later appeared in the Bible. Priestly interpretations in Babylon as to how the world was made are also echoed in Genesis.

Babylonian mathematicians devised a counting system based on the number 60, from which came the 60-second minute and 60-minute hour.

Complex arithmetic calculations, unsurpassed for a thousand years, also gave us

Sport of ancient kings, a lion hunt rages across a frieze *(above)* from Nineveh, seat of once mighty Assurbanipal, last great ruler of the Assyrian Empire. Warriors without rival in the ancient world, the Assyrians were overthrown by a coalition of subject nations in the seventh century B.C. A gilded bull's head *(opposite)* decorates a harp dating back to pre-Babylonian Sumer, unearthed from a tomb in Mesopotamia.

BABYLON
SIXTH CENTURY B.C.

Temple of the New Year Festival

Northern Fortress
Southern Citadel
Ishtar Gate
E-mah Temple
PALACE

Ziggurat Etemenanki
The Merkes
Processional Way
ESAGILA
Temple of Marduk

Canal
Canal
Euphrates

Temple of Shamash
Temple of Ninurta

0   1600 feet
0   400 meters

the 360-degree circle and the 12-month year.

So well established was the culture of Babylon that when barbarians from the north, called Kassites, overcame the city and imposed their rule less than 200 years after Hammurapi, Babylon's way of life prevailed.

When the fierce Assyrians displaced the Kassites some 400 years later, Babylon continued in its role as cultural paragon. It and a coalition of other city-states eventually overthrew the Assyrians in 612 B.C., and Nebuchadrezzar II later brought the city to a new level of grandeur. He built lavish palaces and the Hanging Gardens, which became one of the seven wonders of the ancient world. Shortly after his death Babylon surrendered to Cyrus II (the Great) of Persia. ■

31

ca **3000** B.C.	● Science of survey known in Egypt.	**2686-2160** B.C.	● Egypt's Old Kingdom.		ca **2500** B.C.	● Rise of Indus civilization in Pakistan. Building of wooden boats in Egypt. Fine metalwork in Mesopotamia. Oil pressed from plants in Egypt; flowers and	herbs cultivated for scent. Longshan culture thrives in China.
2697 B.C.	● "Yellow Emperor" in China.		ca **2650** B.C.	● Start of great period of pyramid building; construction of pyramid of Djoser, Egypt.			

The Mysterious Megaliths

Most famous of megalithic monuments raised in ancient Europe, Stonehenge broods in secretive silence at dawn on England's Salisbury Plain.

The permanence of carefully placed stones in Europe attests to one of the most enduring mysteries of the modern world. From the island of Malta in the Mediterranean Sea to the Orkney Islands of Scotland, thousands of free-standing structures called megaliths, or great stones, reveal that a large amount of social organization underlay their construction. The oldest of them date back some 6,000 years.

No one explanation serves for all megaliths; they apparently had a number of purposes.

Some 30 megalithic temples on Malta appear to have contained altars. Numerous obese female figurines discovered there are associated with fertility cults.

In France's Brittany region, home of the greatest concentration of standing stones, some 3,000 of them range from 3 to 18 feet tall and form avenues nearly four miles long.

Some megaliths in Britain were covered with earth to serve as communal burial chambers, or barrows.

Many sites appear to have been constructed as astronomical observatories to mark seasonal passages. In a vaulted burial chamber in Ireland, for example, at winter solstice the rays of the rising sun shine through

ca **2200** B.C. — Beginning of the Bronze Age in Ireland.

2000 B.C. — First settlers arrive in New Guinea. Andean settlements with ceremonial centers thrive in Peru. Afanasievo Neolithic culture begins in southern Siberia.

1674 B.C. — Egyptian capital of Memphis falls to the Hyksos.

ca **1500** B.C. — Shang kingdom flourishes in China. Cuneiform script appears in Asia Minor. First gravel platforms built at Olmec site, San Lorenzo, Mexico.

ca **2200-1700** B.C. — Hieroglyphic writing appears in Far East.

ca **1600** B.C. — First urban civilization in China, Shang Bronze Age culture.

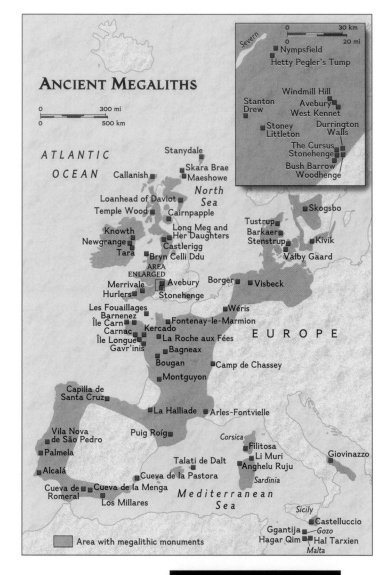

ANCIENT MEGALITHS

a 62-foot corridor, lighting its far end.

The most famous megalith, Stonehenge in southern England, started as a circular ditch, its stone arrangements evolving over 1,500 years to have both solar and lunar alignments. From the center of Stonehenge as the summer solstice begins, one can view the sun rising directly over a 16-foot-tall stone at the end of an entrance causeway.

Stonehenge's builders were farmers and herdsmen who would have been aware of seasonal rhythms and their importance to the fertility of crops and animals.

The massive stones, weighing up to 50 tons each, were quarried 18 miles to the north, then moved to the site on log rollers. There, they could have been lifted into position by ropes, levers, and timber supports. ■

CREATION MYTHS

Ancient Egyptians believed the god Amun created other gods of air, moisture, sky, and earth. The Anasazi in early America thought that their ancestors entered the world through a small opening. The Dogon of West Africa trace their beginnings to a mythical blacksmith who pilfered a piece of the sun. The Inca of Peru called themselves the Children of the Sun.

ca 3000-2750 B.C. | **Early Bronze Age II in Palestine.**

3000 B.C. | **Molded copper ax heads and knives made in Palestine.**

ca 2500 B.C. | **First invaders cross from mainland Europe into Britain. Neolithic civilization in Scotland.**

ca 3000-1500 B.C. | **Indus Valley civilization, or Harappan culture, in today's Pakistan.**

ca 2700 B.C. | **Irrigated fields sustain tens of thousands of people in Mesopotamia.**

ca 2000 B.C. | **First metalworking in Peru.**

The Flowering of Egypt

Ancient Egypt owes its early development to a generous river. The Nile nurtured Egypt's land, fed its people, carried their commerce, and shaped their beliefs. The Egyptians may have adapted for their own needs much of the earlier Sumerian technology in irrigation, metallurgy, writing, and use of the wheel and plow, and civilization along the Nile grew rapidly. After a number of provinces were brought together around 3100 B.C.

Royalty's remnants tell of life in ancient Egypt. A stone pharaoh joins hands with two female deities. Inscribed sandstone columns of a coronation hall at the Temple of Amun at Karnak left little open space for aisles *(right)*.

ca 1894-1595 B.C. **First dynasty of Babylon.**

ca 1500 B.C. **Iron weapons become common in the Near East. Aryans of Europe invade India.**

ca 1482 B.C. **Cretan fleet carries wood from Lebanon to Egypt.**

ca 1240 B.C. **Moses gives the Ten Commandments to his people.**

ca 1700 B.C. **Ukrainian pottery reaches China.**

ca 1400-1100 B.C. **Mycenaean civilization at its height.**

Wedded to eternity, Pharaoh Ramses II *(top)* and his wife Nefertari live immortalized in art. A tomb inscription praised the graceful queen: "Possessor of charm, sweetness, and love." Limestone was floated to pyramid sites *(right)* and then dragged onto land to raise everlasting monuments to pharaohs.

by a shadowy figure we call Menes, Egypt remained united for most of the next 3,000 years.

The real flowering of ancient Egyptian culture came in three waves known as the Old Kingdom (about 2686 to 2160 B.C.), the Middle Kingdom (2040 to 1674 B.C.), and the New Kingdom (perhaps 1558 to 1085 B.C.).

Waves of great achievement were interrupted by periods of strife and disunity, often brought about by drought and famine. But while prosperity reigned, complex societies emerged with social structure, intellectual achievement, and intricate art. Egyptian carvings, statues, and monuments still endure.

Believing their souls could live forever if their bodies were preserved, the Egyptians devised methods of embalming, or mummifying. At first they were reserved for the pharaohs, but by 2300 B.C. they were available to anyone who could afford them.

Pharaohs were entombed within pyramids. The Great Pyramid of Khufu, built over a 20-year period, stands 482 feet high. Construction by some 100,000 men involved emplacing 2.3 million blocks of stone, averaging two and a half tons in weight. The tomb of King Tutankhamun contained nearly 5,000 objects of art from the 14th century B.C.

Into New Kingdom tombs went a text now known as the Book of the Dead, rendered in the unique Egyptian writing known as hieroglyphics. Aimed at guiding the deceased to the next life, it has ultimately guided us to greater understanding of ancient Egyptian culture. ∎

35

ca 2040-1674 B.C. • Egypt's Middle Kingdom.

ca 1500 B.C. • Knossos, Crete, destroyed.

ca 1250 B.C. • Warrior elites begin to emerge in Europe.

ca 1100 B.C. • Phoenicians develop alphabetic script (basis of all European scripts).

1595 B.C. • Hittites conquer Babylon.

ca 1450 B.C. • Composition of Vedas begins—earliest Indian literature.

ca 1140 B.C. • First Phoenician colony in Africa at Utica.

ca 922 B.C. • Israel splits into Israel and Judah.

America's First Civilization

Between 1200 and 400 B.C., America's first-known civilization arose in Mesoamerica, the region stretching from central Mexico to the Pacific shores of El Salvador.

More than 3,000 years ago, the Olmec built elaborate ritual centers with earthen pyramids, walled plazas, even ball courts for competitions.

Olmec art was highly stylized—pear-shaped stone heads with slanted eyes and thick lips. The largest heads, perhaps depicting rulers, were

as much as 10 feet tall and weighed several tons. They were shaped from basalt gathered near volcanic mountains miles away and then hauled to settlements. From quarries far to the south, the Olmec also brought jade and jadeite and carved them into exquisite figurines depicting spirit forces. They were often part jaguar and part human.

The Olmec lived in several settlements that were dependent upon each other for different resources.

814 B.C.   City of Carthage is founded.

ca 612 B.C.   Coalition of Babylonians, Scythians, and Medes sacks the Assyrian capital at Nineveh.

558-529 B.C.   Reign of Cyrus the Great, founder of Persian Empire.

ca 500 B.C.   Theseum erected in Athens. Carthaginian tombs near Tipasa are constructed.

ca 750 B.C.   Kush conquers Egypt.

ca 563-483 B.C.   Life of Indian religious teacher Siddhartha Gautama, founder of Buddhism.

509 B.C.   Roman Republic founded.

One settlement established on fertile soils provided ample food; another had special clays used in ceremonies; another controlled the stone carved into monuments.

Analysis of charred leftovers of meals indicates that these people were planting corn by 2250 B.C. Studies of household garbage reveal that they also ate ample supplies of fish, shellfish, and turtles.

By 800 B.C. the first small Olmec settlements had merged into large communities with various social rankings and powerful rulers. Besides creating Mesoamerica's first recognizable art style, the Olmec devised a system of writing. They also established managerial skills for governing a large urban society.

The Olmec vanished from the archaeological record about 400 B.C., but their culture laid the groundwork for civilizations that would follow, such as the Maya and the Aztec. ■

Velvety blanket of vegetation in Mexico covers a 3,000-year-old site of the Olmec, among the first Americans to design ritualistic centers and raise pyramids. Two pyramids separated by a walled plaza are among nearly a hundred mounds here.

Stone heads weighing several tons (*opposite*) are thought to have honored leaders. A 26-inch tall statue (*opposite, above*) may depict an athlete in a ritual game played with a rubber ball.

NEW FOOD IN AMERICA

The Olmec planted corn as early as 2250 B.C. Women stripped away the dry kernels by rubbing the cobs together and then ground them on a stone grinder. Dough was moistened and flattened into thin disks, then baked over a wood fire. Along with beans and squash, corn of many varieties (*left*) dominated the Mesoamerican diet and bolstered trade, eventually finding its way all over the world.

ca **2000** B.C. Hurrians, a people of unknown origin, are settling all over Syria and Mesopotamia.

1391-1353 B.C. The reign of Amenhotep III, Egypt's "Golden Age."

1000 B.C. Crude anchors evolved in the Mediterranean.

The Villanova culture flourishes in Italy. **1000-600** B.C.

ca **1500—1250** B.C. The Hebrews live in bondage in Egypt.

ca **1010-970** B.C. Hebrew alphabet developed from earlier Semitic script.

1000-774 B.C. Great period of Tyre in Phoenicia.

994 B.C. In Central Europe, Teutonic tribes move westward to the Rhine River.

776 B.C. First Olympic Games held in Greece.

ca 650-560 B.C. Greek poet Sappho, lives on the Isle of Lesbos.

609 B.C. End of Assyrian Empire.

604 B.C. Nebuchadrezzar II claims the throne in Babylon.

551 B.C. Birth of Confucius.

550 B.C.

Arabs cross the Red Sea and settle in Ethiopia.

500 B.C. Caste system established in India.

Hinduism

From times of earliest human thought, people have always sought explanations for the mysteries of birth, death, and calamity. Neandertals buried food along with their dead some tens of thousands of years ago, suggesting belief in some kind of life beyond death. The search for explanations of want and plenty, joy and loss, probably resulted in the first religions.

Hinduism is generally thought by scholars to be the oldest of the major religions still practiced today.

With the Aryans of Europe, who invaded India around 1500 B.C., came the idea that many gods are responsible for the gifts of nature. The warmth of the sun, the nurturing rains, the very air they breathed are each contributed by a separate deity.

One major Existent One, known as Brahma, reigns over them all. Next in importance are Vishnu, the preserver; and Shiva, the destroyer, who rules over life and death.

The principles of the Hindu religion were preserved in hymns known as the *Vedas*. Chanted as an oral tradition, they were not written down until much later, in the ancient language of Sanskrit.

The conquering Aryans subdued the native Indian populations. And perhaps because of continued friction between the two groups, a caste system of social ranking was established. According to this arrangement, persons of upper stations in life limited their associations with those of lower stations. Movement could take place between the levels but not,

according to Hinduism, within a single lifetime.

Hindus believe in cycles of life in which all creatures move either up or down on the evolutionary ladder, according to the amount of merit they achieve. Thus a virtuous person of the lowest "untouchable" caste may die and be reborn in a higher caste, or a foolish man may return in the next life as a monkey.

One myth tells of a woman afire with jealousy who was reborn as a chili plant, destined to burn throughout that existence. Whatever lies in store depends on one's karma, the good or bad fruit of one's actions. We reap according to what we sow. ■

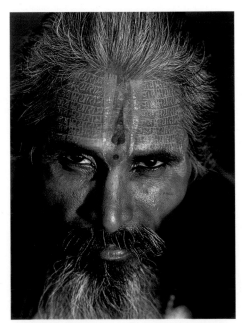

Human protector, Krishna, in this Hindu painting *(left)*, punishes a many-headed serpent spirit king for poisoning a river. Cowherds and maidens cheer their hero from the banks, and serpent nymphs plead for mercy. Banishment is the sentence. Tattooed devotions mark the forehead of a modern Hindu holy man *(above)*.

- **ca 1550 B.C.** Mycenaeans trade by sea throughout the Mediterranean. The Hittites capture Aleppo, in present-day Syria.
- **1500 B.C.** The first historical period begins in China under the Shang dynasty.
- **1504 B.C.** Period of expansion under Thutmose I in Egypt.
- **1300 B.C.** Spokes of chariot axle wheels increase from four to six in Egypt. First settlers arrive in Fiji, Samoa, and Tonga.
- **1100-900 B.C.** The first Chinese-language dictionary is compiled.
- **ca 900 B.C.** Kingdom of Kush becomes independent of Egypt.

The Rise of Judaism

A group of Middle Eastern semi-nomads known as Hebrews, convinced that God had promised them a homeland, were the originators of Judaism. According to tradition, their patriarchal leader Abraham received a call to leave the deserts of Mesopotamia, today's Iraq, and enter the land of Canaan, later called Palestine.

In return for their devotion to the one God they called Yahweh, Abraham and his followers were to be a people who would have a special relationship with the creator of heaven and earth.

Descendants of Abraham's grandson Jacob founded the 12 tribes of the Hebrews. Jacob was also called Israel, and the tribes became known as the Children of Israel, or Israelites. They settled in Canaan until a famine drove them to Egypt, then controlled along with Canaan by the Hyksos, an Asiatic power. There the Israelites apparently prospered until the pharaohs restored Egyptian power and enslaved the Israelites.

After Moses led the Children of Israel out of bondage in Egypt, they wandered the Sinai Peninsula on their way back to Canaan. During this period Moses acquired a religious covenant at Mount Sinai. It contained the written words that established the principles and beliefs of Judaism. From Sinai the Israelites invaded Canaan, conquering its cities. To the south lived the Israelites' most formidable enemy, the Philistines.

Battles against the Philistines turned in Israel's favor under three

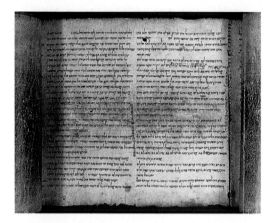

powerful kings: Saul, David, and Solomon. King David united the many tribes into the nation of Israel. His heir, Solomon, built great palaces, fortresses, and the first temple in the capital city of Jerusalem, and Israel became a political power. Judaism as a religion was observed mostly as rituals held in the temple.

The struggles of the Israelites were not over. When Solomon died, the kingdom divided into two parts with Samaria, the capital of Israel, in the north and Jerusalem, the capital of Judah, in the south. The northern segment fell to the Assyrians in 721 B.C., and the smaller southern kingdom succumbed to the Babylonians in 587 B.C.

The leading families of Judah, though scattered to other lands and without a temple in which to worship, held onto their religion through weekly meetings in which teachers, or rabbis, read and interpreted the sacred texts. This observance of their religion through weekly meetings rather than temple rituals continued even after Cyrus II (the Great) of Persia let the Jews return to their homeland, setting the basis for a religion that could be practiced anywhere in the world. ∎

THE MENORAH

Lions guard Torah scrolls above two menorahs in fourth-century gold-fused glass (above). A seven- or nine-armed candelabrum's burning candles recall that, although scattered, Jewish people are sustained by the guiding light of their God. Ritually lighting the candles of a menorah is an important part of the family holiday of Hanukkah. It joyously commemorates the rededication of the temple to the worship of one God, after the Jews triumphed over a Syrian king who tried to eradicate the Jewish faith.

"Put off thy shoes...," the Hebrew leader Moses (opposite) is told at the place of the burning bush at Mount Sinai, holy ground to Jews who hold that here God revealed himself to His people. A mosaic recalls the event in a chapel believed to be at the same location. Dead Sea Scrolls (above), written around 100 B.C. and hidden by early persecuted Jews, were found in modern times. They detail the religion's history and aspirations.

650 B.C. Introduction of iron technology to China.

605-520 B.C. The life of Lao-Tse, founder of Taoism.

581 B.C. Nebuchadrezzar II burns Jerusalem.

539 B.C. Greeks defeat Carthage.

590 B.C. Delphic Games first celebrated, in Greece.

559 B.C. Cyrus II (the Great) becomes king of Persia and reigns until 529.

522 B.C. Beginning of reign of Darius I in Persia.

2000 B.C. 　Cotton grown in Peru.

ca 1400 B.C. 　Siberian axes and lances imitated in China.

1300 B.C. 　The construction of the great rock temples of Abu Simbel begins in Egypt. First settlers arrive in Melanesia.

ca 922 B.C. 　Israel splits into Israel and Judah.

ca 1400-1100 B.C. 　Ramparts of the Acropolis, in Athens, are built.

800 B.C. 　Homer writes the *Iliad* and the *Odyssey*.

China's Splendid Isolation

Hemmed in by the Himalaya to the west, an ocean to the east, and jungle and desert elsewhere, the Chinese built their culture in relative isolation. Near the southeast coast of China, timber houses on wooden pilings were constructed over marshes 7,000 years ago, and evidence of some of the earliest rice cultivation in Asia has been found there.

Many early Chinese settlements grew along the banks of two great rivers, the Yellow and the Yangtze, which provided fertile soils as well as frequent, devastating floods.

While farmers in the warm, moist

The first dynasties brought stability to war-torn regions of China and fostered the emergence of art. A pendant of nephrite, a form of jade, takes the delicate shape of a writhing dragon *(below)* from the Eastern Zhou dynasty. Deadlier rendering, a fierce face glares from an ax blade *(above),* found in a Shang tomb with 48 victims. Its bronze craftsmanship serves as a reminder of the Shang practice of human sacrifice.

south were growing rice, those in the drier central highlands of the north lived on millet, wheat, some rice, fish, and meat, including the flesh of domesticated pigs and dogs.

All settled people had to contend with barbarians who lived in the hills nearby and raided frequently. To protect themselves, the villagers built moats around their settlements.

Because China's early villages were isolated by rivers and mountains, communities developed their own distinctive styles of pottery and housing. Carvings of nephrite and other attractive stones for rituals and

755 B.C. Solar eclipse in China sets the first verified date in Chinese history.

539 B.C. Persian conquest of Babylon.

517 B.C. Canal built from the Nile River to the Red Sea.

558 B.C. Zoroaster begins his work as prophet.

536-515 B.C. Pediments of the Temple of Apollo at Delphi constructed in Greece.

509 B.C. Tarquin the Proud, last of Rome's Etruscan kings, is deposed.

EARLY WRITING

Writing began with pictures that delivered information, such as a stick figure of a man, a tree, or an animal. To simplify and save space, symbols began substituting for the pictures. Writing advanced when the symbols began representing the sounds of human speech instead of being a shortened version of a drawing. An exception was Chinese writing, in which each symbol stood for an object, not a sound. The first-known Chinese script, used in messages to ancestors, has been found on animal bones *(above)*.

decoration have been dated back more than 5,000 years.

According to Chinese tradition, silk from the threads of worms that ate mulberry leaves was made into sleek cloth around 3000 B.C. Bronze casting began around 2000 B.C.

Constant strife was part of the early Chinese way of life. As communities grew larger, some became dominant over others, and the first Chinese dynasties appeared: the Xia, Shang, and Zhou. Shang warriors fought from chariots and wore cumbersome body armor.

With regional centralization came a measure of peace, and the civilization grew more sophisticated.

Under the Shang, urban centers arose that produced a complex writing system and great works in bronze and jade.

One's status and rank in the society was indicated by ownership of intricate carvings of jade. Kings, at the top of the ladder, also served as priests for the community. ■

Rams' heads with horns, hooves, and beards in exquisite detail decorate this ritual bronze vessel *(below)*, cast in the square shape often used by the ancient Chinese. Jade, a bridge to immortality, bears dragons *(left)* on a *pi* disk, used in burial rites along with other jade pieces.

2000 B.C. — Locks and latches come into use in Egypt.

ca 1450 B.C. — Development of Brahma worship in India.

ca 810 B.C. — Phoenicians establish Carthage.

ca 1500 B.C. — Iron weapons become common in Near East.

ca 1250 B.C. — Egyptians build the temple at Karnak.

ca 800-700 B.C. — Chariots introduced into Italy by Etruscans.

The Kingdom of Kush

The first high civilization in sub-Saharan Africa emerged along the middle Nile in the second millennium B.C. Its builders were known as the people of Kush, or Nubians. They were black Africans who occupied the land surrounding the southern portion of the river just after the First Cataract and extending farther south for several hundred miles.

The great kingdoms forged by the pharaohs of Egypt nearer the mouth of the Nile long dominated the culture of Kush, although the Kushites main-

THE ADVANCE OF METALS

Part of a gold Scythian pectoral *(above)*, pulled from a tomb in present-day Ukraine in 1971, dates back some 2,400 years. Much older, an 11,500-year-old pendant of pure copper was found in a cave in what is now Iraq. The forming of copper ore into tools goes back at least 9,000 years. Seeking stronger materials, people in the Fertile Crescent and beyond formed the first bronzes before 4000 B.C. The Kushites went from stone to iron, in the first millennium B.C., as ironworking skills spread westward.

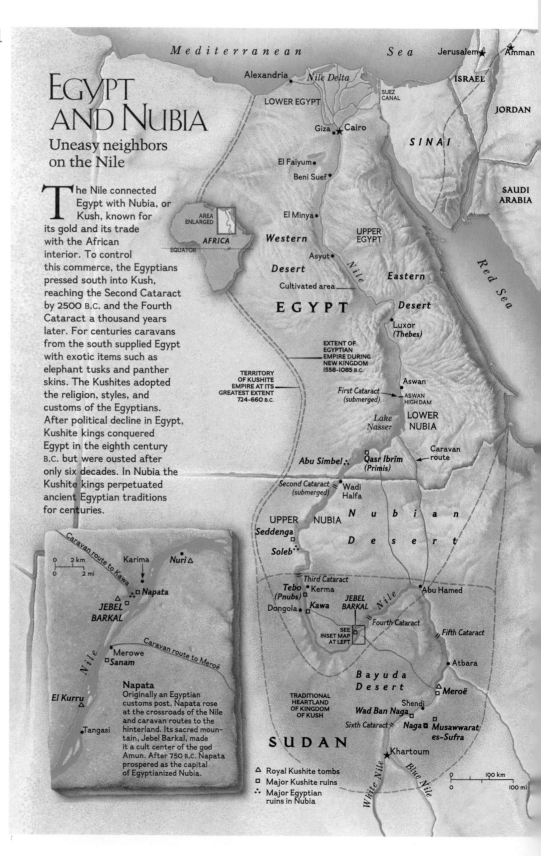

EGYPT AND NUBIA
Uneasy neighbors on the Nile

The Nile connected Egypt with Nubia, or Kush, known for its gold and its trade with the African interior. To control this commerce, the Egyptians pressed south into Kush, reaching the Second Cataract by 2500 B.C. and the Fourth Cataract a thousand years later. For centuries caravans from the south supplied Egypt with exotic items such as elephant tusks and panther skins. The Kushites adopted the religion, styles, and customs of the Egyptians. After political decline in Egypt, Kushite kings conquered Egypt in the eighth century B.C. but were ousted after only six decades. In Nubia the Kushite kings perpetuated ancient Egyptian traditions for centuries.

Napata
Originally an Egyptian customs post, Napata rose at the crossroads of the Nile and caravan routes to the hinterland. Its sacred mountain, Jebel Barkal, made it a cult center of the god Amun. After 750 B.C. Napata prospered as the capital of Egyptianized Nubia.

△ Royal Kushite tombs
□ Major Kushite ruins
⸫ Major Egyptian ruins in Nubia

700 B.C. Native Americans of the Adena culture build large mounds in what is now southern Ohio for burial places and as temple platforms.

612 B.C. Medes and Scythians sack Nineveh.

ca 604 B.C. Lao-tzu, Chinese philosopher and founder of Taoism, is born.

ca 552 B.C. Confucius is born.

526 B.C. First codes of law issued in China.

500 B.C.-A.D. 200 Period of Nok culture begins in northern Nigeria.

Long controlled by dynasties of the lower Nile, the dark-skinned Kushites conquered their oppressors in the eighth century B.C. Prisoner of war, a bound Kushite *(below)* appears on a tile from a northern palace. Defeated in turn after 60 years, the black pharaohs adopted Egyptian customs and styles, building steep-sided pyramids *(below, right)* at sacred Jebel Barkal.

tained a degree of independence. The Egyptians influenced the Kushites in matters of religion and language, and in the practice of building pyramids. From Egyptian hieroglyphics they devised their own Kushite script.

As Egypt's power went into decline, the Kushites threw off the Egyptian yoke, struck north, and by 750 B.C. had conquered their oppressors, maintaining control of them for nearly a century.

Near their first capital, Napata,

although Jebel Barkal remained an important religious center. The new capital, Meroë, developed into a busy urban center made wealthy by extensive trade in copper, gold, iron, ivory, and slaves. Artifacts indicate trade from as far north as Rome and as far east as China.

As the Kushites of Meroë grew stronger, their own gods replaced those borrowed from the Egyptians, and a royal cemetery of distinctive pyramids arose near the capital.

the Kushites built an elaborate temple to the god Amun at the base of a sandstone butte called Jebel Barkal, lining the approach to it with recumbent rams, symbols of Amun's power.

When defeat by the Assyrians drove the Kushites out of Egypt, they relocated their capital 300 miles southeast on a fertile floodplain surrounded by iron ore deposits,

Tombs of some six dozen Kushite kings have been excavated and their chronology determined.

Environmental degradation by aridity, overgrazing, and deforestation may have contributed to the Kushites' decline. In A.D. 350 the forces of Aksum in the Ethiopian highlands destroyed Meroë; extinguishing the thousand-year Kushite flame. ■

<table>
<tr><td>ca 2000 B.C.</td><td>Bronze Age begins in Europe. First use of sails on seagoing vessels in the Aegean. Bronze casting begins in China.</td><td>1950 B.C.</td><td>In Assyria building of a great temple and palace begins at Mari. In Egypt armies of Pharaoh Sesostris I invade Canaan. Decline of the empire of Ur in Mesopotamia.</td><td>1920-1850 B.C.</td><td>In Anatolia, Assyrian merchants establish a colony at Cappadocia.</td></tr>
</table>

ca 1894 B.C. Amorites found dynasty at Babylon.

Europe's First Civilization

Around 2000 B.C., with empires in the Middle East long in flower, the first advanced civilization in Europe emerged on the Mediterranean island of Crete. The people there probably came from somewhere to the east, but over the centuries they gained a unique identity by acquiring considerable wealth and influence through

Between the mountains of Crete, fertile plains yielded enough grain, timber, and olive oil for export, first to the Aegean islands and later to the eastern Mediterranean. In return the Minoans imported gold, ivory, gems, and perhaps linens from Egypt.

They became skilled at crafts, and their finely decorated pottery and

colorfully designed wool textiles were dispersed over a wide area. Gold and silver drinking vessels, as well as daggers with hunting scenes inlaid on the blades in gold and silver, have turned up in the graves of Mycenaean rulers on the Greek mainland.

With the wealth acquired in trade, the Minoans built large cities and

trade. Today we know them as the Minoans, because of legends surrounding one of their kings, Minos.

Minoan coastal communities developed steadily, while mainland Greece languished, perhaps because of frequent barbarian harassment.

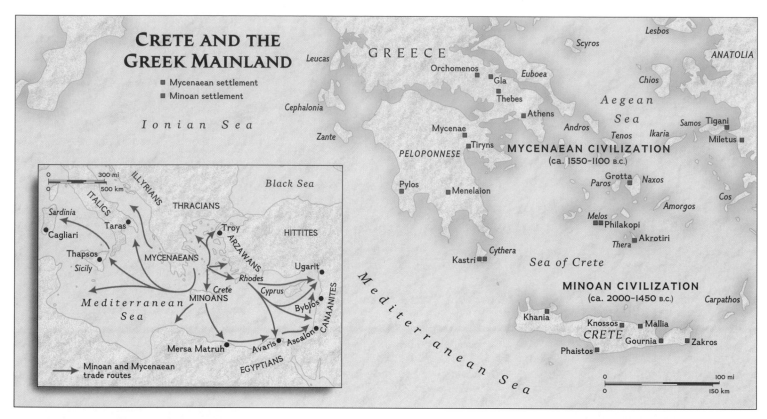

CRETE AND THE GREEK MAINLAND

- ■ Mycenaean settlement
- ■ Minoan settlement

MYCENAEAN CIVILIZATION (ca. 1550–1100 B.C.)

MINOAN CIVILIZATION (ca. 2000–1450 B.C.)

Minoan and Mycenaean trade routes

great palaces, connecting them with paved roads.

The most famous city was Knossos, where activity was centered in an incredible 1,500-room palace spread over five acres. It held apartments and workshops for craftsmen, kitchens, storehouses, bathrooms with toilets, ceremonial chambers, and two levels of underground rooms and passages.

Around 1500 B.C. Crete's well-ordered society faded. A volcanic eruption and earthquakes buried flourishing settlements on the island of Thera not far away. Then, about 50 years later fiery destruction of many Cretan cities occurred. Theories suggest the Minoans, weakened by natural disasters, were attacked and subdued by the warlike Mycenaeans. ■

A fleet appears on a section of a fresco from once prosperous Akrotiri on Thera (opposite, above). Ancient seagoing traders gathered wealth and raised temples such as one now in ruins on Cape Sounion in the Aegean (left). From the Minoans, Europe's first advanced civilization, came the legend of Theseus defeating the bull-man, Minotaur, depicted on a vase from the sixth century B.C. (above). A gold mask (opposite) commemorates a king of the Mycenaeans, the people who succeeded the Minoans.

First settlers arrive
in Micronesia.

1800 B.C.

Founding of the first
dynasty in Babylon; its
1830 B.C. armies conquer the city-
states of northern and
southern Mesopotamia.

Reign of Babylon's
Hammurapi begins.

1792 B.C.

The Mycenaeans

Around 1550 B.C., before the fall of Crete and its cities, the Mycenaeans began building a rich civilization of their own in southern Greece.

This culture was centered at the city of Mycenae, the home of Agamemnon, the king who led the ancient Greeks into the Trojan War, according to the Greek poet Homer. Fact and fiction probably combine in the long legend of the ten-year war, which the Greeks fought against the city of Troy, in present-day Turkey, over the stolen princess, Helen.

During this time period, numerous warrior groups had established separate chiefdoms on the Peloponnese, the lowermost peninsula of the Greek mainland. Within a century they had overpowered the more mercantile

Spartans wore high crests as shown on a bronze figurine *(above)*. Lion hunt on a blade *(below)*, recovered from a tomb, reveals the aggressive spirit of the Mycenaeans, skilled in hunting and warring. The legendary Greek wanderer Ulysses is reunited with his faithful wife on a terra-cotta sculpture *(opposite)*.

society to their south.

While the Minoans were merchants and traders who didn't bother to build fortifications on their home island, the Mycenaeans were warriors who hunted wild boars and lions when they weren't skirmishing with their neighbors.

Each group had its own hilltop fortress commanding surrounding farmlands, and dozens of these citadels—including Corinth, Tiryns, Olympia, Pylos, Sparta—were scattered around the Peloponnese.

The main fortified community was an impressive stronghold called Mycenae, from which the civilization takes its name. Built on a small rise on the Plain of Argos, Mycenae was ringed by 26-foot-wide walls. The

Dynasties
13-17 in Egypt.

1783-1550 B.C.

ca 1766 B.C.

Founding of the Shang
dynasty in China.

1700 B.C.

The third phase in the
building of Stonehenge
begins in England.

1700-1400 B.C.

Height of the Cretan
civilization; trading
develops with Cyprus,
Egypt, and Syria.

1558-1085 B.C.

Egypt's New Kingdom.

only entrance was a gate beneath two magnificently carved stone lions that are now in ruins, their heads no longer present.

Skilled at seagoing, the Mycenaeans traded wine, olive oil, and pottery throughout the Aegean and eastern Mediterranean and occasionally took what they wanted through piracy and raids. With the fall of Crete, they wrested control of trade routes once dominated by the Minoans, subsequently growing in wealth and power.

Fond of gold imported from Egypt, the Mycenaeans produced their own craftsmen who fashioned golden cups, flowers, jewelry, and inlaid swords. When chieftains and members of their families died, they were buried in deep shafts amid their accumulated treasures.

For some 300 years the fierce Mycenaeans dominated life in the northern Mediterranean. Then they mysteriously faded, perhaps eclipsed by a people from the north called Dorians. The Dorians were armed with strong weapons of iron instead of bronze. The Greek peninsula was plunged into a dark age of cultural chaos and stagnation that lasted several centuries.

Upon the emergence of the land of Greece from its period of eclipse, the seeds planted by the Minoans and Mycenaeans grew into a classical civilization that at one time spread across the earth and is still admired and emulated today. ■

7

1

ca 200 B.C.-A.D. 400
**The Hopewell
culture is centered in
eastern North America.**

3

ca 300 B.C.
**The Maya begin
constructing temples.**

9

ca 200 B.C.
**The Nazca of Peru
build aqueducts
and reservoirs.**

8

AROUND THE WORLD

1 Europe: Bulwark of defense, Roman soldiers stood as firm as this quartet in a second-century relief at the Louvre in Paris. At its largest in the second century A.D. the Roman Empire stretched from Britain to the Persian Gulf and the Caspian Sea.

2 Europe: Alexander of Macedon, whom the admiring Romans first dubbed Alexander the Great, spears an enemy at the pivotal Battle of Issos, recorded on a Pompeian mosaic.

Alexander carried Greek thought throughout the Middle East and beyond, across three continents into northern India.

3 Europe: Contact with many races in what became known as the Hellenistic period brought a new realism to Greek art. Sculptures of everyday scenes included two Greek women playing the popular game of knucklebones.

The Classical Age

2

ca A.D. 115
The Roman Empire extends from northern Africa to Asia and Britain.

ca A.D. 250-550
Barbarians sweep out of Asia and northern Europe.

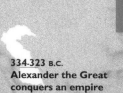

334-323 B.C.
Alexander the Great conquers an empire stretching from Greece to western India.

4

ca 200 B.C.
The Silk Road is established between traders in Europe and the Far East.

ca 450 B.C.
Athens is the center of achievement during the Golden Age of Greece.

ca 4 B.C.
Jesus of Nazareth is born in Judaea,

206 B.C.-A.D. 220
During the Han dynasty invention flourishes in China.

A.D. 320-467
Arts and sciences blossom during India's Gupta Empire.

10

5

6

4 Asia: Reconstructed during the Ming dynasty from remains of earlier fortifications, the Great Wall stretches some 2,000 miles, averages 25 feet in height, and is topped by a paved roadway 15 feet wide.

5 Asia: In this statue the guardian of an early Japanese Buddhist temple tramples a demon. In A.D. 538 Buddhism made its way from China and spread throughout Japan.

6 Asia: Art flourished and Buddhism became popular in the reign of the Gupta kings in the fourth and fifth centuries A.D. This richly carved gate to the Great Stupa at Sanchi, India, tells stories from the life of the Buddha, the "Enlightened One."

7 North America
Serpents loomed large in early American cultures.

Adena or Hopewell people left a snake-shaped earthen effigy more than a thousand feet long, winding across the landscape in what is now Ohio.

8 South America: At its height around A.D. 400, the Moche kingdom stretched nearly 400 miles down the coast of present-day Peru. Important to royalty, Moche metalworkers devised a process for coating copper masks, like this one, with gold.

9 North America: A temple seems to slumber in the mist at ancient Tikal, once a Maya metropolis that covered 50 square miles.

10 Asia: Nativity scene brightens a rock wall at Göreme, in today's Turkey, once a center for Christian worship.

The Classical Age: 500 B.C. to A.D. 500

Civilization, like all levels of achievement, requires constant practice. Experience is instructive. Knowledge feeds more knowledge. The first civilizations were single bright lights widely scattered, the beams of their progress barely reaching one another, if at all. Between 1000 and 500 B.C., as empires grew larger, they began to link up and exchange ideas.

As the world grew more sophisticated, it entered what historians call the classical age, approximately 500 B.C. to A.D. 500. Within that thousand years life became more cultured, more comfortable, and more complicated in numerous locations. New developments occurred in the performance of government and war. Art flourished and claimed considerable importance in the lives of people. Science advanced, as did philosophy. Great thinkers emerged—Confucius in China; Buddha in India; Socrates, Plato, and Aristotle in Greece.

These manifestations of the human intellect occurred roughly within the same space of time over much of the globe. Empires, each with its own unique imprint, grew in southern Europe, India, eastern Asia, western Africa, the Middle East, and Central America, with little or no contact among them. Vast realms spread their tentacles in the few centuries before and after the birth of Christ. Persian, Greek, and Roman powers rose and fell, and China and India were united under single systems for the first time. The Moche and the Maya in the Americas were slower to follow suit, but they also rose to prominence within the classical age.

The eastern Aegean was the site of a confluence of ideas, as cultural influences made themselves felt both from the nearby shores of Egypt and Syria and from as far east as India. The first great power of the classical age in this region was Persia, which came to dominate Mesopotamia, Egypt, and Asia Minor, and to threaten Greece.

The Mycenaean Greeks had fallen into a dark, historically quiet period that had lasted several centuries, but remnants of their earlier cultural flare fed a rebirth around the eighth century B.C. Hilltop chiefdoms expanded into larger political entities—city-states called *poleis,* capable of raising armies and establishing colonies on distant shores. Although frequently warring against one another, they united temporarily against the common Persian threat.

About the same time the Greek city-states struggled with divisiveness, a number of separate realms clashed in India. By the fifth century B.C. the number had been reduced. A century later all had been absorbed into the first great Indian Empire.

In the Far East, then virtually unknown to the Mediterranean world, seven warring states competed for supremacy. Prevailing eventually was the state of Qin, which gave its name to a China united for the first time.

The bickering of the Greek city-states would eventually lead to their combined defeat by Philip II, king of Macedon in the north. Much admired by Philip, the Greeks, or

Hellenes as they called themselves, did not lose their culture but rather expanded it. Philip's son Alexander defeated the Persians and made their wealth his own. In a 13-year period of amazing conquest he won victories on three continents—Europe, Asia, and Africa. His long campaign spread Hellenistic thought, language, and art from Egypt to Tashkent, from Asia Minor to the Indus River.

Alexander's empire was broken up among his generals after his death, but Greek ways had considerable influence on the next rising power, the largest and most enduring of them all. Rome's defeat of the Macedonians established its armies as the new force in the Mediterranean. Eventually Roman legions extended the realm until Rome commanded all the shores of that inland sea and had outposts as far north as the land they called Britannia, today's England. Roman control over this vast area brought a measure of stability known as *Pax Romana,* or Roman Peace, that lasted more than two centuries.

For all the bloodshed that came with consolidation of communities, tremendous accomplishments accompanied the massing of territory and wealth. Great structures arose to serve enlarged constituencies. The Greeks built well-proportioned buildings such as the Parthenon. To bring water to cities and to enable travel throughout their empire, the Romans constructed aqueducts and hard-surface roads. To unify and protect his lands, the Chinese emperor Qin Shi Huang ordered that roads, canals, and other public works be built. The people of Aksum in today's Ethiopia raised obelisks more than a hundred feet tall as tributes to their culture's importance.

Accompanying the expansion of empire was the expansion of minds to encompass new ideas. The Greek sophists raised debate to an art form. The Chinese philosophers discussed one's obligations to others. In India a ruler turned away from war and promoted nonviolence.

Just as progress seemed to be mounting in a great flame in Europe, it was all but snuffed out by the barbarians. Some were roving tribes stuck in time; others were advanced nomadic societies. A constant bother at borders, the barbarians gained strength in huge confederacies and rolled over civilizations that had grown corrupt.

Art cast its glow on civilizations in the classical age, when ideas flourished, sculpture blossomed, and Greeks—emoting through masks such as this *(above)*—gave birth to drama. Life began moving beyond mere subsistence and into realms of comfort, culture, and philosophy.

Overleaf: Ideas spread with the growth of empires. Greeks moving westward built new theaters, including one restored at Segesta, Sicily, that still pleases patrons today.

Inventions, startling for their time, were inspired by both war and peace. Roman catapults, powered by twisted hair or gut, bombarded the enemy with heavy missiles. The Chinese built an earthquake detector in the second century A.D. that showed when an earthquake had occurred and in what direction.

Great empires butted heads and power changed hands, but there was a growing sense of kinship with a wider community. Many corners waited to be explored, but the world had become a smaller place. ■

500 B.C. Susrata (Indian surgeon) performs cataract operations. Semitic people from Arabia migrate to Eritrea and Ethiopia, trading ivory, spices, and incense. Darius I of

Persia starts building king's highway from Ephesus to Susa. Paracas culture flourishes in Peru.

ca 499 B.C. First use of iron in Africa.

ca 499-494 B.C. Ionian War

ca 495-406 B.C. Life of Sophocles, poet and playwright.

494 B.C. Magadha Kingdom expanded to be the most powerful kingdom on the Ganges plain.

492 B.C. Second Persian expedition across the Hellespont.

Athens and New Ways of Thinking

The merging of societies in classical times kindled many new ideas, but in Greece, reason and inventiveness rose to new levels. The main setting for this imaginative surge was Athens, which by the fifth century B.C. had emerged as one of the largest, most powerful, and innovative of the Greek city-states.

All the Greek communities had long lived under the threat of invasion by Persia, and in 480 B.C. the giant war machine from the east succeeded

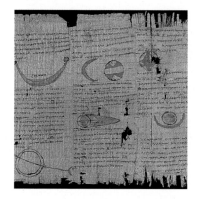

in plundering and burning Athens. But the Greek factions pulled together long enough to win important victories, and the Persians never again launched a full-scale attack. Victory over the common enemy and dominance over its Greek neighbors gave Athens a strong sense of confidence.

Strong mind, strong body, the ideal of the ancient Greeks, inspired worship of Athena, goddess of war and wisdom *(right).* Protected in the ashes of a warehouse fire, the long-buried statue retained gleaming eyes of semi-precious stones. Notes on a second-century B.C. papyrus *(above)* reflect an ancient mind grappling with celestial science. Symbol of Greek achievement, the Parthenon, temple to Athena, endures on the Acropolis at Athens *(opposite).*

486-465 B.C. India provides mercenaries for Persian wars
against the Greeks.

ca 486 B.C. Death of the Persian
King Darius.

482 B.C. Magabyzus puts
down rebellion by
Babylonians.

481 B.C.

Beginning of warring
states era in China.

ca 480 B.C. Voyage of Carthaginian
admiral Hanno along
West Africa. Persian
fleet of King Xerxes
annihilated at Salamis.

At the same time, there arose a new concept in governing—participation by common citizens.

"We are called a democracy, for the administration is in the hands of the many and not the few...," said Pericles, leader of Athens in its golden age of accomplishment near the middle of the fifth century B.C.

Monarchy by a single strong ruler had been the way of nations for centuries, giving way slowly to oligarchy, or rule by a few. Originally, the Greek word "tyrant" meant no more than the lord, or absolute ruler, of an

OLYMPIC GAMES

Personal excellence was important to the Greeks, so the Olympic games, held every four years, became a popular event. The games began in 776 B.C. as a competitive sprint in the city of Olympia, then grew into a week of trials involving athletes from all over Greece. The tradition lasted 12 centuries before a Christian Roman emperor outlawed the games as pagan in A.D. 394. In 1896 the now international Olympics were revived.

area. The Athenians made it a word to despise, a situation to be avoided, and insisted that government was the business of every male citizen over the age of 18.

"We alone regard a man who takes no interest in public affairs not as harmless, but as a useless character," continued Pericles. A popular assembly debated laws to be passed and regulations to be made. It was led by ten "generals," chosen in annual elections, and Pericles was the most influential of them for 15 years. He encouraged the

57

480-470 B.C. ● Sculptures of the Temple of Aphaea carved.

480-406 B.C. ● Life of Euripides, poet and playwright.

468-457 B.C. ● Temple of Zeus at Olympia constructed.

460 B.C. ● Birth of Hippocrates, Greek physician and "father of medicine." Sabine chief Appius Herdonius raids Capitol in Rome. Sabine and Aequian wars.

construction of monuments to Athens's greatness, including the Parthenon that commanded the Acropolis, the highest part of the city.

Proud of their past and present, the Athenians became impassioned with excellence in oration, architecture, sculpture, drama, and personal physique. Clever speaking was seen as the vehicle for success, and skilled orators flocked to the city to train others in their art.

Suddenly, old ways of doing things were questioned and argued. Greek theater throughout the peninsula originally consisted of a masked chorus and a leader singing praises to the gods, but in Athens the leader began having dialogue with others on the stage. Gradually the chorus faded into the background as the actors addressed problems in life so fundamental that some of the plays written then are still performed.

Debaters and thinkers distrusted any custom and convention, arguing that people could better their condition through the use of logic and persuasive language. This brought the very laws of the polis into question, which sometimes resulted in accusations of treason.

Socrates had defended his native Athens as a soldier and magistrate, but his public arguments about flaws he perceived in the government rankled some leading citizens. Convicted in 399 B.C. of corrupting the youth and blaspheming the gods, Socrates was given the choice of repudiating his beliefs or being put to death. True

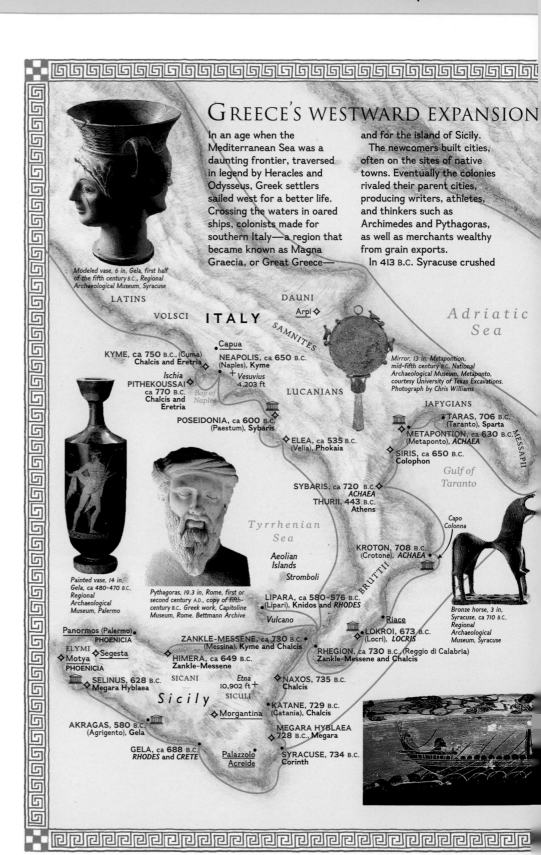

GREECE'S WESTWARD EXPANSION

In an age when the Mediterranean Sea was a daunting frontier, traversed in legend by Heracles and Odysseus, Greek settlers sailed west for a better life. Crossing the waters in oared ships, colonists made for southern Italy—a region that became known as Magna Graecia, or Great Greece—and for the island of Sicily.

The newcomers built cities, often on the sites of native towns. Eventually the colonies rivaled their parent cities, producing writers, athletes, and thinkers such as Archimedes and Pythagoras, as well as merchants wealthy from grain exports.

In 413 B.C. Syracuse crushed

Modeled vase, 6 in, Gela, first half of the fifth century B.C., Regional Archaeological Museum, Syracuse

Mirror, 13 in, Metaponion, mid-fifth century B.C. National Archaeological Museum, Metaponto, courtesy University of Texas Excavations. Photograph by Chris Williams

Painted vase, 14 in, Gela, ca 480-470 B.C. Regional Archaeological Museum, Palermo

Pythagoras, 19.3 in, Rome, first or second century A.D., copy of fifth-century B.C. Greek work, Capitoline Museum, Rome. Bettmann Archive

Bronze horse, 3 in, Syracuse, ca 710 B.C. Regional Archaeological Museum, Syracuse

LATINS
VOLSCI
ITALY
DAUNI
Arpi
Adriatic Sea
SAMNITES
Capua
KYME, ca 750 B.C., (Cuma) Chalcis and Eretria
NEAPOLIS, ca 650 B.C. (Naples), Kyme
Vesuvius 4,203 ft
Ischia
PITHEKOUSSAI ca 770 B.C. Chalcis and Eretria
Bay of Naples
LUCANIANS
IAPYGIANS
POSEIDONIA, ca 600 B.C. (Paestum), Sybaris
TARAS, 706 B.C. (Taranto), Sparta
METAPONTION, ca 630 B.C. (Metaponto), ACHAEA
ELEA, ca 535 B.C. (Velia), Phokaia
SIRIS, ca 650 B.C. Colophon
Gulf of Taranto
SYBARIS, ca 720 B.C. ACHAEA
THURII, 443 B.C. Athens
MESSAPII
Tyrrhenian Sea
Capo Colonna
KROTON, 708 B.C. (Crotone), ACHAEA
Aeolian Islands
Stromboli
BRUTTII
Panormos (Palermo)
PHOENICIA
LIPARA, ca 580-576 B.C. (Lipari), Knidos and RHODES
Vulcano
Riace
ELYMI
Motya Segesta
PHOENICIA
ZANKLE-MESSENE, ca 730 B.C. (Messina), Kyme and Chalcis
LOKROI, 673 B.C. (Locri), LOCRIS
RHEGION, ca 730 B.C. (Reggio di Calabria) Zankle-Messene and Chalcis
HIMERA, ca 649 B.C. Zankle-Messene
SELINUS, 628 B.C. Megara Hyblaea
SICANI
Etna 10,902 ft
NAXOS, 735 B.C. Chalcis
Sicily
SICULI
KATANE, 729 B.C. (Catania), Chalcis
Morgantina
AKRAGAS, 580 B.C. (Agrigento), Gela
MEGARA HYBLAEA 728 B.C., Megara
GELA, ca 688 B.C. RHODES and CRETE
Palazzolo Acreide
SYRACUSE, 734 B.C. Corinth

ca 450 B.C. ● **Brisk gold trade between Libya and West Africa. Specialized woodworking tools appear along northwest coast of Canada and Alaska.**

449 B.C. ● **Roman republic grows in power; earliest Roman code of laws.**

438 B.C. ● **Completion of the Parthenon in Athens.**

ca 415 B.C. ● **The first five books of the Bible (the Hebrew Torah, traditionally ascribed to Moses) given the form in which we have them today. Hindu mythology codified in the Ramayana.**

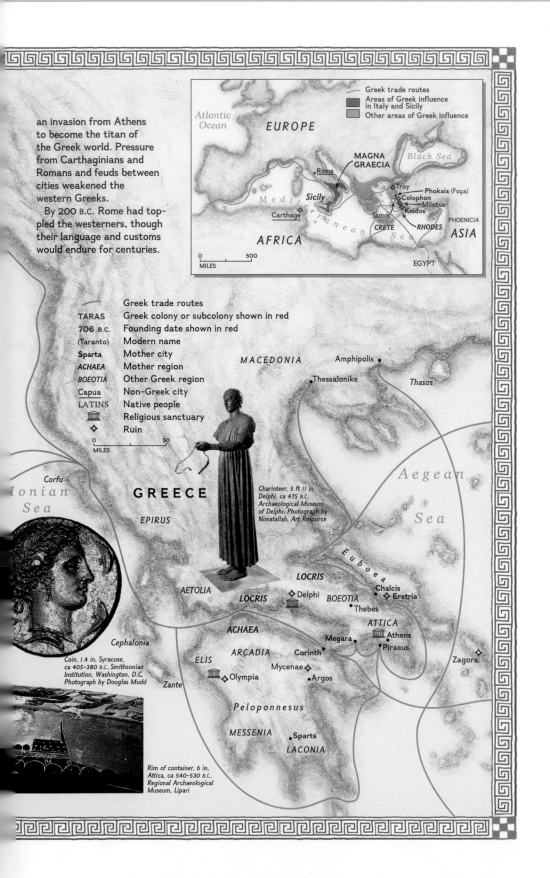

an invasion from Athens to become the titan of the Greek world. Pressure from Carthaginians and Romans and feuds between cities weakened the western Greeks.

By 200 B.C. Rome had toppled the westerners, though their language and customs would endure for centuries.

Greek trade routes
Areas of Greek influence in Italy and Sicily
Other areas of Greek influence

Atlantic Ocean — EUROPE — Black Sea — MAGNA GRAECIA — Rome — Sicily — Carthage — Mediterranean Sea — Troy — Phokaia (Foça) — Colophon — Miletos — Knidos — Samos — CRETE — RHODES — AFRICA — ASIA — PHOENICIA — EGYPT

0 — 500 — MILES

TARAS — Greek trade routes
706 B.C. — Greek colony or subcolony shown in red
(Taranto) — Founding date shown in red
Sparta — Modern name
ACHAEA — Mother city
BOEOTIA — Mother region
Capua — Other Greek region
LATINS — Non-Greek city
— Native people
— Religious sanctuary
— Ruin

0 — 50 — MILES

MACEDONIA — Amphipolis — Thessalonike — Thasos

Corfu — Ionian Sea — GREECE — EPIRUS — Aegean Sea

Charioteer, 5 ft 11 in, Delphi, ca 475 B.C. Archaeological Museum of Delphi. Photograph by Nimatallah, Art Resource

Coin, 1.4 in, Syracuse, ca 405-380 B.C., Smithsonian Institution, Washington, D.C. Photograph by Douglas Mudd

Cephalonia — AETOLIA — LOCRIS — LOCRIS — Delphi — BOEOTIA — Thebes — Chalcis — Eretria — Euboea — ATTICA — Athens — Piraeus — Megara — ACHAEA — Corinth — Zagora — ELIS — ARCADIA — Mycenae — Argos — Zante — Olympia — Peloponnesus — MESSENIA — Sparta — LACONIA

Rim of container, 6 in, Attica, ca 540-530 B.C., Regional Archaeological Museum, Lipari

to his truth, he chose death, drinking hemlock in prison.

In medicine, Hippocrates founded a school that looked into the causes of diseases instead of simply blaming them on evil spirits. Aristotle split science into categories such as biology and physics and studied them all. Herodotus, the first historian, not only recorded events but also wrote of the customs and habits of people. Phideas created statues of great beauty and majesty. Friend of Pericles, he also supervised the building of the Parthenon and contributed the temple frieze, along with an ivory-and-gold statue of Athena.

For all the exercising of brains, attention was focused on fitness as well. Men visited gymnasiums to exercise, wrestle, and keep "a sound mind in a sound body."

The advantages of Athenian glory were not for everyone. Women's instruction was limited to homemaking, and neither they nor slaves—who made up a fifth of Athens's population—were allowed to vote.

Nevertheless, Athens in the fifth century B.C. was a place of achievement that may be unparalleled in human history. Athens's golden age would last less than a hundred years as wars and city-state rivalries gradually wore down the city's intellectual exuberance, but the creative energy in that short time would affect the world for centuries to come.

Mighty Rome copied the art of Greece, borrowed its gods, and imitated its representative government. ■

● Adena people in Ohio reach peak of their civilization. High point of Etruscan political power and civilization in Italy. Persians take rice, peaches, apricots to western Asia.

ca 500 B.C.

● Athenians, at the Battle of Marathon, beat the Persians, bringing an end to the First Persian War. Athenian shrine at Delphi is the first marble building in Greece.

490 B.C.

● Pericles governs Athens.

ca 460-429 B.C.

● Plague at Athens kills a quarter of the citizens.

ca 480 B.C.

● Athenians build the Long Wall to connect the city with its port Piraeus, making Athens impossible to blockade by land alone.

458-456 B.C.

The Emergence of Rome

Primitive farmers and herders were the first occupants of the hills on either side of the Tiber River, on the Italian peninsula west of Greece. In the eighth century B.C., when the Persian Empire was still expanding and Greek city-states were emerging from their dark age, those earliest residents of Rome were dominated by a group known as the Etruscans.

Little remains aboveground from the time of the Etruscans, whose exact origins are unknown. In tombs of the wealthy, however, they left evidence of lives filled with music, chariot races, athletic contests, and a lively art. Pleasureful though their lives may have been, the Etruscans were not welcome along the Tiber.

By 509 B.C. the Romans had driven the Etruscans out of the city and replaced their monarchy with a Roman republic, led by two consuls

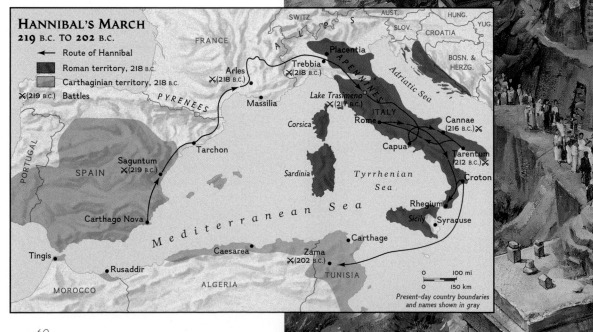

HANNIBAL'S MARCH
219 B.C. TO 202 B.C.

→ Route of Hannibal
■ Roman territory, 218 B.C.
■ Carthaginian territory, 218 B.C.
✕(219 B.C.) Battles

0 — 100 mi
0 — 150 km
Present-day country boundaries and names shown in gray

447 B.C.	Reconstruction of the Athenian acropolis begins with building of the Parthenon.	406 B.C.	Deaths of Euripides and Sophocles bring the great age of Athenian drama to an end.	297-280 B.C.	First lighthouse is built, the Pharos of Alexandria, a 425-foot-tall marble tower, considered one of the seven wonders of the world. A fire at the base reflected off bronze mirrors to create a beacon.	206 B.C.	Rome gains control of Spain.
431-404 B.C.	Great Peloponnesian War between Athens and Sparta.	ca 325 B.C.	End of La Venta, center of Olmec culture in Mexico.			200 B.C.	Germanic tribes reach the lower Danube River.

elected by popular assemblies.

Rome became the leader in a loose confederation of Latin cities in central Italy, united against their Etruscan foes and the surrounding primitive tribes, such as the Sabines and Volsci. Rome expanded its territory, and by 280 B.C. the Italian peninsula was united under that city's government. The remaining Etruscans were absorbed into Roman culture.

The new emerging power in the Mediterranean was viewed with alarm by the Phoenician city of Carthage in north Africa, which had been battling the Greeks for centuries. Rome and Carthage began a series of conflicts known as the Punic Wars, "Punic" being the Roman word for "Phoenician."

Rome first drove the Carthaginians from Sicily in 241 B.C., then clashed with them again, beginning in 219 B.C. when the skillful Carthaginian general, Hannibal, came overland from Spain to attack Italy. Although never defeated in the field over 12 years, he was forced to withdraw from Italy when the Romans stirred up trouble in his homeland.

By 202 B.C. Rome had destroyed Carthage and occupied northern Africa. When the Romans subdued the Macedonian Greeks a half century later, Rome controlled the entire Mediterranean area. ∎

Best known by their tombs, the Etruscans, who dominated early Roman tribes, enjoyed art, music, and games. In this painting, a funeral cortege carries a body to its burial cave in the ancient city of Norchia, while athletic contests on the plateau above serve as a memorial to the deceased.

● Athens sacked by Sulla.

87 B.C.

● Chinese pull back
behind the Great Wall.

68 B.C.

● Julius Caesar wins
his first major victories,
in Spain.

61 B.C.

● The Chinese conquer
Central Asia.

59 B.C.

● Julius Caesar
conquers Gaul.

49 B.C.

● End of Egypt's
Ptolemaic dynasty.

30 B.C.

The Roman Empire

According to legend, Rome was founded by Romulus, who was suckled as an infant by a she-wolf, along with his twin brother Remus, whom he later killed for challenging his authority. Rome lived up to that fratricidal legend as its influence widened and rival generals battled each other.

Although the assemblies still met and magistrates went through the motions of administration, real power in Rome rested increasingly in the hands of military men. Chief among them was Julius Caesar, who had gained popular support with bloody victories in Gaul (western Europe), Asia, Egypt, and Africa.

Ruling as a virtual dictator while promising to restore the republic, Caesar angered opponents, who assassinated him in 44 B.C. His successor, Augustus, rather than press for new conquests, pacified the empire and cloaked it in grandeur.

At its largest in the second century A.D. the Roman world stretched from England to the Persian Gulf and the Caspian Sea. Roman theaters entertained in Africa, Roman aqueducts carried water in France, Roman country villas with indoor latrines sprang up in Britain. Hard-surface Roman roads tied much of the empire together. Stone walls to keep out barbarians were built along the Danube, beyond the Rhine, in Syria, and in northern Africa. Hadrian's Wall snaked across northern England from sea to sea.

At first the conquering Romans let local client states govern themselves. Later, Roman governors were

ROME'S HARD ROADS

The Romans tied their empire together with some 50,000 miles of hard-surface roads to move troops quickly to far frontiers. Rivers were bridged, valleys filled, and mountains bored for a route usually straight as an arrow and cambered for drainage. Workers tamped the base and built up the roadbed with alternate stone and concrete in strata, which gave us the word "street."

assigned to faraway districts to oversee legal affairs. Rome grew rich from looted cities and widespread taxation, but for about two centuries much of the known world experienced stability and orderliness.

Free men in any country in the empire could become Roman citizens. Roman law prevailed, which called for people to draw up contracts in their dealings with each other; such contracts were enforceable in the courts. Some enlightened Roman monarchs insisted on efficient administration and speedy justice everywhere.

Watching over this widespread tranquillity were the Roman legions, perhaps the most efficient military machine in history. The extensive frontiers were guarded by an army of some 300,000, stationed in permanent camps. Whether a citizen volunteer or a recruit from the provinces, the legionary was a professional soldier steeped in discipline, clothed in armor, and led by military tacticians.

4 B.C. Death of Herod the Great, traditionally associated with the birth of Christ and Massacre of the innocents.

A.D. 2 First surviving census figure for China, 57.7 million.

A.D. 27 Jesus is baptized by John the Baptist.

ca A.D. 30 Crucifixion and resurrection of Jesus Christ.

A.D. 43 Roman invasion of Britain.

Mighty in warfare, vigilant in peace, the Romans built miles-long fortifications to deter invaders. Hadrian's Wall *(opposite)*, part of which still stands, stretched from sea to sea, across the land named Britannia, to resist savage northerners. Bulwark of defense, the Roman soldier stood as firm as this quartet in a second-century relief at the Louvre in Paris *(above)*. Other structures served in peacetime. A graded aqueduct 90 feet tall *(right)* near Segovia, Spain, still carries water to this formerly Roman city.

ca 50 B.C. Buddhism begins to spread along the Silk Road from India to China.

44 B.C. Julius Caesar is assassinated

A.D. 45 Birth of Pan Chao (sister of Gen. Ban Chao), historian, poet, astronomer, mathematician, and educator.

A.D. 56 Amphitheater at Leptis Magna built, one of the largest in the Roman Empire, seating some 25,000 people.

A.D. 58 Emperor Ming Ti introduces Buddhism into China.

A.D. 70 Romans destroy the Jewish Temple in Jerusalem.

Closing with the enemy, a legionary first hurled a javelin, then fought man to man with a short thrusting sword while protecting himself with a wooden shield rimmed with iron. If he survived 20 years of this, he was paid well in plunder, bonuses, and a pension in land. Foreign recruits were rewarded with Roman citizenship.

The capital itself also flourished in Rome's heyday. Caesar built a second Roman Forum of grand public buildings. His successor, Augustus, built another. Shrines and monuments were raised to gods borrowed from the Greeks.

Stately arches loomed above generals parading home after foreign conquests. Citizens relaxed in grand, heated public baths built by the Emperor Caracalla; and 50,000 spectators could be seated in the

THE ROMAN EMPIRE

Greatest extent at the time of Trajan, A.D. 117

0   400 mi
0   400 km

A.D. 74 — Gen. Ban Chao begins silk trade with Roman Empire.

A.D. 105 — First use of paper in China.

A.D. 165 — Roman Empire ravaged by smallpox epidemic.

A.D. 200 — Artist Wei Fu-Jen, considered greatest Chinese calligrapher.

A.D. 82-132 — Empire of China ruled by a succession of women.

A.D. 132-135 — Jewish revolt in Israel attempts and fails to establish an independent state.

A.D. 184 — Han China is disrupted by "Yellow Turbans" rebellions.

massive Roman Colosseum to watch games and gladiators. Gardens and villas of the rich adorned the city, although the poor lived in several-story tenements that sometimes collapsed and frequently caught fire.

It was the Golden Age of Rome, a time of power and wealth and—for the great mass of people—freedom from war and traumatic changes in government. Edward Gibbon, an 18th-century historian, called it "the period in the history of the world during which the condition of the human race was most happy and prosperous."◼

Monument to Roman engineering, the Colosseum *(left)* could hold 50,000 spectators. Underground cages and cells contained beasts and humans doomed to mortal combat on an open field of sand —*arena*—used to soak up the blood. A second-century Roman mosaic *(below)* records gladiators urged on by trumpet, horns, and a hydraulic organ. A Pompeii couple hold a tablet and a papyrus roll *(opposite, above).*

| A.D. 256 | Roman province of Gaul is overrun by Germanic invaders from the Rhine frontier. | A.D. 300 | Settlement of eastern Polynesia. Rice becomes main staple food of southern Chinese. Beginning of early eastern Polynesian culture. Classic period of Maya art begins. | A.D. 350 | Christianity reaches Ethiopia. | A.D. 396 | St. Augustine becomes bishop of Hippo, in Africa. |

A.D. 293 — Emperor Diocletian reorganizes Roman Empire.

A.D. 335-375 — Classic period of Hindu India.

A.D. 375 — Central Asian Huns attack eastern Europe.

The Decline of Rome

Gradually the military gained the upper hand in Rome, and the civilian government was little more than a figurehead. The loss of any form of democracy and control from the assembly led to excesses by some leaders, which undermined public confidence.

Meanwhile, barbarians continued to attack the borders. Constantly repulsing them was costly. Resources might have been sufficient to maintain the frontiers, but they were wasted in battles between rival emperors.

After Diocletian became emperor in A.D. 284, he decided the empire was too large for any one person to govern and divided it into two parts, the eastern and the western provinces, with an administrator for each.

The empire's strength shifted eastward, and when Constantine became emperor of the eastern empire, he moved his capital to Byzantium—now Istanbul, Turkey—and renamed the city after himself: Constantinople. Slowly the Roman Empire drifted irreversibly apart.

Situated favorably for commerce and defense near both the Black and the Aegean Seas and supported by the growing Christian religion, the eastern empire continued to thrive for many centuries.

The western half gradually shrank before the continued attacks by Germanic tribes. Besieged by Picts and Saxons, the Roman legions melted away from Britannia at the beginning of the fifth century A.D. Visigoths swept through Gaul and invaded Italy around A.D. 400, then sacked Rome

Amid the remnants of past glories, citizens of Rome cower before the conquering Visigoths who pillaged the

itself in 410. Vandals overran it again in 455, and the last emperor in the city of Rome was deposed by a German chief in 476. In 493 a

Germanic kingdom was established in Italy, and the western part of the Roman Empire was finished.

Once a world capital and home to

A.D. 399 First known female surgeon, the Roman Fabiola, dies.

A.D. 400 Inca established along parts of South American Pacific coast.

A.D. 404 Latin version of Bible completed.

A.D. 409 Vandals take part of Spain and establish their capital at Toledo.

A.D. 409-416 Christians allowed to worship freely in Persia.

A.D. 500 The Ghanaian Empire becomes most important power in West.

Who Were the Barbarians?

Throughout Roman history and during the time of all early civilizations, great sweeps of wild land still existed, occupied by barbaric nomads given more to roving and raiding than building permanent structures. They harassed the great powers continually, sometimes destroying everything they had accomplished, although progress in technology would eventually advance again.

In a huge migration during the late fourth and early fifth centuries A.D., Goths and Huns swept out of the Eurasian northwest, and Angles, Saxons, and Vandals moved down from northern Europe. Able to travel light and fast, sometimes in large confederacies, they were formidable fighters, using short bows when on horseback and sabers at close range.

The Chinese and the Persians as well as the Romans battled against these "uncivilized" people from the north. The Chinese dynasties collapsed before them, but assimilated the northerners into their culture. The Romans were defeated and their capital burned. Only the Persians, better mounted and armored than the horsemen of the steppes, successfully defended their northern borders from the barbarians; yet they later fell to Arab invaders from the south.

As the savage nomads conquered, however, they began to enjoy the fruits of civilized living. Often they lost their warrior edge, setting the stage either for defeat by other forces or, as in the case of the Franks, the gradual formation of organized civilizations of their own. ■

powerful city for three days in A.D. 410.

perhaps a million people, Rome eventually shrank to a population of around 17,000. Cows grazed where Julius Caesar had reigned supreme. ■

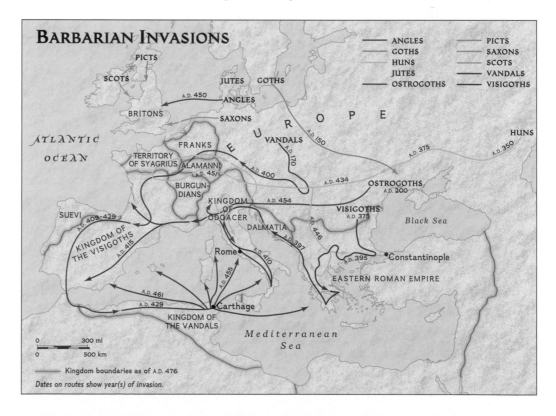

BARBARIAN INVASIONS

ANGLES
GOTHS
HUNS
JUTES
OSTROGOTHS
PICTS
SAXONS
SCOTS
VANDALS
VISIGOTHS

PICTS
SCOTS
JUTES GOTHS
A.D. 450
ANGLES
BRITONS
SAXONS
EUROPE
ATLANTIC OCEAN
FRANKS
TERRITORY OF SYAGRIUS
ALAMANNI A.D. 451
BURGUNDIANS
KINGDOM OF ODOACER
VANDALS A.D. 150
A.D. 170
A.D. 400
A.D. 454
A.D. 434
OSTROGOTHS A.D. 200
HUNS
A.D. 375
A.D. 350
SUEVI
A.D. 409-429
KINGDOM OF THE VISIGOTHS A.D. 415
DALMATIA
VISIGOTHS A.D. 375
A.D. 446
A.D. 397
Black Sea
Rome
A.D. 410
A.D. 395
Constantinople
EASTERN ROMAN EMPIRE
A.D. 461
A.D. 429
A.D. 455
Carthage
KINGDOM OF THE VANDALS
Mediterranean Sea

0   300 mi
0   500 km

—— Kingdom boundaries as of A.D. 476
Dates on routes show year(s) of invasion.

500 B.C. ● The start of wet rice culture in Japan.

446 B.C. ● Athens and Sparta, two city-states, sign 30-year peace treaty.

440 B.C. ● Celtic tribes begin invasions of Roman and Greek territories.

367 B.C. ● Beginning of one hundred years of war between Carthage and Sicily.

339-338 B.C. ● Fourth Sacred War between Macedonia and Athens.

332 B.C. ● Alexander the Great invades and conquers Egypt.

The Might of Persia

Persia's fortunes rose and fell over the centuries, its boundaries expanding and contracting, but as a political institution its monarchy continued for some 2,500 years.

Its beginnings can be traced to around 1000 B.C., when a number of nomadic peoples, including the Persians and the Medes, drifted into today's Iran from somewhere in the east. Both enjoyed organizational success until the Persians overcame and absorbed the Medes around 550 B.C.

Leading the Persians at that time was a keen military strategist known as Cyrus the Great, a member of the Achaemenid family, which controlled the throne for several hundred years.

The empire gained some cohesion under Darius I, another Achaemenid, who united the many cities and tribal groups into a single Persian nation during his reign from 522 to 486 B.C. He adopted a unified coinage, thereby simplifying the widespread economy. Egypt and northwestern India were added to the empire.

The famed 1,600-mile Royal Road

and numerous secondary roads were built to speed the military to trouble spots, but they aided the travels of merchants as well.

Imperial Persia had 20 provinces that were ruled by satraps, or governors. The realm prospered for more than two centuries, with four capitals. Excavations at one of the cities, Persepolis, reveal evidence of great wealth, grand architecture, and extravagant works of silver and gold.

Additions to Persia's vast holdings came to a halt when Darius's attempts at invading Europe only partially succeeded. Although the Persians once destroyed Athens, they were never able to conquer Greece.

Persian rule over a wide area was successful partly because it was tolerant of local ways and other religions. After their conquests, the conquerors attempted to retain local legal systems, customs, and religions, so long as they did not threaten the regime.

Royalty kept its eyes on far-flung provinces through inspectors—actually state spies—who reported on activities that might lead to revolt before it could happen. Word traveled quickly, thanks to a courier system of hard-riding messengers on graded roads, with rested horses at stations spaced out along the route.

Zoroastrianism, the Persian religion, sought no converts. After Babylon was annexed, for example, the Jews who had been exiled there were allowed to return to Jerusalem. Based on the teachings of the prophet Zoroaster, about whom little is

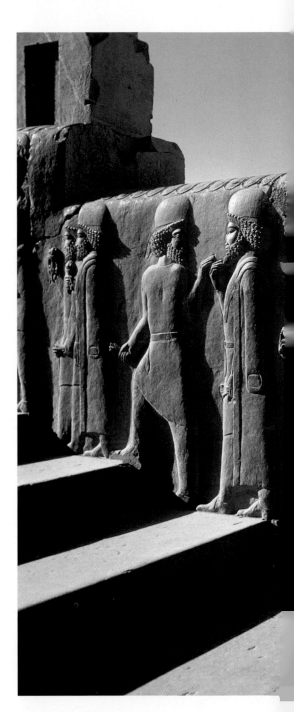

known, the religion teaches obedience to one virtuous deity who is in conflict with another power that represents evil.

Zoroastrianism espouses ethical conduct toward other people,

300-100 B.C. ● The growing city of Teotihuacan comes to dominate the Valley of Mexico.

ca 200 B.C. ● Hopewell period begins in eastern North America. The people are skilled workers in wood and stone.

ca 112 B.C. ● The Silk Road opens across Central Asia, linking China to West.

37 B.C. ● Mark Antony marries Cleopatra.

Party guests locked in stone ascend steps at Persepolis to enter a banquet hall. Persia ruled over 23 nations before Alexander the Great defeated the empire and built Greek cities on former Persian lands. A medallion *(opposite)* found at Ai Khanum in Afghanistan shows both Greek and Asian influences.

rewarding adherents with prosperity in this life and immortality in the next.

A strong force within the Persian hierarchy, Zoroastrianism also influenced other religions, including Judaism, Christianity, and Islam.

It is still the religion of the Parsis, a people descended from Persian refugees who sought freedom from Muslim persecution between the eighth and tenth centuries A.D. They settled principally in Bombay, India. ■

338 B.C. ● Battle of Chaeronea gives Macedon control of Greece.

336 B.C. ● Death of Philip II of Macedon, father of Alexander the Great.

334 B.C. ● Aristotle founds the Lyceum.

333 B.C. ● Viet Kingdom in lower Yangtze Valley destroyed by the Chinese.

332 B.C. ● Egypt conquered by Alexander the Great.

Alexander the Conqueror

Persia met its match in one of the great military leaders of all time, Alexander of Macedon, whom the admiring Romans first dubbed Alexander the Great. The city of Athens helped shape Greek thought, but Alexander carried it throughout the Middle East and beyond, with conquests that dipped into northern India.

Defeating Persia with the help of a united Greece had been the dream of Alexander's father, Philip II of Macedon, when he conquered the divided city-states in 338 B.C. At that time Alexander was 18 years old and leading a cavalry charge in the decisive battle at Chaeronea. When an assassin's knife killed his father two years later, Alexander became king of Macedon at the age of 20 and leader of the unified Greek army.

Philip II is believed to have developed the phalanx, a tight cluster of foot soldiers that moved into battle holding their shields close together and wielding spears so long that those held by men in the fifth rank extended beyond the men in the first rank. As long as the formation held, enemy soldiers were confronted by a surging wall, bristling with pikes.

In 334 B.C., with a force of 30,000 foot soldiers and 5,000 cavalry, Alexander left the Macedonian capital of Pella on an expedition that would last more than a decade.

Although a century and a half had passed since the Persians had burned Athens, the Greeks still sought vengeance. Led by Alexander, they defeated the forces of Darius III, who was later killed by his own men after he had fled. The young conqueror claimed all Persian lands and wealth for himself and his troops, although he took little booty personally.

"Avenge Greece," he shouted as he torched rich Persepolis, later

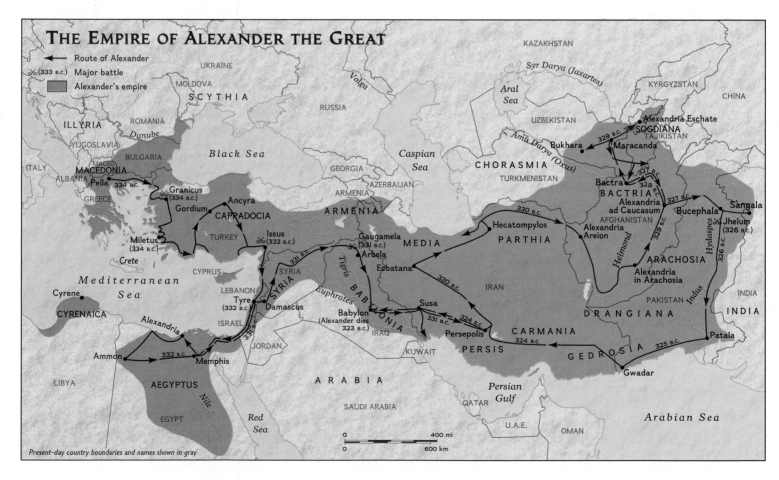

THE EMPIRE OF ALEXANDER THE GREAT

→ Route of Alexander
⚔ (333 B.C.) Major battle
▓ Alexander's empire

Present-day country boundaries and names shown in gray

0 400 mi
0 600 km

323-30 B.C. ● Ptolemaic dynasty flourishes in Egypt.

322 B.C. ● The Stoic school is founded by Zeno of Cyprus, on the principle that virtue, based on knowledge, is the only good. Aristotle dies; Theophrastus becomes head of the Lyceum.

321 B.C. ● Chandragupta Maurya takes the throne of Magadha and expands his rule over northern India.

320 B.C. ● Egypt takes Libya as a province.

Alexander, far left, spears an enemy as Persian ruler Darius III flees in his chariot at the pivotal Battle of Issos, recorded on a Pompeian mosaic.

regretting the act. The treasures there, he observed, would burden 5,000 camels and 20,000 mules.

Although seeking to enrich his homeland, he also wanted to maintain unity throughout his conquered realm. After his first major victory in Asia at Granicus, he spread the word that he came as a liberator, not as a conqueror.

Many cities that had been founded by Greek colonists centuries earli-er welcomed him. As he conquered Egypt and Babylon and drove his forces for thousands of miles across three continents, he sought the loyalty of local peoples by worshiping at their shrines.

Always he championed Greek ways, founding cities on the Greek model. Chief among them was Alexandria in Egypt, which became a cosmopolitan learning center that guided science for centuries. In the wake of his conquests came thousands of Greeks, seeking their fortunes and becoming merchants and administrators. In the process they spread Hellenistic thought throughout the Mediterranean and western Asia.

Alexander pushed into India and might have gone farther had his troops not rebelled and demanded to return home. On the way, he died of a fever at the age of 32, having run out of worlds to conquer. ■

250 B.C. Hebrew scriptures translated into Greek in Alexandria.

241 B.C.

Rome gains control of all Sicily.

240 B.C. The first Greek comedy is written in Latin for a Roman audience.

227 B.C. Sicily, Sardinia, and Corsica constitute Roman provinces.

226 B.C. Temple of Virtue and Honour built at Rome.

200 B.C. In Peru, large-scale geometric and animal shapes, known as the Nazca Lines, are scratched out in the desert.

The Alexandrian Empire in Pieces

The empire that Alexander had taken over broke into separate parts in less time than it had taken him to conquer it. Within a few years a power struggle among his generals divided the realm three ways, with the Antigonid family ruling Macedonia, the Seleucids ruling present-day Syria, the Ptolemies ruling Egypt.

Of the three, Egypt with its wealth and sea power was initially strongest. Its capital was moved from Memphis to Alexandria, and Ptolemy extended his interests into Palestine, where he confronted the Seleucids, the empire with the largest territory of the three. At sea he struggled with the Antigonids for control of the Aegean.

All three leaders were Macedonian generals with strong Greek, or Hellenistic, influences. The Greeks pouring out of their homeland in search of fortune found prominent positions as government officials and administrators or entered business in the widespread cities, which held mixed Greek and local populations. A Hellenization of much of the entire region gradually took place. Greek became the elite language, and Greek education was sought by the upper classes. Far from Greece in today's Uzbekistan, near the Chinese border, a Greek dynasty ruled a country called Bactria for two centuries.

165 B.C. ● Judas Maccabaeus recaptures Jerusalem from the Greeks. The Jews' cleansing of the Temple forms the basis of Hanukkah.

149-146 B.C. ● Third Punic War; Rome founds province of Africa.

43 B.C. ● The orator Cicero is put to death for denouncing Mark Antony.

A.D.14 ● The Pont du Gard aqueduct is built by the Romans in southern France.

● Rome sacks Corinth.
146 B.C.

30 B.C. ● Egyptian farmers produce much of the grain needed to feed people throughout the Roman Empire.

wholly died out among the people.

By successfully connecting this reestablished religion with the throne, the Sassanians created a Persian unity that allowed them to avoid the constant turmoil between aristocrats and the central government that Rome had experienced and which had brought about frequent usurpation and assassinations in the Roman capital. The Sassanian example had some influence on later European governments. ■

Contact with many races in what became known as the Hellenistic age brought a new realism to Greek art. Exquisite details bring life to a gold ceremonial ibex *(below)* from distant Bactria, ruled by Greeks for two centuries. Alexander's empire fragmented after his death, but the Greek influence prevailed as job-seekers followed in his path. Sculptures of everyday scenes include two Greek women playing the popular game of knucklebones *(opposite)*. Architect of the age was the father of Alexander, Philip II of Macedon, killed before he could begin his plan of conquest. The recently found tomb that produced this wreath of gold oak leaves *(left)*, may have held Philip II's remains.

Greeks now found themselves members of not just a polis but a cosmopolis, a larger community that in their minds included the whole civilized world—and a fairly stable one at that. Self-proclaimed cynics with no particular attachment to any kingdom proclaimed themselves citizens of the world.

In 250 B.C. people from central Asia carved out a Parthian kingdom in eastern Persia. In the middle of the second century B.C. the Parthian king Mithradates I, setting out to reestablish the Persian Empire of three centuries earlier, managed to consolidate the lands between the Caspian Sea and the Persian Gulf, overpowering the Seleucids.

In the meantime Macedon, which had allied with Hannibal in 215 B.C. against upstart Rome, was attacked in 146 B.C. in retaliation and made a

Roman province. When Cleopatra VII, the last of the Ptolemy family, was defeated by Augustus in 30 B.C., all of Alexander's heritage was in Roman hands, and the Hellenistic grip on the Middle East was finally broken.

Rome, however, in all its power and glory was never able to subdue the Parthians of Persia. A Persian way of life had persisted in the countryside more than in the city. As Greek influence faded, the culture and language of Persia revived.

The dynasty of Mithradates lasted nearly 300 years; it was unseated in A.D. 226 by a Parthian rebel named Ardashir, a member of the Sassanian family.

Ardashir cultivated a consciousness of Persia's past greatness and rekindled strong belief in Zoroastrianism, a religion that had never

486-465 B.C.   ● Reign of Xerxes in Persia.

480 B.C.   ● Carthage develops a naval fleet and takes part of the Mediterranean. Greeks defeat the Persians in the sea battle of Salamis.

465-400 B.C.   ● Reign of Artaxerxes I in Persia.

367 B.C.   ● Aristotle joins the Athenian Academy.

China, a World Apart

Just as the Mediterranean world knew nothing of the Chinese in the early Classical period, the Chinese believed they were the only civilized people on earth.

When the Zhou dynasty took over from the Shang dynasty in the 11th century B.C., they retained most Shang cultural traditions. Holders of a huge domain, they set up vassal states ruled by regional lords, a system that continued for 300 years.

By 800 B.C., however, rebels overran the capital city of Hao. By 700 B.C. the Zhou kingdom had split into many different kingdoms, some of them walled.

During this time of constant strife,

Still vigilant after 2,200 years is a terra-cotta archer unearthed near the tomb of China's first emperor, Qin Shi Huang. Such statues were designed to protect the dead ruler, but immortality for the Qin, or Ch'in, dynasty came only in the name of the nation it unified— China. Living marksmen hurled bronze arrowheads *(above),* their wooden shafts long since disintegrated.

280 B.C. ● A giant bronze statue of the Greek sun god Helios is built in the Rhodes harbor.

264-241 B.C. ● First Punic War; Rome defeats Carthage and takes most of Sicily.

218 B.C. ● Second Punic War begins with Hannibal's march from Spain to Italy.

ca 100 B.C. ● Germanic people move into Celtic territory in western Europe.

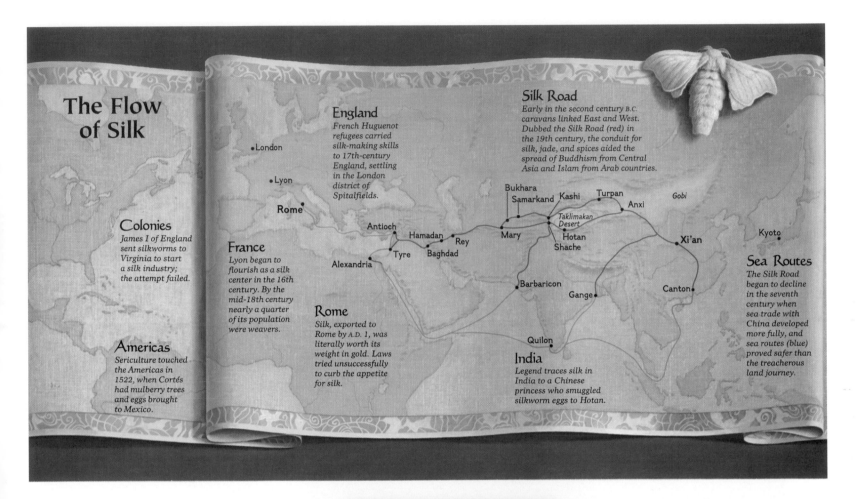

The Flow of Silk

England
French Huguenot refugees carried silk-making skills to 17th-century England, settling in the London district of Spitalfields.

Colonies
James I of England sent silkworms to Virginia to start a silk industry; the attempt failed.

Americas
Sericulture touched the Americas in 1522, when Cortés had mulberry trees and eggs brought to Mexico.

France
Lyon began to flourish as a silk center in the 16th century. By the mid-18th century nearly a quarter of its population were weavers.

Rome
Silk, exported to Rome by A.D. 1, was literally worth its weight in gold. Laws tried unsuccessfully to curb the appetite for silk.

Silk Road
Early in the second century B.C. caravans linked East and West. Dubbed the Silk Road (red) in the 19th century, the conduit for silk, jade, and spices aided the spread of Buddhism from Central Asia and Islam from Arab countries.

India
Legend traces silk in India to a Chinese princess who smuggled silkworm eggs to Hotan.

Sea Routes
The Silk Road began to decline in the seventh century when sea trade with China developed more fully, and sea routes (blue) proved safer than the treacherous land journey.

Map labels: London, Lyon, Rome, Antioch, Tyre, Alexandria, Hamadan, Baghdad, Rey, Mary, Bukhara, Samarkand, Kashi, Turpan, Anxi, Gobi, Taklimakan Desert, Hotan, Shache, Xi'an, Kyoto, Barbaricon, Gange, Canton, Quilon

the philosopher Confucius was born in 551 B.C. At roughly the same time that the Greeks of Periclean Athens were debating good government, Confucius was suggesting that the success of a society depended on the moral quality of its leader. No rulers took his advice during his lifetime, but his followers formed a school of Confucianism that espoused the ideals of honest and morally responsible leadership.

By the end of the fourth century B.C. seven major states remained. Within the next century the Qin state in the northwest reigned supreme. The scattered states were united for

THE SILK CONNECTION

Europe and the Far East began to get acquainted as early as the second century B.C., when commerce began to flow along a system of pathways known as the Silk Road. The fine cloth developed in China from the threads of certain worms became popular in Roman courts. Gold, glass, and metals made their way back eastward. Journeys were perilous through the rugged mountains that had long separated cultures. Deerskin boots similar to those worn by a modern Chinese horseman (left) have been found in ancient graves and could have been worn by ancestors who traveled the Silk Road.

Cicero's gives first speech: "Pro Quinctio." — 81 B.C.

70 B.C. — Birth of Virgil, Roman poet.

19 B.C. — Virgil dies, leaving the *Aeneid* almost complete.

15 B.C. — Good quality tableware made in Roman Gaul (France) and sent to Britain.

A.D. 65 — St. Mark's Gospel is written.

A.D. 70 — Titus destroys Jerusalem and suppresses Jewish revolt. First Diaspora. St. Matthew's Gospel is written.

Reconstructed during the Ming dynasty from remains of earlier fortifications, the Great Wall stretches some

the first time and the Qin, or Ch'in, dynasty gave China its name.

The first emperor, Qin Shi Huang, ruled as an absolute monarch, breaking up the old feudal system with its regional lords. He controlled everything with a central government and forced his old rivals to move to his capital, Xianyang, so he could watch them closely. His autocratic

notions of leadership collided with Confucianism, so he banned any teaching of that school of thought and burned its books.

Although a harsh taskmaster who worked his people to exhaustion on roads, canals, his palace, and his eventual tomb, the first emperor brought uniformity to Chinese life. He standardized such things as cur-

rency, weights, measures, and a system of writing, and established the tradition of a strong, central bureaucratic government that persists to this day. But the discontent he created by excessive state service brought on civil war after his death, and the Han dynasty took over in 206 B.C.

The Hans restored Confucianism and, although they repressed rival

Jews revolt in Egypt.

A.D. 115

ca A.D. 100 Settlement of
Hawaiian Islands.

A.D. 122 Construction of
Hadrian's Wall begun
in Roman Britain.

Birth of Galen, physi-
cian, in Greece.

A.D. 130

A.D. 132 Chang Heng,
Chinese scientist
and mathematician,
invents the world's
first seismograph.

2,000 miles, averages 25 feet in height, and is topped by a paved roadway 15 feet wide.

doctrines, brought a stability to China that lasted some 400 years. During that peace and prosperity, arts and technology flourished, and Buddhism was introduced from central Asia.

Under the Han the Chinese developed the ship's rudder, initiated the first accurate mapmaking techniques, invented papermaking, and established that a year has 365.25 days.

So stable was the empire under the Han that merchants previously fearful of barbarian raids were able to venture farther on trade routes, and contact with Persian and Roman worlds increased. Eventually pressure from confederacies of barbarians beat back civilized China, contributing to division and disorder. ■

JAPAN EVOLVES

Japan, one of the oldest nations in the world, evolved in relative isolation. In the third century B.C. the Yayoi culture introduced by ancient Koreans became dominant. Around the third century A.D. the female shaman Himiko, "Sun Princess," ruled portions of Japan. She sent ambassadors to China, by then an established civilization, and Chinese influence touched the islands for several centuries. Near the end of the fourth century A.D. a tribe called the Yamato became dominant in Japan. Yamato emperors ruled for nearly four and a half centuries. In A.D. 538 Buddhism made its way from China to spread throughout Japan. A guardian of an early Japanese Buddhist temple tramples a demon (above).

ca **300** B.C. ● Moche civilization begins on northern coast of Peru. Yayoi civilization develops in Japan.

200 B.C. ● Etruria falls to Romans.

196 B.C. ● Hannibal forced to flee into exile due to unpopular political reforms.

72 B.C. ● Pirates defeat Roman fleet off Crete.

30 B.C. ● Cleopatra commits suicide.

India's Golden Age

For hundreds of years—through the reign of Ashoka, who united the entire subcontinent except for the very southern tip before he died, and the later Chandragupta I, who brought India under his control in A.D. 320—peace was more common than strife in India. The subcontinent was protected from barbarian invasions out of the steppes by Iranian barons whose sturdy horses capable of bearing armored warriors were a match for the nomads.

While there were disorders within the Gupta Empire, between the fourth and fifth centuries A.D., they did not seem to disrupt cultural creativity. For in this period, art, science, and literature flourished in such a way that the Gupta age is seen as the high point of India's past.

Sculptures from that "golden age" set the style for later Indian art. The Sanskrit language was established and used in religious ceremonies and classical literature.

The Gupta kings ruled lightly, allowing defeated local rulers to continue governing their lands so long as they paid the conquerors ceremonial deference. The older Hinduism had replaced the newcomer Buddhism as the dominant religion, but religious tolerance allowed the two to coexist.

Hindu doctrine held that adherence to the *Vedas,* or scriptures, was more important than living according to the edicts of any king. Law books called *Dharma shastras* were written, detailing how people should conduct themselves according to the circumstances within their castes. Faithful adherence to correct behavior, it was believed, would move the soul farther up the ladder in a new incarnation.

The reign of the Guptas was a time of prosperity and stability through foreign trade and agricultural productivity. This golden age of India blossomed so that it influenced life beyond its borders as merchants and missionaries traveled abroad.

Neighboring cultures in Burma, Sumatra, Malaya, Siam, and Vietnam emulated Indian civilization, which had as much influence on the East as Hellenism had on the West. ■

Languid glance of a celestial nymph in the Ajanta caves fell only on bats and tigers for 1,400 years until India's exquisite paintings were rediscovered in 1904. Art flourished and Buddhism became popular in the reign of the Gupta kings in the 4th and 5th centuries A.D. A richly carved gate to the Great Stupa at Sanchi, India *(right),* tells stories from the life of the Buddha, the "Enlightened One."

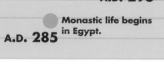

A.D. 226 Sassanians seize control of the Parthian Empire.	**A.D. 296** The Picts first appear in history.
A.D. 42-67 St. Peter is the first pope.	**A.D. 285** Monastic life begins in Egypt.

A.D. 325 The Nicene Creed, a summary of Christian doctrine, is adopted at the first Council of the Christian Church.

A.D. 450 Angles, Saxons, and Jutes begin to conquer Britain.

MAURYAN DYNASTY

India is the flowering of a civilization that began after Aryan pastoralists invaded the subcontinent around 1500 B.C. In the fourth century B.C. Alexander the Great marched into the land, but a nobleman named Chandragupta Maurya led a revolt and created the Mauryan Empire, later defeating Alexander's former general Seleucus. Chandragupta was left in possession of what is now northern India, Pakistan, and part of Afghanistan. Chandragupta's grandson, Ashoka, united almost the entire subcontinent. His laws were carved on pillars topped by a sculpture of four lions *(above)*, which is an Indian national symbol today.

● More Celts arrive in
Britain; iron introduced.
The Mon people enter
Burma from the East.

ca 500 B.C.

500 B.C. ● Start of rice cultivation
in India.

499 B.C. ● Gallinazo and Salinar
cultures flourish in Peru.
Persian Empire at its
height. Etruscan Empire
at its height in Italy.

499 B.C. ● Revolt of the Ionian
Greeks against
Persian rule.

The Birth of Buddhism

Buddhism began in India when a young prince named Siddhartha Gautama—later called the Buddha, or the Enlightened One—began sharing by example his vision of an enlightened life. Exact dates surrounding his life are not known, but he is believed to have been born around 563 B.C. in today's Nepal.

Privileged at birth, he is said to have grieved at the suffering of others, which caused him to search for a better way of life.

The young prince introduced the idea that through inner discipline one could find peace. Through meditation he had determined that the suffering in people's lives stemmed from the craving of sense pleasures. The way to avoid cravings was to follow an Eightfold Path to inner holiness by cultivating right views, right aspirations, right speech, right conduct, right livelihood, right effort, right-mindedness, and right concentration.

Behavior determined one's karma, the law of cause and effect. Nirvana, the perfect, peaceful state in which cravings and wrong inclinations have been expunged, could be achieved through meditation, discussion, humility, and denial.

The new religion, called Buddhism, held considerable appeal to people who had sought a way out of life's frustrations and become discontented with the ritual animal sacrifices of the Brahman religion, in which salvation through knowledge was available only to a chosen few.

For nearly half a century the

Paintings of *bodhisattva*, saints that help others gain nirvana, gaze from walls of a cave along the

497 B.C. ● Death of Pythagoras, Greek philosopher and mathematician.

496 B.C. ● In Italy, Romans defeat the Latins in battle at Lake Regillus.

494 B.C. ● In Rome the plebeians rebel against the patricians, gaining political rights.

485 B.C. ● Gelo becomes tyrant of Syracuse.

ca 400 B.C. ● Copper smelting begins in Mauritania, western Sahara; sharp arrowheads are made.

ancient Silk Road, evidence of the early spread of Buddhism by merchants.

Buddha wandered in a region along the Ganges River, teaching, and died at about the age of 80.

Buddhism eventually split into three main streams of thought, the Theravada, the Mahayana, and the Tantric. The Theravadans stress the brotherhood of Buddhist monks, the *sangha,* as the principal means of achieving rightness and eventually nirvana, although the layman can earn merit in that quest by supporting the monks.

The Mahayana, a movement begun about the first century, teaches the existence of souls called *bodhisattva,* those who had achieved sainthood but had declined entering nirvana so they could help all beings achieve liberation.

The Tantrics, which emerged around the sixth century A.D., expands the number of supernatural deities beyond the *bodhisattva,* including demons who can be called upon for help through rituals.

Hinduism eventually prevailed in India, but Buddhism spread into China and from there into Japan and many other nations. Although it celebrated ordinariness, Buddhism in its early forms had no rituals for the ordinary events of life—such as birth, coming of age, marriage, and death.

Strict adherence to Buddhism, with an emphasis on a life of inner equanimity amid ever changing outer phenomena, requires an unusual individual, but the peace its adherents can achieve has helped it become one of the world's great religions. ∎

500 B.C. ● Zenith of Greek choral music.

305 B.C. ● Ptolemy II builds great library in Alexandria.

202 B.C. ● Hannibal is defeated at Zama, in Tunisia, by Romans.

146 B.C. ● Carthage is destroyed.

332 B.C. ● Work begins on Alexander the Great's new city of Alexandria.

260 B.C. ● Emperor Ashoka converts to Buddhism.

183 B.C. ● Hannibal commits suicide.

63 B.C. ● Romans conquer Judah.

Early North American Cultures

Thousands of years ago, according to one theory, people crossed a land bridge from Asia to North America and spread rapidly to nearly every corner of the North and South American continents. Eventually they developed vastly different cultures, depending on the terrain and the climate where they settled.

The most recent group of immigrants from Asia, who came some 5,000 to 6,000 years ago, developed a specialized life in the frozen North. The predecessors of the Athapascans and Eskimos, anatomically similar to the Asians of today, wrestled a nomadic living from a severe region that is nevertheless rich in animal life. They used small tools of sharp stone for scraping hides and sewing warm clothes. They also introduced the bow and arrow to a continent where the spear had been the chief weapon for thousands of years.

In the Great Plains, with its massive herds of herbivores, nomads never progressed beyond the technology of hunters and gatherers. In the eastern woodlands, however, emerged the Adena society, groups that lived on smaller mammals and native plants and specialized in trade. Succeeding them with similar inclinations was the Hopewell culture that dominated much of eastern North America. Goods passing from community to community came from far-flung points such as present-day Florida and the Rocky Mountains.

Earthen burial mounds of the Hopewell were sometimes hundreds of feet long and thirty feet tall, snaking across the landscape so conspicuously that 19th-century observers thought they were the forts of some lost civilization. Art objects left within the tombs hint at individuals with wealth and high office.

Evidence indicates that the Hopewell died out around A.D. 400, and the Mississippian culture emerged, named for the valley where it reached its apogee.

Like the Adena and Hopewell, the Mississippians traded extensively but also cleared and maintained land to farm maize and beans. Their ample food crops supported communities as large as Cahokia, spread over more than five square miles with a population of some 30,000.

Cahokians built more than a hundred earthen mounds, including a terraced one that rose 100 feet and covered 16 acres.

31 B.C. ● Cleopatra's forces, led by Mark Antony, are defeated at Actium.

27 B.C. ● Augustus becomes first emperor of Rome.

A.D. 116 ● Roman emperor Trajan completes conquest of Mesopotamia.

A.D. 271 ● Magnetic compass is used in China.

A.D. 350 ● Invention of the stirrup, China.

A.D. 372 ● Buddhism is introduced into Korea.

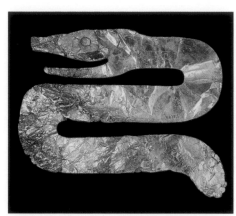

Other early attempts at urban societies in North America sprang up in the southwestern desert around the time of Christ, perhaps due to some contact with the more advanced societies in Mesoamerica.

Challenged by an arid, unkind environment in what is now New Mexico, the Anasazi practiced inventive agricultural techniques centuries later and built cliffside dwellings that sometimes contained more than 200

Adena or Hopewell people left a snake-shaped earthen effigy *(below)* more than a thousand feet long in Ohio. A Hopewell tomb yielded a snake cut from a thin sheet of mica *(above)*.

separate rooms. Their dams and canals irrigated fields of corn, squash, and beans. Although they had neither carts nor horses, they built hundreds of miles of roads, connecting their far-flung communities.

Artisans created tools and jewelry with turquoise inlays and pottery with black-on-white designs. By 1300 the Anasazi had abandoned their dwellings, perhaps because of drought or raids by nomads. ■

ca 150 B.C. ● Settlers from the Polynesian islands of Tonga and Samoa move westward to other islands.

ca 132-131 B.C. ● Olympeion, in Athens, is completed.

73 B.C. ● Spartacus's Slave War in Italy.

51 B.C. ● Cleopatra becomes Queen of Egypt.

37 B.C. ● Roman Senate appoints Herod the Great as King of Judaea.

The Nazca and the Moche

In South America sophisticated cultures developed early along the coastline of what is now Peru. In fertile highlands and along rivers, complex societies were forming as early as 3000 B.C. By 1800 B.C. they had developed pottery, and over the next thousand years they worked metals and built large temples.

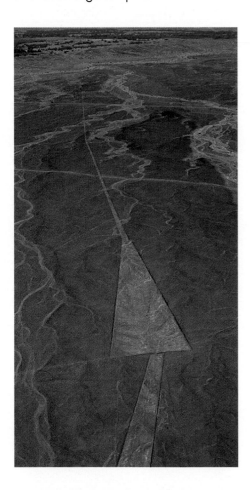

Beginning around 200 B.C., the Nazca molded a culture out of a nearly rainless coastal plain in what is now southern Peru, building aqueducts and reservoirs to make use of groundwater. They lived in homes of tied cane, plastered with mud. They traded, fished, hunted, and grew an assortment of fruits and vegetables.

Their most enduring legacy consists of the curious Nazca Lines, figures hundreds of feet long, etched into the ground. Some are animals: hummingbirds, whales, and spiders. But the most mysterious are the rectangles, spirals, trapezoids, and concentric ray systems—all made by digging a ditch to expose lighter soil below, then banking dark gravel against the indent.

The lines have long puzzled archaeologists. Did they mark ritual pathways and join sacred sites, or were they connected in some way with astronomical observation and worship? Evidence is strong that they somehow relate to precious water.

Although the Nazca culture lasted several centuries, paintings on recovered pottery from later periods imply an increasing emphasis on warfare, perhaps indicating that the Nazca were eventually overcome by more powerful forces to the east.

The Moche also lived on the coast of Peru beginning about A.D. 100, harnessing Andean runoff with elaborate canals. They farmed corn, beans, squash, and peanuts, raised llamas and guinea pigs for meat, and fished in the ocean from reed boats.

At its height around A.D. 400, the Moche kingdom stretched nearly 400 miles along the coast, connected by roads that 900 years later would be used by the Inca. Like the Nazca, they traded with people far beyond their own boundaries. They had no writing but left records of their culture through elaborate decorations on pottery. Expert craftsmanship and finely worked gold testify to the wealth of this society's elite.

Whether by natural disaster or by powerful enemies, this culture disappeared, leaving artwork as its legacy. ■

Geometric figures left by the Nazca, long puzzling to scholars, may relate to water. Broad bands in the desert (above) converge at a center point, maybe a ceremonial site. At another location, a series of triangles and trapezoids (left) hug seasonal watercourses, invaluable to dryland farmers. Important to royalty, Moche metalworkers devised a process for coating a copper mask with gold (opposite).

ca A.D. 1 The saddle first used in China.

A.D. 50 In Mexico, the city of Teotihuacan is laid out in a rectangular grid, and the Pyramid of the Sun is built.

A.D. 127 In Egypt, Ptolemy publishes his first book on astronomy.

A.D. 360 Scrolls start to be replaced by books.

480 B.C. Second Persian invasion of Greece. Greeks of Sicily defeat Carthaginians at Himera.

479 B.C. Death of Confucius.

304 B.C. Seleucus gives up his claim on India to Chandragupta in exchange for 500 elephants.

247 B.C. Arsaces I founds Kingdom of Parthia.

200 B.C. The Romans first use concrete.

The Mysterious Maya

Despite being cut off from centers of learning elsewhere on the globe, the Maya of the Americas built an impressive, long-lasting civilization with accomplishments similar to those in Asia and the Mediterranean. From humble, practical beginnings, their technology steadily progressed, as shown in the remains of the village of Cuello in today's Belize.

By 1200 B.C. the floors of Cuello's pole houses were plastered, with cooking pits at one end. As centuries passed, the village became larger and more formal, with courtyards and burial tombs and carvings that indicated a royal segment of society.

By 600 B.C. Maya at numerous locations in Central America were building massive pyramids. By A.D. 100, when the Roman Empire was in full swing, some Maya cities were already in decline.

Despite those earlier successes, the Classic Period is generally considered to be between A.D. 250 and 900, when out of tropical forest the Maya created complex societies. Maya farmers terraced hillsides, dug canals, and raised fields in marshy areas. They crossbred wild grain to produce a sizable ear of maize—corn— a staple crop that was deified.

City planners laid out urban areas in precise patterns with plazas, government buildings, and apartment complexes for the elite. Architects designed mansions, pyramids, and palaces so grand that the first Europeans to see

them thought the area had been colonized by ancient Egyptians.

Skilled craftsmen and artisans created inscriptions and jade figurines that challenged the splendor of ancient Asia and Africa. Scribes recorded events in a hieroglyphic writing that was unique to the Maya.

The land of the Maya was the Yucatan Peninsula, which juts into the Gulf of Mexico. Today its broad base includes parts of Mexico, Guatemala, Belize, Honduras, and El Salvador. The northern part of this arm receives scanty rain that falls on thin soil. Between May and October bountiful moisture falls on the southern part, creating a dense rain forest. The Maya had cleared much of the vegetation for their fields, which supported life in the cities.

KEEN WATCHERS OF THE HEAVENS

The Maya were a people attuned to the passage of time. They studied the regularity of change in the heavenly bodies, which allowed them to create a calendar. Even their buildings were constructed to honor astronomical movements and important dates. A temple at Chichen Itza is aligned so that at the spring and autumn equinoxes a serpentlike shadow slithers toward a stone serpent head. At Tikal, Venus and Jupiter align directly over the tip of a pyramid.

Lesser numbers of Maya lived in volcanic highlands where occasional eruptions—while threatening their homes and fields—created fertile soil and yielded glassy obsidian, valued for arrow points. Nearly 3,500 archaeological sites have been identified, ranging from great cities such as Tikal and Chichen Itza to mounds of rubble.

Unlike the Persians and the Romans, the Maya never created a vast contiguous empire under a single leader. Their societies consisted of large city-states, each with its own ruler who was considered divine. Mayapan was a walled city of some 12,000 people. Tikal covered an area of nearly 50 square miles and had a population of 55,000.

Trade existed between cities and over long distances: salt from northern Yucatan, wood and feathers from the interior, native obsidian from Guatemala. Large pieces of pottery in the style of the great metropolis of Teotihuacan in central Mexico have been found in Tikal, a thousand miles away by foot. Goods were borne on people's backs or in canoes, for the Maya possessed neither wheels nor beasts capable of pulling them.

Cities fought each other as royalty vied for power and influence, and perhaps sought captives for human sacrifices at important rituals. But incessant war interrupts social creativity, and the accomplishments of the Maya suggest they had long periods of stability.

The massive stone pyramids

Plague, followed
by fire, in Rome.

79 B.C.

Death of Roman
Emperor Augustus.

A.D. 14

Pontius Pilate serves as
Procurator of Judaea.

A.D. 26-37

Buddhism reaches
China.

A.D. 50

The Colosseum
in Rome opens to the
public; it holds some
50,000 people.

A.D. 80

End of Han dynasty
in China.

A.D. 220

Period of civil war and
chaos in Roman Empire.

A.D. 235-284

From this observatory at Chichen Itza ancient astronomers scanned the heavens, seeking information to guide Maya activities.

A.D. 238 ● Revolt in Africa against Roman rule begins half a century of unrest.

A.D. 320-467 ● Gupta dynasty forges empire in northern India.

A.D. 330-340 ● Beginning of conversion of Kingdom of Askum in Ethiopia-Eritrea to Christianity by Bishop Frumentius.

A.D. 386 ● Ambrose, Bishop of Milan, introduces hymn singing.

A.D. 376 ● Huns invade Russia.

A.D. 399 ● Chinese Buddhist historian, Fahsien, begins his journey through India.

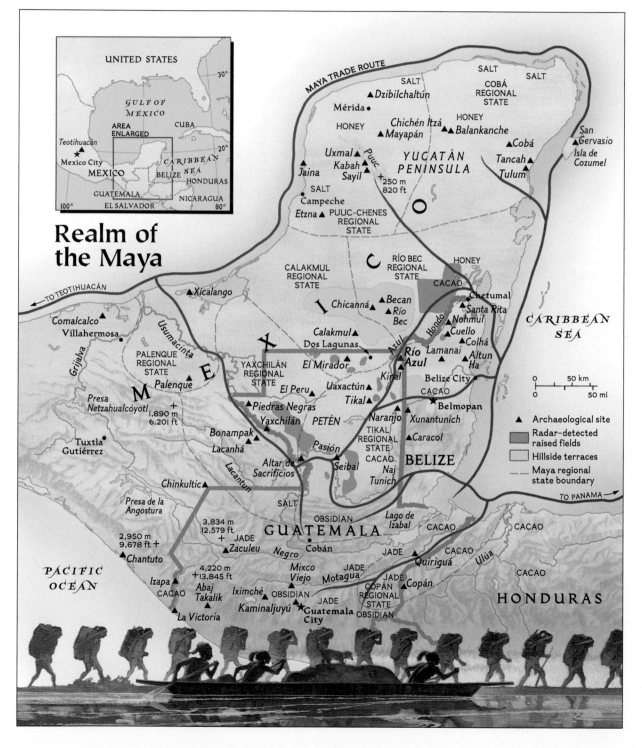

Realm of the Maya

Never a single empire, the Maya raised dozens of great centers in present-day Mexico, Guatemala, Belize, and Honduras. Spreading across some 100,000 square miles, the Maya lowlands flourished during the Late Classic Period, A.D. 600-900, shown here. The cities were supplied by farmers practicing complex agricultural techniques and by extensive trade networks. Goods were transported by canoe and by bearers on packed-dirt paths or sometimes on raised roads. Total population may have numbered 12 to 16 million. Major cities held sway over neighbors with whom they shared architecture and ceramic styles.

▲ Archaeological site

◼ Radar-detected raised fields

◻ Hillside terraces

--- Maya regional state boundary

A.D. 400 Christianity becomes official religion of Roman Empire.

A.D. 432 St. Patrick introduces Christianity to Ireland.

A.D. 455 Attila the Hun attacks western Europe.

A.D. 489 Large Buddhist temples built in China.

A.D. 497 Franks convert to Christianity.

ca A.D. 500 Indian mathematicians introduce the zero (0).

A temple slumbers in the morning mist at ancient Tikal, once a Maya metropolis that covered nearly 50 square miles.

entombing Maya royalty sometimes towered more than 230 feet. The Maya kept written records of their world, carved in stone or printed in folded books of pounded bark or deerskin, some of which survive. Their astronomers calculated the length of the solar year and the lunar month. They were able to predict eclipses, which required advanced mathematical skills.

Around A.D. 900, for reasons not yet clear, Maya civilization collapsed, probably due to its own success. Population increases in the region may have caused a depletion of natural resources and a reduction of the soil's fertility.

For whatever reason, a highly sophisticated civilization that had endured for more than a thousand years came to an end, and once splendid Maya temples, plazas, and pyramids now are cloaked in dense tropical growth.

Today, however, more than four million descendants of the ancient Maya live in the lands of their ancestors, many still feeling connected to the earth in traditional Maya ways. ■

MYSTERIOUS METROPOLIS

When the Maya civilization was probably at its height, the largest city in the ancient Americas was Teotihuacan on the central plateau of Mexico. Home to 125,000 people by A.D. 600, it controlled trade in the Mesoamerican region until its temples and palaces were destroyed between A.D. 650 and 750. The city was laid out in a precise grid and fed from well-tended fields nearby that produced corn and beans. Its Aztec name means "Place of the Gods." Little is known about the Teotihuacanos themselves.

Construction of Moche pyramids in Peru.

A.D. 1

Rising of peasants in China; rebels called "Red Eyebrows."

A.D. 18

Earliest datable iron-working in Zambia.

A.D. 20-96

Birth of Pliny, writer, in Rome.

A.D. 23

Caligula is murdered.

A.D. 41

The Rise of Christianity

In the first century A.D. the Jews in Judaea chafed under Roman rule. They objected to Roman taxes, and they believed they were chosen to observe God's laws, uncontaminated by other cultures. Their scriptures predicted that a savior would be born who would lead them out of bondage.

Around A.D. 27 Jesus of Nazareth began to teach, drawing attention to himself by saying that the kingdom of God was within. Some people believed him and became his followers, or disciples. Strict observers of Jewish doctrine, however, said that some of Jesus's actions, such as dining with "unclean" people and forgiving people of their sins, violated their sacred laws.

Jesus outlined his moral teachings in a sermon, later known as the "Sermon on the Mount," delivered on a hill near the town of Tabgha: Blessed are the meek; not only should you not kill, you should not even be angry with your fellowman; thinking adultery is the same as committing adultery; if a man strikes the side of your face, offer him the other side as well. With such teachings, which ran contrary to prevailing attitudes then as now, Jesus called for restraint and brotherhood in a time of social and political turmoil.

Jewish resistance to Roman rule reached its zenith at the hill called Masada **(below)**, where 961 people committed suicide when defeat by the legions became imminent. Nativity scene brightens a rock wall at Göreme, in today's Turkey, once a center for Christian worship **(opposite)**.

A.D. 45 Severe droughts and plagues of locusts in Hsiung territory.

ca A.D. 50 Red-glazed pottery begins to be produced in the Cevennes.

Nero commits suicide.
A.D. 68

A.D. 117-138

Hadrian is emperor of Rome.

Earliest known Sanskrit inscriptions in India.
A.D. 150

After a triumphal entry into Jerusalem during a festival commemorating Israel's deliverance from Egypt, Jewish leaders noted Jesus' growing popularity with alarm.

Authorities had him arrested and tried before a Roman governor, Pontius Pilate. Pilate found him guiltless, but Jews opposed to Jesus insisted that he be crucified. Pilate acceded to their wishes, and the Romans carried out the execution.

Jesus was forced to carry his cross up a hill called Golgotha. Crucifixion was an excruciatingly slow form of execution, normally reserved for

slaves and non-Roman criminals.

Declared dead, Jesus was laid in a tomb. But three days later his apostles announced that he had arisen from the crypt and had spent time among them.

This report renewed the faith of his followers that he would someday return in glory to grant everlasting life to anyone who believed in his teachings of love, forgiveness, and universal brotherhood.

The message had considerable appeal to pagans living in the Hellenized cities of Syria and Asia Minor. Believers such as a former

tentmaker named Saul of Tarsus, later called Paul after his conversion on the road to Damascus, traveled far, spreading the word that salvation through Jesus was available to anyone who believed in him.

In the Greek language Jesus was referred to as Christos, the Christ—"the anointed one"—and the growing movement became known as Christianity.

So persuasive was Christianity's message of devotion to a power higher than government that the Romans considered it subversive, banned it, and persecuted those who continued

A.D. 167   Terrible plague inflicts illness and death throughout Roman Empire.

A.D. 189   In China, to put an end to the influence of eunuchs at the imperial court, the army massacres them.

A.D. 203   Hippodrome constructed in Byzantium.

ca A.D. 215   Oriental trade with Roman Empire in decline.

ca A.D. 220   Goths begin entering Balkans and Asia Minor.

A.D. 230   Succession of Sujin, tenth emperor of Japan.

to observe their religion in secret, even for sport putting Christians into arenas with wild beasts to be killed.

When the Roman Empire divided, Constantine converted to Christianity. He legalized its practice with the Edict of Milan in A.D. 313, giving tolerance to persecuted Christians.

Some 80 years later Christianity became the official religion of the Roman Empire. Its popularity gradually spread to all of Europe and beyond, and today it has more adherents than any other religion. ■

WORSHIPING UNDERGROUND

Because the ancient Romans outlawed Christianity and observances of it were extremely dangerous, early Christians had to meet in secret *(above)* and to devise codes for identifying themselves to other believers. A simple rendering of a fish became the symbol that marked one as a follower of Jesus. In Rome itself, Christians took advantage of a Roman law, which held that burial places were sacred, to operate under the noses of their persecutors. They met for worship in the Jewish catacombs deep under the streets of the capital city.

Hunters, bearing torches and hidden behind shields, corral lions and leopards for bloody

A.D. 238 ● Goths begin incursions into Roman Empire.

A.D. 244 ● Peace between Persia and Rome.

ca A.D. 290 ● Gupta Kingdom established in Bengal.

A.D. 300 ● In Germanic monasteries, bowling is used as part of religious ritual.

A.D. 308 ● Constantine takes Gaul.

sport, possibly against Christians in Roman arenas, in this third-century mosaic from the former Roman city of Hippo Regius in North Africa.

6

10

1325
**The Aztec begin building
the city of Tenochtitlán.**

ca 986
**The Vikings
settle Greenland.**

7

4

11

AROUND THE WORLD

1 **Africa:** In the Islamic bastion of Cairo, Egypt, Muslim mystics, or Sufis, chant Allah's name in a mosque. Islam spread Arab architecture and ideas to much of the known world in the seventh and eighth centuries.

2 **Asia:** The beauty of karst hills in southwestern China belies the tragedy of the fleeing emperor Minghuang in a painting that marks the twilight of the Tang dynasty.

3 **Asia:** Remnants of Khmer glory emerge in Cambodia with the clearing of jungle from old Angkor. Grim faces guard the Gate of the Dead at Angkor Thom, part of a complex of temples in what was a thriving metropolis for more than 500 years.

4 **Africa:** Rumors of a glittering city of wealth and culture called Timbuktu excited Europeans until early

Isolated Realms

771
Charlemagne spreads the system of feudalism.

527
Justinian becomes head of the Byzantine Empire.

1095
Pope Urban II launches the First Crusade.

2

1211
Genghis Khan and his Mongol forces enter China.

618-907
Under the Tang dynasty, the Chinese Empire expands.

632
After the death of Muhammad, Islam spreads.

1113
The Khmer begin the construction of the temple of Angkor Wat.

9

ca 1240
The Empire of Mali is founded.

1

3

explorers viewed the desert metropolis. "Nothing but a mass of ill-looking houses, built of earth," wrote one.

5 Asia: Genghis Khan, lord of a mighty empire, led nomadic horsemen like this one to conquer most of the known world. Stirrups gave them stability for firing arrows in any direction.

6 Asia: Small-boat raiders prepare to board Mongol ships invading Japan. Two attempts to conquer the islands were repulsed, once by a typhoon that drowned some 100,000 men.

7 Europe: Harassing all England and northwest Europe were fierce Vikings, whose raids by sea are recorded in a medieval manuscript.

8 Europe: Unity came to Europe at the sword of Charlemagne, crowned Holy Roman Emperor by the pope in a 14th-century miniature shown here.

9 Asia: In the successful First Crusade, Christians used catapults and mobile bridges to rout Muslims from Jerusalem. Later Crusades failed to retake the Holy Land.

10 North America: Keeping the gods happy and the world in balance required numerous sacrifices in blood, the Aztec believed. Here, a priest cuts the heart from one sacrificial victim as a previous victim lies below.

11 North America: Cortés, aided in negotiations by his interpreter and mistress Malinalli, center, makes a pact with the Tlaxcalan for help against the Aztec.

Religion, the Empire Builder: 500 to 1400

The establishment of large empires between 500 B.C. and A.D. 500 had offered the prospect of widespread unity. That prospect collapsed as fierce barbarian nomads swept over both Europe and Asia and left their cultures in disarray.

In the fifth century Europe was plunged into what has been called the Dark Ages, as progress slowed for several centuries. Later, in the middle of the 14th century, the population was devastated by the bubonic plague. The flowering of culture in India was also curbed—by different forces—when outside invaders broke the Gupta Empire into petty kingdoms. The Parthians of Persia resisted the barbarians but in doing so built up such strong frontier defenses that they weakened the central government, which later fell to Muslim armies. China, at first overcome by the Hsiung-nu of the steppes, recovered more quickly than regions to the west. Absorbing the invaders, it managed to become the most culturally and technologically advanced region in the world by the early 12th century.

Religion, always present, had become a major political force. Hinduism, which had been supplanted by Buddhism in India, reasserted itself in this place of its birth. Its return probably led to India's conquest by Arab Muslims, because the caste system did not allow a united front to form against the invaders. Buddhism, which had traveled from India to China, followed trade routes to Korea and Japan and was part of the cultural growth of those two countries.

Jews spread over Europe and Africa in a large-scale diaspora, or dispersion, living in small, separate communities and bringing a variety of skills to their host cities. Christianity was the basis of the Byzantine Empire, the eastern portion of the former Roman Empire that held on after the western portion had collapsed. The religion became so widespread on the continent that, when Charlemagne conquered central Europe and forced the vanquished to accept Christianity, the pope crowned him head of what would be called the Holy Roman Empire. Some Christians began to blame Jews for the death of Jesus and to persecute them and discriminate against them.

The most influential religion of the time was Islam, founded in Arabia in the seventh century A.D. by the Prophet Muhammad. Within a relatively brief span of time, a gigantic empire grew quickly from humble beginnings. The first Muslims were wanderers of the desert. But as the religion caught fire, its followers set out in all directions to seek converts. Fierce warriors who believed death in battle sent them to heaven, they conquered armies sometimes far superior in number. Within a century after Muhammad's death Arab influence had spread to three continents.

In Islam's wake came progressive civilizations with great centers of art and learning. Islam stimulated cultures of many lands with extensive trade and a common language, which was Arabic. The Arabs adopted the scientific knowledge about astrology and medicine developed by the Greeks. Some Muslim caliphs, or rulers, became patrons of learning, organizing translations of Greek and Indian treatises on science and philosophy into Arabic.

But the Arabs did not merely borrow from other cultures. Arab mathematicians devised new ways of looking at arithmetic. They used letters to represent unknown numbers and called the system *al-jabr*—algebra. Improved paper, invented in China, made its way to Europe through Muslim Spain, as did new foods and new words that eventually enriched the English language. Still, Christianity in Europe chafed at Islam's presence in Spain and the Holy Land, and the Crusades against the Muslims were launched. Although they ultimately failed in the Middle East, the Crusades helped Europeans absorb Arab accomplishments. Ultimately, Islam's influence helped propel Europe out of its cultural slump.

During Europe's period of isolation, culture and learning were kept alive mostly in Christian monasteries. With war and turmoil all around them, some of the most deeply religious persons had chosen to live simple and prayerful existences in secluded settlements. Such communities sprang up all over Europe and in parts of Africa. By growing their own food, weaving their own cloth, and creating their own pottery, monks were basically self-sustaining, and in a time when mere existence was a struggle outside their walls, the monasteries had no shortage of members. Education was a part of their holy duties, so most monasteries maintained libraries of classic works, as well as collections of paintings and sculpture.

Progress did not grind to a complete halt in Europe. The iron plowshare came into increasing use, which allowed farmers to turn more soil for food crops. Clothes were pressed on ironing boards, the smoothing done with a heated rock. New sources of mechanical power were the windmill and the water mill. The horse collar allowed horses to pull heavy loads twice as fast as oxen without choking themselves.

China's rise to new accomplishment came with reunification under the Sui dynasty in 581. The benefactor was Yang Chien, who cut taxes and reduced the amount of time men were obligated to serve in the army. His irrigation schemes improved agriculture and helped make the country wealthy again. After his death, improvement of a Grand Canal system that linked the main rivers in China also added to prosperity by allowing safe and free movement of goods. A peasant rebellion against a return to high taxes ushered in the Tang dynasty, under which China flourished for nearly 300 years. The silk trade grew, a system of printing was devised, and gunpowder was invented.

Promising to deliver lands won from the Muslims, Christian crusader Godfrey of Bouillon kneels before Emperor Alexius in Constantinople, today's Istanbul. With a fervency that marked an age of religious empires, Europeans marched to the Middle East to regain the shrines of Christendom.

Overleaf:
Ancient walls at Nicaea housed Christianity's first ecumenical council. Later the stones sheltered Muslim Turks against Christians battling to regain the city in the First Crusade.

Meanwhile, the powerful Khmer dominated southeast Asia and built their magnificent Hindu-inspired capital at Angkor. In sub-Saharan Africa in today's Mali, Timbuktu and Jenne-jeno grew into cities of thousands that became significant centers for commerce and Islamic learning. Farther south, Great Zimbabwe raised magnificent stone structures without the use of mortar. In the Americas the Aztec of Mexico took thousands of human prisoners and sacrificed them to Aztec gods. The Inca of Peru considered themselves descended from the heavens and called themselves the "Children of the Sun." ■

529 St. Benedict of Nursia founds the Monastery of Monte Cassino and the Benedictine Order.

530 Gelimer becomes king of Vandals in North Africa.

531 The Franks occupy Thuringia. Childebert defeats the Visigoths in Spain. Mazdak is put to death with 100,000 followers.

534 The Kingdom of Burgundy, founded nearly a century earlier, is annexed by the Franks.

535 India's Gupta Empire collapses.

Evolution of a Culture

Long after the fall of the western Roman Empire in the fifth century, the eastern portion centered in Constantinople retained its Roman identity. The shrunken empire remained prosperous, situated advantageously along both land and sea trade routes. It continued to battle a long-time adversary, Persia, and it fought to keep the barbarians at bay.

A CITY'S SPECTACULAR CHURCH

The greatest building of the Byzantine Empire was Hagia Sophia, meaning "Church of the Holy Wisdom" in Constantinople (above). **Vaulted, spacious, and streaming with light inside, it was simple in appearance on the outside, in keeping with Eastern Orthodox philosophy that the soul deserves more attention than the outer body. Furnishings of gold, silver, and ivory; marble carvings; and rich mosaics that once decorated its walls have largely disappeared. The ten thousand people involved in the church's construction finished it in only five years, from 532 to 537. After the city fell to the Muslim Turks in 1453, the victors turned it into a mosque and added minarets.**

The Roman emperor, Constantine, had taken for his capital a thousand-year-old Greek town called Byzantium, renaming it Constantinople. To secure it against enemies, he quickly built walls. To Romanize it he built Christian churches and public buildings and commissioned works of art.

Under Justinian, who reigned from 527 to 565, some expansion took place. A strong ruler who relied on his beautiful actress wife, Theodora, for advice, he codified Roman law to increase its influence, at a time when people were drifting back to a reliance on custom and tradition. He maintained a shaky peace with Persia and recaptured North Africa, much of Italy, southern Spain, and the islands of the western Mediterranean. But shortly after Justinian's death, the juggernaut of Muslim armies pushed the frontier back again and steadily pressured the empire from the east. From the north the Bulgars flooded into the Balkan Peninsula and formed a second, constant threat.

Increasingly isolated from Europe, the former eastern Roman Empire took on an identity of its own. Reverting partly to its original name, it came to be known as the Byzantine Empire—Greek speaking, culturally mixed, and for a time, the hub of Christianity. New art and architecture developed out of the fusing of many cultures. New ideas also developed in both politics and religion that eventually led to theological differences with the Christians of western Europe, who followed the lead of Rome. ■

ca 537 Arthur, King of the Britons, is killed in battle at Camlan.

ca 540 Ethiopian scholars begin to translate the Bible into their language.

540 St. Benedict formulates his monastic rule.

542-594 Plague hits Europe, halving its population.

ca 543-556 Church of St. Germain-des-Prés founded in Paris.

544 Berbers revolt in North Africa.

MAXIMIANVS.

The glories of the Roman Empire were partly restored by the Byzantine emperor Justinian, flanked by officials in a mosaic at Ravenna, Italy.

An Empire Fed by Trade

In rural provinces around Constantinople a loyal peasantry and work force, which doubled as an army when needed, produced valuable crops and trade goods—olives, wine, and skillfully worked gold. These were exchanged for ivory, spices, and other luxuries from India and Arabia; grain from Egypt; silks from China; and slaves, furs, and other goods from Russia. Despite occasional border skirmishes with the empire's Muslim adversaries, trade was more common than war.

Goods flowed in and out of Byzantium, and the riches that accompanied them often stayed. The trade network was extensive. Silk found in a Viking grave in central Sweden had probably been fashioned into cloth in Byzantium. For centuries, Constantinople was the center of the wealthiest and best governed realm in Christendom. Byzantine currency enjoyed universal prestige for some 700 years.

Justinian had carried on the refurbishment begun by Constantine, raising even more Christian churches and decorating them lavishly—including the elaborate Hagia Sophia, the empire's greatest building. But as Constantinople gained prestige, competitive forces arose in Europe.

The Frankish king Charlemagne had conquered territory that included modern-day France, the Netherlands, Germany, and most of Italy, forcing the conquered to convert to Christianity. In 800 he was crowned emperor of the so-called Holy Roman

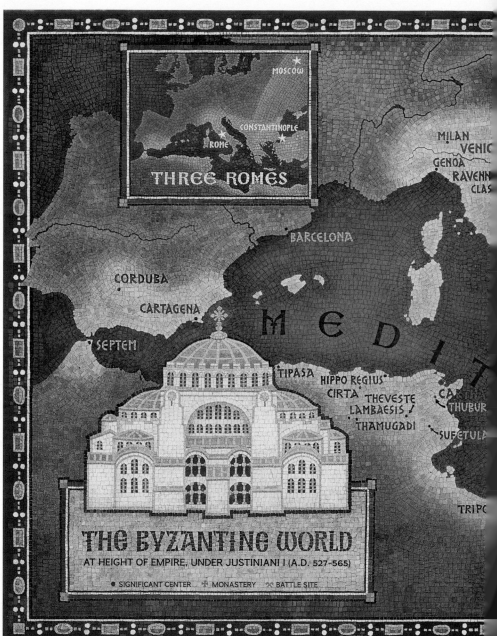

THREE ROMES

THE BYZANTINE WORLD

AT HEIGHT OF EMPIRE, UNDER JUSTINIANI I (A.D. 527-565)

● SIGNIFICANT CENTER   ✝ MONASTERY   ⚔ BATTLE SITE

Empire by a grateful pope in Rome. The Byzantines ratified the pope's action, since according to the split that had occurred more than 500 years earlier, the Roman world was technically still two sectors, east and west, governed by two different heads. But the cooperation that existed when Diocletian created the two-headed empire was no longer alive. Byzantium had become its own empire, and the Franks had carved

● Romans occupy south-east quarter of Spain.
554

● Franks conquer Bavaria.
556

● Huns invade Thrace, Macedonia, and Greece.
558-59

● In France civil war breaks out among the Merovingians.
561

● Christianity reaches the Fezzan.
565

out a new power. Latin had virtually disappeared as a common language, giving way to Greek in the east and German and the Latinate Romance languages in the west.

And there were many religious differences. For example, a Byzantine emperor took a stand against the worship of Christian images, or icons, and banned the use of them as idolatrous. Many Christians who continued to pay homage to icons they held as sacred were persecuted. Although the ban was withdrawn, the bitterness over it fueled the ever widening rift between what would become the Roman Catholic Church and the Eastern Orthodox Church. ■

Nepal gains indepen-
dence from Tibet.

879

Germany is invaded
by the Hungarians.

889

ca 900-1300

Anasazi cultural
advances constitute a
move toward urbanism.

Maya relinquish their
settlements in the
Mexican lowlands
and move into
Yucatan Peninsula.

900

Algiers is founded
by the Arabs.

935

Lapps enter Norway.

950

The Twilight of an Empire

The Byzantines made one more successful attempt at expansion during their long, rich tenure as a cultural capital. Beginning in 863 under a vigorous Macedonian dynasty, they took back from the Arabs several great Roman cities of the past—Antioch, Alexandria, Beirut, Caesarea. By 976 the warrior-emperor Basil II had driven the Muslims back to the gates of Jerusalem.

In the north he defeated the Bulgarians, and their territories became Byzantine provinces. He also defeated the Georgians, Armenians,

administration that feared its power, the military began to experience reverses. The Normans drove them out of Italy, and the Seljuk Turks defeated them at Manzikert, sending them back toward Constantinople. More territory was lost, sometimes to new states rising in Europe after the breakup of Charlemagne's empire.

Christianity's divisions intensified about this same time as well. The rivalry between Roman pope and Eastern Orthodox patriarch broke into the open, aggravated by a dispute over who had jurisdiction in

owners of their own land, they had always been willing to fight for it. As taxes increased, they were forced to sell their holdings to the wealthy and become serfs. Loyalty was transferred to the landlord, now adhering neither to land nor to empire.

When the city that had withstood assaults for centuries finally fell to a foreign power, it was not to Turk or Muslim but to Christian crusaders from Europe in 1204. Byzantine culture continued for another 150 years or so until the empire was taken over by the Turks in the 15th century. ■

Center of culture, walled Constantinople **(opposite)** sat on the Bosporus, connecting Europe and Asia. Seat of the newly emergent Christian religion, remnant capital of the Roman Empire, it was the dominant city of the Mediterranean world. A 13th-century manuscript shows how a volatile liquid, ignited and aimed at an enemy warship **(left)**, helped the Greeks protect the city in 941.

MEDITERRANEAN CAPITAL

For 11 centuries, dating from the time Constantine dedicated it as the eastern capital of the Roman Empire in A.D. 330, the city of Constantinople reigned as predominant in the Mediterranean. Perched on the European side of the Bosporus, the narrow inlet that separates Europe and Asia, it melded the best of both cultures into a distinctive identity in art, architecture, and learning. Hundreds of churches adorned its streets, along with handsome palaces, mansions, hospitals, and schools. Carefully walled, it had successfully withstood 17 sieges by the early 13th century, before it was sacked by Christian crusaders in 1204.

and Normans, turned an eye toward retaking Italy, and dreamed of moving into North Africa. The empire, by now more Byzantine than Roman, had extended its territory in many places nearly to the borders of Rome's former glory.

Seriously overextended, weakened by lack of funds from a civilian

Italy—the Byzantines who had long held it or the pope after the Normans had retaken the peninsula?

The empire was further weakened by a change in its social setup. The military strength long derived from the loyal peasant-warriors was undermined by the rise of a landed aristocracy. When the peasants had been

580 ● Slavs begin to settle in the Balkans.

584 ● Mercia, one of the kingdoms of Anglo-Saxon England, is founded.

585 ● Reconstruction work begins on China's Great Wall.

593 ● First printing press is invented, in China.

ca 600 ● Hohokam culture begins to emerge in the North American Southwest. Height of Maya civilization.

Muhammad and the Birth of Islam

The world's newest major religion, which quickly became one of its greatest empires, began in the Arabian Peninsula, an area so unknown at the time that early geographers drew its coastline but left its interior blank. When the Prophet Muhammad was born late in the sixth century A.D., the desert was a place of wandering tribes and caravan trading centers. People worshiped nature spirits and honored numerous gods housed at a shrine in Mecca.

The orphaned Muhammad lived first with his grandfather; then with an uncle, working hard as a shepherd, camel driver, trader, and merchant and earning the name *al-Amin,* "the trustworthy." At the age of 25 he married Khadijah, a rich widow 15 years his senior. For some years he lived a life of domestic contentment, sired four daughters, and had the leisure to contemplate the destiny of man.

According to tradition, one night in the year 610 as he reflected, he saw a vision and heard a voice that demanded his obedience to the one god, Allah "that teacheth man that which he knew not."

The idea of monotheism had been spreading in the Middle East through both Judaism and Christianity. Arab and Jew counted Abraham as a common ancestor. At about the age of 40 Muhammad saw another vision that commanded, "Muhammad! Thou art the Messenger of God, and I am Gabriel!" Thenceforth his mission was to spread the idea of one god.

The theology concerning proper

Byzantine army is
604 defeated at Edessa,
in Greece.

605-10 Chinese build Grand
Canal to link Yangtze
with the Yellow River.

607 First Japanese ambassadors visit China.
Unification of Tibet.

612 All Jews in Spain are
ordered to be baptized.

618 The Sui emperor Yang
Di is assassinated in
China. The Li family, utilizing Turkish support,
rebel against the Sui,
occupy Changan, found
the Tang dynasty.

ca 620 Copper wire is in use
at Dambwa, Zambia.

conduct was revealed to him gradually and written down as the Koran, the word of God as revealed to Muhammad. In an Arab world that believed death was the end of existence, he preached with eloquence that the faithful would enjoy a glorious afterlife and that the wicked would burn in hellfire. He urged those who made wealth their goal in life to share with the poor. Most dangerously, he deplored the worship of the idols at Mecca—worship that enriched members of his tribe through the selling of concessions. Enraged at

THE HEGIRA, FLIGHT INTO TRIUMPH

The beginning of the Muslim calendar dates from Muhammad's flight from his enemies in Mecca in 622. This journey from his home city of Mecca to the oasis city of Yathrib 250 miles north is known as the Hegira and marks the beginning of Islam. The great escape has achieved legendary proportions. In one story, Muhammad's pursuers passed by a cave where the Prophet had hidden because a spider had spun a web completely across the entrance.

seeing their profits shrink, they began stoning and beating converts.

Warned of a plot on his life, Muhammad fled on a journey that crystallized his beliefs and marked the start of the religion called Islam, which means submission to the will of Allah. Within a decade he progressed from fugitive to religious leader with a large following. ■

Devoted Muslims circle the sacred Kaaba at Islam's holy city of Mecca, where Muhammad began his ministry. Early miniaturists depicting the birth of the Prophet in a golden flame (opposite) avoided the sacrilege of showing his or his mother's face.

623 End of internal fighting in China; all China is united under the Tang dynasty.

626 Abbey of St. Dènis, Paris, is founded. In Egypt the Byzantine emperor Heraclius I expels the Persians.

629 Alleged date of foundation of first mosque in Canton.

630 Knowledge of arithmetic and medicine reaches Tibet from China.

630-40 Arab pirates active in Red Sea.

Spreading Allah's Word

From Mecca, Muhammad fled from his enemies to the oasis city called Yathrib, 250 miles to the north. There he gathered more followers. The new religion was popular for its broader concept of humanity. Offering hope to the poor and disenfranchised as well as to the privileged rich, it appealed to the common people.

Although it condoned polygamy in a land where men died young and women needed protection, it improved the treatment of women. It recognized their property rights and guaranteed them equal footing with men in the afterlife.

As Islam's numbers grew and Muhammad's power was recog-

633 Spain becomes an elective kingdom of the Visigoths. In England the Mercians under Penda defeat the Northumbrians.

634 Chomsongdae Observatory, constructed in southern Korean Kingdom of Silla, remains the oldest known observatory in East Asia.

639-48 China conquers Turkestan and Korea.

645 Buddhism reaches Tibet.

645 In Egypt Byzantine forces recapture Alexandria. In Japan the Taikwa edict of reform nationalizes land and reorganizes the government.

nized, he formed the first Islamic state. Yathrib became Madinat al-Nabi, "the city of the Prophet," and later became known as Medina. The first military actions of Islam's faithful were against caravans from Mecca because of that city's persecution of Muhammad and its opposition to his ideas. In 630 he took Mecca itself

so believers sought new converts by word and by sword. Expansion of Islamic rule by war was seen as a sacred duty, known as *jihad.*

Ill-equipped in comparison with some military troops of the day, these Arab warriors were inspired by zeal and by the assurance that dying in holy battle meant instant entry into

Islam spread Arab architecture and ideas to much of the known world in the seventh and eighth centuries. Of medieval Islamic palaces in Spain, only the Alhambra still stands *(left).* Mosques became churches after the Moors were driven from Andalusia in

1492; at Mezquita *(opposite),* hooded Christians gather under Moorish arches. In the Islamic bastion of Cairo, Egypt, Muslim mystics, or Sufis, still chant Allah's name in a mosque *(opposite, below).*

THE DOME OF THE ROCK

Shrine for three faiths, the golden, glistening Dome of the Rock in Jerusalem, surrounded by prayerful Muslims during Ramadan *(below),* is sacred to Muslim, Jew, and Christian as the spot where Abraham nearly sacrificed his son as an act of faith in the one God. Completed in 691, it is also considered by Islam to be built over the rock from which Muhammad ascended into heaven.

with a force of 10,000 and set an example of leniency for the vanquished that would continue in future Muslim campaigns and aid in their success. Pagans could embrace Islam. Christians and Jews could keep their faith if they paid a tax.

Muhammad died two years after taking Mecca, but his successors urged the faithful not to despair. Allah was all-powerful, they said. Muhammad was only a messenger, as had been Abraham, Noah, Moses, and Jesus before him. The Koran urged propagation of the faith,

paradise. Persia fell, as did Egypt, Morocco, and finally Spain, but Muslims were prevented from marching into France by the forces of Charles Martel, leader of the Franks.

Nevertheless, within a century after Muhammad's death, calls to prayer five times a day could be heard from minarets from the Atlantic Ocean to the border of China, north into Spain and Russia. Arab fleets made the Mediterranean a Muslim sea. Islam spread southward into Indonesia through trade and missionary work. ■

The Arabs conquer
Cyprus.

649

ca 650 Babylonian Talmud, a
record of Jewish law, is
finalized. Hopewell peo-
ple established along
the upper Mississippi
River. Teotihuacan in
Mexico thrives as an
important trade center.

Byzantine fleet defeated
by Arabs off the
Egyptian coast
near Alexandria.

655

The Chinese go to war
against Korea.

661

In England King Oswy
of Northumbria aban-
dons the Celtic Christian
Church, accepting
Roman Christianity.

664

Islam's Contributions

Simple and nomadic though their
beginnings may have been, the
Arabs were no ragtag conquerors.
"The ink of scholars is more precious
than the blood of martyrs,"
Muhammad had said, and learning
followed in the wake of Islam's
advance. Interested in the lands they
conquered, the Arabs absorbed new
ideas and contributed their own.

Ibn Sina (Avicenna) of Bukhara
wrote his *Canon,* which became the
principal medical textbook in Europe
for the next 500 years. The philosophies of the Moorish Ibn Rushd
(Averroës) influenced prominent
European thinkers such as Roger
Bacon and Thomas Aquinas.

Men of knowledge—Muslims,
Christians, and Jews alike—gathered
in centers of learning, copying classic
texts into Arabic, discussing, experimenting, and collecting all known
information about mathematics,
medicine, natural sciences, and
astronomy, rendering their findings
in illustrated textbooks. Arab naviga-
tors and astronomers brought the
compass from China and perfected
the astrolabe.

Foods from the scattered world of
Islam found their way to European

Elaborate filigree and
figures of mathematical
symmetry marked the
work of Muslim
builders. At the king's
palace in Fes,
Morocco, colorful tile
and carved plaster
cover walls *(right).* A
collection of motifs
(opposite) includes four
kinds of arches and sta-
lactites of wood and
plaster, calligraphy on
walls, and arabesques
of sinuous lines. The
basic compass, tile-
cutting hammer, and
straightedge worked
patterns into tiles. Art
adorns a hand-lettered
Koran *(far right).*

673 The Arabs start an unsuccessful, five-year siege of Constantinople.

674 Arabs occupy Crete.

675 Bulgars settle south of the Danube, founding their first empire.

682 Chinese withdraw from Korea.

687 Pepin becomes Mayor of the Franks and effective ruler of their kingdoms.

tables—apricots, rice, and *sukkar*—sugar. Arab words were incorporated into the English language: "cipher," "logarithm," "algebra," "almanac," "soda," and "zenith."

Arab tapestries, tiled domes, luxurious carpets, and paintings spread over the Old World. Arab art became known for its intricate designs and beautiful handwritten scripts. Brocades from the looms of Muslim Sicily garbed the wealthy in Europe. The pointed arch, developed in Persia, made its way through Islamic influence to Europe and

began showing up in lofty cathedrals. The Taj Mahal in Agra, India, one of the loveliest buildings in the world, was built by a Muslim emperor over a period of some two decades as a tomb for his beloved wife.

Perhaps the biggest impact of the Arab Empire was the cohesiveness it gave to culture. Arabic became the learned, and therefore the common, language from Baghdad to the Alhambra in Spain. Over three continents, the faithful worshiped the same God, and lived by the same principles in the Koran. ■

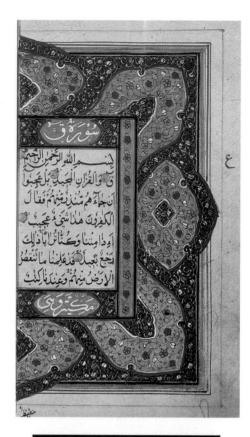

AN EMPIRE DIVIDED

In 634 Omar was selected as caliph, or successor, of the Muslim community. Even though Omar was assassinated a decade later, the caliphate remained in the Ommayad family until 750, when the Abbasid dynasty came into power. The Abbasid caliphs transferred matters of religious importance to local experts in Islam, men called *ulema*. Muslims still submitted matters of interpretation to the *ulema*, but the direct line of spirituality from supreme leader to willing follower had been lost. The Abbasids ruled until 1258. As the empire expanded, central control was strained by disputes, and dynasties arose in other locations: Spain, Egypt, Persia, and today's Turkey. Islam ceased being the exclusive province of Arab leadership.

589 Arabs, Khazars, and Turks invade Persia, but they are defeated. Under King Authari and Queen Theodelinda, the Lombards are converted to Roman Catholicism.

592 Mutiny of Roman troops in Europe.

596-617 Nectan MacDerili is the first Pictish king converted to Christianity.

598 The first English school is thought to have been founded at Canterbury.

598-601 Truce between Lombards and Byzantines.

ca 600 Laws passed in Ireland against women going to battle. Important period of art and literature in Ireland begins.

The Sui Reunite China

Just as the Roman Empire had collapsed before invading barbarians, pressure from nomads of the steppes helped bring down the Han dynasty in A.D. 220 and plunged China into a long period of disunity and discord.

The period might be compared to what is sometimes called Europe's Dark Ages, in which central control was lost, but with some important differences. Although like Europe, China broke into separate localized kingdoms, each vying for power over the other, the society as a whole absorbed the barbarian invaders and continued its own customs. And the nomads, who were not administrators, allowed the landowners to continue the bureaucracy.

For three centuries China experienced political disunity and civil strife. During this time of trial, Confucianism, more a code of ethical conduct than a religion, proved inadequate for the spiritual needs of the Chinese. Buddhism—which infiltrated through traders from India—began to fill this religious vacuum.

Confucianism remained the basis of the educational system. Taoism, a philosophy of a more mystical nature, offered some rivalry. But the adaptable Chinese incorporated benefits from all three that enriched their

disparate society spiritually, intellectually, and culturally.

Cooperating with Turks in A.D. 552, the Chinese destroyed the barbarian Juan-juan confederacy, although the Turks then set up a northern dynasty as threatening as the conquered one had been. Dynastic quarrels created disunity among the Turks, and in 581 the Sui dynasty swept

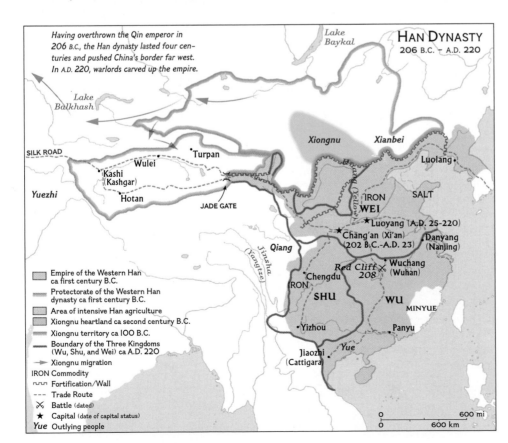

Having overthrown the Qin emperor in 206 B.C., the Han dynasty lasted four centuries and pushed China's border far west. In A.D. 220, warlords carved up the empire.

HAN DYNASTY
206 B.C. – A.D. 220

Lake Baykal
Lake Balkhash
SILK ROAD
Wulei
Turpan
Kashi (Kashgar)
Yuezhi
Hotan
JADE GATE
Xiongnu
Xianbei
Luolang
IRON
SALT
WEI
Luoyang (A.D. 25-220)
Chang'an (Xi'an) (202 B.C.-A.D. 23)
Danyang (Nanjing)
Qiang
Jinsha (Yangtze)
Red Cliff 208
Wuchang (Wuhan)
Chengdu
IRON
SHU
WU
MINYUE
Yizhou
Panyu
Jiaozhi (Cattigara)
Yue

Empire of the Western Han ca first century B.C.
Protectorate of the Western Han dynasty ca first century B.C.
Area of intensive Han agriculture
Xiongnu heartland ca second century B.C.
Xiongnu territory ca 100 B.C.
Boundary of the Three Kingdoms (Wu, Shu, and Wei) ca A.D. 220
Xiongnu migration
IRON Commodity
Fortification/Wall
Trade Route
Battle (dated)
Capital (date of capital status)
Yue Outlying people

0   600 mi
0   600 km

604 First written constitution in Japan.

610 Muhammad has a vision in which the Archangel Gabriel commands him to proclaim the one true god, Allah. In China, a network of canals allows rice to be traded widely.

611 Persian armies capture Antioch.

612 Monasteries of St. Gall and Bobbio founded.

616 Adaloald becomes King of the Lombards.

Workers build a dike to contain a swollen river, part of the massive public works that expressed power in imperial China.

away the last of the northern barbarian states, reuniting China.

Under the previous system of separate kingdoms, defense of the home territory had required conscription of people into local armies for long periods of time, and taxes were high. The first Sui emperor, Yang Chien, reduced taxes and the length of required military service, and he set up irrigation schemes that increased production of food crops.

Under a second Sui emperor, Yang Di, the Grand Canal was rebuilt, which facilitated movement of grain and trade between the east-west Yangtze Valley of the south to the capitals of Changan and Luoyang in the north.

Rivaling the Great Wall as an engineering feat, the Grand Canal helped China become prosperous.

Unfortunately Yang Di also insisted on construction of palaces and pleasure parks for himself and levied taxes against future years to pay for them. The peasants rebelled and killed Yang Di in 618.

The reunifying Sui dynasty had lasted less than 40 years. ■

620 Isle of Man annexed by the kingdom of Northumbria.

622 Official beginning of the Hijra era in the Muslim calendar.

625 Muhammad begins dictating the Koran.

628 Peace made between Medina and Mecca.

630 Peace made between Byzantium and Persia. Muhammad captures Mecca and sets out the principles of Islam.

635 The Muslims begin the conquest of Syria, which takes three years, and of Persia, which takes eight years.

Expansion by the Tang

The Tang dynasty, which replaced the Sui in 618, continued the administrative policies of its predecessors, but with an eye toward expanding the Chinese Empire. Within 50 years Chinese armies had ventured into India, central Asia, and Afghanistan and set up protectorates in Sogdiana, Ferghana, and eastern Persia, areas directly north of India.

In the north the Tang occupied northern Korea and exerted considerable cultural influence on Japan. In the south they dominated what is now Vietnam. The Chinese Empire had never been so vast. Lands under its control and on its periphery adopted Chinese language, culture, and political institutions.

This period of power and stability fostered literature, the arts, and many new inventions, so that the Tang years are sometimes referred to as China's golden age. Books proliferated after a system of printing on moveable wood type was introduced. By carving images into a block of wood, pictures and text could be stamped onto many pages instead of being painstakingly drawn on each. Porcelain, made from different clays, was invented by the Chinese, with brilliant, three-color glazes attained by the Tang. Gunpowder was created accidentally by a scientist who was trying to make a potion to ensure everlasting life. Used first in fireworks for entertainment and to frighten an enemy, it later became a weapon.

With the northern borders protected by Tang expansionism, caravans plodded regularly along the trails that made up the Silk Road to the West.

The creation of poetry achieved heights never again equaled. Chinese poets praised the glories of the northern capital city, Changan, and the beauty of the courtesan Yang Guifei, the favorite of the emperor Ming-huang. Unfortunately she convinced him to give considerable power to a frontier general, An Lu-shan, who revolted in 755 and captured the capital. Fleeing the rebel, the emperor was forced by his own soldiers to give up the beautiful Yang Guifei to the enemy. Her betrayal and subsequent execution were events immortalized in poetry and drama.

The Tang regime continued until 907, but the population shifted from the north to the fertile Yangtze Valley in the south, where new farming methods produced surpluses in grain.

When in 907 the Tang dynasty disappeared, China was split once again, into ten regional kingdoms and six dynasties. ■

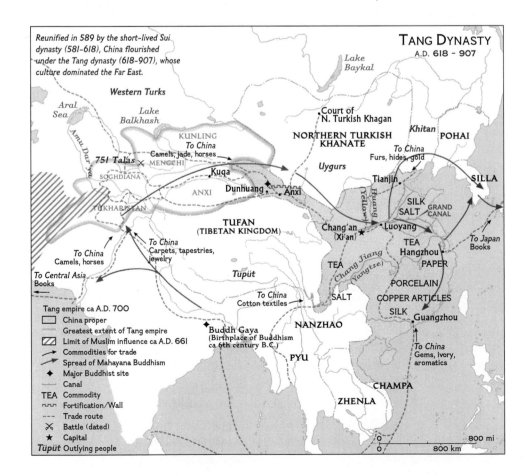

Reunified in 589 by the short-lived Sui dynasty (581-618), China flourished under the Tang dynasty (618-907), whose culture dominated the Far East.

TANG DYNASTY
A.D. 618 - 907

Lake Baykal

Western Turks

Aral Sea

Lake Balkhash

Amu Dar'ya

KUNLING
To China
Camels; jade, horses

Court of N. Turkish Khagan

NORTHERN TURKISH KHANATE

Khitan

POHAI

To China
Furs, hides, gold

751 Talas × MENGCHI

SOGHDIANA

Kuqa

Uygurs

Tianjin

SILLA

Dunhuang

Anxi

ANXI

Huang (Yellow)

SILK SALT

GRAND CANAL

TUKHARISTAN

To China
Carpets, tapestries, jewelry

TUFAN (TIBETAN KINGDOM)

Chang'an (Xi'an) ★

Luoyang

To Japan Books

To China
Camels, horses

Tüpüt

TEA

Hangzhou

TEA

Chang Jiang (Yangtze)

PAPER

To Central Asia
Books

To China
Cotton textiles

SALT

PORCELAIN

COPPER ARTICLES

SILK

Guangzhou

Tang empire ca A.D. 700

☐ China proper
☐ Greatest extent of Tang empire
▨ Limit of Muslim influence ca A.D. 661
→ Commodities for trade
⇢ Spread of Mahayana Buddhism
◆ Major Buddhist site
--- Canal
TEA Commodity
〰 Fortification/Wall
--- Trade route
× Battle (dated)
★ Capital
Tüpüt Outlying people

♦ Buddh Gaya
(Birthplace of Buddhism ca 6th century B.C.)

NANZHAO

PYU

To China
Gems, ivory, aromatics

CHAMPA

ZHENLA

800 mi
800 km

The beauty of karst hills in southwestern China belies the tragedy of the fleeing Emperor Ming-huang in a painting that marks the twilight of the Tang dynasty (opposite). A more tranquil twilight reflects in today's quiet waters (opposite, below).

643 Muslims conquer Tripoli.

691 Dome of the Rock is completed in Jerusalem; considered by Islam to be built over the rock from which Muhammad ascended into heaven.

700 Collapse of Moche civilization in Peru.

771 Charlemagne, son of Pepin the Short, becomes King of the Franks.

ca 790 Vikings invade the British Isles; for the next two centuries these raiders will ravage villages and monasteries throughout Europe.

800 Invasion of Bohemia by the Franks.

843 By the Treaty of Verdun the Carolingian Empire is partitioned.

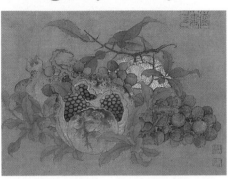

ca **960** Star of David first appears as symbol of Judaism.

974 Earliest authenticated earthquake in Great Britain.

994 City of Delhi is founded by the Tomaros.

ca **1000** Stone for first statues at Easter Island is quarried. First Viking settlement on Newfoundland. New Zealand is populated by ancestors of present-day Maori.

1066 Normans and Saxons clash at the Battle of Hastings.

Prosperity Under the Song Dynasty

Beginning in 960, the Song dynasty reunified most of China, but ultimately it could not hold the north against a Tatar people known as the Khitan tribes. A corruption of that name led Europeans to refer to China as "Cathay," a term introduced by Marco Polo. Driven southward, the Song controlled only central and southern China. Distant places like northern Korea and Vietnam were no longer Chinese holdings.

In their more limited territory—perhaps because of it—the years of the Song dynasty were prosperous. The fertile south produced more food than the mountainous north. In middle of the eighth century, the total Chinese population was 60 million. By 1100 the population had grown to more than 110 million, two-thirds of whom lived in central and southern China.

Trade and industry boomed, and the capital, Hangzhou, became the world's greatest city. A growing urban middle class patronized art, drama, and storytelling. The evolution of exquisite porcelain continued.

A development in the bureaucracy added to stability. Appointments in administration previously had been based on one's social standing, not necessarily on merit. This was replaced by state examinations for the recruitment of officials, elevating the best and the brightest.

Because trade with western lands was curtailed by loss of control over the northern land routes, the Song became a maritime power, trading by sea with southeastern Asia,

Their empire shrunken by invading northern tribes, the Chinese became even more prosperous under the Song dynasty by concentrating their efforts in the fertile south. A thriving urban middle class acquired refined tastes, supporting artwork such as this painting of fine fruit **(above).** Cut off from overland routes, the Song built ships for far-flung trade by sea. A 17th-century watercolor on silk **(opposite)** portrays a Song emperor shipping pierced rocks and misshapen trees for artistic construction.

Indonesia, India, and the Persian Gulf. Merchants became immensely wealthy and set up complex commercial systems that included banks, credit systems, and paper money.

As Europe during this time was still in a period of stagnation, China was perhaps the world's greatest power—its culture, the most splendid.

Landed gentry, made fat by prosperity, acquired large estates and then rented land to peasants at high rates. They reaped peasant rebellion. Bureaucrats who, like the gentry, had been made complacent by economic success, neglected the military.

The Song fell to the Mongol hordes in 1279. ■

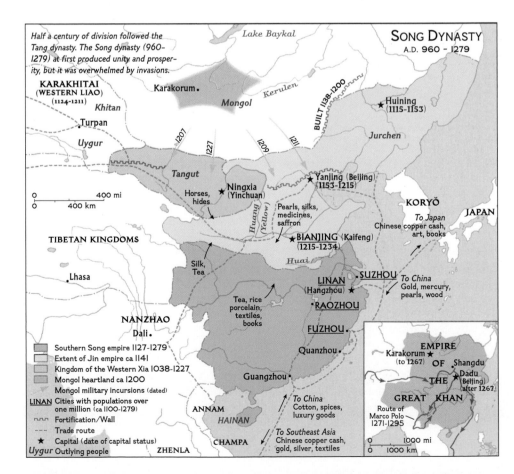

Half a century of division followed the Tang dynasty. The Song dynasty (960–1279) at first produced unity and prosperity, but it was overwhelmed by invasions.

SONG DYNASTY
A.D. 960 – 1279

Southern Song empire 1127-1279
Extent of Jin empire ca 1141
Kingdom of the Western Xia 1038-1227
Mongol heartland ca 1200
Mongol military incursions (dated)
LINAN Cities with populations over one million (ca 1100-1279)
Fortification/Wall
Trade route
★ Capital (date of capital status)
Uygur Outlying people

1094 El Cid, Christian soldier of fortune, takes Valencia.

ca 1100 First universities established in Europe at Salerno, Bologna, and Paris. Toltec build their capital at Tula.

1182 Jews banished from France by Philip II.

1210 St. Francis of Assisi founds Franciscan Order of Friars, emphasizing poverty and repentance.

1232 China is first to use rockets in warfare.

800 Charlemagne is crowned Holy Roman Emperor by a grateful Pope Leo III on Christmas Day in Rome.

802 Vikings dominate Ireland.

ca 850 Groups of Jews begin to settle in Germany, start to develop their own language—Yiddish.

863 Creation of Cyrillic alphabet in eastern Europe.

868 *The Diamond Sutra,* earliest known complete woodblock-printed book with woodcut illustrations, is printed in China.

The Splendors of the Khmer

Over several centuries, the influence of India and its Hindu and Buddhist religions had traveled along trade routes into Indochina, where the Southeast Asian state of Funan had become established. One of Funan's vassal states, which Chinese chronicles refer to as Chen-La, eventually overthrew its masters. The Chen-La people, later known as the Khmer, established an empire that dominated the southern half of the Southeast Asian Peninsula between the 7th and 13th centuries

A.D. Touched by Indian styles but expanding on them, the Khmer created some of the world's grandest structures and art.

At first, after winning their independence, the Khmer struggled internally, with numerous factions vying for power. Around 800 a prince named Jayavarman II began consolidating the empire. The capital of Jayavarman and his successors shifted from one location to another until it finally settled on the north shore of

the Tonle Sap, or Great Lake, in today's Cambodia. Named Yashodharapura, it was the capital of the Khmer from around 900 until the 15th century, when it became known as Angkor.

Although both major religions infiltrated the area, the Khmer of early empire first embraced Hinduism. The massive temple, Angkor Wat, dominated the plain where today the remains of 72 temples and monuments tell of the metropolis that once

930   Cordoba becomes the seat of Arab learning, science, commerce, and industry in Spain.

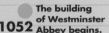

977-983   Compilation of 1,000-volume Song dynasty encyclopedia.

1052   The building of Westminster Abbey begins.

1123   Death of poet Omar Khayyam in Persia.

1204   Constantinople falls to Christian crusaders.

1206   Military genius Temujin is named Genghis Khan—universal leader—by nomadic tribes of Mongolia.

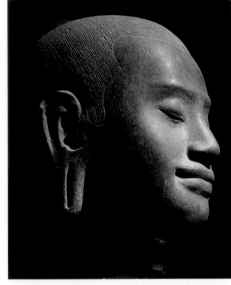

Remnants of Khmer glory emerge in Cambodia with the clearing of jungle from old Angkor. Grim faces guard the Gate of the Dead at Angkor Thom *(opposite)*, part of a complex of temples in what was a thriving metropolis for more than 500 years. A more serene visage may be seen in a stone likeness of Jayavarman VII, one of the Khmer's greatest rulers *(above)*. A benevolent king and decisive general, he rallied the Khmer after their defeat by the Cham in the 12th century and conquered most of southeastern Asia.

existed. Inscriptions on the walls of the Bayon temple provide glimpses into the lives of the Khmer. They show fishermen casting their nets from small canoes, a hawker releasing his hunter, market vendors and buyers, spectators at a cockfight, a lively group aboard a riverboat.

The city of Angkor spread over an area twice the size of today's Manhattan and supported perhaps a million people. A central government oversaw a uniform society that used an elaborate hydraulic system for transportation and rice cultivation.

A complex system of canals and reservoirs retained and distributed the water that fell seasonally, allowing the Khmer to obtain two or even three harvests a year. Even the Siem Reap River was diverted to fill one of the reservoirs.

In the dry season the reigning king made war against the Cham to the north or the Siamese to the west, for glory, treasure, and slaves. The Cham destroyed the capital in 1177, which was rebuilt by Jayavarman VII.

The Khmer may have outgrown their elaborate complex. Perhaps they overextended their ability to feed themselves. For whatever reason, the energetic construction of the empire's earlier days ceased. The last major temple was dedicated to Buddhism by an emperor who felt the Hindu gods had failed his people in their defeat by the Cham.

The Siamese finally captured and sacked the capital in the late 14th and 15th centuries. And shortly thereafter the Khmer abandoned their once glorious city. ■

TAPESTRIES IN STONE

Relief from an Angkor wall depicts a Khmer scene of battle *(left)*. Temple wall decorations stand among the greatest expressions of Khmer art. Thousands of carvings—some 1,700 of graceful celestial maidens on Angkor Wat alone—decorate nearly every surface of Angkor's temples. Lengthy panels with lifelike figures tell Hindu myths and depict visions of both blissful and hellish afterlife. One 160-foot-long relief, symbolizing immortality and the king's beneficence, uses multiple images of the same character to give a sense of motion, like frames of a movie.

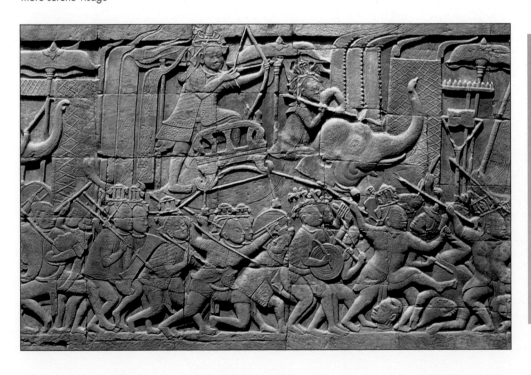

Mali Rules West Africa

After A.D. 900, Muslim dynasties that had spread over North Africa stimulated trade southward into the Sahel, giving rise to a number of African states. The kingdom of Ghana flourished from the 8th to the 11th centuries in western Africa north of the Niger and Senegal Rivers. In its decline it was overthrown by two of its subject peoples, the Susa and later the Keita.

Around 1240 the Keita warrior-king Sundiata expanded his territory and established the Empire of Mali, which became the most important of the sub-Saharan Muslim realms. Sundiata's grandson Mansa Musa brought Islam to the empire and expanded its territory and wealth.

At its height, Mali extended from the Atlantic Ocean eastward to the far-north bend of the Niger River, covering most of what is now Gambia, Senegal, Guinea, and modern Mali.

Mansa Musa became renowned throughout Islam and Christendom for his wealth, brilliance, and the artistic achievements within his realm. In 1324 during a pilgrimage to Mecca, he took so much gold with him that the currency of Cairo was depressed.

The capital of the Mali kingdom was Timbuktu, a thriving, walled city of thousands. It was Mali's intellectual hub as well as its chief trade center. From the north via camel caravans,

1306 — Jews are expelled from France.

1317 — In France, women are excluded from succeeding to the French throne, through the Salic Law.

1337-1453 — The Hundred Years' War between England and France.

1339 — Construction begins on the Kremlin in Moscow.

1400 — Death of Chaucer, first great English poet.

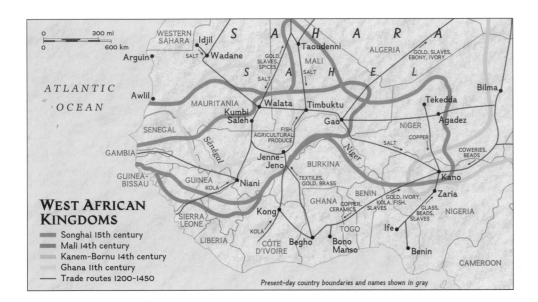

WEST AFRICAN KINGDOMS

- Songhai 15th century
- Mali 14th century
- Kanem-Bornu 14th century
- Ghana 11th century
- Trade routes 1200–1450

Present-day country boundaries and names shown in gray

came salt, copper, and luxury items from Fes. From the south came food, ivory, and gold. "Caravans come to Timbuktu from all points of the horizon," wrote a historian.

Upriver from Timbuktu a second important city in Mali was Jenne-jeno, the oldest-known city south of the

Sahara, with beginnings in the third century A.D. By 800 its population may have been around 10,000, profiting from trade on the Niger. In Mali's heyday, trade goods from the south and west came overland to Jenne-jeno and were then shipped downriver in large canoes to

Timbuktu. Surpluses of rice and other crops from Jenne-jeno's flooded Niger delta and fish from the river helped supply the desert with food.

The long-standing rule of Mali's kings was upheld by a mixture of military force and diplomatic alliances with local leaders. Royal judges dispensed justice through a tolerant legal system. Royal bureaucracies levied taxes and controlled trade.

In 1464 the province of Songhay rebelled, bringing the more than 200-year-old Empire of Mali to an end. ■

Reflecting the endurance of the Islamic faith, this turreted mosque stands in Djénné, Mali, a short distance from the even older town of Jenne-jeno. In the 14th century devout Muslims hailed the town as a center of religious learning, and merchants flocked to its prosperous trade. Rumors of a glittering city of wealth and culture downstream, called Timbuktu, excited Europeans until early explorers viewed the desert metropolis. "Nothing but a mass of ill-looking houses, built of earth," wrote one, sketching his impressions (opposite).

LEARNING IN TIMBUKTU

Mali's capital, Timbuktu, became not only a thriving center for trans-Sahara trade but a hub of Muslim scholarship as well. The ruler, Mansa Musa, commissioned the renowned Arab architect and poet, al-Sahili, to build the great Friday Mosque. This religious building was a university of its day, drawing teachers and students in law, logic, rhetoric, and other specialized subjects. Even after the empire's fall, Timbuktu remained an intellectual center. A visitor in 1512 noted that books fetched more profit than any other merchandise.

Mongols: Few But Fierce

Since earliest history, settled and civilized people in organized communities had contended with raids from primitive, warlike nomads who generally lived as pastoralists in rugged high country. Sometimes these intrusions completely disrupted societies, such as the Roman Empire and China, which suffered numerous barbaric attacks. One last time, from the 13th to the 15th centuries, civilization had to endure the successful invasion by primitive people when the Mongols conquered an empire that in scope and range exceeded anything that had come before it.

Because the barren land of the central Asian steppes from which they originated was not highly productive, the Mongols were never a numerous people. Their success as conquerors was due to their excellent horsemanship, endurance, ferocity in battle, and superior military tactics.

In their male-dominated, warrior society Mongol men took the best food for themselves and trained from childhood in archery and physical combat. They hunted on horseback, honing their skills as swift, deadly cavalrymen who were able to loose arrows with great accuracy at full gallop. Even so, their impact would have been merely regional had it not been for the leadership of a military genius named Temujin, later

known to the world as Genghis Khan.

Son of a minor Mongol chieftain, Temujin's early life was a struggle for survival and an exercise in brutality. His father was poisoned by Tatar tribesmen. Gathering allies, Temujin defeated the Tatars. In revenge he killed all but the smallest males and enslaved the women and children. As his power grew and alliances shifted, he gradually brought the 30-some

Lord of a mighty empire, Genghis Khan, pictured on a plaque *(opposite, below),* led nomadic horsemen to conquer most of the known world. Stirrups gave them stability for firing arrows in any direction *(below).*

At the great warrior's death in 1227, mourners killed anyone met by the funeral procession *(opposite)* to keep the location of Genghis Khan's grave a secret.

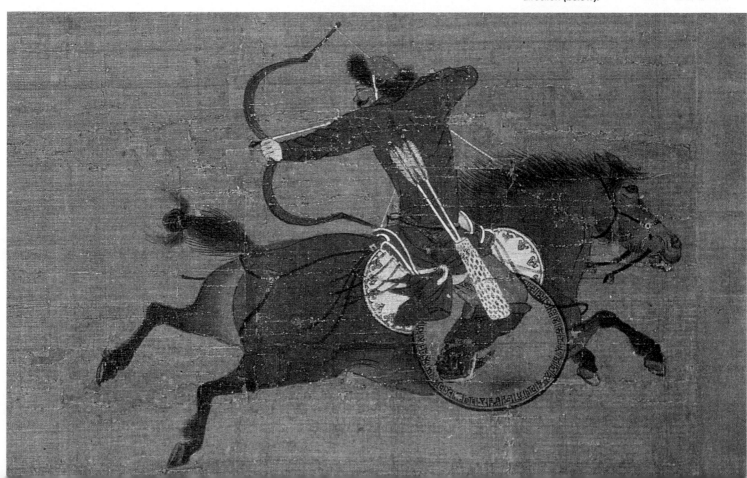

1195 Famine occurs in England.

ca 1200 City of Cuzco founded by Inca leader Manco Capac.

1204 Water-powered lumbermill appears at Evreux, Normandy.

1209 Treaty between England and Scotland.

1215 King John seals the Magna Carta; approaches pope to have it annulled later that same year.

nomadic tribes of Mongolia under his control, killing in the process his own blood brother, who had opposed him. In 1206 the tribes named him Genghis Khan, universal ruler.

He turned first to China, defeating the kingdom of Xi Xia, which controlled oases along the lucrative Silk Road between China and lands to the west. The Xi Xia refused help in a later campaign, so eventually Genghis ordered them exterminated, and an entire people virtually disappeared from history.

Moving farther into China, he first

took bribes aimed at fending off his attacks, then sacked and massacred inhabitants anyway. Returning to Mongolia, he built a capital at Karakorum, then defeated rivals to the west.

When the shah at Samarkand killed envoys sent by Genghis to negotiate, Genghis avenged the insult by defeating the shah's forces, even though they were superior in number to his own. Continuing westward, he overran central Asia, Afghanistan, Persia, and parts of Russia.

Genghis's army may never have

● Pope Gregory IX establishes the

1233 Inquisition.

ca **1240**
● Keita warrior-king Sundiata expands his territory and establishes the Empire of Mali, which became the most important of the sub-Saharan realms.

1252
● Florence strikes the first gold coins (florins) to be issued in the West since the fall of Rome.

ca **1254**
● Explorer Marco Polo is born in Venice.

1258
● Abbasid rule of Islamic Empire ends.

exceeded 110,000 men, but they were mobile, loyal, and disciplined. When necessary, troops from conquered states were incorporated into the forces and rewarded with booty.

Turks perhaps outnumbered native Mongols in Genghis's armies, and the Turkic language became the language of the invaders. Fear preceded rampages by the Mongols, who were known to slaughter the vanquished and were rumored to cannibalize the enemy dead.

Genghis died in 1227, but his successors continued to expand Mongol territory. By the late 13th century the empire stretched from the borders of Hungary to the Sea of Japan. ■

MONGOL WEAPONRY

A mounted Mongol was a formidable force, a superb horseman armed with a lance, saber, dagger, a bow with at least two quivers of arrows, and a shield on his arm to protect his face. Some of the arrowheads, shown here, were designed to make a whistling sound to terrify the enemy. Each warrior kept as many as four horses so that he would always have a fresh, speedy mount available. Using catapults in siege warfare, warriors would lob not only rocks but also diseased human carcasses into their enemies' strongholds.

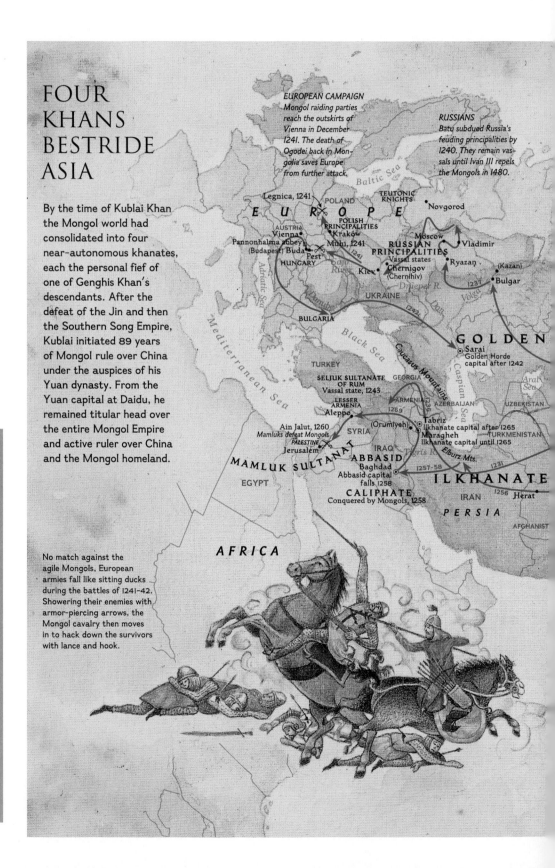

FOUR KHANS BESTRIDE ASIA

By the time of Kublai Khan the Mongol world had consolidated into four near-autonomous khanates, each the personal fief of one of Genghis Khan's descendants. After the defeat of the Jin and then the Southern Song Empire, Kublai initiated 89 years of Mongol rule over China under the auspices of his Yuan dynasty. From the Yuan capital at Daidu, he remained titular head over the entire Mongol Empire and active ruler over China and the Mongol homeland.

EUROPEAN CAMPAIGN
Mongol raiding parties reach the outskirts of Vienna in December 1241. The death of Ogodei back in Mongolia saves Europe from further attack.

RUSSIANS
Batu subdued Russia's feuding principalities by 1240. They remain vassals until Ivan III repels the Mongols in 1480.

No match against the agile Mongols, European armies fall like sitting ducks during the battles of 1241-42. Showering their enemies with armor-piercing arrows, the Mongol cavalry then moves in to hack down the survivors with lance and hook.

The Mongol Empire

Inspired by Persian astronomers, Kublai Khan commisioned an observatory to be built in Daidu. There the armillary sphere was used to measure angles between celestial objects. Under Kublai's 34-year rule, China makes many great strides in science.

Extent of Mongol empire in 1294

JAPANESE CAMPAIGNS Two failed attempts, in 1274 and 1281, to invade Japan frustrate Kublai Khan's desire to expand his empire beyond the seacoast.

RUSSIA — Lake Baikal — (Bayan-Ovoo) — (Ulaanbaatar) — MONGOLIA — Karakorum (Harhorin) Mongol empire capital 1235-1267 — Shangdu — KORYO — NORTH KOREA — SOUTH KOREA — JAPAN — Kyushu — Takashima, 1281

KAZAKSTAN — ORDE — ASIA — ALTAY MOUNTAINS — Daidu (Beijing) Mongol empire capital founded, 1267 — (Doudian) — Jining — Yellow Sea — GRAND CANAL

CHAGHATAI KHANATE — EMPIRE OF THE GREAT KHAN — XI XIA Conquered by Mongols, 1227 — CHINA — Yellow — JIN EMPIRE Conquered by Mongols — Kaifeng — Jin capital falls, 1233 — Fancheng (Xiangfan) — Hangzhou Song capital falls, 1276 — Xiangyang — Jingdezhen — PACIFIC OCEAN

Markand (Samarqand) — AJIKISTAN — TIBET — SOUTHERN SONG EMPIRE Conquered by Mongols, 1279 — Yangtze

KASHMIR Vassal state by 1286 — HIMALAYA — Brahmaputra — Pearl River

DELHI SULTANATE — INDIA — PAGAN Vassal state, 1287 — (Bagan) Pagan — MYANMAR (BURMA) — DAI VIET Vassal state, 1287 — LAOS — VIETNAM — South China Sea

HORSES MEET ELEPHANTS Their horses shy in terror when mongols face a Burmese army mounted on 2,000 elephants.

KHMER EMPIRE — THAILAND — CAMBODIA — CHAMPA Vassal state, 1287

MONGOLS IN JAVA Two years before his death, Kublai Khan sends a fleet of 1,000 ships against the island kingdom of Java. Facing intrigue and ambush, the Mongols once again return in defeat.

INDONESIA — JAVA

Major battle — Mongol military route — Present-day city names in parentheses — Present-day country boundaries and names in gray — 0 400 MILES

Mighty Kublai Khan was master of a vast domain.

Ogodei, the third son of Genghis Khan, became the Great Khan of the Mongol Empire upon the death of his father. He completed the overpowering of the Chin dynasty of northern China, but the most spectacular campaign was made by Genghis Khan's grandson Batu, who invaded Europe.

Northern Russian principalities were defeated in a lightning winter campaign in 1237-38, the only successful winter campaign against Russia in history. Kiev fell in 1240. In 1241 a German-Polish army was annihilated in Poland, and all Europe lay before the seemingly unstoppable fighting machine. Batu's forces might have reached the Atlantic had it not been for the death of Ogodei in the Mongol capital of Karakorum. Batu headed eastward to safeguard his position in the line of succession.

The Mongols were tolerant rulers. Parts of the empire were assigned to regional administrators, with the requirement that they recognize the

1308 Papal court moves to Avignon.

1325 Aztec begin to build their capital city of Tenochtitlán.

1336 Founded by Harihara I, the Hindu Empire of Vijayanagar, in India, becomes focal point for resistance to Islam.

1348 Persecution of Jews in Germany after the Black Death causes many survivors to migrate to Poland. Emperor Charles IV founds University of Prague.

1352-53 Ibn Battuta, Berber scholar, travels across Africa and writes an account of all he sees.

MARCO POLO, TRAVEL WRITER

Europe's knowledge of the Orient was fed by the travels of Venetian Marco Polo, who went to Beijing with his father and uncle in 1271. There the Kublai Khan took a liking to 17-year-old Marco, sending him on missions to distant places. Golden tablets (above) from Kublai Khan assured his safe passage. After 17 years at the court of the khan, the Polos returned to Venice, where Marco's written accounts about China's magnificence astonished Europeans.

supreme authority of the Great Khan. Buddhists, Muslims, and a Persian sect of Christians known as Nestorians were welcome in Mongol courts. To regain Jerusalem, the Roman Catholics attempted an alliance with the Mongols against the Muslims, but problems arose over the pope's claim to universal authority.

Although the Mongols had no written language, Genghis Khan respected writing and enlisted literate people to transliterate spoken Mongolian, using the alphabet of another language. Thus was the Mongolian code of law written down.

In 1260 a Mongol force was defeated by the Mamalukes of Egypt, and the idea of Mongol invincibility was put to rest. With the death of the Great Khan Möngke, the unity of the

huge empire was broken when western areas in Persia and Russia began operating as separate states.

The nature of the empire also changed with the ascension of Kublai Khan, another grandson of Genghis Khan. Completing the conquest of China, Kublai Khan moved the capital to Beijing and enjoyed a life of luxury. An attempt to take Japan was thwarted when his invading fleet encountered a typhoon. The storm destroyed much of the fleet, a storm that the Japanese called *kamikaze*, the "divine wind."

1358 Peasant uprising in France, known as the Jacquerie.

1377 Papacy, in person of Pope Gregory XI, returns to Rome.

1381 Both the Peasants' Revolt in England and the antitax riots in Paris seen as reactions to economic changes caused by the Black Death.

1397 Kalmar Agreement unites three Scandinavian Kingdoms of Denmark, Norway, and Sweden.

The Mongols never created a distinctive civilization, borrowing instead from other cultures and blending in with them. Kublai Khan ruled as a Chinese emperor, and the Mongols in China began to lose their martial qualities. After his death the empire broke apart further. The Chinese retook their land, but the Mongols in Russia had kept their warlike, nomadic ways and stayed in control there for some 200 more years.

Mongol power surged once again in the late 14th century when Timur the Lame, the ferocious ruler of Samarkand who claimed to descend from Genghis Khan, conquered Persia, Iraq, Syria, Afghanistan, and part of Russia. He attacked India, sacking Delhi in 1398 and killing most of its people. He turned his army toward China but died on the way there in 1405, ending the era of Mongol conquest.

Over the next two centuries firearms neutralized somewhat the athleticism that had marked Mongol success in battle. The Chinese and Russians, who had suffered most from their incursions, were able to control the fierce herdsmen of the steppes. ■

Small-boat raiders prepare to board Mongol ships invading Japan. Two attempts to conquer the islands were repulsed, once by a typhoon that drowned some 100,000 men. Attacking Mongols pierced the hands of Japanese women *(opposite, below)* and hung them from their ships' hulls. A gracious welcome awaited European Marco Polo, whose travels were sanctioned by the Mongol lord, Kublai Khan. Some of Marco Polo's reportage led to illustrations of headless people *(opposite, above)* by Europeans still isolated in their homelands.

521 Boëthius, Roman scholar, introduces Greek musical letter notation to the West.

531 Chosroes I becomes King of Persia.

537 Hagia Sophia, greatest building of the Byzantine Empire, is completed.

542 Ly Ben leads Vietnamese rebellion against China.

ca 594 Buddhism becomes the official religion in Japan.

607 Emperor Yomei completes Japan's Horyuji Temple, oldest surviving wooden building in the world.

Anglo-Saxons and Normans

The Germanic tribes exerting pressure on the western Roman Empire in the fourth and fifth centuries were themselves being pressured by fierce Huns from the Russian steppes. Pushed from the east, the Angles and Saxons moved into Britain. Some 500 years later, a group of Vikings moved into northwestern France across the channel from Britain and became known as Normans. The groups would clash over control of the island.

With the end of Roman authority in the early fifth century A.D., the Angles and Saxons quickly established dominance in Britain. Resistance to them by native Britons probably continued for some time, giving rise to the legend of Arthur, a native British king gallantly fighting against the heathen foe.

Many of the Romanized Celts were pushed back into Wales and Ireland. Others were probably absorbed into the society of the victors. The West Saxon code of 694 provides for "Welshmen" as substantial landowners and those who performed errands for the Saxon king.

Various invading groups carved out their own territories in Britain. At one time there were seven kingdoms: three ruled by Saxons, three by Angles, and one by the Jutes. Vying for supremacy over all Britain, they fought each other frequently. By the eighth century they fought the Vikings as well, who invaded from the north. Although warlike, most all the invaders were farmers who sought fertile valleys in which to grow crops

627 — T'ai Tsung the Great becomes Emperor of China. During his rule, arts and letters flourish.

711 — Islamic armies invade southern Spain.

ca 750 — Pharmacology and medicine become two separate sciences.

791 — Byzantine Emperor Constantine imprisons his mother for her cruelty.

820 — Persian mathematician Musa al-Chwarazmi develops algebra.

1055 — Seljuk Turks capture Baghdad.

and graze their animals.

By the late ninth century the fierce Saxons had prevailed, absorbing the Angles and Jutes and restricting the Vikings to an area called the Danelaw in northeastern England. Even that was eventually won from the Vikings, and after 954 England was one kingdom. But one more major battle would determine which group would rule it.

In the 11th century Edward the Confessor was the Saxon King of England, although—being related through his mother to the Normans across the channel—he was pro-Norman. When a powerful Saxon earl named Godwin revolted unsuccessfully, Edward banished him and named William of Normandy as his heir to the throne. Godwin's son Harold returned to England and rose in power but, according to chroniclers, acknowledged William's eventual right to the kingship.

When Edward died in 1066, however, Harold quickly had himself crowned king of England. Now there were three laying claim to the throne: William of Normandy, originally named heir; Harold the Saxon son of Godwin, already crowned; and King Harald Hardraada of Norway, who took the opportunity of Edward's death to invade northern England.

Harold sped to the north and defeated the Norwegian, then raced south again to meet William, who had invaded across the channel. Wearied by battle and travel, the Anglo-Saxon, or English, forces of Harold fell to the Normans.

Saxon nobility was shattered, Norman barons were awarded large estates, and French was spoken in court. But the Anglo-Saxon population dominated, and eventually so did the English language, which absorbed considerable French content. ■

Battling for Britain, Normans and Saxons clashed at Hastings in the pivotal fight of 1066. Showing his face to dispute rumors of his death, William cheered the Normans to victory, here depicted in tapestry (below). Harassing all England and northwest Europe were fierce Vikings, whose raids by sea are recorded in a medieval manuscript (opposite).

529 Justinian's Code of Civil Laws, the Codex Vetus, is issued.

543 First official Christian mission is established in Nubia; the site would become the foundation of a major cathedral in later centuries.

595 First authenticated record of decimal reckoning in India.

618 China's Grand Canal is completed.

651 Uthman establishes committee to collate and revise the Koran.

700 Nazca society falls under the influence of people from highlands to the east, and their culture begins to fade.

Charlemagne, Holy Roman Emperor

Europe after the decline of the Roman Empire was occupied by scattered groups of Germanic tribes. Among these, the Franks emerged as the strongest. A series of Frankish kings gradually amassed more and more territory into one realm until the one who came to be known as Charlemagne ruled a vast domain in the eighth century.

The Franks had achieved some measure of unity nearly 300 years earlier, around A.D. 500, when Clovis of the Merovingian dynasty defeated rival Frankish chieftains and became king of what is now southwestern Germany and France. He also became Roman Catholic, helping to spread Christianity in Europe. After his death and the division of his kingdom among his sons, these Merovingian kings gradually lost control of their holdings, which came to be administered by men called "mayors of the palace."

One of these mayors, Charles Martel, led a Frankish force against the Muslim army that was moving into Europe through Spain. After his victory at Tours in A.D. 732, in which he was hailed as the defender of Christendom, the Franks became united politically behind Charles and his family, later known as the Carolingians. In 751, with the backing of the Frankish nobles and the blessing of the Christian church, Charles's son Pepin the Short deposed the reigning Merovingian and became king of the Franks.

In return for the church's blessing,

Unity came to Europe at the sword of Charlemagne, here crowned Holy Roman Emperor by the pope in a 14th-century miniature (above). Under Christianity, society stratified into social classes. Nobles ruled vassals who were served by serfs, with the king supreme over all. Lowly serfs labored in their lords' grainfields (below), and chopped wood to heat houses they shared with livestock (opposite), seeking hope in the church for a peaceful afterlife. The bejeweled book shown here (opposite, right) was a legacy of the Carolingians, enshrining holy words.

Pepin struck against the church's enemies, forcing the heathen Lombards to withdraw from Rome and granting a strip of land in central Italy to Pope Stephen II. As a result, the papacy's power in Italy grew, and it was bound even closer to the Franks and distanced from the Byzantine Empire in Constantinople, a division that would deepen through the years.

In 771 Pepin's son Charles, later called Charlemagne, or Charles the Great, became king of the Franks and expanded their borders to include what is now Germany, France, northern Spain, and most of Italy, forcing defeated people to accept Christianity. Once when the vanquished failed to convert, he rounded up 4,500 Germans and beheaded them all in one day. He also defended the pope against

- ca 700 — Temple I, in Tikal's Great Plaza, is built by Maya ruler Ah Cacao for his funerary monument.
- 748 — First printed newspaper appears in Beijing.
- 748 — Arab fleet destroyed during attack on Cyprus.
- ca 771 — System of Arabic numerals is first called "Arabic" when the Indian numeral system is introduced into the Arab world.
- ca 800 — First castles built in western Europe.
- ca 810 — Of Hindu origin, the rosary is first mentioned in Arabic literature.

opposing nobles in Rome. In gratitude, the pope crowned him Holy Roman Emperor in A.D. 800.

Sometimes called the "Father of Europe," Charlemagne brought to Europe a unity it had not known since earlier days of the Roman Empire. Although barely literate himself, he respected learning and encouraged the founding of schools in cathedrals and monasteries. He granted land to nobles who would support him politically and militarily and created an atmosphere in which craftsmen could settle and work in his kingdom.

A large man—his remains indicate he was about six feet, four inches tall—he created stability by the strength of his personality. When he died, his empire became a patchwork of kingdoms controlled by rulers who passed the land to heirs. What had been a united Europe became a number of independent kingdoms. ■

ca 500 — First Scottish kingdoms established. Aztec civilization active in Mexico. Maya cities flourish in Yucatan Peninsula. Thule people move into Alaska.

ca 520 — Rise of mathematics in India.

527-565 — Reign of Justinian.

529 — Ratisbon becomes the capital of Bavaria. St. Benedict founds a monastery at Monte Cassino, south of Rome.

534 — Malta becomes a Byzantine province.

570 — Byzantium and Persia establish a 50-year peace.

Feudalism

The twin needs of societies for military protection and for food production often gave rise to the political system known as feudalism. In a feudal system, land was parceled out to people in exchange for services as well as the payment of rent.

Feudalism was a class system, in which the status that a person held in society depended in large part on the amount of land he controlled.

At the top rung of the ladder was the king, who granted land to nobles in exchange for their support. At the bottom were the peasants who worked the land for masters.

Feudalism has appeared in China, Persia, and Byzantium, but its most systematic, widespread, long-standing tenure was in Europe, beginning in the eighth century. It found its roots in the policies of Charlemagne, who sought the support of powerful nobles by granting them large estates. The nobles sought to guard those estates and the king's realm by doling out parcels of land to lesser lords, who served as knights in time of conflict. The lesser lords in turn contracted peasants to work their land, producing the wealth by which they could outfit themselves with expensive armor and sturdy mounts, therewith to serve their king. Charlemagne also kept vast, well-stocked estates for himself, scattered over Europe as way stations in making his rounds.

"Wherever capable men are found," he ordered, "give them woodland to clear"—and the forests of Europe were leveled to create the manors of the feudal age. The more manors that could be supported, the more knights were available for military duty, and thus did Charlemagne maintain a powerful fighting force.

The economic success of this

Bowmen close on a stag in an illustration from the age of feudalism, when hunting reigned as the sport of the gentry. Woe to poachers who encroached on reserves set aside for the royal chase. As seen in a medieval *Book of Hours*, a castle—in this case the original Louvre, built in the 12th century *(opposite)*, serves as counterpoint to the everyday lives of workers in the fields.

LIFE IN THE CASTLE

The life of a lord and his family in the manorial castle was not as luxurious as modern imagination would have it. Windows were mere slits in the walls, and the rooms were cold and drafty. Fires for cooking and heating often made the rooms smoky as well. Animals were kept within castle walls, a practice that added their odors to smells of indoor latrines. There were few furnishings, and stone or earthen floors grew cold in winter.

- **570** Persians overthrow Abyssinian rule in Yemen.
- **ca 600** Irish art and literature flourish. Rise of Huari in Peru.
- **ca 618-26** Islam preached in Canton, China.
- **622** Muhammad flees from his enemies in Mecca to the city of Yathrib, 250 miles to the north.
- **ca 640-711** Arabs, spreading the Muslim faith, expand across northern Africa.
- **650-683** Chinese Empire reaches apogee under Kao Tsung, Tang emperor.

system of mutual dependency in Europe was enhanced by two developments. The moldboard plow bit deep into the soil, turning it efficiently. The horse collar allowed horses to pull plows much faster than oxen, without being choked. Faster cultivation meant more grain could be produced, important to the manor in trading for goods that it could not produce, such as salt and metals.

Lords and knights grew rich off tolls, taxes, and produce generated from the labor of their serfs, then willed the land to their heirs. In the medieval social pyramid beneath the ruling nobility were the clergy and members of religious orders, merchants and craftsmen, and peasants.

Central to the system were the castles of the major nobles, in militarily defensible positions and garrisoned with a contingent of professional troops for the nobleman's personal protection. In Charlemagne's time manor houses were most likely simple—square towers encircled by wooden walls.

As the centuries passed, they became stone fortresses with turrets and slitted windows from which archers could shoot attackers. They were moated bastions, accessed only by crossing a drawbridge.

In case of an outside threat, the peasants could retreat to the safety of the castle and aid in its defense. Otherwise they lived in simple, dirt-floored huts and worked from dawn to dusk, seeing to the master's land first, tending to their own when time

● First Arab coinage.

695

● Polynesians first settle in Cook Islands.

ca **700**

● Opposition to the use of images in Byzantine churches becomes official policy of Leo III and Constantine V.

720

● Charlemagne at war with the Saxons.

772-76

An apothecary of medieval times *(below)* sold purgatives, tonics, and other medications plus kitchen spices. Surgeons' tools included saws and bloodletting knives *(bottom).* In happy times a 15th century feast for a well-turned lady *(opposite)* might feature pheasant, with dinner music performed on an oboelike instrument.

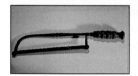

allowed. They plowed his soil and planted his crops, harvested his wheat for bread and beer, butchered hogs for winter, felled trees and split wood for fuel. They also worked on the lord's roads, bridges, and walls.

Thus, although feudalism provided an effective military organization and some security for all parties, it thrived on inequality. The aristocratic classes enjoyed wealth and leisure on the backs of serfs. "What the peasant

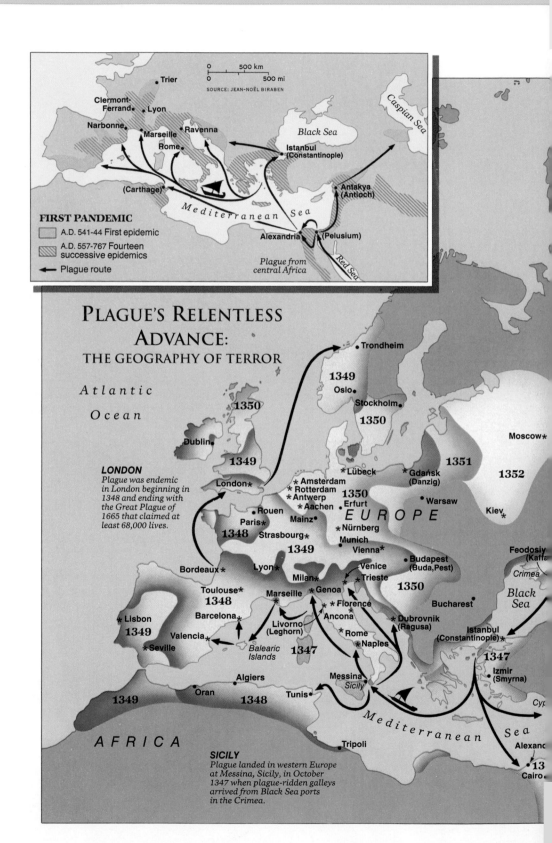

0   500 km
0   500 mi

SOURCE: JEAN-NOËL BIRABEN

FIRST PANDEMIC

☐ A.D. 541-44 First epidemic

▨ A.D. 557-767 Fourteen successive epidemics

← Plague route

Trier
Clermont-Ferrand
Lyon
Narbonne
Marseille
Ravenna
Rome
Black Sea
Caspian Sea
Istanbul (Constantinople)
Antakya (Antioch)
(Carthage)
Mediterranean Sea
Alexandria
(Pelusium)
Red Sea
Plague from central Africa

PLAGUE'S RELENTLESS ADVANCE:
THE GEOGRAPHY OF TERROR

Atlantic Ocean

1349
1350

Trondheim
Oslo
Stockholm
Moscow★

Dublin

1350

1351

1352

LONDON
Plague was endemic in London beginning in 1348 and ending with the Great Plague of 1665 that claimed at least 68,000 lives.

London★
★Amsterdam
★Rotterdam
★Antwerp
★Aachen
Lübeck
Gdańsk (Danzig)
Warsaw
Kiev★

1349
1350
Erfurt

1349
Rouen
Paris★
Mainz
EUROPE
Nürnberg
Munich
Vienna★
Budapest (Buda,Pest)
Feodosiy (Kaffa)
Crimea

Strasbourg★

1348
Lyon★
Milan★
Venice
Trieste

1350
Bordeaux★
Toulouse★
Marseille★
Genoa★
Florence★
Ancona
Dubrovnik (Ragusa)
Bucharest
Black Sea

1348
Barcelona★
Livorno (Leghorn)
Rome★
Istanbul (Constantinople)★

★Lisbon
1349
Valencia★
★Seville
Balearic Islands
1347
Naples★
1347

Algiers
Messina *Sicily*
Izmir (Smyrna)
Cyp

Oran
1349
Tunis★
1348
Mediterranean Sea
Alexan

Tripoli
13
Cairo

AFRICA

SICILY
Plague landed in western Europe at Messina, Sicily, in October 1347 when plague-ridden galleys arrived from Black Sea ports in the Crimea.

● Japanese capital moved from Nara to Kyoto.

794

● Teotihuacan civilization in Mexico collapses.

ca 750-800

● Pope Leo III crowns Charlemagne Holy Roman Emperor.

800

● Cahokia (in present-day Illinois) becomes largest town in North America.

1050

● Pope Urban II calls for a holy war to regain the Holy Land.

1095

● Building begins on Chartres Cathedral, establishing Gothic architecture in western Europe.

1154

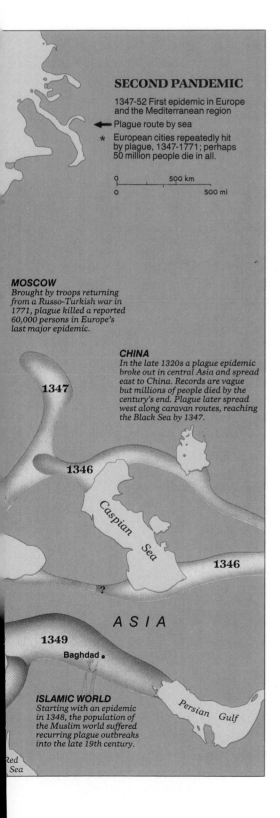

SECOND PANDEMIC

1347-52 First epidemic in Europe and the Mediterranean region

→ Plague route by sea

✱ European cities repeatedly hit by plague, 1347-1771; perhaps 50 million people die in all.

0   500 km
0   500 mi

MOSCOW
Brought by troops returning from a Russo-Turkish war in 1771, plague killed a reported 60,000 persons in Europe's last major epidemic.

CHINA
In the late 1320s a plague epidemic broke out in central Asia and spread east to China. Records are vague but millions of people died by the century's end. Plague later spread west along caravan routes, reaching the Black Sea by 1347.

1347

1346

Caspian Sea

1346

ASIA

1349

Baghdad ●

ISLAMIC WORLD
Starting with an epidemic in 1348, the population of the Muslim world suffered recurring plague outbreaks into the late 19th century.

Persian Gulf

Red Sea

produces in a year, the lord wastes in an hour," the serfs lamented. Religion was their comfort, but even here they adhered to the feudal system, praying to saints to intercede for them with God, just as they petitioned their lord instead of their king.

Most peasants owed heavy debts to their masters and could not even leave the manor without permission. Always they were watched over by stewards, who made sure that they fulfilled their service obligations.

Most serfs rarely worked their way out of bondage. One example was the son of a serf freed by Charlemagne who became the archbishop of Reims.

The feudal system became even more firmly established after Charlemagne's death in 814. Within two

generations his empire collapsed, and much of Europe disintegrated into numerous small fiefdoms.

The security offered by the castle became critical to lord and serf alike as new waves of marauding warrior groups—Vikings and Magyars— swept through Europe with no unified force to oppose them.

More and more towns sprang up, giving birth to markets where peasants could sell surpluses, which could eventually buy them their freedom.

Some peasants simply slipped away from the manor and became mercenary soldiers or set themselves up as free persons. Gradually European landowners found it more profitable to hire day laborers to do their work than to maintain a peasant and his extended family. ■

ca 700-900 Pueblo people live in houses aboveground in eastern Arizona.

732 Charles Martel is hailed as the defender of Christendom after his victory at Tours.

777 Charlemagne, victorious over the Saxons, holds his first Diet.

ca 800 Rise of Kingdom of Ghana in West Africa.

801 Charlemagne prohibits prostitution.

814 Building of Doge's Palace is begun in Venice.

The Fury of the Vikings

The economic success of the feudal system meant that considerable wealth had accumulated in Europe, England, and Ireland. As the unity of Charlemagne's Empire began to collapse in the late ninth century, this wealth became vulnerable to raids from fierce invaders out of territories that are now Norway, Sweden, and Denmark. The Vikings were pitiless warriors but also traders and farmers, who sometimes settled in the areas they explored. Coming from a watery world of lakes, streams, fjords, and islands, they were excellent mariners and shipbuilders. They ventured fearlessly seaward in trim, graceful craft that withstood heavy swells.

As early as the first century the Roman Tacitus commented on mighty fleets of Swedish ships "having a prow at each end."

Those high, carved prows became harbingers of doom around the end of the eighth century when Vikings began moving southward. Perhaps prodded by overcrowding at home, where rocky lands offered limited opportunities for farming, the Vikings were drawn to England's deeper soils like magnets, as they were to the rich monasteries that had become repositories for Christianity's treasures as well as its tenets.

Surprise was the ally of the Vikings, for their numbers were seldom large. With their shallow-draft ships they could swoop quickly onto coasts or speed upriver to inland settlements. Fearless in battle, they believed that if killed in combat they would be borne by warrior-maiden Valkyries to Valhalla, the Viking heaven, where they would dine on pork and the honey-flavored, fermented drink called mead. Pagans, they slaughtered churchmen even as they robbed their monasteries.

For 250 years, from the 9th to the 11th centuries, the Vikings sacked Europe's manors, towns, and churches, as Christians huddled together and prayed, *"A furore Normannorum libera nos, Domine*—From the fury of the Northmen deliver us, O Lord!" Nothing seemed to hold them back, certainly not fear, for they ventured over open sea all the way to Iceland and Greenland and probably even made brief stops on the North American coast.

Sailing around the Spanish coast, they entered the Mediterranean to strike at the continent's underbelly. And east of their homeland, they

Norsemen wreaked havoc on Christian monasteries, which held church treasures during Europe's Dark Ages.

889 Khmers start to build capital city at Angkor, Cambodia.	**891** Monks write the history of England in *Anglo-Saxon Chronicle*.	**ca 900-1150** Hohokam culture flourishes in Arizona and New Mexico.	**ca 969** Orthodox Christianity is established by Vladimir, Grand Prince of Kieva, as the official religion in his realm.	**976** Warrior-emperor Basil II drives the Muslims back to the gates of Jerusalem.

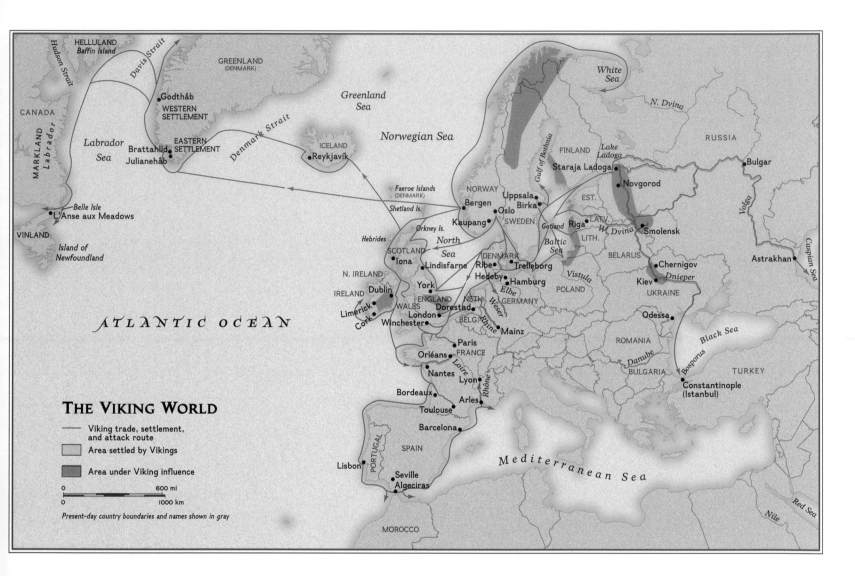

THE VIKING WORLD

— Viking trade, settlement, and attack route

▢ Area settled by Vikings

▢ Area under Viking influence

0   600 mi
0   1000 km

Present-day country boundaries and names shown in gray

ruled the first Russian state.

The brutal image of the Vikings has overshadowed the more positive aspects of their culture. They traded as often as they raided, bringing southward valued goods such as furs and walrus ivory.

They were skillful in decorative arts, especially wood sculpture and metalsmithing. Their poetry espoused such ideals as freedom, courage, loyalty, and honor.

An Arab chronicler encountering Norse traders on the Volga described them as the "filthiest of God's creatures," yet perfect physical specimens, "tall as date palms, blond and ruddy." Viking wives knew rights that other medieval women could scarcely imagine. They owned land, ran farms while their husbands raided, kept their maiden names, and could divorce by simply stating it to witnesses. Compared to feudal Europe with its delineations of class, Viking society was highly egalitarian.

"Who is your master?" a Frankish messenger called out to a Viking band sailing up France's Eure River. "None," came the reply from the sleek ship. "We are all equals."

As they spread out over wider areas, the Vikings created outposts, thereby losing their mobility and the element of surprise. In this more static position they were eventually driven out of England by Alfred the Great, and on the continent they were forced to accept the overlordship of French kings. Some adopted Christianity and became absorbed into local populations. ◼

● Monastery founded at
1098 Citeaux in France; start
of Cistercian Order.

● Decline of empire
in Ghana. Rise
ca **1100** of Inca in Peru.

● Louis VI is King
of France.
1108-1137

● The Chin dynasty is
founded by Akuta
1115 in China.

Knights of the Christian Crusades

To Christians in medieval Europe, Palestine where Jesus had lived and died was Holy Land. After it was taken by the Muslims in the seventh century, Christians were still allowed to make pilgrimages to their sacred sites. But when Seljuk Turks, also Muslims, overran Palestine in the late 11th century, safe passage for

With stirruped feet, Crusader Godfrey leads knights to holy battle (*above*). **The success of the Frankish knight as an effective fighting machine followed the invention of the stirrup, although its origins are lost to history. With his feet in stirrups, a knight could withstand the shock of impact and stay on his horse when his long lance made contact. An armored man on a horse—itself armored—charging headlong with a lance was a tanklike weapon. Thus, it could be said that the stirrup ushered in the Age of Chivalry.**

Christians was no longer possible.

In 1095 Pope Urban II called for a holy war to regain the Holy Land. Thousands responded, but their disorganized efforts met with defeat and massacre by the Turks. A more organized force later managed to capture Jerusalem in 1099. Several more Crusades would follow during the next 200 years, none of them as successful as the first.

The Christian Crusades came at a time when knighthood had reached its full expression in Europe. The system of military recruitment through a landed aristocracy, set up by Charlemagne, had produced a cult of gentleman warriors whose code of conduct became a romantic ideal.

Training for knighthood began early, with youths serving as pages at about age 12, then as squires or apprentices to knights at age 14. Training included horsemanship, archery, wrestling, and the use of sword, shield, and lance.

Education emphasized Christian piety, honor, respect for women, and protection and compassion for the helpless. A novice was expected to become proficient at hawking, chess, and writing poetry. At 21, if found worthy, he could be dubbed a knight in an impressive ceremony.

The aura of selfless and chivalrous service made knights natural recruits for campaigns to regain the Holy Land. In seeking an army for the First Crusade, Pope Urban had urged volunteers "…to strive to expel that wicked race from our Christian

ca 1115-42 French scholar Peter Abelard makes Paris a center of religious learning.

1135 At Poissy, France, the flying buttress is first used. Henry I, King of England, dies.

1138 In France, Louis VII marries Eleanor of Aquitaine.

1149 A university is founded at Oxford, England.

ca 1150 End of Hopewell culture in North America. First paper made in Europe.

In the successful First Crusade, Christians used catapults and mobile bridges to rout Muslims from Jerusalem. Later Crusades failed to retake the Holy Land.

1151 In Mexico, Toltec Empire comes to an end.

1152 Louis VII secures the dissolution of his marriage with Eleanor of Aquitaine.

1167 Alcohol distilled from wine at Salerno, Italy, in the first certain instance of this technique.

1168 In Mexico, the Aztec begin to migrate.

1174 Saladin declares himself sultan in Egypt.

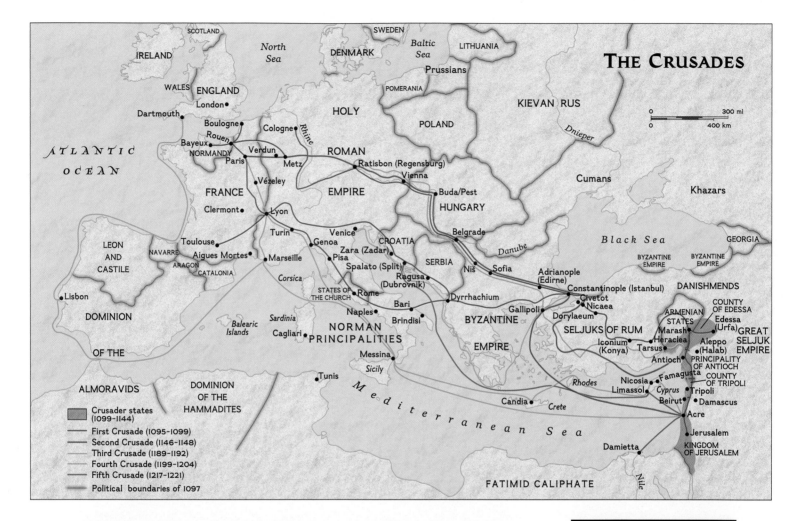

THE CRUSADES

SCOTLAND
IRELAND
North Sea
SWEDEN
DENMARK
Baltic Sea
LITHUANIA
Prussians
POMERANIA
KIEVAN RUS
WALES
ENGLAND
London
Dartmouth
HOLY
Cologne
ROMAN
POLAND
ATLANTIC OCEAN
Boulogne
Rouen
Bayeux
NORMANDY
Verdun
Rhine
Ratisbon (Regensburg)
Vienna
Dnieper
Paris
Metz
EMPIRE
Buda/Pest
Cumans
Khazars
FRANCE
Vézelay
HUNGARY
Clermont
Lyon
Turin
Belgrade
Black Sea
GEORGIA
LEON
AND
Toulouse
Venice
Danube
BYZANTINE
EMPIRE
BYZANTINE
EMPIRE
NAVARRE
Aigues Mortes
Genoa
CROATIA
Niš
Sofia
Adrianople
(Edirne)
DANISHMENDS
CASTILE
ARAGON
Marseille
Pisa
Zara (Zadar)
SERBIA
Constantinople (Istanbul)
ARMENIAN
STATES
COUNTY
OF EDESSA
CATALONIA
Corsica
Spalato (Split)
Ragusa
(Dubrovnik)
Civetot
Nicaea
Marash
Edessa
(Urfa)
GREAT
Lisbon
STATES OF
THE CHURCH
Rome
Dyrrhachium
Gallipoli
Dorylaeum
SELJUKS OF RUM
Heraclea
Aleppo
(Halab)
SELJUK
EMPIRE
DOMINION
Balearic
Islands
Sardinia
Naples
Bari
Brindisi
BYZANTINE
Iconium
(Konya)
Tarsus
Antioch
PRINCIPALITY
OF ANTIOCH
OF THE
Cagliari
NORMAN
PRINCIPALITIES
EMPIRE
Rhodes
Nicosia
Limassol
Famagusta
Cyprus
COUNTY
OF TRIPOLI
Tripoli
ALMORAVIDS
DOMINION
OF THE
HAMMADITES
Messina
Sicily
Tunis
Mediterranean Sea
Candia
Crete
Beirut
Damascus
Acre
Damietta
Jerusalem
KINGDOM
OF JERUSALEM
FATIMID CALIPHATE
Nile

300 mi
400 km

- Crusader states (1099-1144)
- First Crusade (1095-1099)
- Second Crusade (1146-1148)
- Third Crusade (1189-1192)
- Fourth Crusade (1199-1204)
- Fifth Crusade (1217-1221)
- Political boundaries of 1097

THE CHILDREN'S CRUSADE

A pitiful misadventure was the Children's Crusade of 1212, when masses of youngsters in Europe decided to free the Holy Land. Led by a charismatic French lad named Stephen of Cloyes, thousands left by ship from Marseilles, only to be sold into African slave markets by greedy ship captains. Many German children marching overland died of hunger and disease. Others turned back, and none reached the Holy Land. This Crusade may have given rise to the legend of the Pied Piper of Hamelin, who lured a band of children away from their homes.

● **1190** Teutonic Order of Knights, a military society, set up in Germany to defend Christian lands in Palestine and Syria.

● **ca 1190** End of first period in which flat-topped mounds built as bases for temples in Mississippi.

● **1192** Minamoto Yoritomo becomes shogun of Japan.

● **1202** Early English Gothic style established.

● **ca 1220** Emergence of first Thai kingdom.

lands....Christ commands it. Remission of sins will be granted for those going thither...."

In the Crusades themselves, as in any war, there were examples of both valor and cruelty. The Muslims were said to admire the courage of the "Franks" as they called all crusaders, and when the Christians conquered the city of Acre, they stared at the departing Turks with admiration, remembering their fierce defense.

When the Christian leader King Richard the Lionheart of England was ill, the Muslim leader Saladin sent him fresh fruit and snow from the mountains, and there was some discussion of a peace between the two that would involve the marriage of Richard's sister and Saladin's brother. And yet, when terms of Acre's surrender displeased Richard, he allowed the slaughter of 2,700 Turkish hostages within sight of their comrades at Jerusalem.

And between battles, besieged Turks lowered hooks over the walls to haul up crusaders' bodies, loot them, and toss back the carcasses.

Success in the First Crusade strengthened the Church's influence and increased the self-confidence of western Europeans. When forces that remained in Palestine failed to hold on to crusader territory, the Second Crusade was launched less than 50 years after the first. It failed, however, to regain what had been lost.

Jerusalem itself fell to the Muslims in 1187, and the Third Crusade could not regain it. In the Fourth Crusade the western Christians turned against the eastern Christians of the Byzantine Empire and sacked Constantinople. Gradually Europeans lost interest in the Crusades, concentrating instead on political and economic matters in their homelands.

Although the Crusades failed in their intended purpose of liberating the Holy Land from the "infidels," some good came of them. Contact with the highly advanced civilizations of the Muslims and the Byzantines stimulated Europeans and helped bring them out of their stagnation. Exposure to goods from the East— rugs, tapestries, spices, and exotic foods—opened up trade routes, and European standards of living began improving for the first time since the days of the ancient Roman Empire. ■

Crusaders flocked to Constantinople, afoot, on horseback, and in high-prowed ships **(right)** before their final assaults against Muslim infidels. The Christian influence on the region around this noble city, then the richest in Europe, can still be seen in the ruins of churches in central Turkey, like the one shown here **(opposite)**.

ca 1344 — Hanseatic League claims membership of almost all large German towns along the Baltic and North Seas.

1368 — The Persian poet Hafiz publishes the love poem, *The Diwan*.

1369-1372 — In China, rebellion led by Chu Yuen-Chang overthrows the Yuan dynasty and founds the Ming dynasty.

The Ottoman Turks conquer Bulgaria.

1397 — Union of Kalmar unites Norway, Denmark, and Sweden under Eric of Denmark.

The Hundred Years' War

From the time William of Normandy defeated Harold at the Battle of Hastings and took over the crown of England, monarchs on both sides of the English Channel disputed ownership of territory. By the early 1300s England claimed possession of Flanders, with its profitable markets in the north, and the large, rich area in southwest France known as Gascony.

In 1337 matters came to a head when Philip VI of France laid claim to Gascony and Edward III of England declared himself king of France, events that set off what is known as the Hundred Years' War. It was a dreary century for Europe. The inequalities of feudal times often boiled into open violence between the peasantry and the privileged. A disagreement over election of a pope resulted in two popes simultaneously.

Germany was in pieces, the Swiss were rebelling against Austrian overlords, the Byzantine Empire was overwhelmed by the Turks, and a quarter of Europe's population was wiped out by plague.

The Hundred Years' War between England and France actually lasted more than a century, from 1337 until 1453, but fighting was not continual. The English won most of the important battles, including Crécy in 1346 and Agincourt in 1415. By using the new longbow, they could loose arrows from 400 yards away with deadly effect, while the French were still using short-range crossbows. English forces also began experimenting with gunpowder, firing missiles through a long tube lighted by a match. By the end of the Hundred Years' War, cannons were in use, which rendered both knightly armor

English longbows defeat the crossbows of the French at Crécy *(opposite)* in the Hundred Years' War. The English burned French leader Joan of Arc at the stake *(below)*, but she inspired her people to eventual victory.

● **1398** Timur (the Lame) sacks Delhi.

● ca **1400** Establishment of Malacca as major commercial port of southeast Asia.

● **1420** Filippo Brunelleschi starts work on Florence Cathedral, in Italy.

● **1432** The Thai sack Angkor; the Khmer abandon their capital.

● ca **1450** Inca city of Machu Picchu is built.

● ca **1452** The painter Leonardo da Vinci is born.

and town fortifications ineffective against assault.

Inspired by a young French girl named Joan of Arc, the French experienced a turn for the better. She led them to victory at Orléans but was captured by the English and eventually burned at the stake. Her courage continued to be an inspiration for the French, who drove the English out of France, except for the port of Calais. ■

THE GROWTH OF GUILDS

Dyers learned their craft under the careful eye of a master *(above).* As commerce stimulated the growth of European cities, merchants and craftsmen established guilds that set standards and rules for creating products and regulating trade. Membership did not come easily. An apprentice could serve up to 12 years before becoming a master and having the guild stamp of quality on his products. Merchants formed guilds also to deal with political superiors who charged heavy taxes. Sometimes guilds became monopolies that made it difficult for journeymen craftsmen to become masters.

● **1326** Moscow becomes the seat of the Patriarch in place of Kiev.

● **1328** England acknowledges Scotland's independence.

● **1336** In southern India the Hindu kingdom of Vijayamagar is founded.

● **1338** England and the Roman Empire form an alliance with the Treaty of Coblenz.

● **1349** The Black Death reaches northern Russia.

The Aztec Kingdom

One of the most brilliant and accomplished of early American civilizations may also have been its most cruel. When the Mexica, or Aztec as we know them now, first migrated from northern Mexico into central Mexico, they were a relatively minor tribe but extremely warlike.

For protection against their many enemies, and because of signs that seemed to fulfill their prophecies, they took refuge on an island in Lake Texcoco. And in 1325 they began building a city that became the capital of an empire.

Primitive in comparison with their

Dress signified rank among Aztec men. Every captive taken added to a priest's raiment *(right, top row)*. Officials wore knee-length mantles *(third row)*. And feathers adorned army leaders *(bottom row)*. A human skull covered with mosaics evoked a feared god *(below)*. Remnants of a water garden of the Aztec capital, Tenochtitlán, still exist *(opposite)*.

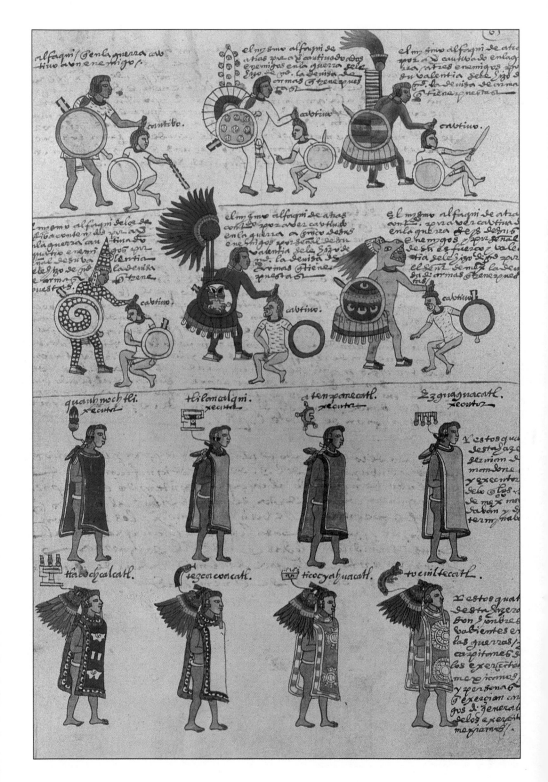

1368 — **Ming dynasty founded** in China.

1378-1417 — **Great Schism** in the West.

1380 — **In England John Wycliffe and others translate the Bible into English. Catherine of Siena, Christian mystic, dies in Rome.**

1389 — **Epic defeat of Serbs by Ottoman Turks at Kosovo.**

predecessors who had constructed great pyramids, the Aztec quickly copied the culture and technology of others. They built up their island city into an impregnable fortress, interlaced with canals and connected to the shoreline by causeways. With mud raised from the lake bottom, they created floating gardens where they grew maize, pumpkins, beans, tomatoes, peppers, avocados, and limes.

By the early 15th century the Aztec had greatly expanded their territory by a simple strategy. They allied with powerful neighbors against smaller groups and then,

THE AZTEC MARKETPLACE

In Tlatelolco, a sister city to Tenochtitlán, crowds of up to 60,000 thronged to the marketplace to trade in the wealth of the empire. Stalls were organized according to the offerings—food, ceramic figurines, flowers, sharp blades made of obsidian, jewelry made from jade and turquoise. To the wealthy elite were offered jaguar skins, finely worked gold, slaves, and capes of brilliant feathers. Market police patrolled to keep order; judges seated on shaded platforms ruled on trade disputes.

once conquest was complete, turned on and defeated their former allies.

Within a hundred years of establishing their capital, they controlled all of central and southern Mexico. Conquered people had to pay tribute in gold, silver, jade, and bird feathers, important in Aztec decorations and ceremonies.

Using this wealth of conquest, they built up Tenochtitlán into a city of temple-pyramids, palaces, and extensive marketplaces.

At the head of their complex political system was the emperor, who held great power but had to consult

145

● Portuguese sailors
1434 round Cape Bojador off
the coast of West Africa.

● Gutenberg begins
1440 to use movable type
in Germany.

● Building at Great
1450 Zimbabwe, southern
Africa, is at its height.

● Spanish Inquisition
1480 introduced to root
out heretics.

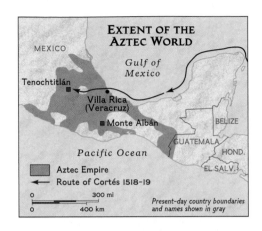

EXTENT OF THE AZTEC WORLD

MEXICO

Gulf of Mexico

Tenochtitlán

Villa Rica (Veracruz)

■ Monte Albán

BELIZE

GUATEMALA

HOND.

Pacific Ocean

EL SALV.

Aztec Empire

← Route of Cortés 1518–19

0 ____ 300 mi
0 ____ 400 km

Present-day country boundaries and names shown in gray

with a council of nobles before making important decisions. Serving under the emperor were military chiefs who governed local areas. The most powerful members of Aztec society were the royal family, nobles, military chiefs, and priests; next were farmers, merchants, and warriors. All men served in the army from the ages of 17 to 22. Some became career soldiers because even a peasant, through his accomplishments, could rise to the level of army commander. Military prowess was important, since the Aztec waged wars almost incessantly, often for the purpose of obtaining captives for human sacrifice.

They worshiped many deities who represented the forces of nature. The earth, in Aztec eyes, was a great square floating on an endless sea. By day the sun rose in a sky laid out in tiers, like the view from the inside of a pyramid. By night it traveled in the underworld.

Keeping the gods happy and the world in balance required numerous sacrifices in blood, the Aztec believed. Tens of thousands of captives were bent backward over an altar at the top of the Great Temple in

Tenochtitlán, slits were made with an obsidian knife under their ribs, and their beating hearts were ripped out. In one four-day celebration, 20,000 captive humans were killed in this way in view of Aztec citizens and foreign dignitaries.

Another period of mass sacrifices probably marked an unsettled period of time in Aztec history. In the mid-15th century the city was struck by a series of calamities—deadly disease that attacked the lake's animal life, unseasonable frosts that wiped out crops, and drought and famine that reduced citizens to eating dry husks and the flesh of vultures.

In one serious military defeat, the ruler Axayacatl led 20,000 Aztec and 12,000 other warriors against the Tarascans of Michoacan. Only 200 Aztec warriors returned home.

By 1500, however, the Aztec had established perhaps the largest empire in the Americas, with some 15 million people in at least 38 provinces.

Skilled artisans created stone sculptures, turquoise mosaics, intricate relief, obsidian masks, ceramic statuary, and storytelling murals. Using small picture symbols, writers produced poetry and legendary accounts of their brief but glorious history. ■

A priest cuts the heart from a second sacrificial victim as the first lies below.

1463-1479 • War between Ottoman Empire and Venetians.

1483 • Martin Luther, Protestant reformer, is born.

1492 • Moors are driven from Andalusia, and former mosques become churches as Moslem rule ends in Spain. Columbus reaches the Caribbean.

1497 • Italian navigator John Cabot reaches North America.

1498 • Vasco da Gama rounds Cape of Good Hope.

The Aztec Fall to Old World Conquerors

When Hernán Cortés led his powerful army toward the Aztec capital of Tenochtitlán in 1519, the Spaniards were dazzled by what they saw. As they approached on a causeway, a low skyline of homes was overshadowed by pyramids, 78 major structures dominated by the Great Temple itself. Nearby were separate palaces and a zoo belonging to the emperor, Moctezuma II. Around the city's center were neighborhood subdivisions, each with its own military school and minor temples. Walled houses opened onto streets or canals. Around the city were floating gardens growing food for the city.

At its height, Tenochtitlán probably held 150,000 to 200,000 people. Fortunately for the Spaniards, the exacting of tribute and the frequent raids for sacrificial captives had built up resentments in Aztec provinces, which lent support to the foreigners.

In years before the arrival of the Spaniards, Tenochtitlán had been led by a number of effective rulers—chief among them, Nezahualcoyotl, who reigned 40 years. A great warrior, he was also a humane lawgiver, an architect, a poet, and a philosopher. Had he ruled when Cortés arrived, the history of Mexico might have been written differently.

Instead, the emperor was Moctezuma, who vacillated on what to do about the newcomers, giving Cortés time to gather allies.

They were not hard to find. Millions of peasants, members of subject tribes such as the Totonac and the Tlaxcalan, had been forced to provide tons of foodstuffs regularly to the capital and its satellites.

Even before the Spaniards arrived, outlying tribes had begun to rebel, and the Aztec had to fight frequently to retain control over them. The client states saw the Spaniards as deliverers from the Aztec and joined forces with the superior weapons and battle tactics of Cortés.

Tenochtitlán fell in 1521, and the mighty Aztec Empire came to an end. ■

Cortés, aided in negotiations by his interpreter and mistress Malinalli, center, makes a pact with the Tlaxcalan for help against the Aztec.

2

9

4

1607
The first successful
English settlement in North
America is Jamestown. ●

1

11

1492
Columbus is the first
European explorer
● **to reach islands in the Caribbean.**

10

ca 1450
The Inca build the
● **city of Machu Picchu.**

AROUND THE WORLD

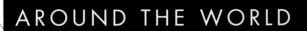

1 Europe: Columbus gained financial backing from the Spanish monarchy for his daring venture: to sail west to reach the rich trade goods of the East.

2 North America: Europeans began staking claims in the Americas. Micmac Indians and Samuel de Champlain hunted game birds as they explored for France up the St. Lawrence River and founded Quebec.

3 Asia: As trade between East and West increased, such cloth, painted with Indian women and flowers, from Calicut, India, may have brightened European drawing rooms.

4 Australia: Aboriginal cave paintings like this one suggest visits from Europeans during the age of exploration, when nations sent ships and hardy souls to points unknown, searching for commodities of trade.

New Links and Contacts

1643
Louis XIV begins a
72-year reign as
King of France.

1618-1648
The Thirty Years' War
pits Catholics against
Protestants in the
Habsburg Empire.

1558
Elizabeth I
becomes Queen
of England.

1588
The Spanish Armada
is defeated by England
off the coast of France.

1517
Martin Luther sparks
the Reformation in Europe.

ca 1450
Florence is the
birthplace of the
Renaissance.

1453
The Ottoman Turks
sack Constantinople
and rename it
Istanbul.

1480
Under Ivan the Great,
Russia breaks free of the Mongols.

1644
Beijing's Forbidden City
is completed during
the Ming dynasty.

1631
Shah Jahan begins
construction of the
Taj Mahal in Agra, India.

7

6

ca 1500
The exportation of
Africans as slaves to the
New World begins.

3

8

5

1652
Cape Town is founded
by the Dutch.

1642
Abel Tasman
discovers Tasmania.

5 Asia: Indian hands gathered the pepper that brought the Portuguese. Through the profitable spice trade, the Portuguese controlled an area on the west coast of India that they called Goa.

6 Europe: Elizabeth, the daughter of Henry VIII and Anne Boleyn, became queen. As Elizabeth I, she ruled ably for nearly half a century during the period

when England began to establish itself firmly in the New World.

7 Asia: In the 13th century the Ottoman Turks became known as the Ottomans, after Osman I. Greatest of Ottoman sultans, Süleyman the Magnificent held land in three continents and threatened Central Europe.

8 Asia: Center of the Chinese cosmos, the Forbidden City was built in the early 1400s during the Ming dynasty. It sheltered the emperor with several walls and a moat shaped like a Tatar's bow.

9 Asia: The Japanese developed a distinctive national style under military rulers such as Tokugawa Ieyasu, first in a long line of shoguns.

10 Central and South America: Artisans hammered and shaped metals or cast them into molds. Soldering and fastening, they created such masterpieces as this figurine.

11 North America: Makah tribesmen sew shut the mouth of a lanced whale to keep it buoyant.

12 Europe: In Russia, onion-shaped roofs copied Byzantine domes, but they shed snow better.

Broadening Horizons: 1400 to 1700

Human development seems to creep along at a slow pace for hundreds of years, then take a giant leap forward. The end of the Ice Age spurred such a surge. The rise of city-states, with the accompanying desire for conquest, brought a melding of cultures. Similarly, in the mid-1400s the defeat and disintegration of the Byzantine Empire seems to have contributed to the growth of the Renaissance in Italy. When Constantinople fell to the Muslim Ottoman Turks, many scholars who had nurtured the Greek and Roman classics there took flight and resettled in Italy, particularly in Florence. They helped feed the intellectual revival that had been alive in Italy since the 13th century and that would eventually stir Europe out of its cultural doldrums. After a long period of adhering to church-centered points of view, Europeans began to explore new ideas.

Few historic changes happen abruptly. The Ottoman Turks did not plug up classical thought at the Bosporus only to have it burst free at the Arno. But the de-emphasis of Greek and Latin studies in an area freshly defeated and its re-emphasis in an area undergoing rebirth are coincidences not easily ignored. In Florence and elsewhere earthly matters were being looked at with new eyes. Painting, architecture, writing, religion, politics, and daily life were caught up in a fever of change, one that proved contagious. A passion for new directions swept into the rest of Europe, which had been simmering in lethargy. Asia, not Europe, had long been the center of accomplishment. Islam was the most expansive religion in the world, still making new converts. China's advancements and attractive cities made Europe look backward and drab. In some areas the Turks, advancing westward out of Anatolia, were greeted as progressive liberators.

In Christian monasteries the writings of ancient Greece and Rome had been preserved and translated, but the monasteries had also preserved the ideal of poverty and humility. With the Renaissance came the attitude that one might be wealthy and virtuous, using one's resources to help others. The quality of this life on earth, as well as the quality of an afterlife, gained importance. The desire for wealth is as old as material comforts, but true capitalism took root in the Renaissance. The Roman Catholic Church's total control over people's tastes lessened. Fifteenth-century Europe was in its adolescence, still acknowledging religion's parentage but increasingly challenging it and pushing its limits.

But the parent remained important, as the Reformation would show. Ultimately challenges to certain practices in the Catholic Church led to protests and the creation of numerous Protestant churches. Torture and killing in the name of God reached horrendous proportions as zealots on both sides insisted that their way of worship was right. Wars between Protestants and Catholics raged over Europe, and boundaries changed. Carving out earthly kingdoms for the church of one's preference fed the growth of the nation-state.

Both religion and capitalism helped spur another important development. Alarmed at the spread of Islam, European Christians wondered if they might sail on the oceans far enough to attack the Muslims from a different direction, gaining converts in the process. Businessmen also pondered the profits that might be possible if they traveled by sea to buy and trade in the eastern spices and silks that were becoming popular in Europe. Both motivations sent Europeans seaward to find new routes to the Orient.

Travel before 1500 had been land-centered. As ships and navigational equipment improved, sailors ventured farther offshore. Two voyages changed history. In 1488 Bartolomeu Dias proved that it was possible to sail around the coast of Africa. Four years later Christopher Columbus headed west into the unknown and bumped into a new world. Up to that point the major civilizations had occupied perhaps a quarter of the earth's land surface. For comparison, imagine space voyagers in the 21st century discovering a planet that was habitable, reachable, rich in resources, and unspoiled.

First Spain, then Portugal, England, France, and the Netherlands grew wealthy off the New World, and the booty they brought back changed the economy of the Old. Meanwhile, trade in the East was increasing contacts between different parts of the globe, not all of them welcome.

Australia had been the sole province of the Aborigines for millennia until European explorers began nosing their ships along the shores of that large land-mass. And on the small islands of the Pacific, hunter-gatherers did not always greet the likes of Magellan with respect. Both China and Japan, quite content with their cultures, regarded Europeans as barbarians and tried to minimize contact with them.

Contacts, for good or ill, would not be denied. Isolation was not a long-standing option. Isolation had left the native peoples of the Americas behind in technology, and the better-armed and armored invaders rolled over them with little difficulty. Russia found itself cut off from the advancements of the age and struggled mightily to catch up.

It was a time of fast-paced change and shifting boundaries. Nations rose and fell in rapid succession. Portugal went from economic powerhouse to vassal state in less than a century. Through trade, the Dutch developed in 70 years from a few Protestant provinces fighting for survival to a first-class sea power.

As the stakes rose, so did the political manipulations. Marriages among European monarchies, undertaken for diplomatic and strategic reasons, sometimes reached conjugal absurdity. Adults were matched with children. Youths were wed to the elderly. To counter the expansionist plans of England's Henry VIII, Mary of Scotland was betrothed to the Dauphin of France when she was six and he four. Thanks to carefully arranged marriages by the Habsburgs, the boundaries of the Holy Roman Empire shifted around Europe for nearly 400 years.

Not all the movement was happening in Europe. In this period the Ottoman Empire rose to its greatest power, the Moguls took over India, and China remained a paragon of civilized living. Asia and Europe were now more balanced in the weight of their influence, and the continents of the earth were linked as never before. ■

A cultural revival in Europe brought an appreciation of artistic endeavors. Here a painting shows three women trilling the pipe and plucking the lute to the tune of "I will give you joy."

Overleaf:
Much as the love of beauty wafted northward during the Renaissance, "The Birth of Venus" by Botticelli shows the maid rising from the sea on a scallop shell, as zephyrs blow her toward a mantle of flowers.

● Peoples of the West
Indies are still living in
1400s the New Stone Age.

● Geoffrey Chaucer dies.

1400

● By the Treaty of Radom,
1401 Poland and Lithuania
are united.

● Timur (the Lame),
Mongol conqueror from
1402 Central Asia, defeats
Ottomans at Battle of
Ankara in Turkey.
European adventurers
begin conquest of the
Canary Islands.

● China's Ming dynasty
carries out a series of
1405-1433 seven grand exploratory voyages, probably to
impress foreigners with
their power. Fleets sail
to Sri Lanka, India,
Africa's east coast, and
the Arabian Peninsula.

Renaissance in Europe

It has often been noted that the death of one thing brings life to another. So it was when Constantinople fell to the Turks in 1453, signaling the end of the thousand-year Byzantine Empire. The demise of that cultural stronghold helped feed a rebirth, or renaissance, of culture in Europe.

For hundreds of years the church had been the purveyor and the patron of Europe's artistic tastes. All art and learning carried a strong religious theme. Challenging the precepts of Christianity could be dangerous; condemned heretics were some-

times burned at the stake. Europeans tended to see all worldly matters through the prism of religion.

Into this closed-minded atmosphere crept the intellectual open-mindedness that had characterized ancient Greece and Rome. The study of those civilizations and their classical literature had continued in the Byzantine Empire throughout the Middle Ages. Some Byzantine scholars moved to Italy, which maintained close contacts with Constantinople through trade, and Italian scholars, in turn, often studied in Constantinople.

But with the fall of that city to the Muslim Ottoman Turks, many scholars living there took their classical manuscripts and fled to other lands, particularly to Italy. Their ideas about virtue and the value of questioning authority landed on fertile ground. Italy, more than other European countries, was steeped in reminders of a classical heritage with its many ruins of Roman buildings, arches, and amphitheaters. It was also an area of active commerce, where people with wealth became interested in supporting new ideas and artistic activity.

"Good Government," a fresco in Sienna, exalted free travel and ample work opportunities and a serenity little known in frequent municipal strife.

1406 Chinese army attacks Vietnam.

1409 Leipzig University is founded.

1420-1467 Policy of religious toleration by Zain al-Abidin, Sultan of Kashmir, later venerated as a saint.

ca 1423 In India, severe famine occurs in the Deccan Plateau.

1425-1435 Reign of Hsuan Tsung, Ming Emperor; has throne name of Hsuan-te.

1427-1772 Le dynasty in Vietnam.

Unlike the rural, feudal system found elsewhere in Europe, Italian economic activity was centered in urban areas. Whereas northern Europe had lords and manors, who were dependent on agriculture, Italy had towns that produced textiles and luxury goods. Many of them became city-states that resisted the rulership of emperors and kings and fought each other for power and control. A sense of independence grew.

The cities also fought internally, as resentments in the lower classes sometimes boiled into violence.

Revolts were usually crushed by the ruling classes, but sometimes the wealthy tried to win the loyalty of the people by making city improvements and providing entertainment. Sometimes this included encouraging the production of fine art to engender civic pride.

The Medici and the Borgias, both influential families, became patrons of culture. New public buildings were designed. Works of sculpture and painting were commissioned. The influences of the ancient writings added to this creative energy. Those

writings emphasized the dignity and worth of the individual. People began to put less emphasis on the afterlife and think more about the significance of this life on earth.

Paintings became more realistic; sculptures, more lifelike. Writing dealt with people facing everyday problems and situations. Architecture took on the graceful lines and balance of classical times.

The new attitudes spread from Florence to other Italian cities, and then to northern Europe. The Renaissance was under way. ■

The Inca Empire
expands further
1438 in Peru.

1440-1493 Reign of Frederick III,
Holy Roman Emperor.

1440 City of (Old) Goa, India,
is founded. Sidi Yahya
Mosque is built
in Timbuktu.

ca 1441 Cocom power collapses
in Mexico.

1449-1473 Shogun Yoshimasa is
patron of the arts.

1449-1453 Constantine XI is
Byzantine Emperor.

Expansion of the Renaissance

The Renaissance in Europe did not happen overnight. What began in Italy, and particularly in Florence, gradually affected life throughout the continent from the 13th through the 16th centuries. And although the collapse of the Byzantine Empire helped stoke the interest in classical ideas, the spark was struck at least a century earlier.

Florence had been the home of writers Dante and Boccaccio and the birthplace of Petrarch. All three wrote in Latin, but also in Tuscan, the Italian language of Florence. Dante's speculations on politics and his literary masterpiece, *The Divine Comedy;* Petrarch's literary and religious writings; and Boccaccio's defense of the moral worth of poetry became accessible to a broad range of people in the last half of the 14th century.

With the renewed interest in the classics—perhaps inspired by the questions raised in contemporary writings, as well—painting and sculpture also began to change.

Independent-minded artists, funded by wealthy families and not by the clergy, broadened their subject matter and made it more realistic. Painters departed from the flat, one-dimensional style of medieval art and began to

In Florence the wool manufacturers' guild annually clothed the poor *(right)* and funded projects such as Brunelleschi's dome, which dominated the city skyline *(opposite).* In front of it, Giotto's bell tower looms over the baptistery entered through Ghiberti's famous doors. During the Renaissance in Florence, carvings, frescoes, statues, and architecture evidenced a tremendous explosion of creativity.

HEIGHT OF THE
RENAISSANCE 1492
☐ Holy Roman Empire

0   100
MILES

1519 Death of Italian Renaissance artist Leonardo da Vinci. In India, Guru Nanak founds Sikhism.

1519-1522 Mexico conquered by Hernán Cortés.

1520-1550 Spanish conquistadors take most of South America (excluding Brazil) and much of present southern United States.

1520-1566 Ottoman Empire is at its peak.

1520 Moctezuma II, ruler of Mexico, is killed accidentally.

1526 Babur, the first Mogul emperor, invades India.

show more realistic human forms and facial features.

In the early 1300s Giotto painted frescoes on the life of St. Francis of Assisi, depicting people with strong emotions. Sculptors such as Michelangelo Buonarroti studied anatomy to more accurately recreate the human body in stone, as the ancient Greeks had done. Statues began to show veins and detailed musculature.

Architecture began drifting from the practical and pointed Gothic style to the more graceful, flowing lines of ancient Greece and Rome. Filippo Brunelleschi studied Roman ruins before creating his eight-sided dome for the Florence cathedral, considered by many to be the greatest engineering feat of the time.

Despite these departures from religious centrism, even the popes became interested in the new culture. Pope Pius II, who was himself a writer of distinction, authorized construction of buildings in the new style of archi-

A preliminary design of "Virgin and Child with St. Anne" shows the depth of Leonardo da Vinci's art.

tecture. Subsequent popes began rebuilding Rome and the Vatican with domes and paintings of the period.

The Renaissance was not a change realized only in retrospect. Writers and artists of the time talked about what was happening among themselves. Gradually their ideas spread to the rest of Europe. The

French invaded Italy in the late 1400s and were attracted to Italian art and fashions. Italian diplomats who were sent elsewhere in Europe spread their new sense of values.

The development of movable type by Johannes Gutenberg, based on Chinese and Korean inventions, aided the diffusion of ideas by speeding the proliferation of books. As the new way of printing spread, some northern Europeans sponsored Italian writers and painters to make use of their talents outside Italy.

Henry VII invited Italian scholars to come to England and teach classical literature. Thomas More wrote *Utopia*, criticizing his society and speculating on a system in which everyone was equal and prosperous.

Many of William Shakespeare's plays were based on the events of ancient Rome, involving figures such as Julius Caesar and Antony and Cleopatra. Dutch artists combined Italian technique with their own artistic traditions, painting realistic portraits and scenes of peasant life. Flemish painters created scenes from the Bible and daily life in sharp, realistic detail. Jan van Eyck developed the use of oil as a painting medium, which made colors richer. The French excelled in architecture, building graceful castles in the Loire River Valley south of Paris. The French physician-monk Rabelais wrote *Gargantua* and *Pantagruel*, adventure stories about two giants that poked fun at the church, universities, and other institutions. ■

EUROPEAN USE OF MOVABLE TYPE

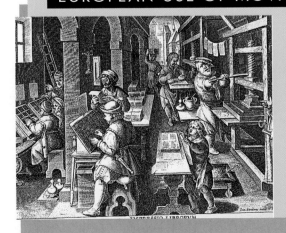

Printers prepare type and press pages in a 1570 engraving *(left)*. Johannes Gutenberg's Bible was the first large book printed in Europe. These same techniques allowed more books to be printed and distributed. Letters were cast in metal and arranged in a tray to spell words, then moved to another tray for reuse. Printing invented by the Chinese had an entire page carved in a block for pressing the image onto paper.

1527 Sweden becomes Lutheran.

1532 Francisco Pizarro defeats the Inca after killing their leader, Atahualpa.

1533-84 Reign of Ivan the Terrible, in Russia.

1564-1642 Life of Galileo Galilei, astronomer and scientist.

1565 St. Augustine, Florida, is founded by Spanish colonists.

1588 Defeat of Spanish Armada off south coast of England.

A New Way of Regarding Life

Art and literature were not alone in the changes wrought by the Renaissance. The new way of thinking touched many levels of European society, from manners to political manipulations.

The moral values that were gaining strength during this time led to a movement called humanism. This philosophy put greater emphasis on the human than on the divine. Humanists agreed with the Greek philosopher Protagoras, who wrote that "man is the measure of all things."

In Italy, educated people realized that the study of the ancient writers offered fresh insights into how people should conduct themselves. At first in Florence and then throughout the Italian Peninsula, these ideas were expressed in poems, essays, histories, and letters dealing with questions of morality and virtue.

Baldassare Castiglione, a diplomat and scholar, wrote *The Courtier*,

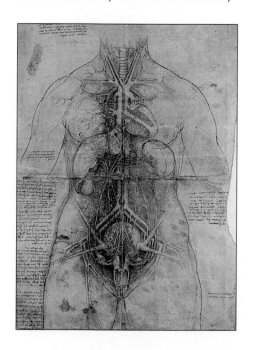

a treatise on manners that became a handbook on how to be the ideal gentleman. It was translated into French, English, and other northern languages and circulated widely.

Similar works were produced and were equally popular, including *Governour* by Englishman Sir Thomas Elyot, which suggested how men of social distinction and privilege should devote their efforts to public service.

Knowledge of the classics became the basis of education over all of Europe. Whether teachers were bona fide humanists or merely pedantic schoolmasters, Latin literacy was reinforced as the mark of an educated person and was a means of personal advancement.

The position of women in society improved as well. Aristocratic families had their daughters tutored at home, sometimes by noted humanist scholars. Wealthy merchant families sent their daughters away from home to attend convent schools.

Some women had opportunities to play prominent roles. For example, after her husband was captured in battle, Isabella d'Este ruled the small Italian territory of Mantua with such skill that scholars and artists were attracted to her court.

Or take the case of Lucrezia Borgia, daughter of Pope Alexander VI, who established a court at Ferrara that drew some of the best thinkers, poets, and artists of the time. Although her father involved her in several marriages of political convenience and her brother killed one of

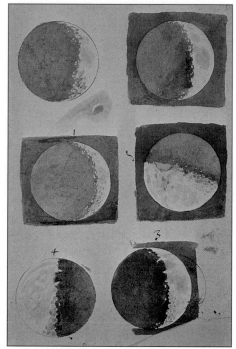

Questioning ideas long accepted, Renaissance thinkers pushed the limits of science as well as art. Some of Galileo's ideas departed from the official church view of flawless heavens—for example, his theories based on telescopic views of a moon pocked with craters *(above)*. The artist Leonardo da Vinci dissected corpses at night to avoid censure, and with his precise hand recorded the inner workings of humans, including a female torso *(left)*.

her husbands, Lucrezia herself has been cleared by modern research of accusations of crime and vice. She devoted her later life to education and charitable works.

The ideal person in Renaissance times became one who knew something about everything. The "universal man," or woman, or "Renaissance person" was a well-traveled individual knowledgeable in art, music, science, literature, and philosophy.

Not surprisingly, such attitudes led to advances and speculations in

159

1638 | First printing press reaches America.

1646 | The English colonize the Bahamas.

1666 | Isaac Newton measures the moon's orbit.

1670 | The founding of the Hudson Bay Company to trade in North America forms the basis of a huge fur-trading empire, later to be part of Canada.

1673 | French explorers Jacques Marquette and Louis Joliet reach headwaters of the Mississippi River and descend to present-day Arkansas.

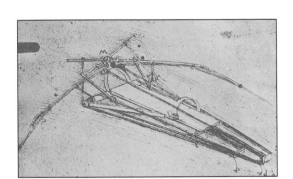

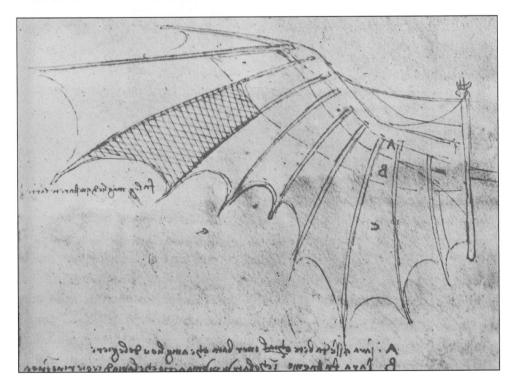

Leonardo sketched ideas for machines that would let men fly, some 400 years before the first airplanes (left). As God's touch enlivened Adam on Michelangelo's Sistine Chapel ceiling (opposite), new ideas sparked Renaissance imaginations. Festivals featured pomp and pageantry that bordered on bacchanalia (opposite, below).

a person's involvement in government and business was morally defensible. A virtuous rich man, they argued, could enhance society with patronage of buildings and the arts and make life more comfortable for the poor. Since this was a welcome message to the wealthy, many humanists found employment as tutors for children of the well-to-do, as secretaries to princes, and as administrators in towns. So popular and well stated were the new ideas that even popes and tyrants found them attractive.

For all the divergence from church science and technology. Leonardo da Vinci was not only one of the finest artists of the Renaissance but also perhaps the best example of a Renaissance man. He advanced the science of hydraulics, and his notebooks include drawings of human anatomy, mechanical diggers, artillery—and even the principles of flight some 400 years before airplanes were invented.

Other matters of science were explored by scholars such as Copernicus, who deduced a circular orbit by planets around the sun. This idea was so divergent from the then current view of the church—that the earth itself was the center of the universe—that Copernicus was afraid to publish his observations until just before his death.

In other ways, also, the new ideas clashed with church doctrine. For example, clerics had idealized poverty and the way of the cloister for centuries. Now humanists proposed that

MACHIAVELLI AND STATECRAFT

The floodgates of new attitudes were decidedly opened when statesman and political philosopher Niccolò Machiavelli wrote *The Prince* in 1513. He analyzed the discordant politics in Renaissance Italy and suggested that rulers could justify using force and deceit in holding on to power. While some charged that Machiavelli was justifying immoral behavior, his book influenced the politics of his time and gave rise to the description even today of a ruthless politician being "Machiavellian."

1677 Ice cream becomes a popular dessert in Paris.

1681 First oil street lamps are used in London.

1685 Edict of Nantes is revoked in France.

1689 Opera introduced to Munich.

1690 English set up a trading post at Calcutta.

1692 In the West Indies, an earthquake destroys the city of Port Royal in Jamaica.

thinking of Medieval times, Europeans did not turn away from religion during the Renaissance. The devout carried new thinking into their theology, seeking a more worldly church and a more personal faith.

In the 16th century this process of searching and questioning led to a spiritual crisis on the Continent known as the Reformation. ■

1517 Fernão Pirés de Andrade, Portuguese, is the first modern European to visit Canton. Babur makes reconnaissance raids on India. Expedition under

Francisco Hernández de Córdoba explores the Mexican coast.

1519 Firearms introduced into China by the Portuguese.

1521 Peace treaty between Venice and Turkey renewed. First conversions of Filipinos to Christianity.

1522 Five-year truce between Poland and Russia. The Ottomans take Rhodes.

Reformation and Reason

From its humble, furtive beginnings in ancient Rome, when Christians worshiped literally underground in catacombs, Christianity had become a powerful institution.

When the Roman Emperor Constantine moved his capital to Byzantium, Italy had been thrown into chaos. Through the years, the leaders of the church, the popes, helped restore social order.

In dealing with barbarian invaders, squabbling barons, and strong-willed kings, the more than 150 popes who ruled Christendom between Constantine and the time of the Renaissance became not just religious leaders but also statesmen, heads of armies, and politicians.

In 1309 French Pope Clement V,

Blessing new ideas, popes such as Borgia Alexander VI **(above)** boosted learning and art in the 15th century. But corrupt practices, such as payment for forgiveness of future sins, weakened the moral leadership of the church and led to protests that divided Christianity into different creeds **(opposite)**.

under pressure from King Philip, moved his residence from Rome to Avignon. Throughout the "Babylonian Captivity" as the popes' 68-year absence from Rome was called, and in the Great Western Schism, which followed when two—and briefly three—popes held office at the same time, the reputation of the papacy began to slip.

In 1417 a church council finally forced the resignation of all three popes, then elected a pope everyone could agree with. By this time, however, the moral influence of church leadership had been weakened.

Financial issues raised eyebrows even further among believers. To raise money for its large administrative structure, unpopular church taxes were levied. Almost all services of the church required the payment of fees. Church positions could be bought.

Although many popes were virtuous and altruistic, for others the pursuit of power and luxury had become paramount. Pope Leo X spent heavily not only on wars to drive out foreigners and on improvements for the Vatican, but also on pleasures such as lavish banquets, during which birds flew out of pies and naked children climbed out of puddings.

To many educated people in Europe, one of the most objectionable practices was the selling of indulgences—paying money for a pardon from sins, including some not yet committed.

In the late 1300s in England, Oxford University scholar John

Wycliffe criticized the church's wealth and its hierarchy of clergy.

In Bohemia, Jan Hus led a movement aimed at reforming corrupt church leadership. In 1415 a church council, after promising Hus protection to hear his views, had him burned at the stake.

The man who truly touched off the religious Reformation in Europe was a practicing Catholic and a university professor at Wittenberg, Germany, named Martin Luther. He became convinced that salvation was a gift direct from God that could not be bought or sold and did not require the intercession of a church official.

On October 31, 1517, he nailed to the door of the Wittenberg castle church a list of 95 theses that questioned the granting of indulgences.

Luther intended merely to spur an academic debate on the subject. Instead he touched off a religious

1523 Russian ambassador visits Rome. First school for Indians started at Texcoco, Mexico.

1524 Charles de Bourbon invades Provence. Rebellion is aborted in Egypt. Giovanni Verrazano reaches Newfoundland and Belle Isle; he may be the first to realize that the Americas are continents.

1525 Peace between Henry VIII and France.

1526 Babur invades India. All Spanish vessels ordered to voyage in groups because of pirates.

ca 1530 Annually 4,000-5,000 slaves shipped from the Congo.

● Citadel of Jerusalem
is completed.

1532

● Civil war in Denmark.

1533-37

● Uprising in Ireland is led
by Thomas, Lord Offaly.

1534-35

● Lima, Peru, founded
by Pizarro. Conquest
of Inca Empire complete.
Thomas Cromwell
appointed visitor-
general of English
monasteries.

1535

● First printing press
established in Mexico.

1537

● St. Thomas Becket's
shrine at Canterbury
is destroyed.

1538

revolt, a massive protest against the church's policies, which came to be known as Protestantism.

The church founded on Luther's tenets of faith was the first of the Protestant denominations and was called Lutheranism. He and other reformers simplified church doctrine and rituals and called their church leaders not priests but ministers, who preached from the Bible and conducted services in the local language instead of Latin.

Protestantism broke into numerous sects as different interpretations were

After religious war and persecution had raged across Europe, an age of tolerance ensued, which allowed citizens to travel and express their opinions and ideas openly *(above)*.

applied to biblical passages.

Ulrich Zwingli, leader of the Reformed Church in Switzerland, created a church-run state that banned the Catholic mass and forbade the use of music in worship.

The followers of John Calvin believed in a particularly rigid brand of predestination.

The Anabaptists disagreed so rad-

Learned scientific treatises, such as Isaac Newton's 17th-century book on gravitation and dynamics *(right)*, became influential.

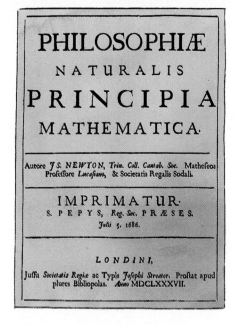

PHILOSOPHIÆ
NATURALIS
PRINCIPIA
MATHEMATICA.

Autore *JS. NEWTON*, *Trin. Coll. Cantab. Soc.* Matheseos
Professore *Lucasiano*, & Societatis Regalis Sodali.

IMPRIMATUR.
S. PEPYS, *Reg. Soc.* PRÆSES.
Julii 5. 1686.

LONDINI,

Jussu *Societatis Regiæ* ac Typis *Josephi Streater*. Prostat apud
plures Bibliopolas. *Anno* MDCLXXXVII.

1539-1541   ● Printers in Paris and Lyons go on strike.

1542   ● Jesuits start work in Goa.

1550   ● Cattle introduced into South America.

1570   ● In Japan, Nagasaki nominated as the port for overseas trade.

● Rebellion in Ghent.
1539-1540

1546   ● Spanish gain control of Yucatan Peninsula.

ically with civic authority that they refused to hold office or bear arms.

In 1534 Henry VIII declared himself head of the Protestant Church of England when the pope would not grant him a divorce. This more radical variant of the Catholic Church became part of the Protestant movement when Henry's young son, Edward, was assisted in governing by a Council of Lords, most of whom were Protestant. Some believers who thought the church still not reformed enough became known as Puritans.

To counter Protestantism, the Catholic Church reinvigorated the Inquisition to forcibly uproot its opponents. The Lutherans formed the Schmalkaldic League, which fought the pro-Catholic Holy Roman emperor Charles V. Religious wars raged across Europe from 1545 to 1650.

Although the Inquisition spelled the end of the Renaissance in Italy, it did not kill intelligent thought continent-wide. At the height of religious conflict Galileo Galilei, using a telescope improved for astronomical use, confirmed the observations of the deceased Copernicus.

The Frenchman René Descartes applied science to philosophy and the art of debate.

English philosopher Francis Bacon argued for careful observation and systematic gathering of information in answering questions about nature.

These intellectual bright spots in the midst of narrow-mindedness were part of what is known as the Age of Reason.

THE GREGORIAN CALENDAR

Since the time of Julius Caesar the Christian world had been using the Julian calendar, which had 365¼ days. Actually the earth orbits the sun every 365.2422 days, so by the 16th century this had displaced the vernal equinox—the date when day and night are exactly equal—by 10 days. In 1582 Pope Gregory XIII corrected the error by changing October 5 into October 15. Future error was prevented by determining that an extra day would be assigned to February in years divisible by four; but in century years, such as 1600, the extra day would be added only in those centuries that could be divided by 400.

Science and theology coexisted and sometimes clashed, but neither one of them replaced the other.

Europeans wearied of warfare over religion, which slowly abated. The Catholic Church looked inward and reformed its worst abuses.

Out of the conflict came many different forms of Christian belief. ■

Division in Islam

Like the Christian church during this historical period, the other major religion to influence Europe—Islam—was also divided by ideology.

The split began with the death of the prophet Muhammad, founder of Islam, in 632. His followers named Muhammad's father-in-law and close associate, Abu Bakr, to succeed him.

However, Muhammad had left one daughter, Fatima. In 656, when the time came to elect a new caliph, or leader of Islam, a great argument broke out. The more fundamentalist group—known as Shiites—felt that Fatima's husband Ali, a cousin of Muhammad, should be the new caliph and that the leaders of Islam should always be descendants of Muhammad's own family.

The opposing group believed that any outstanding follower of Islam should be eligible for the caliphate.

Ali was elected, but his opponents set up a rival regime led by a military leader named Muawiya and planned to seize control of all Islam.

Although Ali had the stronger army, he attempted to negotiate a settlement. While at prayer, Ali was murdered by a former supporter, and Muawiya succeeded to the position of spiritual leader. The Shiites countered by claiming the caliphate for Ali's son Husain.

When Muawiya died in 680, Husain and a small party set out from Mecca so he could assume the caliphate. But Muawiya's son Yazid had taken charge, and his cavalry intercepted Husain and killed him.

The Shiites, now centered in Iraq and Persia, never again acknowledged the caliph's authority.

Most Muslims today belong to the original group of Muhammad's followers that opposed the initial Shiite challenge. This dominant group in Islam are called Sunnis, or "followers of the way." ■

1415 · Henry V of England lays claim to the French throne, invades France, wins Battle of Agincourt.

1441 · Second Ottoman siege of Byzantium.

1456 · Ottoman Turks occupy Athens.

1470 · First printing press in France set up at the Sorbonne.

1478-92 · Algiers is founded by the Arabs.

Columbus and the New World

For centuries Europeans had been content to travel overland to contact other civilizations in the known world. The open sea was, by all accounts, a fearsome place with monsters and other fantastic horrors. Most seagoing ships stuck close to coastlines. A number of geographers believed the earth was round, but they disagreed on its size.

In the 15th century, economics, religion, and the very nature of the Renaissance prompted mariners to venture into the unknown and begin one of the greatest periods of exploration the world has ever known.

With Muslim armies pressuring Eastern Europe, Christians were worried about the spread of Islam. Some thought they might outflank the Muslim Empire by sailing around the great land to the south—Africa—and attacking Islam from a different direction. In addition, they wanted to win more souls for Christ.

Trade also spurred exploration. Through the Crusades and overland commerce, Europe had acquired an appetite for Eastern goods—silks, jewels, and spices. Spices from the Orient were used in cosmetics, medicines, and especially in meat, to improve its flavor or to preserve it by smoking and then curing.

Trading in these goods could replenish national treasuries, even

A determined man who pressed his case for years, Columbus *(top)* finally gained financial backing from the Spanish monarchy for his daring venture: sailing west in ships like this modern replica *(above)* to reach the rich trade goods of the East. When his voyage struck previously unknown lands, Columbus named one island Dominica *(opposite)*, because he found it on a Sunday.

while frequent wars and the maintenance of splendid courts drained European coffers.

The Venetians, a maritime power in the early 1400s, controlled trade through the Mediterranean, but with the fall of Constantinople these routes from the East were cut off. Europeans wanted desperately to find new ways of reaching commodities of the East.

Aiding these aspirations was a man who seldom went to sea. Early in the 1400s Prince Henry, third son of Portugal's King John I, set up a school at Sagres on the southwest tip of Portugal to study sea travel.

Henry improved the compass and made alterations in ship design. Ships gained multiple masts and sturdy sails. He became known as "the Navigator," financing expeditions along the African coast and analyzing the results.

Among the sailors coursing the west coasts of both Europe and Africa was a navigator and commercial agent from Genoa, Italy, named Christopher Columbus. Years of observation and discussions with other mariners had convinced him that one could reach the trade-rich Orient, the East Indies, by sailing west across the Atlantic.

The Portuguese king turned down Columbus's request for ships but secretly sent one out to test the theory. It returned after days of sailing west

1480 ● Mongols have been driven from Russia.

● First printing of the Koran in Arabic.
1485 Virupaksa II of Vijayanagar murdered by his son.

1486-1502 ● Rule of Aztec Emperor Ahuizotl; Aztec Empire at height of power in Mexico.

1487 ● On site of present cathedral of Mexico City, 20,000 persons are sacrificed to the god Huitzilopochtli.

1488 ● Ming emperors order rebuilding of the Great Wall to defend China from northern invaders.

1504 ● In Germany, the watch is invented by Peter Henlein of Nuremberg; it has a single hand.

without ever reaching land.

King Ferdinand and Queen Isabella of Spain also at first turned down Columbus's repeated requests, dismissing him completely in 1487. Then, heartened by the expulsion of the Moors from southern Spain in 1492, they relented and outfitted Columbus with three ships. On August 3 he sailed from the coastal city of Palos to the Canary Islands off the coast of Africa. Departing there on September 6, he went for weeks without sighting land, his crews increasingly fearful and mutinous. On October 12 they arrived at an island

in the Caribbean. Believing he had reached India, Columbus called the natives there "Indians."

After three months' exploration, Columbus returned in triumph to Spain, where he was showered with honors. In three subsequent voyages he reached the continent of South America and touched Central America, as well. Some opposed him in the Spanish court, and a rebellion in a New World colony resulted in his return to Europe in chains.

A measure of royal favor was eventually restored, and he derived some income from his discoveries, as

originally promised. He died in 1506, still believing he had reached the East Indies by sailing west, disappointed that he had not found civilizations that would enrich him through trade. The islands he discovered, and for a time the coastline he encountered, were called the West Indies.

Between 1497 and 1503 Italian Amerigo Vespucci explored there and suggested that the land might be separate from Asia. A German publisher proposed that the area be called America in his honor, and it was. But it was Columbus who had introduced the New World to Europeans. ■

1488 Duke Humphrey's Library opened at Oxford.

1492-1547 Life of Vittoria Colonna, Italian poet.

1492 Cairo devastated by plague: 12,000 persons are said to have died in one day.

1493 In West Africa, the Songhay Empire reaches its greatest extent under Askia Muhammad.

1494 Charles VIII of France enters Rome after a triumphal march through Italy.

1495 Jews expelled from Portugal.

Discovering the Earth's Dimensions

Many voyages down the west coast of Africa finally paid off for the Portuguese. In 1488 Bartolomeu Dias sailed around the tip of Africa, thereby proving that there was an end to that large continent.

For a decade domestic troubles at home kept the Portuguese from capitalizing on Dias's discovery. Finally in 1497 Vasco da Gama set sail with four ships, two of them outfitted to haul trade goods. They sailed around Africa's southern end, renamed by the Portuguese king the Cape of Good Hope for the promise its discovery held, and landed at Calicut on the southwestern coast of India. The voyage took more than two years and although da Gama lost two ships and half his crew, it was successful.

Subsequent voyages took the Portuguese to the Moluccas, also called the Spice Islands for their richness in those products, located between Indonesia and New Guinea. They pushed on to China and Japan and set up trading and missionary posts. From Ceylon, now Sri Lanka, they brought back tea and spices. To protect their monopoly in eastern trade, they established naval bases at key points—Hormuz at the entrance of the Persian Gulf, Malacca at the straits leading to the South China Sea, and Goa just off the west coast of India. In the New World they colonized Brazil.

The Spanish, still believing the lands Columbus had discovered were the back side of Asia, continued their voyages across the Atlantic. The search for a strait that would take them to India showed them only a long, wild, north-to-south coastline. In 1513 Vasco Núñez de Balboa, after hearing rumors of a vast sea to the west, fought his way through jungles at the Isthmus of Panama and from a

NAVIGATIONAL TECHNOLOGY

Sandglass, compass, lodestone, and astrolabe were mariners' tools (above). Improvements in navigational instruments emboldened Europeans to venture onto open seas in the 14th century. The compass, invented by the Chinese two centuries earlier but new to Europeans, told them their direction. By sighting on astronomical bodies with an astrolabe, sailors could determine how far north or south they were.

Earth grew larger as maritime explorers sailed far beyond sight of land (opposite). Ferdinand Magellan (upper left), began his final voyage with a brave broadside (left) as his fleet left Spain in 1519 on a journey that would change the known shape of the world. Magellan died in the Philippines, but one of his five vessels returned to Spain after steadily sailing west, proving the roundness of the globe. Other Europeans began staking claims in the Americas. Micmac Indians and Samuel de Champlain hunted game birds (opposite, below), as they explored for France up the St. Lawrence River and founded Quebec.

● **1497** In Naples, first recorded outbreak of syphilis in the Old World.

● **ca 1500** Maize introduced into Africa from Brazil.

● **1509-1564** Life of John Calvin, Protestant reformer.

● **1499** Muslims in Spain required to conform to Christianity; Arabic books burned.

● **1506-1612** Construction of Basilica of St. Peter's in Rome.

● **1510** First slaves from Guinea reach Haiti.

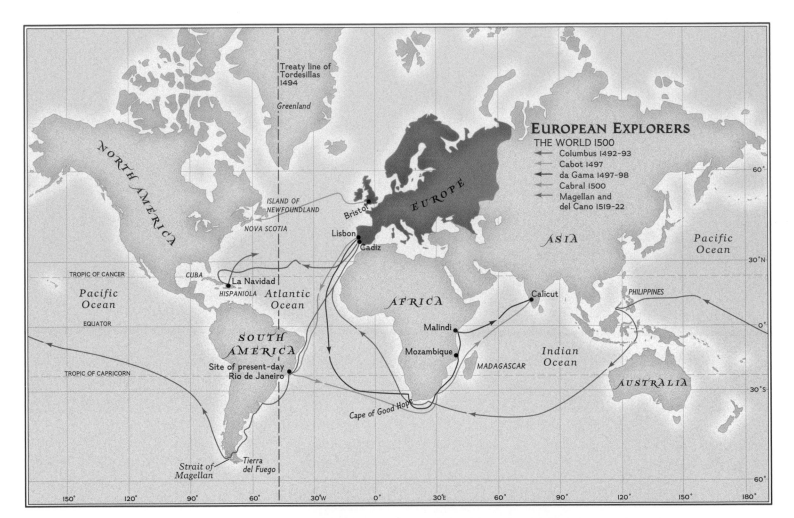

EUROPEAN EXPLORERS
THE WORLD 1500
← Columbus 1492-93
← Cabot 1497
← da Gama 1497-98
← Cabral 1500
← Magellan and del Cano 1519-22

high peak glimpsed a new ocean.

In 1520 Ferdinand Magellan, a Portuguese in Spanish employ, rounded the tip of South America through the straits that now bear his name and continued west. Of five ships that began the voyage, one was wrecked in the straits, one turned back, and two others became unseaworthy. Magellan was killed by natives in the Philippines along with nearly 30 of his remaining crew.

The 18 survivors continued west to Seville, Spain, in the remaining ship, proving not only that the world was indeed round but also that

1521 Edict of Worms outlaws Luther and his followers.

1521-1557 Reign of John III, King of Portugal.

1534 The Ottoman Turks capture Tunis, Baghdad, and Mesopotamia.

1551 Parliament of Paris declines to allow the Jesuits in France. English currency reformed.

1561 Olives first grown in Chile.

1568 Dutch begin revolt against Spanish rule.

Sailing up the river that would one day bear his name, Henry Hudson encountered friendly native people and found rich land later claimed by the Dutch.

Columbus had, in fact, discovered new continents.

Throughout the 1500s the Spanish concentrated on conquering Central and South America, although Hernando de Soto explored the southeastern part of North America and Francisco Vásquez de Coronado ventured north from Mexico as far as Kansas. The first European settlement in North America was Spain's St. Augustine in present-day Florida.

The French, English, and Dutch were relatively late starters. Jacques Cartier sailed up the St. Lawrence River from 1534 to 1542, but he left no French colonies. Samuel de Champlain followed in 1608 and founded Quebec.

The English, preoccupied with fear of the Spanish until they defeated

THE DUTCH TRADING COMPANIES

In the age of European colonization, the Dutch decided that, with their small country and few natural resources, they would focus on trade for economic survival. They designed their ships for carrying large cargoes with small crews. They combined competitive trading companies into the Dutch East India Company and later the Dutch West India Company and gave each of them monopolies in their respective areas—Asia and Africa, and the New World. By the late 1600s the Dutch had a fleet of ships larger than the fleets of England, Portugal, France, and Germany combined and traded on every continent.

the Spanish Armada in 1588, set up the first of their many colonies along the Atlantic seaboard in 1607, at Jamestown, Virginia.

The Dutch developed settlements in Guiana and the West Indies, and in 1626 the Dutch founded New Amsterdam, today's New York.

The New World natives, separated from technological advancements that had occurred in Europe and Asia, were no match for armor, fearsome horses, and superior weapons.

Diseases such as measles, smallpox, and typhus devastated local populations. Malaria moved from Africa to South America.

Whole peoples—for example, the Caribs of the Caribbean—were virtually wiped out by disease, war, slavery, and interbreeding. ■

1551 — Universities of Lima and Mexico founded.

1553 — The French take Corsica.

1554-1557 — War between Ivan the Terrible and Gustavus I Vasa for Finland.

1559-1598 — Struggles between Catholics and Protestants in France.

1560 — The first Puritans preach in England.

1574-1645 — Life of Feng Meng-Lung, Chinese novelist.

The Wealth of Conquest

Although winning souls to Christianity was a stated aim of Spanish conquest in the New World, gold and silver were major attractions as well. These were found among the Aztec when Cortés conquered them; and in Peru, where Francisco Pizarro defeated the Inca Empire. Treasures sailed aboard galleons back to the Old World in such amounts that they caused widespread inflation. Within a century prices in Spain quadrupled, causing hardship and discontent among people with fixed incomes. Prices were also affected, although less drastically, throughout Europe, the Ottoman

New lands and long voyages resulted in a wide distribution of goods and treasures around the world. Chocolate's fame broadened, and Europeans acquired a taste for the frothy drink, called xocatl, that the Mixtec of Mesoamerica used to seal a marriage *(above)*. The Dutch grew rich on far-flung trade; a fleet of East Indiamen loads fragrant sandalwood and spices in the Orient *(below)*.

Empire, and as far away as China. At first the gold and silver came from plunder or barter. Then the Spanish began panning for gold in streams and mining silver in large deposits they had discovered. In Potosí, in today's Bolivia, a boom town of 100,000 sprang up around a mountain laden with silver.

Besides disease and treasures, both flora and fauna were exchanged around the world. The founders of colonies in the New World brought horses, cows, and sheep over on ships and grazed them on their large holdings. The British

● Muskets first used in Japan.
ca 1578

● The Catacombs redis-covered in Rome.
1578

● Rialto Bridge built in Venice.
1587-91

● Japan invades Korea with 300,000 men. Seoul and other cities are taken, and the country is devastated.
1592-98

● Population of India estimated at about 100 million.
ca 1600

● Spain is bankrupt.
1607

brought sugarcane to Barbados. On return voyages came American corn, or maize, potatoes from Peru, pineapples from the Caribbean, bananas, sweet potatoes, peppers, peanuts, tomatoes, and new varieties of beans.

Some of the new crops could be grown abroad, and they spread quickly around Europe, Africa, and Asia with beneficial impact. In warm areas of China, sweet potatoes could be grown on hillsides where rice could not. In cooler Europe, the pota-to became a new source of food. In Africa, corn augmented diets. Ultimately the new foods produced a

Conquistadors pillaged New World masks like the one above. Cloth painted with Indian women and flowers (below) from Calicut, India, may have bright-ened European drawing rooms. Indian hands gathered the pepper that drew the Portuguese (opposite, above). Aboriginal cave paintings (oppo-site, below) suggest visits from Europeans.

dramatic increase in populations in China, Europe, and Africa.

Human populations were trans-ferred as well, not always of their own will. At first the plantations of the Americas were worked by indentured servants, who bound themselves to their employers for a certain period of time before gaining freedom. As cash crops of sugarcane and tobacco became more profitable, producers turned to slave labor. During the 18th

TOBACCO SUPPORTS BRITISH COLONY

DUM FUMO VIVO.

Edwd Halford's fine Virginea
The best in Holbeach for a Guinea.

A British tobacconist's label extols the product shipped from Virginia (above). England's toehold in North America can be traced partly to the growing of tobacco. It was John Rolfe in Jamestown who discovered how to cure tobacco. Sir Walter Raleigh then spread its use to England and Ireland. Its sale abroad provided an economic base that helped support the English colony of Virginia.

1608-1674 Life of John Milton, English poet.

1611 The King James Bible is published.

1612 About 10,000 slaves shipped annually from Angola.

1616 Inquisition forbids Galileo to teach.

1616-1624 Plague in Punjab, India.

1618 Sir Francis Bacon made Lord Chancellor. Source of the Blue Nile discovered by Pedro Paez.

century, at the peak of the slave trade, between six and seven million Africans were shipped across the Atlantic under miserable conditions. ■

Australia

The large landmass of Australia managed to elude European exploration and settlement for centuries after other new lands were occupied and exploited. Portuguese, Spanish, and French voyages into the Pacific and Indian Oceans may have brought explorers close to Australia in the early 1500s.

Later, in 1577, England's Capt. Francis Drake was given instructions to search for land in the vicinity of Australia. But, upon entering the Pacific through the Straits of Magellan, he turned northward, toward Peru, instead.

The Dutchman Willem Jansz was probably the first European to reach the coast of Australia in 1605-06. His impressions were of a bleak land promising no commercial gain. In 1642 another Dutch expedition set out to investigate to the west and the south of Australia. Led by Abel Janszoon Tasman, the expedition took Tasman to the south of Tasmania and to New Zealand. Tasman erroneously believed that New Zealand was part of *terra australis*.

William Dampier, a pirating adventurer searching for riches to plunder in the East Indies, visited Australia in 1688. But he found nothing suitable for his purposes. ■

ca **1500** A village of oval stone houses is built on Easter Island.

1535 In England, Sir Thomas More is executed for refusing to take an oath agreeing to the Act of Supremacy.

1536-1540 The Dissolution of the Monasteries in England.

1541-1564 Reformer John Calvin leads Calvinists in Geneva, Switzerland.

1549 The Christian missionary St. Francis Xavier arrives in Japan. First *Book of Common Prayer* used in the Church of England.

Spain Climbs to Power

The Muslim Arabs, or "Moors," as the Europeans called them, who entered Europe through Gibraltar in the eighth century, ruled Spain for nearly 800 years.

Gradually the Christians of Europe won it back city by city and town by town, but the reconquered parts were divided into separate states. The two largest states merged into the Spanish kingdom through the marriage of Ferdinand of Aragon and Isabella of Castile in 1469.

The united forces drove the Moors out of their last stronghold, Granada, in 1492. In that same year King Ferdinand and Queen Isabella commissioned Christopher Columbus to find a new sea route to the East, little knowing that he would find, instead, the New World. It signaled the beginning of a period of Spanish power.

Since it was believed for years that Columbus had found a shortcut to Asia, the Portuguese feared competition on their Asian trade routes and claimed they had a monopoly there. Both Spain and Portugal were Catholic, so the matter was decided by the pope.

With the Treaty of Tordesillas the pope drew a line from north to south in the Atlantic and declared that Spain had rights to everything west of the line and Portugal everything to the east.

But by cutting through the great eastern protuberance of South America, the line prevented the Spanish from settling coastal Brazil as the Portuguese eventually did.

1554 • Founding of São Paulo, Brazil.

1555-1560 • Construction of St. Basil's Cathedral in Moscow.

1562-1591 • Turks raid the eastern African coast.

1564 • Sir John Hawkins's second voyage to the West Indies.

1571 • Tatar raiding party invades and burns Moscow.

1576 • African slaves in South America number 40,000.

Spain quickly exploited the new lands that remained, however. Conquistadors, or conquerors, in search of riches established bases in Hispaniola, Cuba, and Panama and overcame the Aztec of Mexico and the Inca of Peru.

Jesuit and Franciscan priests followed them and set up missions to convert the Indians to Christianity.

Immigrants seeking opportunity were drawn to the new settlements, and Spanish-speaking people quickly populated areas in Central and South America, the Caribbean, and on the Florida peninsula of North America.

From "New Spain" came cargoes of gold and silver, so valuable that they gave rise to piracy on the high seas. Before they began settlements of their own, the Dutch and English preyed on the treasure-laden galleons coming out of the Caribbean.

In 1581 Queen Elizabeth knighted the Englishman Francis Drake more for the Spanish booty he brought home than for being the first of his countrymen to sail around the world. Eventually the Spanish shipped their plundered goods home in convoys protected by warships.

When the stolen treasures of the Amerindian empires ran out, the Spaniards continued to take silver and gold from the earth.

The riches that poured in from the Americas made Spain wealthy. This wealth allowed the nation to build vast fleets of ships and compete with other nations for supremacy at sea. ■

CERVANTES

The Spanish writer Miguel de Cervantes (1547-1616) *(above)* tweaked chivalry in his novel *Don Quixote de la Mancha*. While making fun of the chivalric practices of the recent past, he helped create the art form of the novel. His own life rivaled the adventures in any book. While soldiering, Cervantes's hand was maimed as he fought the Ottoman Turks in the battle at Lepanto. Later, he was captured and held for ransom by pirates in the Mediterranean.

Unity and New World wealth vaulted Spain into prominence, beginning in the late 15th century. The marriage of Ferdinand and Isabella *(opposite)* unified Aragon and Castile to drive out the last of the Moors and freed the nation to explore the high seas. Riches from the Americas filled the treasury, allowing Spain to build a huge fleet. But tempting cargoes led to piracy; and when England's Queen Elizabeth knighted Francis Drake *(right)* for loot taken from Spanish ships, the angry king of Spain prepared to invade.

1556-59 Sir Henry Sidney is vice treasurer of Ireland.

1557 France goes into bankruptcy.

1558 Mozambique replaces Sofala as Portuguese eastern African capital.

1559 Jesuit college founded in Munich. University of Geneva founded.

1560-68 Erik XIV, King of Sweden.

1561 Spire of St. Paul's, the highest in England, destroyed by fire.

The Decline of Spain

Through the riches of the New World and a series of royal European marriages, Spain became the most powerful Old World power in the 16th century. The reign of Philip II, a member of the powerful Habsburg family, extended over Spain, the Netherlands, and part of Italy; and he sought to expand it even more. In the mid-1560s his forces added the islands that they called the Philippines in his honor. In 1578 his relative,

English fire ships strike at the anchored Spanish Armada to set vessels ablaze and thwart an invasion of England. Sea storms further weakened the Spanish fleet.

1562 The Wars of Religion start in France. Treaty of Prague between Emperor Ferdinand I and Turkey.

1568 Yemen taken by Sinan Pasha for Ottoman Turkey.

1569-1573 First Desmond revolt in Ireland.

1570 Elizabeth I of England excommunicated.

1572 Last Inca, Tupac Amaru, captured and executed. Inquisition set up in Mexico.

1576-78 Three voyages of Martin Frobisher reach Baffin Island and Hudson Strait.

King Sebastian of Portugal, was killed in battle against the Moroccans, following which Portugal came under Spanish rule for 80 years.

Some Spaniards were bothered by the enslavement and exploitation of thousands of New World natives. A Catholic missionary, Bartolomé de Las Casas, believed that the Indians' rights should be protected and that Spain should limit itself to spreading the gospel among them.

Others argued that the natives should yield to the more sophisticated Spanish culture. The Spanish crown, attempting to mediate, decreed that the Indians were free, could own land, and could sue Spaniards in Spanish courts, but to do so they must be Spanish citizens and accept Christianity. Many suits were brought against Spaniards in the name of Native Americans, but in far-off America, abuses against the Indians continued to be common.

Angered by British aid to the rebellious Dutch and their piracy against his ships, Philip gathered a mighty fleet in 1588 to invade England, but there his ships suffered heavy losses.

Although the Spanish ships outnumbered the English ships, those of Spain were heavy galleons. The English vessels were more maneuverable, and the sailors were more familiar with the seas in the vicinity of their home island.

The defeat of the Spanish Armada did not in itself spell the downfall of Spanish power, but it marked a turning point. Much of the wealth that Spain had acquired was squandered on war, and after borrowing money from foreign bankers, its colonial income went toward paying off debts. Inflation in Spain priced Spanish products out of world markets. Continued piracy in the Caribbean interrupted the flow of silver from the New World colonies. England had gained control of the Atlantic.

A series of Spanish kings whose reigns were fraught with internal squabbles further weakened Spain, whose period of world power had lasted little more than a century. ■

THE SPANISH INQUISITION

An 18th-century English engraving depicts Inquisition torture in a jail *(above)*. The Inquisition by Catholics to root out unbelievers took place throughout Catholic Europe but nowhere as brutally as in Spain. Great loss of life occurred. Christians accused of heresy—which might include being Protestant or reading books condemned by the Catholic Church—could be tortured until they confessed, then burned alive. Muslims and Jews were also tortured in attempts to convert them, and killed if they did not accept Catholicism.

● **1421** Yong Le, Ming Emperor, builds a new capital city in northern China, today's Beijing.

● Jews expelled from England. **1422**

● **1434** College of Cardinals is reformed.

● James I of Scots assassinated. **1437**

● **1440-1518** Life of Kabir, a leader of the Bhakti movement in India.

● **1448** Frederick of Brandenburg seizes Berlin, making it his capital.

Portugal's Empire of Trade

An early interest in sea exploration gave the Portuguese a head start over other Europeans in trade with the East. It was the first country on the continent to establish an overseas empire. The caravels designed at the maritime school of Prince Henry the Navigator (below) were small but sturdy; and with triangular sails that pivoted around the masts, they sailed close to the wind. Soon after discovering a new route to India from Europe, the Portuguese had extended their trade network to China, Japan, Ceylon, and islands in the Indonesian archipelago. To protect their commerce, by the mid-1500s they had set up more than 50 fortified trading posts along the route. Lisbon became one of the most important ports in Europe.

Portugal never had a monopoly on eastern trade, despite the Treaty of Tordesillas, which supposedly limited Spanish activity. The first visits to eastern ports met with opposition from the Muslims. The Portuguese tried to limit competition through tolls and by

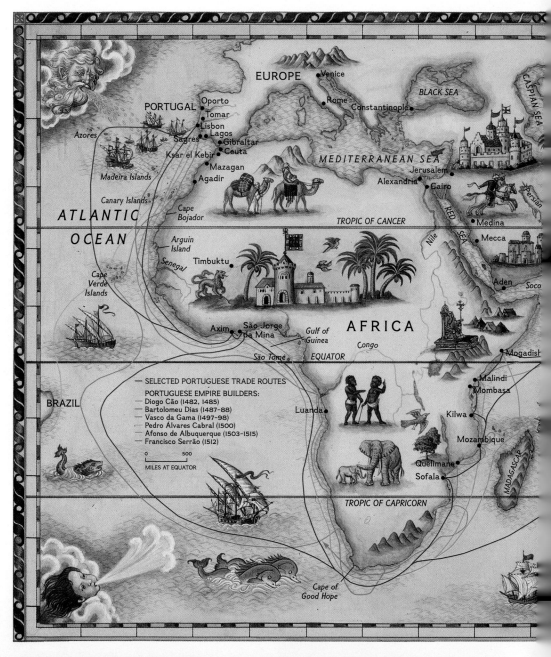

SELECTED PORTUGUESE TRADE ROUTES
PORTUGUESE EMPIRE BUILDERS:
— Diogo Cão (1482, 1485)
— Bartolomeu Dias (1487-88)
— Vasco da Gama (1497-98)
— Pedro Alvares Cabral (1500)
— Afonso de Albuquerque (1503-1515)
— Francisco Serrão (1512)

0   500
MILES AT EQUATOR

1460 Henry VI captured by Edward IV and imprisoned in the Tower of London.

1482 Leonardo da Vinci paints the fresco "The Last Supper" in Milan, Italy.

1485 Henry VII becomes first Tudor King of England.

1501-05 Michelangelo's "David," sculptured in Florence.

1536 Pedro de Mendoza founds the city of Buenos Aires.

1572 Epidemic in Algiers kills one third of the population.

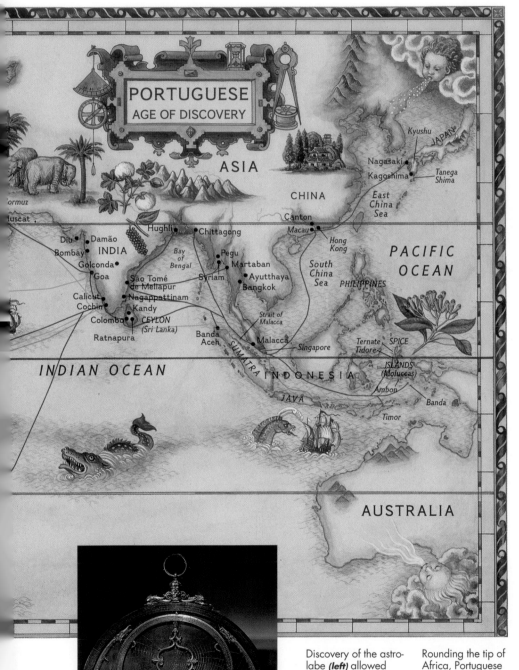

PORTUGUESE AGE OF DISCOVERY

plundering other cargoes, but the sea was big and the ships few.

Arabs, Persians, and Indians continued to haul pepper across the Indian Ocean and through the Red Sea to Europe. But for a century, prior to coming under Spanish rule, the Portuguese had no serious European rivals.

Although some bases such as Hormuz, Goa, and Malacca were taken as outright possessions, the Portuguese were not aggressive in establishing colonies abroad. The home country's population was too small to allow for large-scale emigration, and the wealth garnered from trade seemed adequate.

Gradually colonies were formed in the African bases at Angola and Mozambique, and settlers began arriving in Brazil. There strips of land were divided among wealthy Portuguese who introduced sugarcane, tobacco, coffee, cocoa, and cotton.

Since the local Indian population was not adequate for forced labor, the Portuguese began bringing slaves from their ports on the west coast of Africa, a practice soon copied throughout the Americas. By the late 1600s Brazil was the largest sugar-producing area in the world. ■

Discovery of the astrolabe (left) allowed mariners to know their latitude far out at sea. Early sailors had hugged coastlines, following landmarks such as the high bluffs of Cape Espichel south of Lisbon (opposite).

Rounding the tip of Africa, Portuguese traders dipped into the wealth of the East. From Sri Lanka they gathered gems that included sapphires and a large topaz (right), here swimming in a pool of aquamarines.

179

1561 ● Portuguese monks in Goa introduce printing to India.

1572 ● Francis Drake captures Spanish fleet off Isthmus of Panama.

ca 1580 ● Use of beaver fur for hats in Paris stimulates trade with North America.

1580 ● First Dutch settlement in Guiana.

1587 ● Mary, Queen of Scots, executed.

1600 ● William Shakespeare writes *Hamlet*.

Turmoil in France and Abroad

PARIS

over France were massacred. Civil war continued in France until Henry of Navarre, who had married one of Catherine's daughters, succeeded to the throne.

A longtime Huguenot, Henry of Navarre converted to Catholicism, because it was the dominant religion in the country. In 1598 he granted Protestants some freedom, although his edict would be rescinded nearly a century later and Protestantism would be almost eliminated in France.

In the New World, while the Spanish concentrated on the

France in the latter half of the 16th century suffered under a weak monarchy and a series of religious conflicts. An able leader was lost in 1559 when King Henry II died of injuries received in a tournament that celebrated the end of a long war between France and Spain. His oldest son succeeded him, then died within a year. The next son, Charles, became king at the age of 10 and was dominated by his mother, Catherine, of the Italian Medici family. Although she was Catholic, the court of young King Charles was influenced by the Huguenots, or French Protestants.

The Protestants made such gains that Catherine ordered violent measures, and on St. Bartholomew's Day in 1572 thousands of Huguenots all

In the 1500s Catholics and Huguenots fought in France. Catherine, Catholic mother of the boy king Charles, ordered a massacre that killed thousands of Huguenots in one day (*above*). Cardinal Richelieu (*below*) defeated Huguenot armies and ended the threat. France became a power, celebrated by King Louis XIV, who held extravaganzas such as this gala at the Tuileries Palace in Paris (*opposite*).

THE GREAT PALACE AT VERSAILLES

France's King Louis XIV demonstrated France's greatness by building Europe's most magnificent palace at Versailles near Paris. The finest artists decorated the inside with paintings, sculptures, carvings, and tapestries, while formal gardens, including the fountain of Apollo (*above*), surrounded the outside of the palace. Distrustful of French nobles, Louis forced them to live nearby with their families so he could keep an eye on them. He entertained them with endless rounds of balls, picnics, hunts, plays, and banquets.

1612 John Rolfe starts growing tobacco in Virginia.

1616 The Blue Mosque in Istanbul, Turkey, is completed.

1626 Dutch found New Amsterdam, today's New York.

1652 Dutch found Cape Town in South Africa.

1679 Habeas Corpus Act in England ensures no imprisonment without court appearance first.

Caribbean and South America and the English colonized the Atlantic seaboard, the French settled in the northern portion of the North American continent. For a time, sugar production in the Caribbean was a profitable undertaking, and the European powers sought the islands more than the mainland. France claimed Guadeloupe, Martinique, Grenada, Tobago, and the future Haiti, but its biggest holdings were in northern and central North America.

Long after Samuel de Champlain founded Quebec, Catholic missionary Jacques Marquette and explorer Louis Joliet traveled through the Mississippi Valley in 1673. Nine years later René-Robert Cavelier de La Salle explored the Mississippi to the Gulf of Mexico and claimed the inland area for France, calling it Louisiana in honor of King Louis XIV.

In the Americas the French were different occupants from the English, who settled and farmed, and the Spanish, who gleaned riches from the native population through plunder and slave labor. Frenchmen traded blankets, guns, and wine to the Indians for valuable furs, and they themselves became trappers and hunters and extracted some lumber.

As a result the Indians often became allies of the French, so that when English colonists began moving inland, they met both French and Native Americans as opponents.

Back in France, Louis built up the military to a formidable fighting force and secured his nation's frontiers to roughly what they are today. ■

● Collapse of Chimu
culture in northern Peru.

1470s

● In the Treaty of
Constantinople, Venice
1479 agrees to pay tribute
to the Ottoman Empire
for trading rights in
the Black Sea.

● Portuguese navigator
Diogo Cao explores
1482-84 the Congo River in
West Africa.

● The Ottoman Turks
conquer Albania.

1478

● Parachute invented by
Leonardo da Vinci.

1480

● Birth of Raphael, Italian
1483 painter and architect.

The Wars of the Roses

As the European nations took shape, a few families strove for dominance. Monarchies were based on lineage, with titles passed down to heirs over centuries. Families jockeyed and fought for the power of kingship.

Perhaps nowhere did familial conflict reach such bloody proportions as in England's Wars of the Roses. The Plantagenets had ruled the island nation for more than three centuries. In 1455 a dispute arose between two branches of the family—the House of York and the House of Lancaster— over who rightly deserved to be king. The conflict took its name from the

Royal struggles raged across England for centuries, with losers either killed or imprisoned in the Tower of London (opposite). Deposed King Richard II may have gone to his grave (left) after starving himself. Cheerful warrior Henry V (above) gained British loyalty by winning French lands, but family feuds soon plunged England into chaos with the Wars of the Roses. Victory for Henry VII (below) began the reign of the Tudors.

1483 Ashikaga Yoshimasa completes building of the Silver Pavilion temple, or Ginkakuji, at Kyoto in Japan.

1484 In England, Caxton prints *Morte D'Arthur*, the poetic collection of legends about King Arthur compiled by Sir Thomas Malory.

ca 1485 Isabella of Castile refers Columbus's plan for exploration of the western route to the Indies to a committee.

1485 In South America, the Inca under Topa conquer all of what is now Chile.

1492 Columbus leaves Palos, Spain, for his voyage to the New World.

eventually won although Richard was killed in the deciding fight. His son Edward IV became king, but when Edward died 12 years later, his 12-year-old son Prince Edward was to inherit the throne, under the protectorate of Edward IV's brother Richard, Duke of Gloucester.

The uncle placed the prince and his younger brother in the Tower of London, supposedly for their protection; and when they mysteriously died, he had himself crowned Richard III. Richard III was killed when the last Lancaster heir, Henry Tudor, defeated him in battle. Henry Tudor then became King Henry VII, ending the Wars of the Roses.

His son King Henry VIII brought a measure of stability to England, although he is mostly remembered as the royal rogue who married six times, executed two of his queens, and split from the Catholic Church. ■

PIRACY ON THE SEAS

Early in the 1500s piracy was encouraged by countries who sought thereby to boost their treasuries. Sir Francis Drake had been knighted after bringing Spanish booty back to England from the Caribbean. British buccaneer Henry Morgan, who ranged from the Caribbean to Gibraltar, sacking Spanish cities and capturing money and goods, was made lieutenant governor of Jamaica. Edward Teach, an 18th-century privateer known as "Blackbeard," reportedly wore burning matches in his hair, carried six pistols in battle, and drank a mixture of rum and gunpowder.

respective emblems of the families, a red rose for the Lancasters and a white one for the Yorks.

The nation divided behind each of the claimants to the throne, Richard II

of the House of York and King Henry VI of the House of Lancaster. Battles became massacres, with thousands littering the fields of conflict and prisoners put to death. The Yorkists

● Death penalty imposed in Spain for importing or printing books without permit.
1558

● Tobacco introduced to Europe via Spain and Portugal.
1559

● The Church of Scotland is founded.
1560

● Süleyman the Magnificent, of the Ottoman Empire, dies.
1566

● Reign of emperor Wan Li in China; period of great paintings and porcelain making.
1572-1620

● The first microscope is made by Zacharias Janssen in the Netherlands.
1590

The Tudors and the Stuarts
Elizabethan Period

Henry VIII, of the House of Tudor, declared himself head of the church in England in 1534 when the pope would not allow him to divorce his queen. After marrying Anne Boleyn, his daughter Elizabeth was born, not the male heir Henry had hoped for. During the reign of Henry VIII, the Church of England differed less from the Catholic Church than other Protestant churches did.

It was after Henry VIII's death in 1547, during the reign of his young son by Jane Seymour, Edward VI, that the Protestant Reformation fully came to England. Church services were conducted in English, and church decorations were simplified.

Subsequently, after Edward's death in 1553, his half-sister Mary, daughter of Henry VIII and Catherine of Aragon, became queen. A devout Catholic, she tried to return Catholicism to England, killing many Protestants toward that end.

After "Bloody Mary" died in 1558, Elizabeth, the daughter of Henry VIII and Anne Boleyn, became queen. Elizabeth I ruled ably for nearly half a century during the period when England began to establish itself in the New World. She supported a moderate form of Protestantism and, although some persecution of

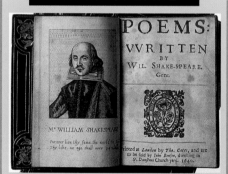

THE GENIUS OF SHAKESPEARE

This book, issued in 1640 and attributed to the actor and playwright William Shakespeare, contained poems not written by him. In the flush of art and literature during the Elizabethan era, his work was the most memorable—and sometimes imitated. Although the plots of many of his plays were borrowed from history or from dramas already performed, the Bard's genius lay in his understanding of human nature, masterful use of English, and character development.

Despite a stormy temperament that meant death or divorce for several wives, Henry VIII *(left)* brought stability to England. The birth of daughter Elizabeth *(below)* disappointed him, but she later ruled well for nearly half a century. Courtiers whispered of plots against Elizabeth by Mary Queen of Scots, shown here *(opposite)* in defeat at the Battle of Langside, after she had attempted, unsuccessfully, to regain her Scottish throne.

Catholics occurred under her reign, she laid the basis for religious tolerance in England. She allowed Catholics to hold their beliefs as long as they were loyal to the Crown.

During Elizabeth's reign, England became a trading nation. Earlier in the 1500s English mariners had been active in the Americas, fishing for cod off Newfoundland, trading with Spanish America, and pirating Spanish ships laden with treasure.

After the defeat of the Spanish

1591 Mercenaries of Spain and Portugal destroy the Songhay Empire in West Africa.

1598 The Edict of Nantes ends civil wars in France.

1600 During the Spanish Inquisition, Giordano Bruno is burned at the stake for saying that the earth revolves around the sun.

ca 1600 Abbas I reigns in Persia; introduces reforms and expands territory.

1614 Native North American princess Pocahontas marries English settler John Rolfe.

Armada in 1588, a stronger, more confident England began thinking of colonizing in the New World.

In 1585 the British landed on Roanoke Island and called the place Virginia, after Elizabeth, the virgin queen who never married. The community failed, as did a second attempt two years later.

Not until 1607 did an English colony succeed in the New World when a group led by Captain John Smith at Jamestown survived disease, hunger, and attacks by Native Americans. Five years later John Rolfe introduced tobacco as a money crop, and the colony prospered.

The first successful English settlement motivated by something other than commercial profit was named Plymouth, in today's Massachusetts. There 102 Puritans seeking religious freedom landed in November of 1620. Native Americans helped them learn to live in the wilderness, although 54 died the first winter. The following November the survivors rejoiced with a feast of thanksgiving.

More English arrived, and colonies began to spread out along the coastline. Meanwhile, England had become active in Asian trade as well. A group of London merchants late in the 16th century formed an

East India Company, and Queen Elizabeth I gave it exclusive rights to trade in the East Indies.

Clashes with Dutch businessmen reached a peak in 1623 when rivals executed ten English traders for trading in the Moluccas. The English East India Company turned to India instead for trade. The anglicizing of the Indian subcontinent over the next three centuries dates from the charter that Elizabeth had given the group of London merchants in 1600.

In many ways, England defined itself during Elizabeth's reign. The nation's defeat of Spain's Armada, its presence in the New World, its

Dutch establish virtual monopoly of spice trade in Indonesian islands.
1619-1624

1621
Charter for Nova Scotia is granted.

1623-1638
The Dutch seize 500 Portuguese and Spanish vessels off the Americas.

1627-28
Catholics besiege Huguenots in La Rochelle on western coast of France.

1630
Dutch colonists invade Brazil.

1634
Flemish painter Rubens paints the "Adoration of the Magi."

growing prosperity, its partial resolution of religious issues—all made the English people proud nationalists.

Art, music, and literature flourished, with many works of art dedicated to Elizabeth.

Textile and iron industries grew, and the queen passed Poor Laws to help those who could not find employment. "Good Queen Bess" was loved by her people and respected by the nobles for her intellect and her indefatigability.

There appeared to be one rival to her crown, and Elizabeth was slow to acknowledge it. Like Elizabeth, Mary Stuart in Scotland had descended from England's Henry VII. Born in 1542, she was named Queen of the Scots as a baby but grew up in France while her mother ruled in her place. When "Bloody Mary" Tudor in England died, the French King Henry II suggested that Queen Elizabeth I was illegitimate and that Mary Stuart, Queen of Scots, was therefore the rightful queen of England. Mary showed no interest in assuming the English throne, but the possibility of future claims by her might have bothered Elizabeth and those around her.

At the death of Mary's French husband Francis II, briefly the king of France, the lovely young woman returned to Scotland in 1561 and served as queen for six years. After a series of castle intrigues, she was forced to abdicate in 1567. She fled to England where she was detained by Elizabeth who was probably convinced by advisors that Mary might

seek the English throne. For 18 years Elizabeth deliberated on what to do with her potential rival. Pressured to approve the execution of Mary, the queen finally had her beheaded.

Ascension of James I

With Elizabeth's death in 1603 the 118-year reign of the Tudor family ended. Ironically, although Mary Stuart had been executed because of the presumed threat of her ascendancy, her only son, James, was the next in line for the throne. He was, of course, a Scot, a fact that did not sit well with the English, who had been battling their northern neighbors for centuries. During James's remaining lifetime the two separate countries shared the same king.

The ascension of James I threw religion in England into confusion again. Mary Tudor had been a Catholic and a killer of Protestants. Elizabeth, a moderate supporter of the Church of England, had executed a number of Catholics on charges of treason and had silenced the Puritans. James was a Scottish Calvinist, although a bit of a backslider. The Puritans hoped that he, with his strict Protestant upbringing, might bring changes in the Church of England, which they considered too Catholic. The Catholics, knowing that his mother had shared their faith, hoped that he might regard them more kindly. The Episcopalians prayed that he would let matters remain as Elizabeth had left them.

James listened to the Puritans but changed nothing. He banished Catholic priests and fined Catholics who did not attend Church of England services. Disappointed, a group of Catholics, including a war veteran named Guy Fawkes, plotted to blow up James and the Parliament while they were in session at Westminster. Word got out, and Fawkes was found in Westminster's cellar and later executed along with the other conspirators. On Guy Fawkes Day, November 5, England still celebrates the plot-foiling with bonfires and fireworks.

Less war-prone than many monarchs, James ended a conflict with Spain, bringing England a 20-year period of peace. A believer in the divine right of kings to do what they pleased, he butted heads with an English parliament that wanted more say in managing the nation. The tension would come to a head when his son Charles succeeded him in 1625. ■

THE KING JAMES BIBLE

The most lasting contribution of James I to the world was his authorization of a new version of the Bible, including the Christian New Testament. The many previous versions differed in text and interpretation and were often riddled with errors. About 50 scholars and clergy were asked to render a uniform version that everyone could accept. They spent three years on research and two more on writing. The resulting King James Version was widely accepted, and no new large-scale revision was done in English until the 20th century.

1637 Japanese shogun Iemitsu bans the Christian religion and expels all missionaries and most traders from his country.

1639 The first American university at Cambridge, Massachusetts, is named after clergyman John Harvard.

1643 Italian physicist Evangelista Torricelli invents the barometer. France establishes a parcel post service.

1648 Spain officially acknowledges an independent Netherlands.

1650 Tea is first served in England.

The English Civil War

From his father, James, the new king, Charles I, inherited not only the English crown in 1625 but also the belief that its word was supreme. The Parliament disagreed.

Unlike his pacifistic father, Charles was eager to go to war with Spain. As had been the custom, Parliament granted the king money for the war, but placed limits on his personal income. This action angered Charles, who became even angrier when an attack on Spain went badly and Parliament blamed the expedition's leader, Charles's good friend, George Villiers, the Duke of Buckingham. When Parliament impeached Buckingham, Charles dissolved Parliament.

But the king could not wage war without money authorized by the Houses of Lords and Commons, and Charles now felt compelled to rescue the French Huguenots, who were besieged by Cardinal Richelieu's Catholic forces. Charles tried to force the wealthiest men of England to lend him money. When several refused, he had them thrown into prison.

Still without sufficient money, he recalled the Parliament. Being in session gave that body the opportunity to debate the king's action against the imprisoned nobles. They gave Charles the money he needed for war but asked that, in return, he agree to a Petition of Right, in which no English subject could be imprisoned without trial. Charles agreed, but there was still no peace.

When Parliament denied him

Earliest Parliaments were called to Westminster to advise the king, as shown in this painting of a 13th-century council.

money other than that approved for war, Charles had his officers collect it anyway. The Parliament unanimously passed a list of grievances against the king; the king, in turn, dissolved the Parliament again and began 11 years of personal rule.

In many ways it was a time of peace and contentment. Charles avoided foreign wars and raised money through customs and through the taxes that he imposed upon his subjects. The wealthy made money but had little say in national affairs.

For years England virtually ignored its many settlers in North America and the Caribbean, caught up as it was in the rift between Parliament and king.

Religion finally forced the eruption

of a civil war. Scotland rebelled against the new Church of England prayer book, which seemed too Catholic, and troops advanced against England.

Charles had to ask for money to fight the Scots; but when he recalled Parliament, that long-idle body made demands on him. In answer, Charles marched to the House of Commons on January 4, 1642, with several hundred swordsmen and demanded the House surrender five of his principal opponents. Forewarned, they had already gone into hiding. His act so outraged citizens that Charles had to flee the city. Armies rallied to both sides, Royalists and Parliamentarians, and the war was on.

The early conflict was indecisive. Then Oliver Cromwell, a member of Parliament, took over the recruitment and training of troops, and the tide turned. Charles surrendered in 1645 and was imprisoned on the Isle of Wight. In 1649 he was tried for treason and executed, maintaining his dignity right to the fall of the ax. England was governed by Parliament as a republic for a decade with Oliver Cromwell as Lord Protector.

Effective as Cromwell had been in leading the army, as ruler he had constant trouble with the Houses. Anarchy followed his death in 1658.

England wanted a king again. Remembering Charles's royal deportment at his execution made it easy to welcome his son back from exile in 1660 and install him on the throne as King Charles II. ■

French King Louis XIV begins construction of his palace at Versailles. Act for the Settlement and Act of Explanation are passed in Ireland; Cornwellians are forced to give up usurped land. — 1662

In Italy, Antonio Stradivari starts to make violins. — 1666

In India, Emperor Aurangzeb bans the Hindu religion and starts to persecute Hindus. — 1669

In protest against alleged unorthodoxy of the Russian church 20,000 persons burn themselves. — 1675-1691

In Denmark, astronomer Ole Romer calculates the speed of light. — 1676

Rise of Asante Kingdom in West Africa. — 1680s

Troubled Times in Merry England

Charles II did not wish to challenge Parliament and meet the fate of his father. And Parliament did not plan to give up the powers it had gained through the civil war.

England became a constitutional

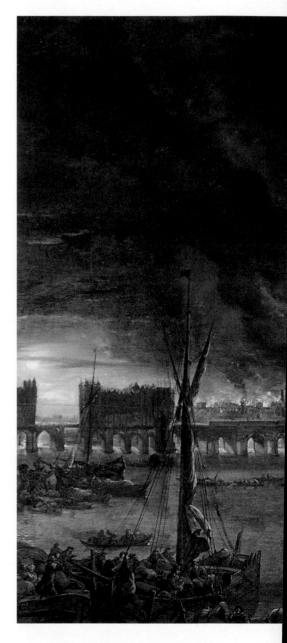

monarchy, with the king's powers limited by laws passed during the conflict with Charles I.

The witty and charming Charles II lived a life of indulgence, openly consorting with mistresses, showing interest in art, science, and entertainment. His subjects, tired of Puritanism, followed his lead and enjoyed dancing, sports, and theater.

Despite the gaiety, a series of calamities lay ahead. In 1665 the bubonic plague struck London in the worst outbreak since the notorious

Black Death in Europe three centuries earlier. Perhaps a fifth of London's population, some 60,000 people, died of the disease carried by fleas from infected rats. The plague was ended by another disaster, the Great

Fire that started at London Bridge and burned out the heart of London. The fire also destroyed the diseased rats.

Competition in worldwide trade continued to spark conflicts with Holland, and major sea battles were fought in the North Atlantic, off the coast of Africa, and in the English Channel. Barely had the ashes of the Great Fire cooled than a Dutch fleet sailed up the Thames to Chatham harbor, burned four British ships, and towed away a fifth.

Charles signed a treaty with Louis

XIV of France to join forces against the Dutch. A closet Catholic, he secretly took money from Louis with the agreement that he would restore Catholicism to England.

He never did, but when his brother James succeeded him as king, James, himself a practicing Catholic, began appointing Catholics to high

● 1683 Formosa (Taiwan) becomes Chinese territory. In North America, first German colonists settle in Pennsylvania.

● 1687 In Greece, Venetians bombard Athens and badly damage the Parthenon.

● 1689 James II is acknowledged as king by an Irish Parliament in Dublin.

● 1694 The French Academy publishes the first French dictionary.

● 1697 In China, the Manchus conquer western Mongolia.

positions. Appalled, Parliament invited an invasion by the Dutch Protestant leader, William of Orange, James's nephew, who was married to James's daughter, Mary.

King James fled as William of Orange advanced toward London. William and his cousin-wife became the king and queen of England. ■

England's bloody civil war diminished the powers of the king and cost many lives, but even more lives were lost to pestilence and fire. Thousands in London died of bubonic plague in 1665, a disaster remembered in a gruesome woodcut of the period *(opposite)*. The plague ended only when a great fire *(above)* burned out the core of the city and destroyed the slums where plague had flourished. Catholics and Protestants still wrangled for high posts, the latter rejoicing when Dutch Protestant William and his English wife, Mary, ascended the throne *(right)*.

1415 Jan Huss is burned as a heretic.

1449-1473 Rule of shogun Ashikaga Yoshimasa in Japan.

1455 Huge temple built to Aztec war god Huitzilopochtli in Tenochtitlán.

1469 The marriage of Ferdinand of Aragon and Isabella of Castile leads to the unification of Spain.

1482 Postal system organized in England with relays of fresh horses every 20 miles.

1506 In Spain, Columbus dies in poverty, still convinced that the lands he has visited are part of Asia.

The Holy Roman Empire

During this period of history, it would be impossible not to take into account the influence of the powerful Habsburg family.

Although Charlemagne had been crowned Holy Roman emperor by the pope in A.D. 800, the empire had broken up shortly after his death, and France and Germany had become separate countries.

More than a century later King Otto I of Germany wanted to revive the old Roman Empire, and in 962 he had the pope crown him Emperor Augustus. By conquering Bohemia,

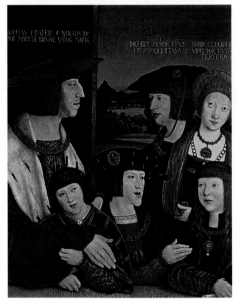

Despite the collapse of the Roman Empire in the fifth century, the concept of a Holy Roman emperor continued almost until modern times. One family, the Habsburgs, held the title almost exclusively for some 500 years through careful marriages and alliances. To further his claim,

Emperor Maximillian I, here with members of his family (above), wed his son Philip to the daughter of the Spanish king and queen. Their son Charles V (right) thus inherited much of Europe, but rule so wearied him that he retired to a monastery.

Austria, and northern Italy, he controlled a large area that was called the Holy Roman Empire. The area was made up of many small duchies, counties, and districts governing themselves, but owing allegiance to the emperor. The popes saw this empire as a means of helping them rule over Christendom.

In fact, however, the popes and the Holy Roman emperors were often at odds, each struggling for power over the other. In the middle of the 11th century, the papacy allied itself with various Italian towns and with the Normans to resist invasions from angry emperors.

In the meantime, the monarchies of France and England were growing more powerful and independent. The popes were forced to negotiate with them to counter the power of the

emperors in Germany. Eventually the Holy Roman emperor was selected by a group of seven electors within the emperor's holdings and was no longer crowned by the pope.

In 1273 the emperor chosen was Rudolf, a member of the powerful Habsburg family that had many land holdings. A Habsburg would hold the title of emperor almost continuously for the next 500 years, passing it down through marriages of expediency and subsequent inheritances.

In the late 15th century, for example, Emperor Maximilian I, a Habsburg, married his son Philip of Burgundy to Joanna, daughter of Ferdinand and Isabella of Spain.

1516   **Juan Diaz de Solis** discovers Plata River estuary, but is killed and eaten on landing by Indians.

1519-21   **Hernán Cortés,** Spanish soldier-explorer, brings down the Aztec Empire in Mexico.

1520   **Ferdinand Magellan,** Portuguese in Spanish employ, rounds the tip of South America through the straits that now bear this name.

1526   **Babur** defeats the sultan of Dehli at the battle of Panipat and becomes first Mogul Emperor of India.

1540   **Hernando de Soto** discovers the Mississippi River.

1567   **Mary Queen of Scots** forced to abdicate because of her Catholicism.

They had a son named Charles, and when Philip died Charles inherited Burgundy and the Netherlands. In 1516 Ferdinand died and left Charles Spain and Naples. Three years later Maximilian I died, and Charles V was then Holy Roman emperor of Spain, Austria, Germany, the Netherlands, and Italy.

Rule of such an empire exhausted him, particularly as he was constantly at war, and when Charles V retired in 1556 his empire was divided among other Habsburgs. His son Philip II took over Spain and the Netherlands, and his

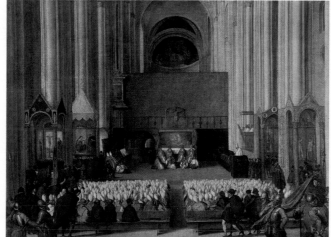

Countering Muslim control of the Mediterranean, a Christian coalition crushed the Ottoman Turks in a naval battle at Lepanto *(top)* in 1571. Challenges to Catholic doctrine led to reforms in the Council of Trent *(above),* which met three times in 18 years.

brother Ferdinand ruled Germany and also Austria.

Into this emerging Europe—with the Holy Roman Empire generally opposed by England and France—came the religious differences of the Reformation to complicate alliances further. Religion was extremely important in early modern Europe. It played a critical part in such events of the people's lives as baptism, marriage, and burial, and it was their hope for salvation and an afterlife.

For centuries the church with its leadership in Rome had been the center of Christianity. When the Muslims

ca 1568-1600 ● Period of National Unification in Japan begins when feudal lord, Oda Nobunaga, captures capital of Kyoto.

1577-1640 ● Life of Flemish painter, Peter Paul Rubens.

ca 1600 ● Women begin to take acting parts on the English stage.

1608 ● Polish soldiers occupy Moscow and set up a puppet government.

1662 ● Over 1,500 Quakers imprisoned in England for refusal to conform to Church of England's demands.

1672-1681 ● War between Russia and Turkey.

Bohemians in Prague throw Catholic officials out a window to protest the razing of Protestant churches.

came knocking on Eastern Europe's door and threatened to control trade in the Mediterranean, the Christians fought them back in Hungary, and the pope called together a league of Christian nations to battle Muslim ships in the Battle of Lepanto just off the coast of Greece.

But it was the spread of Protestantism during the Reformation that caused the bloodiest clashes, as Europe was torn apart by disagreements. The western half of the continent became a patchwork of Catholics, Calvinists, Lutherans, Anabaptists, and many other shades of Protestantism. Catholic leaders, recognizing that excesses had contributed to the rise of the Protestant movement, tried to correct their mistakes in a Council of Trent on the

border between Italy and Germany. Some of the worst abuses, such as the selling of indulgences, were banned. The Council also urged better education for priests, resulting in church colleges known as seminaries. The counter-reforms slowed and sometimes reversed the rush to Protestantism. But it was not enough to stop the the Thirty Years' War between Catholics and Protestants that lasted from 1618 to 1648.

The Catholics, initially led by the Holy Roman emperor Ferdinand II of Germany, prevailed at first, defeating Protestant Bohemia and recovering lands held by Protestants in Germany.

With aid from the excellent army of King Gustavus Adolphus of Sweden, the Protestants began winning important victories. Then the war

became more a contest of great powers than religions, with Spain intervening on the part of the Catholics and Catholic France helping the Protestants because of a long-standing rivalry with the Habsburgs. Peace finally came with the Treaty of Westphalia, by which Catholics and Protestants recognized the right of the others to exist in their own states.

The Thirty Years' War diminished the office of Holy Roman emperor, and the realm was fragmented into some 300 different entities. Germany, center of the empire, had lost nearly a third of its people. Only Austria remained a major force, due to Habsburg possessions there.

When in 1806 Napoleon forced the abdication of Francis II of Austria, the use of the title "Holy Roman emperor," begun a thousand years earlier, finally came to an end. ■

GUSTAVUS ADOLPHUS

King Gustavus Adolphus, the Swedish king who interceded in the Thirty Years' War on behalf of the Protestants, was not only a soldier but also a scholar who had mastered German, Dutch, French, Italian, and Latin. He built his military force of 40,000 men into a modern army of small tactical units, led by professionals and supported by concentrations of light, mobile artillery. Gunners, cavalry, and infantry cooperated in a wedge-shape formation that had great success against the massed squares of pikemen and musketeers more common in his day. No behind-the-lines general, Gustavus Adolphus was killed leading a charge in a victory at Lützen, Germany.

1529 — Ottoman Turks reach the gates of Vienna.

1543 — In Poland, astronomer and priest, Nicolas Copernicus, states that the earth moves around the sun.

1556-1598 — Reign of Philip II of Spain.

1556-1605 — Reign of Akbar, Mogul Emperor.

1576 — Spanish troops in the Netherlands seize and sack Antwerp.

1587 — Hideyoshi bans Christian missionaries from Japan.

The Dutch Grow Rich on Trade

When Columbus sailed to the New World, the Dutch were ruled by a Habsburg, Philip of Burgundy. When Philip died, his son Charles inherited the Netherlands, which at that time included today's Belgium and Luxembourg. The area was known as the Low Countries, because of the low elevation and nearness to the sea. Charles married a Spanish princess, and—when her father died—he became King Charles I of Spain in 1516, which made the Netherlands a Spanish possession.

The Netherlands at that time comprised 17 provinces. High taxes and attempts by Charles and later his son Philip II to centralize the government irritated the Dutch.

The Reformation brought Calvinism to the Low Countries, which met with the disapproval of Catholic Spain. Tensions erupted into riots, and Spain's vicious retribution

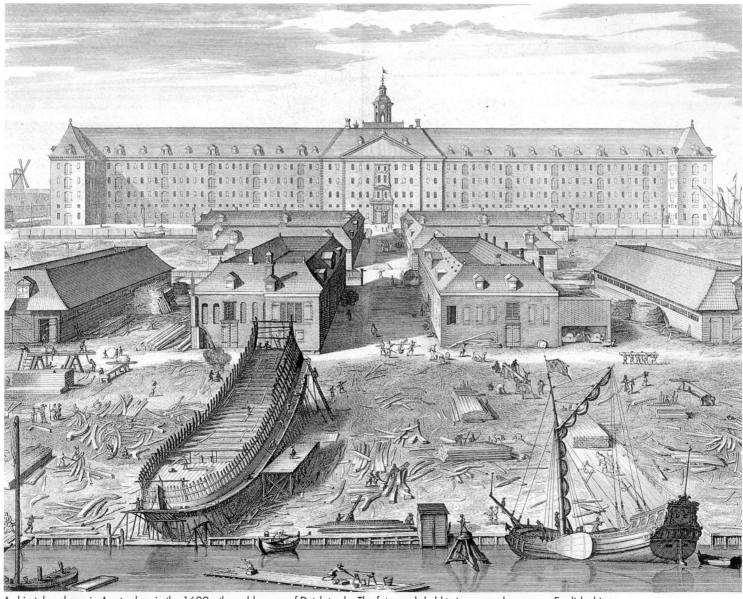

A ship takes shape in Amsterdam in the 1600s, the golden age of Dutch trade. The fat vessels held twice as much cargo as English ships.

● Pompeii is rediscovered.

1592

● Golden age of
Elizabethan literature
1594 begins.

● In England, the East
India Company is set up
1600 to trade with India.

● Russian national assem-
bly meets and selects a
1613 new tsar—Michael
Romanov—the 16-year-
old grand-nephew of
Ivan the Terrible. The
Romanovs would rule
Russia until 1917.

● Life of Jean-Baptiste
Poquelin de Molière,
1622-1673 dramatist.

● First settlers
in Maryland.
1631

resulted in civil war. In 1579 ten Catholic provinces in the south made peace with Spain, but seven northern Protestant provinces banded together in the Union of Utrecht and declared themselves independent. A Twelve Year Truce was signed in 1609, but fighting resumed.

Long before Spain officially acknowledged an independent Netherlands in 1648, the young Dutch nation with few natural resources set its sights on world trade. By 1679 its fleet of ships was larger than those of Spain, Portugal, France, England, Scotland, and Germany combined. The Dutch East India Company was a shadow government, with power to make war and peace, coin money, and establish

Trade fired imagina-
tions among seagoing
nations as they jock-
eyed for rights to com-
merce. Germanic towns
formed the Hanseatic
League to monopolize
markets along the Baltic
and the North Seas.
Houses of rich Hansard
merchants *(below)*, still
in use today, exagger-
ated their size with
false fronts. Success of
the Dutch fired artistic
talent as well. Jan
Vermeer painted scenes
of domestic life such as
"The Lacemaker"
(above) and "The
Painter and His Model
as Klio" *(opposite)*.

colonies. Its port in Batavia, Java—today's Jakarta—was its trade center with China, Japan, India, and Persia. New Amsterdam in America became its clearinghouse for trade between the New World and the Old. The Dutch government grew wealthy from taxes on international trade.

Dutch success stirred resentments among other European nations. Late in the 1600s, the Netherlands fought wars with England over rights to trade. The English took over New Amsterdam, today's New York City. In the Four Days' War at the mouth of the Thames in 1667, the Dutch destroyed 25 English ships, although both sides withdrew after the battle.

By the 1700s fighting had exhausted the Dutch economy, and the growing English and French colonies had restricted access to its profitable markets. The Dutch contin-ued as traders, but their dominance in world markets had ended. ■

NEW AMSTERDAM

Dutch New Amsterdam, founded in 1625, at the mouth of the Hudson River, became the trad-ing center of America. From Europe came glass, cloth, paper, and other finished products. Sugar, rum, and tobacco sailed up from the Caribbean, and furs came from the north. England forbade its ships to trade in the port, but colonial vessels from Virginia and Massachusetts sneaked up the coast to buy duty-free European goods. The English renamed the settlement New York when they took it over in 1664.

1645 The Dalai Lama, religious ruler of Tibet, founds a monastery in Lhasa.

1657 First stockings and fountain pens are made in Paris.

1664 The English seize New Amsterdam in North America from the Dutch and rename it New York.

1665 Bubonic plague strikes London; some 68,000 die from the disease, which is carried by fleas from infected rats.

1666 Great Fire of London.

1679 Father Hennepin reaches Niagara Falls in Canada.

1533 Henry VIII marries Anne Boleyn and is excommunicated by the pope.

Pizarro conquers Peru.

1534 Luther completes his translation of the Bible.

1545-63 Roman Catholic Council of Trent meets in Italy to begin Counterreformation.

1547 French, rather than Latin, becomes the official language of France.

Moguls Conquer India

At the time Europeans were discovering new routes to India, the subcontinent itself was undergoing considerable change. Three hundred years had passed since Genghis Khan had marched across Asia with his fierce Mongol horsemen.

By the mid-1300s the Mongol Empire had broken into numerous domains, reviving briefly before the end of the century when the merciless Timur (the Lame) tried to restore Mongol power. His devastating sack of Delhi in India had brought chaos and disunity to the subcontinent.

Little more than a century later, a descendant of both Timur (the Lame) and Genghis Khan decided to carve out a kingdom in northern India. From out of Kabul in Afghanistan in 1523 came Babur, a Mogul, the name used in India to describe those descended from Turks and Mongols. His warriors on swift horses outmaneuvered the elephants of Indian troops, and he overthrew the Turkish sultanate at Delhi and controlled the central part of northern India.

Despite his conquests, Babur was never happy in India, and his Mogul Empire was never consolidated. In his memoirs he wrote: "Hindustan is a country of few charms. Its people have no good looks; of social intercourse, paying and receiving visits, there is none; of manners none....There are no good horses, no good dogs, no grapes, muskmelons or first-rate fruits, no ice or cold

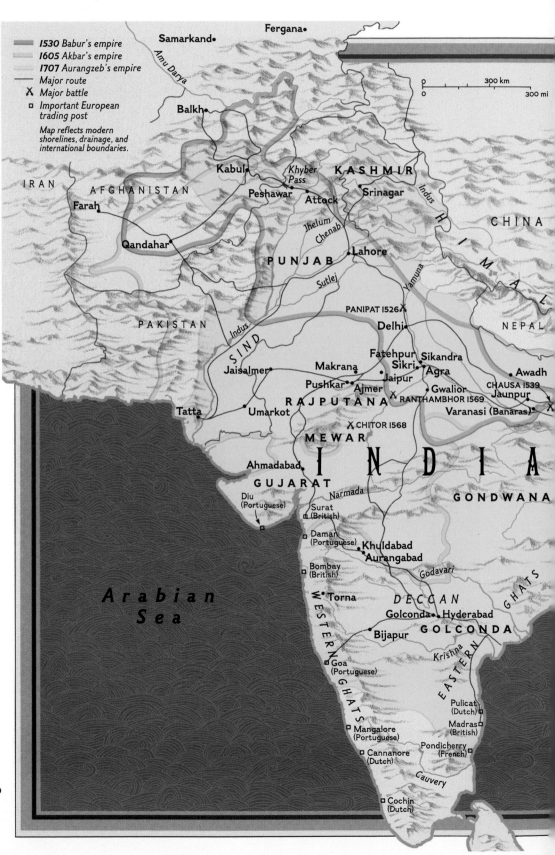

1530 Babur's empire
1605 Akbar's empire
1707 Aurangzeb's empire
— Major route
X Major battle
□ Important European trading post

Map reflects modern shorelines, drainage, and international boundaries.

First wheat crop in Chile.

1553

First grapes produced in Chile.

1555

France's King Henry II dies of injuries received in a tournament celebrating the end of a long war with Spain.

1559

Madrid made capital of Spain.

1560

1560s-1590s During the French Wars of Religion, the Protestant minority is in conflict with Catholic majority.

Francis II of France dies.

1561

THE MOGUL EMPIRE

The Moguls amassed a realm of as many as 150 million subjects. Babur hailed from Central Asia, where, unable to pluck the plum of Samarkand, he turned south and from Afghanistan took northern India. His heir, Humayun, lost most footholds but regained a base for his son Akbar, who ruled from Bengal to Persia. Painting attained great heights under his successor Jahangir and architecture under Shah Jahan. But forces from the south took their toll on the last Great Mogul, Aurangzeb, who saw inexorable dissolution set in.

Chronology

Color bars indicate reigns of Babur, Akbar, and Aurangzeb.

BABUR 1483-1530

1483 **Babur** *is born in Fergana.*
1526 **Babur** *defeats Ibrahim, Sultan of Delhi, at Panipat.*
1530 Death of **Babur,** *accession of son Humayun.*

HUMAYUN 1508-1556

1540 Humayun defeated by Afghan leader Sher Shah, who rules empire.
1555 Humayun retakes Delhi.
1556 Humayun dies; son **Akbar** *enthroned.*

AKBAR 1542-1605

1562 **Akbar,** *a freethinking Muslim, marries a princess of the powerful Hindu province of Rajputana.*
1564 **Akbar** *abolishes jizya, the tax on non-Muslims.*
1605 Death of **Akbar,** *succession of son Jahangir.*

JAHANGIR 1569-1627

1617 Jahangir's son Khurram pacifies rebellious Deccan region and receives title of Shah Jahan.
1627 Jahangir dies; Shah Jahan proclaimed emperor and executes five rivals.
1631 Queen Mumtaz Mahal dies in childbirth; the following year work begins on her tomb, the Taj Mahal.
1657 Rumors of Shah Jahan's imminent death trigger war among four sons. The victor, **Aurangzeb,** *is crowned in* **1658** *and confines his father to the palace.*

SHAH JAHAN 1592-1666

1666 Death of Shah Jahan.
1679 The jizya reimposed.
1681 **Aurangzeb** *departs for the Deccan, remains 26 years.*
1707 **Aurangzeb** *dies.*
1739 Persians massacre the people of Delhi and carry off Peacock Throne.
1862 Death of last of 17 succeeding Mogul rulers, Bahadur Shah II.

AURANGZEB 1618-1707

PORTRAITS ARE DETAILS FROM MINIATURES.

water, no good bread or cooked food in the bazaars, no hot baths, no colleges, no candles, torches, or candlesticks." The sour attitude may have rubbed off on his son Humayun, who became an opium addict and lost the empire to Sher Shah, an Afghan chief. Humayun regained Delhi in 1555. But it was his son, Babur's grandson, Akbar, who pushed back its boundaries. Akbar created a lasting Mogul dynasty that controlled more than half of India and lasted nearly two centuries.

Akbar began by organizing the tattered country into regular provinces, districts, and villages, each with sound administration. He revised taxation, which had been a special burden on the large peasant population. His predecessor, Sher Shah, had demanded a third of every peasant's crop, with the amount determined before seed time, not after harvest. Akbar's system allowed for varying yields and changes in market prices, more fair to the farmer and more profitable in both income and good feeling toward the state. His successful reign had drawn many capable office-seekers from Asia but Akbar also made use of Hindus as administrators, army commanders, and counselors.

Islam had come to India periodically for hundreds of years, and clashes were frequent between the monotheistic Muslims and the polytheistic Hindus.

The philosophical Akbar invited scholars of many faiths to his court

197

and appointed Hindus to high government posts. He married a Hindu princess and allowed his subjects to worship as they pleased.

Unlike his grandfather, Akbar immersed himself in the culture of the conquered land, establishing libraries and schools and encouraging art, music, and literature. The Mogul school of miniature painting became widely known.

People responded to Akbar's benevolent rule. A popular saying was, "The ruler of Delhi is the same as the lord of the universe." Typically, his benevolence did not extend to occasional uprisings, which he fiercely put down, keeping tight control of his empire. His rulership was a time of good government for India. ■

Descended from Mongol warriors such as Timur (the Lame) and Genghis Khan, Babur the Mogul conquered India. Artists recorded his love of contests at a feast that included wrestling between men and beasts *(left)*.

His grandson Akbar so loved horses that a statue said to be of his favorite was placed near his tomb *(above)*. As fair as he was fierce, Akbar tolerated Hinduism and built schools and libraries.

English colony of
Virginia is founded at
1607 Jamestown. Dutch
destroy a Spanish fleet
off Gibraltar.

1608 Samuel de Champlain
founds Quebec.

Etienne Brulé discovers
Lake Huron, first of the
1610 Great Lakes to be visited by a European.

Rapid growth of towns
1611 in Japan.

Thirty Years' War
between Catholic and
1618-1648 Protestant forces.

In London, William
Harvey discovers how
1619 the blood circulates.

Mogul Success and Decline

Mogul occupation brought a melting pot of Arab and Persian thought to India. Muslim architecture mixed with Indian to produce marble buildings with domes, arches, elaborate decoration, and minarets.

A new language, Urdu, emerged that is still spoken in Pakistan and parts of northwest India. It is based

A poem in stone, the Taj Mahal was built by Mogul emperor Shah Jahan in memory of his favorite wife, who died bearing his 14th child.

A painting of the leader at the age of 25 shows him holding a turban jewel *(left)*.

on Hindu grammar, includes many Persian and Arabic words, and is written in Arabic script.

Although most Indians remained Hindu, the upper classes rubbed shoulders with their conquerors and picked up new ways. The Muslim Moguls were also influenced by the Hindus. In violation of Islamic law

THE TAJ MAHAL

The Taj Mahal in Agra, India, was built by Mogul emperor Shah Jahan as a tomb for his beloved wife Mumtäz Mahal, who died in childbirth. Constructed of marble inlaid with precious and semi-precious stones, it took 22 years to complete and is considered one of the loveliest buildings in the world. When Shah Jahan died in 1658 in the prison where he had been placed by his son, he was buried next to his wife.

prescribing strict diet and modest dress, they began to wear elaborate, bejeweled clothing and to indulge in alcoholic beverages.

The peace and prosperity during Akbar's reign drew Europeans who followed Vasco da Gama's route around Africa, seeking lucrative trade in Indian goods. With Akbar's death in 1605 his Mogul inheritors continued to press for territorial expansion, but often did not govern with his customary efficiency. Military and civil service declined under the 22-year rule of Jahangir, who was asthmatic and a heavy drinker.

1621 — Etienne Brulé explores Lake Superior.

1640 — John Eliot's *Bay Psalm Book* is North America's first printed book.

1653 — A hundred colonists arrive in Montreal, increasing the French Canadian population from 600 to 700.

1656 — Jews readmitted to England.

1663 — In Canada, French colonies join together as Province of New France with their capital at Quebec.

1666 — Britain's Sir Isaac Newton devises calculus and begins to formulate laws of gravity.

Shah Jahan restored state discipline, but his attempts at expansion raised taxes on the peasantry, causing many to leave the land. Although best known as the creator of the Taj Mahal, he also rebuilt Delhi as the capital of his empire. Construction there included the Pearl Mosque, where in a delicately built hall of private audience he inscribed: "If there be paradise on earth, it is this, it is this, it is this."

Paradise apparently did not extend to familial relations. When Shah Jahan fell so ill in 1657 that he could not govern, his eldest of four sons took over as ruler; the other three went against him. The victor, Aurangzeb, killed his brothers and imprisoned his father.

Aurangzeb pushed the Mogul frontiers to their greatest extent, but the effort drained the treasury. Unlike Akbar, with his policy of religious tolerance, Aurangzeb destroyed Hindu schools and temples, dismissed Hindu

ORIGIN OF THE SIKHS

The Sikhs, formed in 1519, combined the Islamic belief in one god with Hindu belief in reincarnation, and rejected India's caste system. Sikh men wind their long hair atop their heads and fasten it with a comb, then cover it with a turban. They also wear a steel bracelet and carry a sword, often today a tiny facsimile inset in the comb. What began as a group of religious puritans became a powerful military group that kept the British out of the Punjab region of India until 1849.

● **Great Schism in Russian Church.**
1666

● **Cholera epidemic in China.**
1669

● **Sir Isaac Newton invents the reflecting telescope.**
1668

● **In Germany the League of Augsburg is formed against France.**
1686

● **The first Huguenots settle on the Cape of Good Hope.**
1687

● **William Dampier leads an English expedition along Australia's north-west coast.**
1699

clerks, and reinstated the taxes on non-Muslims. Rebellions began, and he found himself battling not only former allies such as the Rajputans but also the Sikhs and a rising Hindu power called the Marathas.

After the death of Aurangzeb and the shrinking of the Mogul Empire, the Marathas—hill people from western India—appeared ready to inherit the remainder of it. But they were bloodied by Afghans who, sensing opportunity, swept down from the north and then withdrew.

By the beginning of the 1700s the British, French, Portuguese, Danish, and Dutch had set up trading posts along the coast of India and often battled each other for supremacy.

The British, who had concentrated on India after being driven from the Spice Islands by the Dutch, defeated the French, thereby ending France's Indian ambitions.

The British continued battling the Marathas and a southern group called the Mysores well into the 18th century, the Mogul Empire by then reduced to a small kingdom.

In 1803 the Mogul emperor accepted British protection, and in 1805 England's supremacy in India was a reality. ■

Under Akbar, the Moguls reigned over 150 million people in lands that are now India, Pakistan, and Afghanistan. Akbar tolerated Hinduism and ruled a kingdom more wealthy than that of England's Queen Elizabeth I, his contemporary. Miniature painting flourished under his son Jahangir, here shown with courtiers *(left)*. Strict Muslim policies of the emperor Aurangzeb stirred rebellion among Hindus in mountaintop forts such as Torna *(opposite)*.

● Church council orders Bohemian reformer Jan Hus burned at the stake.
1415

● France, with Scots' support, is at war with England.
1423-29

● Azores Islands discovered by the Portuguese.
1431

● Reign of Inca ruler Pachacuti.
1438-71

● The Inca build great fortress at Cuzco.
1440s

Ottoman Turks Carve a Huge Empire

Of the numerous groups of Turkish nomads to emerge from the Central Asian steppes, none was more successful or durable than the Ottoman Turks. They came through Iran and Iraq, picking up the Islamic religion on the way, and settled in Asia Minor in the late 11th century. Not until the 13th century did they become known as the Ottomans, after the tribal leader, Osman I.

Like the Habsburgs, theirs was a dynastic empire passed from father to son, usually with no quarrels about succession. By early Ottoman custom, whoever was first named sultan became the ruler, and his brothers were strangled with a silken bowstring to avoid any disputes.

From a small principality in Anatolia, in today's Turkey, the Ottomans gradually expanded under Osman I. Conquest of the city of Bursa in 1326 and the emirate of Karasi in 1345 brought them to the shores of the Mediterranean. Crossing the Dardanelles, they acquired their first foothold in Europe by capturing Gallipoli. By 1393 Bulgaria became part of their growing empire.

Their early advances were helped by the military feats of others. They moved into Anatolia after the Mongols defeated the Seljuk Turks. Ottoman successes in Bulgaria followed the sacking of Constantinople and the weakening of the Byzantine Empire by its fellow Christians, soldiers of the Fourth Crusade.

A setback for the Ottomans

occurred in 1402 when Timur (the Lame), the last of the Mongol conquerors to reach so far west, crushed their army. A number of areas under Ottoman rule regained their independence then, only to lose it again when Mehmed, and later his son Murad II, reasserted power.

In 1453 the Ottomans ended the 1100-year Byzantine Empire by overrunning Constantinople and renaming it Istanbul. The church Hagia Sophia became a mosque, and a forest of minarets grew in the city.

Moving farther into Europe, the conquering Turks occupied Athens in 1456; and over the next 11 years the remainder of the Balkans—Serbia, Bosnia, and Albania—came under Ottoman rule. Wars with the Venetians at the turn of the century

showed that the Ottomans had become a naval power as well.

Sunni Muslims, they carried out wars against Christians in the name of Allah but also turned east against the Shiites of Iran, whom they considered heretical Muslims. Under Sultan Selem the Grim the Ottomans took Syria and Cairo from the Mamluks, former Islamic slaves who had ruled Egypt for more than 250 years.

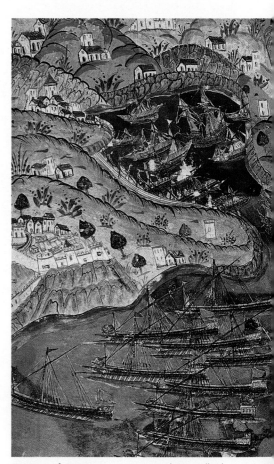

Greatest of Ottoman sultans, Süleyman the Magnificent *(above, left)* held land in three continents and threatened central Europe. His admiral Barbarossa ruled the Mediterra- nean and once allied with the Christian French king to attack Nice *(above)*, held by a vassal of the Holy Roman emperor.

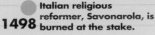

1444 Treaty of Tours between England and France brings peace for two years.

1498 Italian religious reformer, Savonarola, is burned at the stake.

1500 Portuguese explorer Pedro Cabral reaches Brazil.

1507 In Germany, Martin Waldseemüller produces a world map, the first to show South America as separate from Asia and to use the name America after Amerigo Vespucci.

1525 Diego Ribeiro, official mapmaker for Spain, makes first scientific charts covering the Pacific.

1540s Spanish arrive in California.

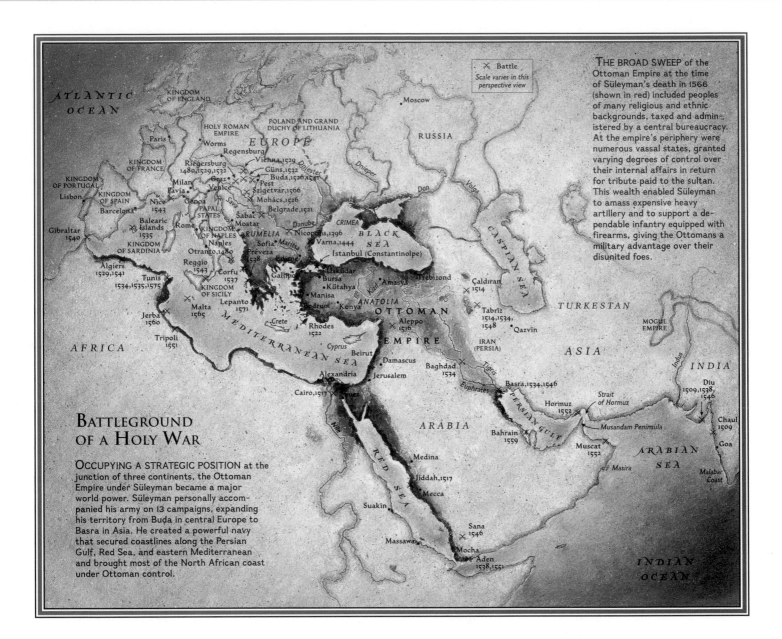

THE BROAD SWEEP of the Ottoman Empire at the time of Süleyman's death in 1566 (shown in red) included peoples of many religious and ethnic backgrounds, taxed and administered by a central bureaucracy. At the empire's periphery were numerous vassal states, granted varying degrees of control over their internal affairs in return for tribute paid to the sultan. This wealth enabled Süleyman to amass expensive heavy artillery and to support a dependable infantry equipped with firearms, giving the Ottomans a military advantage over their disunited foes.

BATTLEGROUND OF A HOLY WAR

OCCUPYING A STRATEGIC POSITION at the junction of three continents, the Ottoman Empire under Süleyman became a major world power. Süleyman personally accompanied his army on 13 campaigns, expanding his territory from Buda in central Europe to Basra in Asia. He created a powerful navy that secured coastlines along the Persian Gulf, Red Sea, and eastern Mediterranean and brought most of the North African coast under Ottoman control.

By the mid-1500s Süleyman I had pushed the empire to its largest extent, so that it stretched along the coast of North Africa to Algiers, north into the center of Hungary, south into today's Yemen, and east to Bahrain. The Ottoman Turks controlled most of the Mediterranean coast and completely ringed the Black Sea.

Turkish warriors from many areas flocked to the Ottoman army for the opportunity to serve Islam and also to participate in conquest.

Firearms were becoming more sophisticated, and the wealth pouring in from conquered areas allowed leaders such as Süleyman to buy heavy artillery and other guns.

At the core of soldier ranks were the elite troops called Janissaries. Often they were formerly Christian youths, taken from conquered villages at an early age. A seven-year training period honed some into ardent Muslims, fanatical fighting machines devoted to the Sultan.

Those more adept at bookwork were steered toward administrative roles. Officials in the Ottoman bureaucracy might be Arab, Greek, Slavic, or Armenian, but all were bound together by the Turkish language and loyalty to the sultan. ■

● Galileo observes
the periodicity of
1581 the pendulum.

● First successful English
colony established
1608 along the Atlantic
seaboard of America at
Jamestown, Virginia.

● **The Japanese**
persecute Christians.
1612-1639

● **Thousands of Huguenots**
die throughout France in
1572 the St. Bartholomew's
Day Massacre.

● Founding of Trinity
College, Dublin.
1591

● Spain agrees to a
nine-year truce in
1609 the Netherlands.

The Downward Spiral of the Ottoman Turks

I n 1565 Süleyman I, known as the Magnificent in Europe and as the Lawgiver in Turkey, failed in an attempt to capture Malta in the Mediterranean. Six years later the Ottoman fleet was beaten in a sea battle at Lepanto, just off the west coast of Greece. The empire quickly recovered, but the defeat at Lepanto marked the end of the Ottomans' westward advances.

By 1600 the empire was fighting on two fronts, Europe and Persia. Although the empire's decline had begun, the Ottomans would be a force in the Middle East for more than another 300 years.

Ottoman culture was geared for conquest, for hauling in booty and training new slaves. Some of the soldiers were paid only by the loot and captives they could gather. If they had no new territory to invade, they grew restless and dissatisfied. Funds were low for quieting them, as inflation had been brought on by silver from the New World.

Trade that the Ottomans had controlled in the Mediterranean shifted to the Americas and to the Far East via sea routes around Africa. As revenues fell and demands increased, the once efficient Turkish bureaucracy became corrupt, its officials taking bribes and neglecting their duties. Discontent rose among the populace, and rebellions sprang up in the far-flung provinces.

Ottoman boundaries began to shrink. A seige of Vienna failed in 1683, and the Turkish army was dev-

● **Jean Nicolet explores** **The French**
1634 Lake Michigan and **establish Montreal.**
reaches St. Lawrence– **1642**
Mississippi Divide ● **Manchus found Qing** ● **The Qing force the**
in Wisconsin. ● **Académie Française** **dynasty in China.** **1645** Chinese to wear ● **Louis XIV takes over the**
1635 is founded. **1644** the pigtail. **1661** government of France.

astated. In 1699 Hungary was lost to the Austrians, who began to challenge the Turks as the major power in the Balkans. Russia seized Ottoman territories along the Black Sea.

It was not until the 20th century, however, that the empire totally collapsed. Just before World War I, the Ottomans ruled areas that are now Syria, Lebanon, Iraq, Jordan, Israel, Saudi Arabia, Yemen, and islands in the Aegean. But during the war, Turkey—the seat of the Ottoman Empire—allied itself with Germany

and Austria. Defeated along with them, Turkey lost the last of its holdings. The Ottoman Empire was the precursor of the modern Turkish Republic, primarily in Asia Minor where the Ottoman Empire had its beginnings 600 years ago. ■

A humpbacked bridge in Bosnia-Hercegovina **(below)** was built in 1566 on Süleyman's orders and was destroyed in 1993 by Croatian guns. Bells pealed in St. Stephen's Cathedral in Vienna **(opposite)** when Süleyman retreated in 1529 after the walled city blocked his way to central Europe. His wife, Roxelana **(left)**, a former slave, ruthlessly ensured that her son would succeed Süleyman as the Ottoman ruler.

○ **Papacy, in person of Pope Gregory XI,**
1377 returns to Rome.

○ **Peasants' Revolt in England.**
1381

○ **University of Heidelberg is founded.**
1385

○ **Life of Ramanand, Indian philosopher.**
ca 1400-1470

○ **Peoples of Sierra Leone reach present locations.**
ca 1400

The Ming Dynasty Rebuilds China

Kublai Khan, who lived like a Chinese emperor after the Mongols took over China in the late 1200s, had no confidence in the local people as government officials. He placed political power in the hands of his fellow Mongols, adding to the hatred that the Chinese people felt for these foreign interlopers.

Under the Mongols much of the land was neglected and went out of cultivation, and cities and industries were destroyed.

After Kublai Khan's death Mongol leadership deteriorated into internal feuds and harsh rule, and a series of Chinese rebellions flared up. Over a 13-year period, a monk named Zhu Yuanzhang drove out the Mongols and restored Chinese rule in 1368.

As emperor, Zhu Yuanzhang began the Ming Dynasty, which would last nearly 300 years. He is credited with being a good ruler but a harsh one, one who executed any government official who opposed him. Nevertheless, he brought prosperity and a resurgence of national pride to China. Ming means "brilliant," and prospects certainly brightened for the Chinese after a long period of exploitation.

The Mongol bureaucrats that had dominated the government were replaced by Chinese, and the examination system that moved people into civil service by merit was restored. Colleges were established for young men—the sons of public officials mostly, but others as well if they showed promise. Candidates for

posts in the civil service or the officer corps of the 80,000-man army had to pass examinations in literature and philosophy. The Confucian scholar, in low profile during the Mongol years, came back into prominence, and knowledge of the Chinese classics was once again a ticket to advancement. Slavery was abolished, large estates were redistributed to the peasants, and taxes were made more equitable, with the wealthy paying their fair share. Perhaps because of Zhu Yuanzhang's background as a peasant, the economic system emphasized agriculture, unlike that of the Song Dynasty, which had preceded the Mongols and relied on traders and merchants for revenues.

Under the Ming many Chinese moved back to the neglected north. Large, devastated areas were reforested. Irrigation and drainage ditches were repaired. Soldiers who had helped drive out the Mongols were settled along border areas with their families, as a defensive measure. Rural reforms brought greater agricultural production and prosperity.

Under the Mongols the Chinese population had dropped 40 percent, to a little more than 60 million. Two centuries later it had doubled. New crops helped feed the new mouths. Sorghum became common in dry areas of the west and northwest. Cotton had been grown in Mongol times but was now cultivated intensely as a money crop. Later from the New World came potatoes, maize, peanuts, and tobacco, which could

Center of the Chinese cosmos, the Forbidden City, built

● At University of Paris an uprising occurs against Pope Benedict XIII.
1405

● Civil war in Germany.
1423

● Emperor Frederick III is the last emperor to be crowned by the Pope.
1452

● Tower of Hôtel de Ville, Brussels, built.
1454

in the early 1400s, sheltered the emperor with several walls and a moat shaped like a Tatar's bow.

be grown in areas where rice could not. With prosperity and population increases, the job market improved, and China began producing larger amounts of products such as tea, silk, handicrafts, and porcelains.

Construction and fine architecture reached a peak under the reign of Yong Le, who ruled in the early 1400s. Fearing the return of the Mongols, he had the Great Wall repaired and in 1421 built a new capital in the north, today's Beijing.

Undistinguished as a city, it had started as a barbarian settlement and had existed for centuries, but the Ming remade it into the center of the Chinese cosmos. The new walled metropolis had nine gates and was laid out in a rectangle, since the Chinese then believed the earth was square. Inside the rectangle was a smaller walled area, the imperial square; inside that square was an even smaller enclosure, the Forbidden City, where the emperor lived.

A number of Ming emperors built elaborate gardens, graceful pavilions, arched bridges, and tall pagodas. Public buildings were adorned with curved roofs and colored tiles.

In the 15th century the Ming expanded their territory. The Mongols had been the first to incorporate areas in the southwest into China, and the Ming army affirmed its control there. It staged invasions into Mongolia and Vietnam and became a sea power, with vast fleets sailing into the Indian Ocean and demanding tribute from foreign ports. ■

1478 — Ferdinand and Isabella establish the Spanish Inquisition, aiming to root out their Muslim and Jewish minorities.

1488 — First major Ikko-ikki, or uprising of Buddhists, in Japan.

1492 — Christopher Columbus lands on Bahama Islands, Cuba, and Hispaniola.

1497 — John Cabot sails from Bristol, discovers Newfoundland, and returns.

The Flowering of the Ming

In 1500 the Ming Empire was the most powerful and advanced state of its time. Italian missionaries, arriving in the 1580s from the grubby towns and religious wars of their continent, thought the Chinese cities with their colored tiles and curved roofs represented a nation supremely civilized.

The arts were in full bloom. Short stories and dramas about romantic love and the pretensions of the newly rich were popular. Chinese silks, teas, carvings, embroideries, and porcelains were coveted items, successfully exported.

The Chinese had been trading internationally for many years. The mariner's compass was described by a Chinese writer of nautical affairs a century before it was mentioned by Europeans. In the 12th century Chinese ships carrying porcelains and silks were sailing regularly to the Red Sea and the Persian Gulf.

Their unique, oceangoing vessels, called "junks," were described admiringly by the Muslim traveler Ibn Battuta in the 14th century: "The large ships have anything from twelve down to three sails made of bamboo rods plaited like mats. A ship carries a complement of a thousand men....The vessel has four decks and contains rooms, cabins, and saloons for merchants."

Under the Ming, China became a true sea power. From 1405 to 1433 the empire carried out a series of seven grand exploratory voyages,

For centuries before Europeans learned the process, the Chinese fired porcelain in conical kilns (above).

probably to impress foreign countries with the power of the Ming. Led by Admiral Zheng He, a Muslim by birth, fleets sailed to Sri Lanka, India, the east coast of Africa, and the Arabian Peninsula. The first trip was undertaken by an armada of 317 vessels. They included 62 baochuan, the largest vessels then known in the world, perhaps up to 180 feet long and 28 feet wide in the beam.

Then, for reasons not entirely

CHINESE PORCELAINS

The fine porcelains of China, some of them eggshell thin, were the envy of the world for centuries. First made around A.D. 900, they were fired in kilns that reached temperatures above 2200°F. The blue-and-white Mings were called "chinaware" in Europe. Not until 1718, after years of experimentation, did the Austrians learn to make such porcelains. By then millions of pieces such as this jar and pouring vessel (opposite) had been exported. Today nearly all porcelains are called "china."

clear, the Ming retreated from maritime activity. Emperor Yong Le, who had authorized the voyages, died and a subsequent emperor stopped the expeditions. Chinese were forbidden from either building oceangoing ships or leaving the country in the ones that remained. The decision may have reflected Ming fear of the continuing threat of the Mongols, and the feeling that resources needed to resist them should not be spent on foreign enterprises. The decision may have been connected also to China's growing policy of isolationism.

The resurgence of Confucianism fed a belief in the superiority of Chinese ways. Discourse with foreigners was considered unfruitful and was actually discouraged. The European traders and missionaries who began sailing to the Far East in the 1500s were tolerated, but rarely allowed into court life.

A Ming mercantile class arose and became wealthy. Chinese commerce was stimulated by the flow of silver from the New World, used to pay for Chinese exports of tea, silk, and ceramics. To satisfy European markets, Chinese businessmen devised a way of mass-producing cheaper types of porcelain.

The Europeans themselves were seen as barbarians, developers of a few novelties that could not compare with the accomplishments of the Chinese and their elegant, organized way of life. ■

1517 Martin Luther nails his 95 theses to the Wittenberg Castle church door, touching off the Reformation in Europe.

1534-42 French explorer Jacques Cartier sails up St. Lawrence River in Canada.

1535 Cortés explores lower California.

1536 Michelangelo begins "The Last Judgment" on the altar wall of the Sistine Chapel.

1545 Opening of the Council of Trent.

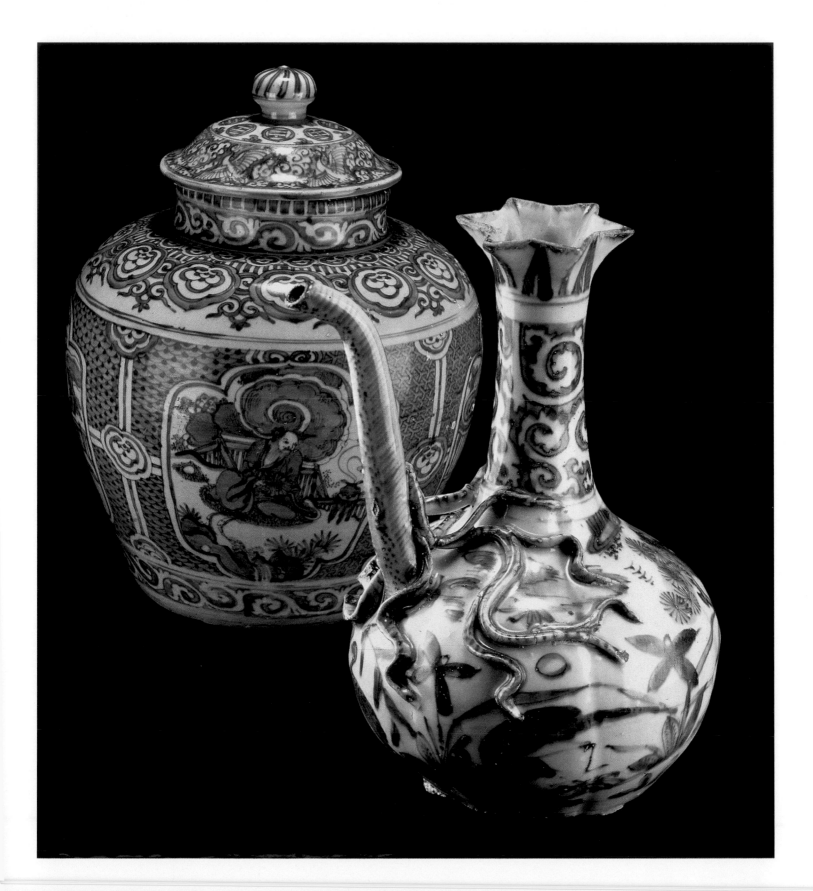

1553 Richard Chancellor journeys from England to Moscow via the White Sea, hoping to establish a new trade route.

1562 Sir John Hawkins starts English slave trade, taking cargoes of slaves from West Africa to the Americas.

1564-1616 Life of English playwright, William Shakespeare.

1565 Süleyman I fails in an attempt to capture Malta in the Mediterranean.

Behind Ming Glitter, Tensions Smolder

Despite China's civilized appearance that so impressed the Europeans, all was not well within the Ming Empire. Prosperity was maintained with harsh discipline, in which out-of-favor political leaders and other "enemies" were beaten to death in public. The seclusion of the Forbidden City worked both ways; outsiders could not get in, but emperors also had little contact with court business. Increasingly they left day-to-day national affairs up to court officials, who grew wealthy by selling favors and bribes. Decisions made often were not in the nation's best interests, and rebellions sprang up in the countryside. Meanwhile Mongols continued to threaten from

Dazzling mark of Ming officialdom, a badge designed for the formal robe of a military officer included gold and silver threads and filaments of peacock feathers.

1568 In Japan, Nobunaga seizes Kyoto.

1577-80 English seaman Francis Drake sails around the world.

1620 Puritans seeking religious freedom land at Plymouth, in today's Massachusetts, to establish a colony.

1631 John Winthrop founds Boston, Massachusetts.

THE MOUNTAIN REALM OF TIBET

A special civilization evolved in the mountain fastness of Tibet, a 16,000-foot plateau fenced by some of the highest peaks in the world. Earliest settlers were probably nomads out of central Asia who migrated into the plains and river valleys. The earliest king is believed to have reigned in the fifth century B.C. In the seventh century A.D. King Songzen Gampo established an empire that extended beyond the mountain ranges into parts of India, Nepal, Sikkim, Bhutan, and China. Buddhism came quickly to Tibet after being founded in neighboring India. Tibetan Buddhism holds that monks of great wisdom and deep spirituality, called lamas, are reincarnations of great lamas before them. The one achieving the highest level of spirituality is the Dalai Lama.

Fortresslike monasteries in the Himalaya provided havens for religion and also served as the nation's focus for artistic and intellectual life. Rising atop Red Hill is the Potala (left), citadel of Tibetan Buddhism and the residence of a long line of Dalai Lamas. The Potala's origins go back more than 1,350 years. When the Mongols conquered China in the 13th century, Tibet submitted as well. Later, Kublai Khan appointed a lama as ruler of the vassal state. In the 15th and 16th centuries, a pattern of monastic tradition began that has lasted for centuries.

the north, and pirates ranged along the coastline.

The Japanese warlord Hideyoshi invaded Korea, a vassal state of China, and aspired to conquer China as well. Huge armies that taxed the resources of the empire had to be sent to counter him.

After 1627 more rebellions broke out in the northwest, following repeated crop failures and famine. Farmers left their fields and entered the hills to become bandits. The leader of one group, Li Zicheng, took over his entire province and began moving beyond it. Another rebel leader, Zhang Xianzhong, ravaged the eastern plain and the Yangtze valley and set up his own kingdom in Sichuan. Manchu tribesmen in the Manchurian northwest began moving about and

striking with impunity. As funds ran short in the central government, salaries went unpaid. Members of the Ming army mutinied. In 1644 they allowed the bandit leader Li Zicheng to enter Beijing almost unopposed, and the last Ming emperor hanged himself rather than face capture.

Loyal Ming army forces stationed in northern China returned to the capital to oppose the rebels. The army leader, Wu Sangui, found his men between those of Li Zicheng and the Manchus, who were approaching from the northeast.

Wu Sangui joined forces with the alien Manchus, and together they defeated the bandit force. Wu later rebelled against his allies, but the Manchus prevailed and ruled China for two centuries. ∎

Inca Empire enters period of expansion.

1400s

Death of Richard II

1400

Peace between Castile and Portugal.

1411

Mongols invade China, capture Ming emperor, then withdraw.

1449

1453 Constantinople falls to the Turks, ending the 1100-year Byzantine Empire. The Turks rename the city Istanbul.

Japan Goes Its Own Way

After centuries of living under the influence of China, Japan began reemerging as a separate civilization around the eighth century. Japanese writing was simplified, and literature was rendered in the island language instead of Chinese. Japanese artists and writers began developing their own styles. Buddhism imported from China and Korea was blended with Japan's Shintoism, which is rooted in a belief that spirits pervade virtually all aspects of nature.

Although Japan had an emperor for hundreds of years, his duties were mostly religious and ceremonial. Real power lay with nobles who handled government affairs.

Administration of the provinces was handled by warlike landlords known as samurai. A feudal system evolved in which the shogun, head of the ruling family, appointed the samurai to run the estates that were worked by rice farmers.

Traditions of the samurai warriors worked their way into Japanese culture much as the cowboy ideal has become part of American thought. Samurai were skilled horsemen, archers, and swordsmen who lived by a code that emphasized courage, honor, and loyalty to a leader.

The use of weapons was considered profane unless guided by purity of thought, so good scholarship was expected as well. Trained to be indifferent to physical hardship and death, samurai were expected to commit ritualistic suicide if their reputations were damaged.

If one substitutes the word "king" for shogun, "knight" for samurai, "peasants" for rice farmers, and perhaps even "pope" for the religion-centered emperor, Japan's feudal system was remarkably similar to that of Europe, with one important difference. The warrior samurai supposedly owed their allegiance to the shogunate, but gradually they began banding together into groups of lords that pledged loyalty to each other.

The samurai class became so powerful they could not be controlled by the shogun. Various groups of samurai battled each other for control of Japan, and in the mid-1400s the islands became embroiled in civil war that lasted for more than a century. ■

The Japanese developed a distinctive national style under military rulers such as Tokugawa Ieyasu *(above),* head of the last of the three shogunates. Modern kayakers in Hiroshima Bay paddle past a torii gate of camphorwood *(right)* that marks a holy space, extending to a Shinto shrine on shore.

1455 The Wars of the Roses begin.

ca 1460 Imperial porcelain works at Jingdezhen, in China, begin to export Ming pottery.

1462-1505 Reign of Ivan III.

1469 Crowns of Aragon and Castile, in Spain, united under Ferdinand and Isabella.

1490 In Venice, Aldo Manuzio founds the Aldine press. It becomes famous for the low cost and high quality of its classical texts, with great clarity of typography.

○ **1498** The third voyage of Christopher Columbus discovers Trinidad and the Orinoco delta.

○ **1500** Black lead pencils used in England.

○ **1503** Leonardo da Vinci paints the "Mona Lisa."

○ **1506** Death of Christopher Columbus.

○ **1509-1547** Reign of Henry VIII.

The Japanese Draw Inward

Out of Japan's long civil war, the house of Tokugawa emerged as the most powerful family and ruled as shogunate for more than 250 years. Rather than use its power to disband the warrior clans or attempt to expand Japan's territory, the Tokugawa dynasty simply controlled the feudal system and let it continue.

Vast territories were held by the reigning family and its supporters. To prevent buildups of local power in other groups, they did not allow samurai to travel from territory to territory and did not allow unauthorized marriages between feudal groups.

All samurai were required to sign oaths of obedience to the shogunate. In a "sword hunt" undertaken in 1588, the peasants were disarmed and restricted to a life of farming. Periodically families who headed outlying provinces were required to live at the shogunate capital of Edo, modern Tokyo, or to leave members of their families there as hostages. Only the Tokugawa family was allowed to communicate with the powerless emperor at Kyoto.

During the civil wars European traders and missionaries began arriving. They brought not only a new religion but firearms, using gunpowder that had been invented in China.

At first samurai scorned guns as the weapons of cowards. But after a leader named Oda Nobunaga defeated a much larger rival samurai force by using muskets, the future of guns in Japan was assured.

Thenceforward, Nobunaga

welcomed the traders, hoping to learn from them about advances in astronomy, cartography, gunmaking, and shipbuilding.

Jesuit missionaries were also held in high regard by Hideyoshi, the military leader who sought unsuccessfully to conquer China. But Christian converts grew to some 150,000 by the late 1500s, which made Japanese leaders fear a gradual infiltration of European ways.

Under the shogunate of Tokugawa, persecution of Christians began. Hidetada, Ieyasu's son, crucified 55 Christians in 1622. When Japanese Christians were

1516 ● Coffee is introduced into Europe.

1517 ● The Ottomans conquer Egypt.

1520 ● Chocolate is introduced into Europe.

1538 ● Henry VIII issues English Bible.

ca 1570 ● The Portuguese set up the first sugar plantations in Brazil.

found to have participated in a revolt in 1637, the shogun Iemitsu banned the Christian religion and expelled all missionaries and most traders from the country.

Japan's leaders began to fear pollution of Japanese thought and ways by all outside contact, and a period of extreme isolation began. The Japanese were not allowed to travel abroad. Those citizens already abroad were not allowed to return. Construction of large, oceangoing ships was forbidden.

Only a handful of Chinese and Dutch were allowed to trade with Japan. Unlike other European visitors the Dutch had not tried to make converts for Christianity. Nevertheless they were restricted in trading activity to one small island in Nagasaki Bay, as far as possible from the heart of Japan. For nearly 250 years the Japanese were virtually cut off from contact with Europeans.

Isolation brought about stability and unity within the country. However, Japan missed advances in mathematics and science that proved beneficial to Europeans. ∎

Japanese initially welcomed ideas brought by Europeans like these Portuguese merchants bearing gifts *(opposite, above)*. But the growing number of Christian converts fed fears of European infiltration and takeover, leading to the crucifixion of 26 Christian missionaries in Nagasaki in 1597 *(opposite, below)*. Japan entered a long period of isolation during which only a few Dutch and Chinese ships were allowed in Nagasaki harbor, seen in this 17th-century map *(left, below)*.

THE CEREMONY OF DRINKING TEA

Tea came to Japan from China, but the ceremony that arose around drinking it became uniquely Japanese. In rustic tea houses around the country, in simple but elegant rooms, the beverage was drunk under strict rules intended to promote purity, harmony, respect, and a tranquil mind. A tea master presided over the ceremony, solemnly preparing, pouring, and presenting the brew to participants, a practice that continues to this day *(above)*.

1576 English explorer Martin Frobisher sets out to find a northwest passage to China, reaches the Canadian coast, and Frobisher Bay is named for him.

1608 French explorer Samuel de Champlain establishes Quebec.

1613 The Globe Theatre in London burns down during a performance of *Henry VIII*, and it is rebuilt within a year.

1635 France declares war on Spain. The French settle Martinique and Guadeloupe.

1643 Louis XIV becomes King of France.

1649 Charles I executed. England is declared a Commonwealth.

1660 Samuel Pepys begins his diary, which he keeps for the rest of the decade.

1672 Holy Roman Empire and Brandenburg join the Dutch in war against France.

1673 Jacques Marquette and Louis Joliet explore the Mississippi Valley.

The Growth of Japanese Cities

The long, unbroken period of peace during Japan's isolation brought changes in the feudal system and resulted in the growth of urban life. All Japan had been divided into fiefs, and because the shogun's fief was larger and more powerful than the others, peace was maintained.

Rice, produced by farmers and delivered to landlords, served as the accepted medium of exchange. The shogun paid his officials in rice, just as the samurai paid their overseers. The rural barter economy depended on the yield of its one crop, a practice that was disruptive in lean years.

Trade, piracy, and the opening of silver mines in the 16th century had started money circulating in Japan. And in the 1600s the minting of money and banking emerged.

With sustained peace, the samurai began finding pleasures and luxuries in towns. A merchant class, once despised in the glorification of spartan samurai life, began to grow. Peasant cooperatives, formed when the landlords were preoccupied in the long years of civil war, gained in numbers and confidence.

In a growing cash economy, frugality had little appeal. To feed the demand for new goods and materials, estates set up workshops and regions began to specialize in certain crafts. Guilds were formed.

The new, prosperous middle class created literature and art. Ritualized tea ceremonies became popular. Zen Buddhism, imported from China, took root in Japan, bringing the simplicity of the countryside into the growing cities. It contributed to a culture that believed in saying more with less. ■

Peace through isolation nurtured the development of Japanese culture. A cash economy fed the prosperity of cities. Religion and recreation took on unique flavors. Zen Buddhism, with its emphasis on beauty and tranquility, originated in China but took deep root in Japan. A Zen garden in Kyoto *(left)*, with its islands of moss and stones, becomes symbolic of the entire universe.

KABUKI DRAMA

Buddhist monks, perhaps the first playwrights of Japan, produced a form of drama called Noh, which grew out of religious dances and taught religious lessons. As a prosperous middle class arose in Japan, a combination of the Noh dramas and the movements of puppet shows resulted in dramatic performances known as Kabuki, theater performed with elaborate, exaggerated movements and highly stylized makeup and costumes *(above)*.

217

1498 Modern-style tooth-brushes are being used in China.

1500 Tennis becomes very popular in France.

1505-07 Portuguese capture Sofala on Africa's east coast, found Mozambique, and begin trade with the Africans.

1508 Antwerp syndicate agrees to buy all the spices the Portuguese can bring back from the Orient.

Conquering the Americas

S pain moved quickly to exploit its new claims in the area that Columbus had discovered in the fall of 1492. The navigator had convinced the Spanish court that he had reached the East Indies. Spanish settlers occupied the island of Hispaniola in the following year so they could advance to the wealth of spices they believed were not far away. From there they moved on to Cuba, Jamaica, and Puerto Rico. Settlement of the South American coast and the Isthmus of Panama began around 1510, despite the onslaughts of unaccustomed diseases and attacks by hostile Indians.

Official motivation for settlement may have been the conversion of heathens to Christianity, but the actual explorations were undertaken by conquistadors, Spanish adventurers bent on getting rich by trade or plunder.

On the coast of Central America, Spaniards heard from the Maya of an incredibly wealthy king farther inland. In 1519 Hernán Cortés sailed from Cuba with 11 ships, 600 men, 10 cannon, and 17 horses. A courageous but ruthless leader, Cortés burned the ships after he landed so that none could desert him.

Word of his forces reached the Aztec king Moctezuma II at the splendid lake capital of Tenochtitlán. Reports were of "supernatural creatures riding on hornless deer, preceded by wild animals on leashes, dressed in iron, armed in iron, fearless as gods."

If the Aztec were awed, so were the members of the invasion force

1510 Medici Pope Leo X starts the Vatican's collection of sculpture.

1521 Martin Luther is excommunicated from the Roman Catholic Church.

1558 Elizabeth I becomes Queen of England.

1588 Defeat of the Spanish Armada.

when they reached Tenochtitlán. The wide causeway leading to the well-ordered city in the lake, with its large plazas and splendid buildings, surpassed anything they remembered in Spain. Unfortunately for the Aztec, legend and superstition led them into disastrous decisions. Moctezuma II apparently believed Cortés was the fulfillment of an Aztec prophecy about a former ruler, Quetzalcoatl, who would return to reclaim his throne. He dawdled instead of attacking the Spaniards with his superior numbers. When he finally did, goaded by the massacre of Aztec officials by a Cortés officer, the invaders were driven away—although Moctezuma II himself was killed. The Spaniards returned with native allies and defeated the Aztec.

The splendid but cruel civilization they had built, with some of its rituals based on human sacrifice, collapsed with the fall of Tenochtitlán. The city on the lake was partially razed, and Mexico City rose in its place.

News of the riches gleaned from the Aztec brought even more Spaniards, searching for gold. Scarcely a decade after the fall of the Aztec, Francisco Pizarro worked his way along the west coast of South America and encountered the Inca Empire in Peru.

Pizarro had even fewer men than Cortés, but in 1532 he defeated the

Treachery felled a mighty empire in Peru, where the Inca had grown surplus crops on garden terraces cut into mountainsides (opposite). Spanish conquistadors lured the unprotected Inca ruler, Atahualpa, into their camp and held him for ransom, killing him after it was paid. At the door of the room that reportedly imprisoned him, a woman spins yarn with a whorl, like that used by her ancestors (above).

Inca by treachery. First he enticed the Inca leader Atahualpa and 6,000 unarmed bodyguards to enter his camp of 160 soldiers. The Spaniards killed most of them and took Atahualpa prisoner. They offered to release him in exchange for two rooms filled with gold and silver, but when the ransom had been paid, they killed him anyway. Leaderless, the Inca Empire collapsed. Pizarro was killed nine years later by rival Spaniards.

The two most advanced civilizations in the Americas had been virtually obliterated 40 years after Columbus discovered the New World. The Spanish remained relatively few in number, but within a generation of their arrival, the areas they occupied were converted to Christianity.

Missionaries followed in the steps of the conquerors and attempted to turn local people to European ways, occasionally succeeding. At a mission in Paraguay Jesuit priests turned a large group of Indians into a productive community made prosperous by trade. Nevertheless, resistance to the invasion of North and South America by Europeans would continue for years, although disease and superior technology would eventually lead to European victory. ■

EARLY AMERICAN METALLURGISTS

Native Central and South Americans panned gold from streambeds or picked it off the ground with balls of sticky clay during periods of low water. They reached underground veins by burrowing narrow 100-foot mine shafts. Processed gold was hammered to flatness and shaped, or cast into forms in the lost-wax process. Using sophisticated techniques, artisans created alloys and solders to fasten items together into gold and silver figurines (above, right), rings, earrings, flasks, and pendants.

1581 — Russian settlement of Siberia begins.

1584 — Archangel, first port on the White Sea, is founded. The potato is introduced into Europe.

1600s — Kalonga Kingdom, north of the Zambezi River, becomes rich through ivory trade. Hausaland dominates trade routes to the Sahara.

1605 — End of Boris Godunov's reign in Russia.

1612 — Stock Exchange is founded in Amsterdam.

1620s — Beginning of Japan's restriction of contact with the outside world.

The Spread of European Colonies

After the plundering of Mexico and Peru, Spanish immigrants—drawn by the promise of wealth—at first congregated in the cities founded by the Native Americans. Later they developed farming and ranching, followed by mining of gold and silver. The Treaty of Tordesillas prevented them from entering Portuguese Brazil.

The Portuguese, originally distracted by the success of their spice trade in the East Indies, eventually established vast sugar plantations in the New World. In the Caribbean and in Brazil, slaves were imported to supply plantations with cheap labor.

On the mainland of North America, the Spanish established the first European settlement in Florida in 1565. After the conquest of Mexico, they had extended their claims into California and New Mexico. They

Pre-European Makah Indians sew shut the mouth of a lanced whale to keep it buoyant. The Makah, like many Native American tribes before the coming of European culture, had impressive technology and rich traditions to support their ways of life.

concentrated their efforts, however, on the wealth of the islands and Central and South America.

The English, French, and Dutch explored regions north of New Spain, raiding Caribbean harbors, and pirating treasure-laden ships en route to Europe. But when the joint-stock investment companies of England and the Netherlands began

to establish colonies as profit-making ventures, the British claimed Jamaica, Barbados, and the Bahamas; and the French occupied St. Kitts, Martinique, Guadeloupe, and modern Haiti.

Like the Spanish and Portuguese, the British and the French imported slaves to work their plantations. The English lined their colonies along the eastern seaboard, and the French occupied the St. Lawrence River in the north and claimed portions of the interior of North America.

Attitudes toward Native Americans varied. The French worked with them in gathering furs. The English treated them with indifference. The Spaniards tried to convert them or force them into labor. The indigenous peoples were decimated by diseases or defeated in war when they stood in the way of European expansion. ■

THE SLAVE TRADE

Arabs, Europeans, and African kings grew rich off the selling of slaves to the Americas. The slave trade began in the mid-1400s and reached its peak with the proliferation of large plantations in the 1700s. Estimates of fatalities among captives packed into the holds of slave ships exceed one million. The number of Africans transported against their will may never be known, but it may have nearly matched the willing migration of Europeans to the New World.

ATLANTIC SLAVE TRADE
1502–1870

NORTH AMERICA

Imported into Middle America 0.2 million

Imported into the U.S. 0.4–0.5 million

Boston
New York
Jamestown

Imported into the Old World 0.2–0.3 million

Liverpool
London
Bristol

EUROPE

Atlantic Ocean

Lisbon
Cádiz

Bahamas
Cuba
Hispaniola
Mexico City
Jamaica
Puerto Rico
Cartagena
Barbados

Imported into the Caribbean 4–5 million

AFRICA

Pacific Ocean

Imported into Spanish South America 0.5 million

SOUTH AMERICA

Imported into the Guianas 0.5 million

EQUATOR

(Recife) Pernambuco
(Salvador) Bahia

Imported into Brazil 3.6–5 million

Rio de Janeiro

Madagascar

Coffee
Cotton
Mining
Rice
Sugar
Tobacco
Main area of slave origin
Movement of slaves

Buenos Aires

From Mozambique and Madagascar

● **1624** Richelieu becomes chief minister of France.

● **1657** Tokugawa Mitsukuni begins compilation of *History of Japan*.

● **1661** First banknotes are issued in Stockholm, Sweden.

● **1664** The Dutch force the King of Siam to give them monopoly of deerskin exports and sea trade with China.

● **1670s** French settle in Senegal.

● **1688** An earthquake destroys Smyrna in Asia Minor.

● **1696** London weavers riot to protest cheap cloth imports from India.

EUROPE CLAIMS NORTH AMERICA
CA 1750

Land Claims and Exploration

▢ ←	Denmark (Vikings)
▢ ←	Great Britain
▢ ←	France
▢ ←	Russia
▢ ←	Spain
▨	Disputed area
⚓	Spanish fort or presidio

0 — 800 km
0 — 800 mi

1400 Death of Richard II

1400s Expansion of Aztec Empire in Mexico. In the Hawaiian Islands taro, a starchy root vegetable, is cultivated.

1403 Chinese encyclopedia, in 22,937 volumes, is compiled (only three copies made).

1405 Cheng Ho, with Chinese fleet, visits Indochina and reaches Arabia.

1444-1460 Palazzo Medici, in Florence, is built.

The Expansion of Russia

Russia lived long under the shadow of others. Its principal city of Kiev was overrun and destroyed by Mongols in 1240, and the land Kiev had controlled was split in two. The eastern part came under the jurisdiction of the Mongols, while the western part was absorbed by Catholic Lithuania and eventually became part of Poland. For centuries hostile neighbors would isolate Russia from scientific and cultural developments in Europe, including the Renaissance and the Reformation.

Moscow eventually emerged as Russia's new political center. The Mongol khan made Ivan I the grand duke of Russia, basically a tax collector exacting tribute from his people for the benefit of the Mongol overlords. With the backing of the khan, he expanded his territory of Muscovy to collect even more taxes. His leadership acquired legitimacy among the taxpayers when he received the backing of the Russian Orthodox Church. Christian orthodoxy had spread to Russia during the heyday of the Byzantine Empire.

Ivan III, known as Ivan the Great, was grand duke from 1462 to 1505 and liberated Russia by renouncing his allegiance to the Mongols. The khan's forces were unable to take the well-fortified Kremlin to reassert their authority. By 1480 the Mongols had been driven from Russia.

Since the Byzantine Empire had fallen in 1453, Russian churchmen had developed the idea that Russia would become the "third Rome," after Constantinople and the original Rome on the Tiber River. They claimed that Ivan III was a descendant of a brother of Caesar Augustus. The churchmen

Rough-and-ready Cossacks, shown here in "The Cossacks of Zaporozje," established self-governing communities in Ukraine during the Time of Troubles.

● **1448-1488** Thailand expands under King Trailok.

1449 War between England and France, resulting in France recovering Normandy, except for the Channel Islands.

1466 Birth of Erasmus, Dutch scholar and leader of revival of learning in northern Europe.

● **1467-77** Onin War in Japan.

● **1471-1493** Emperor Topa Inca expands Inca Empire into Bolivia, Chile, and Argentina.

● **1513** Vasco Núñez de Balboa discovers the Pacific Ocean.

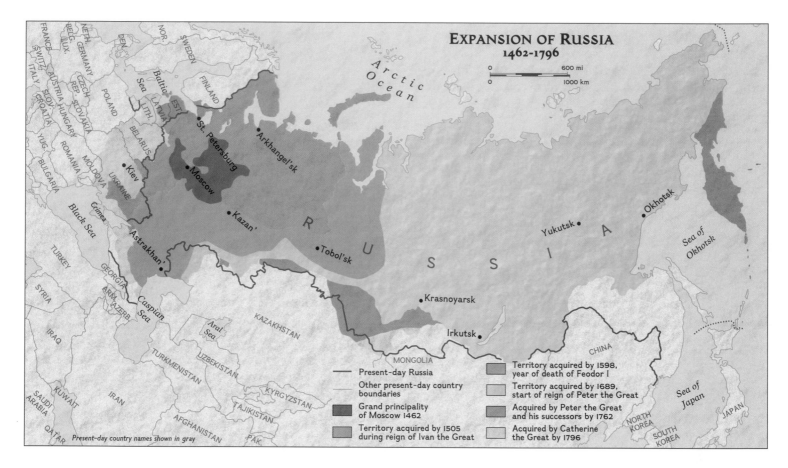

EXPANSION OF RUSSIA
1462-1796

- — Present-day Russia
- --- Other present-day country boundaries
- Grand principality of Moscow 1462
- Territory acquired by 1505 during reign of Ivan the Great
- Territory acquired by 1598, year of death of Feodor I
- Territory acquired by 1689, start of reign of Peter the Great
- Acquired by Peter the Great and his successors by 1762
- Acquired by Catherine the Great by 1796

Present-day country names shown in gray

also undertook the role of guardians of the "true faith" of eastern Christian orthodoxy, whose place had been usurped in Constantinople by the Islamic faith of the Ottoman Turks.

To further solidify Ivan III's ties to the old Roman Empire, he married Sophie Paleologue, the niece of the last Byzantine emperor. He called himself "tsar," or caesar. To create a dwelling fit for himself as a caesar, Ivan rebuilt the Kremlin, or fortress, with onion-domed churches and elaborate palaces.

On the military offensive, he nearly tripled the size of Russia's holdings, adding numerous small principalities around Muscovy, and planned to regain the lands absorbed by

Lithuania. It was an ambition not realized in his or several more lifetimes as Lithuania was by then united with robust Poland.

Most powerful of the early tsars

was Ivan IV, who became known as Ivan the Terrible because of the arrests, tortures, and executions he carried out to purge suspected traitors. Always wary of the class of

IVAN THE TERRIBLE

A tense and violent upbringing at a time of political stress in Moscow may have molded the neurotic character of Ivan IV. Grand duke in 1533 at the age of 3, tsar at 17, he may have gone partially mad at the death of his first wife. He married seven times and at one point suggested that Elizabeth I of England marry him, a possibility that she dismissed. After killing his eldest son, Ivan, in a fit of rage in 1581, Ivan IV was overcome with remorse (*right*).

1516-1556 ● Reign of Charles I,
King of Spain.

1521 ● Hernán Cortés captures
Tenochtitlán, the
Aztec capital.

ca 1530 ● Beginning of trans-
atlantic slave trade
organized by
the Portuguese.

1534 ● Henry VIII declares himself head of the church
in England.

1553 ● Queen Mary
brings England
back to Catholicism.

raiding party out of Tatar Crimea invaded and burned the outskirts of Moscow and then retreated. Guns had become superior to bows and arrows on the battlefield, but swift hit-and-run units like those of the

Mongols could still inflict damage. Raiding parties from the steppes would not be stopped until a series of frontier forts was built and manned by the well-mounted Cossacks, who were better-armed than the nomads.

nobles known as boyars, who threatened to take over the throne, he attempted to destroy them.

The boyars controlled about half the country when Ivan IV seized those lands, uprooted the owners, and installed his own supporters. He then terrorized all Russia with agents bent on rooting out any subterfuge.

Nevertheless, early in Ivan IV's rule as tsar he attempted to centralize the Russian government, and he increased trade and contact with western Europe. His armies expanded Russia in all directions. To the east and south he annexed the Mongol lands of Kazan and Astrakhan, although he was not yet totally safe from Tatars, as the Mongols were called in Russia. In 1571 a large

The Spanish establish first European settlement in Florida.
1565

Fifth Huguenot war in France.
1574-76

ca 1578 Oda Nobunaga, a lord of central Japan, becomes leading figure through the use of muskets.

James VI, at the age of 15, is declared of age to rule Scotland.
1581

1595 The Dutch begin to colonize the East Indies.

France and neighboring states make postal agreements.
1601

To the west, Ivan waged war for 25 years with Poland, Lithuania, and Sweden, trying in vain to win Livonia, modern Latvia, so Russia could have an outlet to the Baltic Sea. Although he lost territory to Poland and Sweden, he gained land in Siberia in 1581. He died in 1584 at age 54.

Ivan the Terrible was succeeded by his son Fedor, a weak ruler who died in 1598 without an heir.

In the 15 dark years following Fedor's death, known in Russian history as the Time of Troubles, many Russians moved into the borderlands. In a region called Ukraine, south of Moscow, settlers established their own self-governing communities. Among those pioneers were the skillful fighters known as Cossacks.

Factions jockeyed for the throne, and an ambitious nobleman named Boris Godunov, who had overseen Fedor's reign, had himself crowned tsar. Rivals challenged his right to the office. Noble families struggled for

supremacy. He let half the country be governed by the Boyar Council within his administration.

When famine brought on peasant uprisings, Poland and Sweden intervened, with the Poles entering and occupying Moscow. ■

Throwing off Mongol rule, Russia called itself the "third Rome," assuming leadership of fallen Byzantium's Eastern Orthodox Church. Quarters fit for a caesar mixed religion and wealth at Terem Palace in Moscow (*opposite*). In today's Kremlin Museum the coronation gown of Catherine the Great stands next to an image of that monarch later in life (*opposite, top*). The Cap of Monomakh (*left*) was used to crown tsars from 1498 to 1682. Onion-shaped roofs (*above*) copied Byzantine domes, but shed snow better.

225

1610 In Italy, the first stellar observations with a telescope are made by Galileo.

1612 In Germany, the decimal point is used for the first time in Europe.

1615 The peoples north of China combine to form powerful military organizations, known as Manchus.

1620 First hackney coaches appear in London. Their speed is limited to 3 mph.

1623 Colonists at New Plymouth establish the system of trial by 12-man jury.

Russia Joins the Modern World

When Polish soldiers occupied Moscow in 1608 and set up a puppet government, the outrage was enough to unite the Russian people. In an uprising organized by monks and Cossacks, the Poles were driven out of Moscow, an event helped by civil unrest in Poland.

In 1613 a Russian national assembly met and chose a new tsar. The popular choice was Michael Romanov, the 16-year-old grand-nephew of Ivan the Terrible and son of a patriotic leader named Philaret. The Romanovs would rule from 1613

PETER THE GREAT

His fascination with practical matters and his desire to modernize Russia sent Peter the Great on a trip unusual for a monarch. For 18 months in 1697 and 1698 he traveled in western Europe, dressed as a commoner, visiting factories, hospitals, museums, and almshouses for the poor. He worked as a carpenter in a shipyard and learned some skills even in surgery and dentistry. Thoroughly Europeanized, he returned home intent on changing Russia.

until the Russian revolution in 1917.

Under Michael and his son Alexis, Russia made a slow recovery from the Time of Troubles. Under Alexis, who ruled from 1645 to 1676, Russian lands were extended all the way to the Pacific coast, an addition valuable for the furs that could be exchanged in trade with Europe for military armaments.

A new legal code was adopted, aimed at improving the administration. It also worsened the lot of Russian peasants, or serfs, who were tied to land granted to overlords who

Dedicated to modernizing Russia, halls of institutes, museums, and libraries fill Vasilyevskiy Island in St. Petersburg, new capital established by Peter the Great.

The Paris *Gazette* is founded.
1631

The bayonet is invented in Bayonne, France.
1647

England's Charles I is executed for treason.
1649

English take over Dutch settlement of New Amsterdam and rename it New York.
1664

1667 Four Days' War between the English and the Dutch is fought at the mouth of the Thames. The Dutch destroy 25 English ships; both sides eventually withdraw.

owed military service to the tsar. In contrast to Europe, perhaps due to Russia's isolation from it, Russian serfs steadily lost freedoms after the medieval period and were little better than slaves.

Meanwhile Ukrainian Cossacks revolted against Poland in 1654 and appealed to Moscow for help. After 13 years of war a truce transferred to Russia lands that included Kiev, lost in the Mongol domination some 400 years before.

A formidable personality came onto the Russian scene in 1682 when Peter I, to be known as Peter the Great, became tsar. Nearly seven feet tall, filled with energy and ambition, he is credited with leading Russia into the modern world.

Isolation remained Russia's largest problem, and Peter concentrated on opening a "window on the West." After a long struggle with Sweden, he finally gained Estonia and Livonia, winning in the process a port on the Baltic Sea. At its edge he built a new Russian capital, St. Petersburg, under the direction of European architects.

Peter, who had taken an extended trip through western Europe early in his reign, attempted to remake Russia in the western European mold. He brought in advisers, technicians, and craftsmen from Europe and sent young Russians there to study military and industrial techniques. He also formed a professional army of 300,000 men and organized the first Russian navy.

The civil service was reorganized along western lines, and members of the court were required to adopt western clothes and manners. Old traditions were discouraged; extra taxes were levied against those wearing a beard or national dress.

Peasants were subjected to new taxation and conscripted to military service and public works. Thousands died in construction of St. Petersburg. Under Peter, new industries were founded, and factories, canals, and roads were built.

Russia's huge tsar could be ruthless, but he put his nation on the road to becoming a superpower. He died as dramatically as he had lived, succumbing in 1725 at the age of 53 after diving into the Neva River in winter to rescue drowning sailors.

Catherine the Great, Last Absolute Monarch

One Russian monarch who was given the title of "the Great" was not Russian but, rather, of German descent. Catherine the Great was born Sophie Friederike Auguste von Anhalt-Zerbst. In 1745, at the age of 16, she married the heir to the Russian throne, a weak-minded man and a grandson of Peter the Great.

It was no love match, and the two soon became estranged after both were involved in court scandals. He became Tsar Peter III in 1762, briefly. Six months after his enthronement, Catherine deposed him with the help of a paramour, and Peter III was assassinated nine days later.

Their son, Paul, was next in line, but Catherine made herself empress.

A study in contradictions, she pretended concern for the serfs while making their lives worse and brutally crushing a peasant uprising.

She announced plans to improve education, but the new schools were for the children of nobles only.

Ruthless and cruel, she had courtiers flogged and peasants punished for complaining about their misery. Intelligent and energetic, she nevertheless held her territories together and added to them, accomplishments that earned her the title of Catherine the Great.

She achieved the long-sought Russian goal of gaining a warm-water port on the Black Sea by defeating the Ottoman Turks, by then a declining power.

In the west, Poland was suffering from feuds among its nobility, and she took advantage of the situation. In 1792 she seized the western Ukraine, which became a vast granary for Russia. In connivance with Prussia and Austria, Russia helped see to it that Poland was divided three times, and in 1795 the Polish nation ceased to exist until 1919.

In many ways Catherine the Great continued the modernization of Russia that had been started by Peter the Great. She died in 1796, the last absolute monarch of a major nation in the 18th century.

By that time new ideas about liberty and equality were stirring in western Europe. ■

227

7

11

1775
The 13 Colonies begin
the Revolutionary War
against England.

1800s
U.S. government
forces relocation
of Native Americans.

1

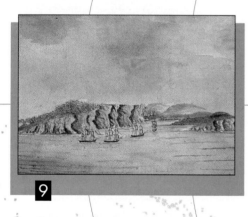

9

2

1810
Colombia is first European
colony in South America
to win independence.

AROUND THE WORLD

1 **North America:** Colonists
jeered and insulted British
troops, and in March 1770
a squad of British soldiers
in Boston was pelted with
stones and snowballs. A
riotous crowd gathered,
and British troops opened
fire, killing five in the
Boston Massacre.

2 **South America:** Simón
Bolívar, dreaming of a
unified South America, led
armies of colonists to throw
off the rule of Spain in
several countries.

3 **Asia:** British traders introduced opium into the Orient
as a trade item. When
Chinese officials banned the
drug and burned British-
owned warehouses filled
with it, the British attacked,
capturing Dinghai in 1840.

4 **Africa:** Built by a French
company, the Suez Canal
opened with festivities in
1869. Measuring 101
miles long and 179 feet

Quickening Change

ca 1770
The industrial revolution begins in England.

1700-1721
Peter the Great expands Russia by winning land in the Baltic.

1700s
Europe's Age of Enlightenment spawns new ways of thinking.

1789
The French Revolution is sparked by a mob in Paris.

1857
A widespread revolt against British control erupts in India.

1850-1864
During China's bloody civil war, millions of people die in the Taiping Rebellion.

1841-1873
British explorer David Livingstone travels in Africa.

1787-1868
Thousands of British convicts are shipped to Australia.

wide, the canal reduced a voyage from Britain to India by 4,000 miles.

5 Europe: In 1876 Britain's Queen Victoria became Empress of India, but Indian nationalistic feelings ran high against British authority.

6 Europe: The industrial revolution inspired English inventor James Nasmyth in 1839 to sketch a vertical steam hammer powerful enough to shape an iron beam, gentle enough to crack an egg.

7 North America: By the end of the 19th century, telephones were being used for pleasure as well as for business.

8 Africa: Struggles for South Africa often had complex racial boundaries. Zulu King Shaka subdued other black clans, and Dutch farmers, called Boers, fought the British over land rights.

9 Australia: Australia interested England in the late 1700s as a depository for undesirables. A ship's officer painted the arrival of the first fleet of convicts in Sydney Harbour in 1788.

10 Oceania: Tattoos and distorted faces greeted Dutch navigator Abel Tasman, the first European to encounter New Zealand, in 1642. His stay was brief as he fought with the

fierce Maori—Polynesians who had reached the big islands by canoe around A.D. 1000.

11 Hawaiian Islands: The Hawaiian Islands saw the end of famed explorer Capt. James Cook, first welcomed and feted by the local people but later killed.

Quickening Change: 1700 to 1900

Since the dawn of complex societies, people generally had lived at the mercy of their governments and the individuals who ran them. Monarchs and their entourages most often reigned like gods, levying taxes, waging wars, living off the backs of people who struggled simply to exist. Corrupt and unfair kings and queens could be overthrown and replaced by other rulers, so some attempts at national harmony could be made. Plots and connivance were part of court life, but for hundreds of years, the common people served royalty, not the reverse.

By the 1700s Europe, fed by wealth from worldwide maritime trade, had divided into a chessboard of nations jockeying for power and influence. Boundaries changed frequently, alliances were made and broken, and strategic marriages occurred so frequently that European politics became a family affair. The death of a monarch with no clear heir brought proprietary claims from nobles in other countries—claims that could shift the balance of power. Wars involving several countries and costing thousands of lives were fought over the question of who had the legal birthright to rule a single nation.

In the midst of this diplomatic intrigue a number of thinkers began questioning the role of government and arguing for the ability of people to determine their own destinies. Feeding these inquiries were scientific advances that were improving lives and adding to the general body of knowledge. The microscope began peering into the world of germs that had caused misery for millennia. Encyclopedias of knowledge were compiled that gathered all known facts for perusal.

Institutions were criticized and new ways of operating society were debated in intellectual salons. The discomforts and disadvantages that had long been the lot of great masses of people were becoming unacceptable, and it appeared possible that with the proper procedures, people's everyday lives might actually improve. Reason threatened to prevail.

But reason had to couple with emotion before rebellion was born. By the middle of the 18th century the excesses of power and the desire for independent thought came together in revolutions against long-established authority. Britain's colonies in faraway North America were growing increasingly restive over taxes they considered unfair. The colonists had long accepted the necessary sponsorship and protection by Britain, and even fought alongside British redcoats against the French. But now the French were defeated, and the Americans were learning to defend themselves against Native Americans. Who needed the faraway British?

Much of the colonial population was composed of Protestant dissenters and independent thinkers who had left Britain as a protest against religious opponents. Their struggles in a harsh new world only fed a desire to throw off authority that seemed detrimental to their own ambitions and interests.

In 1776 a few radical thinkers, backed by a ragtag army of squirrel hunters and tradesmen, did the unthinkable: They declared that rule by one of the most powerful nations on earth had become so unwanted that they were forming their own nation. Furthermore, it would be a nation cast in a new mold, one answerable to the people themselves.

The success of the American Revolution reverberated elsewhere. The French, fed up with famine and national bankruptcy, erupted soon afterwards in a bloody revolt that reached heights of head-severing excess. The specter of royalty laid low alarmed other monarchs who marched on the upstarts. The French people's success in repelling them caused a new realization in military affairs, that citizens who believed in their country and felt a part in its destiny would fight to preserve it. A long history of tyrants employing private armies was coming to an end.

Rebellion and change became a fever that swept the world. South America threw off its Spanish masters. India, where control passed quickly from the Moguls to the British, grew resentful of all outside interference. Greece, where democracy was born, rose up against the occupying Ottoman Turks. China and Japan, long in voluntary isolation against an outside world they once justifiably considered backward, suddenly realized that technology had passed them by. China fought against the European expansionists. Japan changed its ways and joined them.

Meanwhile another revolution was under way that was changing people's lives even more than political metamorphoses—the industrial revolution, a burgeoning of factories and large industries that moved people from the farms to the cities, creating new benefits as well as the social problems of overcrowding, filth, crime, and worker exploitation. With it came a new explosion of technology. The steam engine ran machines that could turn out products faster than individuals could craft them one by one. Harnessed to movable objects, steam quickened the movement of people. Railroads spider-webbed over continents. Thoughts traveled even faster as first the telegraph, then the telephone, came into use. Medicine improved, and diseases that had long plagued humankind were conquered.

Conquered as well were those segments of the globe that had been detached from the new technology. A deadly offspring of the industrial revolution was improved weaponry. Exploding shells, repeating rifles, and metal warships not only changed the nature of warfare but also spelled the doom of less technologically advanced groups long isolated by difficult geography.

In the young United States, Native Americans yielded to the westward advance of settlers. Africa, its social structures riddled by the slave trade and Muslim holy wars, was carved up and divided among European powers. Remote peoples of the South Pacific were finally swept unwillingly into new cultures, their spears and arrows no match for firearms.

It was a time of empire and angst, new benefits and unconscionable cruelty. One thing for certain: A world that had moved in a time-honored rhythm was caught up in a quickening tempo. ■

Mr DE, LA FAYETTE

At the first anniversary of the Bastille's fall, the tables turned on the Marquis de Lafayette, shown bigger than life on a poster *(above)*. Radicals opposed this hero of the American and French Revolutions and head of the French National Guard. After he fled France in 1792, Austrians captured and imprisoned him for five years. *Overleaf:* New Yorkers toppled a statue of King George III as revolutionary fever swept the American colonies. Patriots enriched their coffers with gilt from the statue and molded its lead into 42,000 bullets.

1700 The commode becomes a popular piece of furniture.

1701 "Captain" William Kidd is hanged for piracy.

1702 An ecclesiastical history of New England, *Magnalia Christi Americana,* is published by Cotton Mather.

1702 Serfdom is abolished in Denmark.

1704 *Boston News Letter* is the first newspaper published in America.

Maintaining Europe's Balance of Power

At the beginning of the 1700s, the monarchs of Europe, often related by marriage, jockeyed for power. National borders changed frequently by wars and treaties. As allies changed sides in the struggles for European dominance, the people paid the price in taxes and lives.

France had become a powerful nation, and other monarchs feared the expansionist ambitions of Louis XIV. When Charles II, King of Spain, was dying in the late 1600s, he had no children to succeed him. Claimants to the throne, by royal inheritance, were connected to either the Bourbon family of France or the Habsburgs of Austria.

Britain did not want the French heir to be the Spanish king because that would make France and Spain powerful allies. France did not want the Austrian heir to become king of Spain because that would make allies of two of her traditional enemies.

Louis XIV of France and William III of Britain decided that the new Spanish king should be a Habsburg prince of Bavaria who must agree never to join forces with Austria. The Austrian emperor, of course, was outraged at the agreement.

Just before King Charles died, however, he made a new will, naming a Bourbon, Philip of Anjou, the grandson of Louis XIV, his successor. Louis chose to honor the will, rather than the agreement he had made with William, but he assured Britain that France and Spain would not be allies after Philip ascended the throne. Britain, weary of war, accepted his word.

But when French forces occupied Spanish fortresses in the Spanish

● **Daniel Defoe publishes his famous novel,** *Robinson Crusoe.*
1719

● **In Germany, Johann Sebastian Bach compos-es the** *Brandenburg Concertos.*
1721

● **More than 60,000 die in tremendous earthquake in Lisbon, Portugal.**
1755

● **The British capture Quebec from the French.**
1759

● **Ireland declared insepa-rable from England.**
1719

● **Russia's University of Moscow is founded.**
1755

Netherlands, today's Belgium, as a prelude to invading Protestant Holland, the much-feared collusion between Spain and France appeared to be a reality.

Then came the death of James II, a Stuart and an ousted king of Britain who had fled to France for protec-tion. Louis proclaimed that James's son should be the rightful next king of Britain. This alarmed the British because thousands of Scottish follow-ers of James II, known as Jacobites, stood ready to join France in recap-turing the British crown for the Stuarts.

Outraged at Louis's betrayal and fearful of a takeover of Europe by the two Catholic nations, France and Spain, Britain formed a Grand Alliance with Holland, Austria, and most of the German states. The War of the Spanish Succession began.

War ground on from 1702 until 1713, when the Treaty of Utrecht was signed. Under the leadership of Britain's Duke of Marlborough the Grand Alliance had won important victories. Philip was allowed to remain king of Spain, but both Spain and France gave up territory. The war had drained the French treasury and brought much opposition to the

European armies clashed over inheri-tances early in the 1700s. Amid the dead and dying, Prussians sing a hymn of victory at Leuthen *(above)* after thwarting Austria's claim to a region called Silesia in the Seven Years' War. Two years later the two armies met again in the Battle of Maxen *(opposite).* The war spilled into the New World as Eng-land and France, allied with opposing sides, fought in America.

once popular reign of Louis XIV.

Less than half a century later another war broke out, aimed at curbing a growing power. Charles VI, a Habsburg, archduke of Austria, and emperor of the shrunken Holy Roman Empire, had no sons; and according to empire law and custom, his daughter Maria Theresa could not succeed him. He persuaded other European monarchs, however, to let her do so. When the 23-year-old Maria Theresa inherited the throne in 1740, the ambitious King Frederick the Great of Prussia invaded a part of Austria called Silesia. He was sup-ported in this action by Spain, Bavaria, and Saxony, all countries with royal family members who claimed they had a better right than Maria Theresa to the title of emperor, and by France, where the Bourbons were rivals of the Habsburgs.

Britain, the Netherlands, and

Hungary, concerned about the rise of Prussia, supported Maria Theresa. After seven years of fighting, a peace was signed that allowed Prussia to keep Silesia.

But Maria Theresa wanted Silesia back. So she changed sides, dissolv-ing her alliance with Britain and ally-ing with France and Russia, also alarmed by Prussia's rising power.

The Seven Years' War began in 1756 and involved almost every country in Europe. Major powers fought mostly for control of the seas and of their colonies. In North America, the conflict was known as the French and Indian War because many Native Americans fought on the side of the French.

Britain prevailed, and France ceded to her all of Canada and lands east of the Mississippi. Austria and Prussia worked out their own agree-ment, and Prussia kept Silesia. ∎

1707 England, Wales, and Scotland are joined by the parliamentary Act of Union to form the United Kingdom of Great Britain.

1720 First yacht club established at Ireland's Cork Harbor.

1735 John Peter Zenger, a newspaper editor, is acquitted of libel in New York, establishing press freedom.

1744 First recorded cricket match is held in England.

1744 First national geographic survey in France produces the first map drawn on modern scientific principles.

The Age of Enlightenment

As the monarchs of Europe fought seemingly endless wars over questions of power, a new way of thinking was spreading among thoughtful people. Many intellectuals began to believe that reason could solve virtually every human problem and that a better future was in store.

Scientific advances were also taking place, such as the development of the microscope and the subsequent discovery of the world of bacteria.

Over a 21-year period a 28-volume encyclopedia was published in France, containing all the then current knowledge about science, technology, and history. The period in which many new ideas and discoveries came to the fore was known as the Age of Enlightenment.

Many prominent philosophers believed in the natural law and the purifying effects of nature on people. Englishman John Locke wrote in

1690 that people have natural rights to life, liberty, and property and that they have a contract with their government to help them achieve these. If their government fails them, he wrote, people have a right to break the contract with their government. Such ideas were a formula for revolution.

In the 18th century, Paris became the center of enlightened thought, and many French philosophers admired Locke's writings. Artists,

1753 French troops from Canada invade the Ohio Valley, a British settlement.

1762 Catherine the Great becomes Czarina of Russia.

1769 Scottish machinist James Watt patents modern steam engine.

1778 British and Indian raiders surround and defeat a small patriot garrison near today's Wilkes-Barre, Pennsylvania; the conquest would be called the Wyoming Massacre.

1788 A fleet of 11 ships loaded with 776 prisoners arrives at Botany Bay from England, establishing Australia's first penal colony.

writers, and intellectuals met in salons to discuss ideas.

Those with important viewpoints included François-Marie Arouet, known as Voltaire, who poked fun at hypocrisy and criticized the churches that persecuted people who worshiped differently. And Montesquieu, who wrote *The Spirit of the Laws*, a book that described governments as divided into legislative, executive, and judicial branches, an important influence later in the writing of the Constitution of the United States of America.

The importance of reason in ruling people's lives was challenged by Jean-Jacques Rousseau, who argued for the importance of sentiment. Governments and civilization in general corrupted people, Rousseau believed, so they should change the former if necessary and avoid the latter as much as possible by retreating to the simple pleasures of country life.

Even monarchs were influenced by the new ways of thinking. Catherine the Great of Russia read the works of Voltaire. The French queen Marie Antoinette had a small cottage built for herself and occasionally pretended to lead a simpler exis-

tence. Frederick the Great invited Voltaire to live at the Prussian court and attempted reforms based on enlightened thought, abolishing most torture and urging religious tolerance.

But history would show that real reforms would be forced by the people, through acts of revolution that would take place around the globe. ■

Thinkers in concert *(below)*, Voltaire, arm raised, and a group of intellectual friends met to discuss ideas of the Enlightenment, a movement centered in France. Among notions debated: the natural right of people to improved living conditions under their government. When the French king seemed to ban a reorganized National Assembly from its chambers, members massed in an indoor tennis court *(opposite)* and laid the groundwork for a revolution.

1703 In the Americas, Delaware breaks away from Pennsylvania to form a separate colony.

1725 In Italy, Antonio Vivaldi writes *The Four Seasons*.

1730 Large parts of India are under the control of the state of Maratha as the Mogul Empire weakens.

1740 Employed by the Russians, Capt. Vitus Bering, of Denmark, explores Alaska.

1763 In the American Colonies, Chief Pontiac leads a Native American rebellion against British settlers.

Unrest in Europe

The strong hold that European monarchs long had over their citizenry began to wear thin. Britain's civil war had weakened the authority of the king in favor of the Parliament. When James II had tried to reassert royal authority, he had been driven from the country.

Democracy had not yet arrived; it was merely knocking at the door. Although Parliament included a House of Commons, voting was limited to wealthy property owners, perhaps 4 percent of the population. Some talk of equality and universal suffrage had been raised during the civil war by a radical British group called the Levelers, but it died out.

A cry for justice rang out in several countries as common people began to struggle against inequities. None answered more ardently than the French, weary of an economy ruined by royal wars. During France's revolutionary times, extremists called Jacobins (below) met to condemn the crown, those connected to the crown, or anyone deemed an enemy of the state. A chief architect of this frenzy, Maximilien Robespierre (opposite), instigated the death of thousands before rival rebels executed him in turn.

Grande Séance aux Jacobins en janvier 1792, où l'on voit le grand effet interieure que fit l'anonce de la guerre par le Ministre Linote à la suite de son grand tour qu'il venoit de faire

1789 ● Mutineers on the British ship *Bounty* overthrow their captain after a voyage to Tahiti.

1789 ● George Washington becomes first President of the United States.

1793 ● First free settlers arrive in Australia.

1798 ● Napoleon invades Egypt.

1800 ● Italian physicist Alessandro Volta creates the voltaic pile, a crude battery.

The ordinary Englishman could not claim equality, but the classes mingled and one could improve oneself.

Elsewhere the plight of the common people was often grim. Russian serfs were little better than slaves, working in poverty on the estates of nobles. Catherine the Great admired the egalitarian ideas of the Enlightenment, but when the serfs rebelled, she brutally crushed the effort and their lives remained unchanged.

Peasants in France were better off, and many of them owned their own land. But they had to pay land taxes, feudal dues, a church tithe, and fines to the nobles. As the nobles faced the increasing costs of living in the 17th century, they collected dues from the peasants even more diligently.

The growing middle class in France—the bourgeoisie—consisted of merchants, doctors, lawyers, and other professions. Educated, they had read the writings of the Enlightenment and believed in equality and social justice. Resenting the privileges of the aristocratic class, they were more restless and outspoken than the peasants.

Like the peasants, the bourgeoisie was heavily taxed, while the aristocrats of the country paid relatively little tax. The extravagance of the royal court and the privileged existence of nobles and church officials made the tax inequities especially grating.

Food was scarce, prices were high, and the government was nearly bankrupt. The French treasury had been drained by the wars of Louis XIV.

In 1788 a severe winter brought famine and starvation in the countryside, while in Paris rising food prices brought riots over bread.

The desire for freedom and personal independence extended to colonies and empire holdings as well. In North America British colonists protested paying extra taxes to ease royal debts brought about by the French and Indian War. In Greece, birthplace of democracy, nationalists were chafing under the rule of the Ottoman Turks. The time was ripe for wars of change and independence. ■

IRISH POTATO FAMINE

A disaster increased the hatred many Irish had for their British overlords. British Corn (wheat) Laws kept wheat prices high so landlords could make large profits from crops grown on their land. Most Irish ate potatoes because they could not afford wheat for bread. This sketch *(below)*, published in the *Illustrated London Times*, shows a body being carted away, one of around a million Irish who starved when, in 1845 and 1846, a blight ruined the potato crop. A million others emigrated, mostly to the United States.

1789 Chrysanthemums are first introduced from the Orient into Great Britain.

1789 John Carroll of Baltimore becomes first Roman Catholic bishop to be consecrated in U.S.

1790 Philadelphia becomes the federal capital of the United States.

1791 The Bank of North America is founded.

1792 In England illuminating gas is used for the first time.

The French Revolution

The situation in France had reached the boiling point. The government was out of money, and no one would extend loans to it. The common people were already overtaxed, and nobles refused to pay additional tax. In desperation King Louis XVI called together, in May of 1789, the Estates-General, a French legislative body that had not met for some 175 years.

France was at this time divided into three social classes. The First Estate was the Catholic clergy, the Second Estate was the nobility, and the Third Estate was everyone else. In the Estates-General the three sat separately and each estate had equal voice in affairs, even though the Third Estate represented vastly more people than the other two combined. The first two estates assumed business would be conducted as usual, but the Third Estate asked for a meeting in which each delegate would have one vote. When the king refused this request, the Third Estate began to meet on its own and started to draft a new constitution, one inspired by the egalitarian ideas of the Enlightenment and the experiment in democracy that was taking place in North America after the recent war for independence.

Public support for the new assembly was high, and when the king appeared ready to use force to disband it, a crowd took over an armory called Hotel des Invalides for guns and stormed the prison known as the Bastille in search of powder and shot. Word spread of the crowd's success, and uprisings began all over France, with granaries robbed and manor houses overrun.

Seeing the power of the Third Estate, the other two joined the assembly and the Declaration of the Rights of Man and Citizen was written. It proclaimed new rights (speech, press, and religion) and outlawed arrests and punishment without just cause. All citizens were declared equal, and it was stated: "Social distinctions may be based only upon general usefulness."

When Louis XVI seemed to waiver in his support of the declaration, a mob of Parisian women marched on Versailles, where the king and queen lived, and forced them to move to

The fall of the Bastille marked the beginning of the French Revolution as militiamen and Parisians stormed the prison (opposite). The powers of King Louis XVI eroded, and three years later rebels declared France a republic. Found guilty of treason, the king died at the guillotine after a tearful adieu (above) to his children and his sister, at right. Nine months later, his queen, Marie Antoinette, met the same fate.

1792 Baptist Missionary Society is founded in London.

1793 Board of Agriculture is established in Britain.

1793 John Macarthur begins the breeding of Merino sheep in Australia.

1794 Eli Whitney patents the cotton gin, which makes cotton the chief crop of the American South.

1794 The United States Navy is established.

Dutch surrender Ceylon to the British.
1795

Explorer Mungo Park explores the Niger River.
1795

1795
The U.S. and Spain settle the boundary of Florida in the Treaty of San Lorenzo. It also gives the U.S. the right to navigate the Mississippi River.

George Washington refuses to accept a third term and delivers his Farewell Address.
1796

Jews are granted civil rights in Amsterdam.
1796

The execution machine proposed by Dr. Guillotin beheaded the former king of France, who had declared, "I die innocent," before 20,000 spectators.

Paris so they could be watched.

Over the next two years the assembly drastically altered the government and the way of life. Church properties were confiscated and sold, mainly to the peasants and middle class. A one-house legislature was established whose members were selected by voters, which despite declarations of equality included only men of property.

Louis reluctantly accepted rules for a limited monarchy. News of the revolution stirred unrest in other European countries and alarmed rulers, but an attempt by Austrian and German forces to march against Paris and quell the revolution was halted by French forces.

A group called the Jacobins felt the revolution had not gone far enough. In 1792 they abolished the monarchy and accused King Louis of treason. They then beheaded him on a new machine called the guillotine, a weighted blade falling along grooves toward a victim's neck.

The act outraged European monarchs. Joining in the fight against the revolutionary army were Britain, the Netherlands, and Spain. The Jacobins killed thousands of people whom they declared counter-revolutionaries, a Reign of Terror that continued until one of the leaders, a young lawyer named Maximilien Robespierre, was beheaded.

In 1795 a new constitution was adopted, less radical than that of the Jacobins. Some calm returned. Churches reopened. The new regime favored the well-to-do. Five men elected by the assembly served in the executive branch, known as the Directory. France's troubles calmed but were not over. The economy was in chaos, and the country was still at war with other nations. ■

1804 Alexander Hamilton is fatally wounded in dual with Aaron Burr.

1805 Break occurs between Britain and U.S. over trade disputes in the West Indies.

1806 Holy Roman Empire is dissolved.

1807 First successful steam-boat trip is made on the *Clermont* between New York City and Albany.

1808 Pigtails disappear as a men's hair fashion.

The Conquests of Napoleon

French society was in tatters after the Reign of Terror. Bandits roamed the land. Royalists who wanted the kingship returned were in rebellion. Into this disorder strode Napoleon Bonaparte, a young general who had won victories over armies marching against France.

In 1799 Napoleon, a brilliant military strategist, took over the French government. He helped overthrow the Directory, established a new government administered by three consuls, and was himself named First Consul. He restored internal order and suppressed the royalist rebellion. He rewrote the confusing and contradictory old laws into clear and consistent statutes known as the Napoleonic Code. An admirer of Enlightenment thinkers, Napoleon did not destroy the revolution, but—no friend to representative government—he set himself up as virtual dictator and finally crowned himself Emperor of the French in 1804.

Meanwhile he had expanded his empire to include much of Europe. He abolished the title of Holy Roman Emperor and became ruler of Italy. He named his brother Joseph king of Naples and Sicily and his brother Louis king of Holland. Most of continental Europe was either controlled by him or allied with him.

Only defeats by Britain at sea prevented him from invading the country, so he tried to control British trade. He

Restorer of French pride, Napoleon Bonaparte returned from a campaign in Egypt *(below)* in 1799 to seize control of his nation and restore order. He conquered most of Europe before allied armies left him brooding in defeat *(above)* in 1814.

● Elizabeth Seton founds
Sisters of Charity of
1809 St. Joseph in U.S.

● **Krupp metalworks**
opens in Germany.
1810

● Java is occupied
by the British.
1811

● Venezuela is declared
an independent nation
1811 by Simón Bolívar.

● War of 1812.

1812-1814

NAPOLEON'S EUROPE

KINGDOM OF SWEDEN

KINGDOM
OF DENMARK
AND
NORWAY

Friedland 180

PRUSSIA

HOLLAND

GREAT
BRITAIN

Leipzig 1813
Jena 1806

Waterloo
1815

CONFEDERATION
OF THE RHINE

Prague

Austerlitz
1805

Wagr
180

Paris

Vienna

Fontainebleau

F R E N C H

E M P I R E

ILLYRIAN PROVINCES

Rochefort

KINGDOM
OF ITALY

Lodi 1796

Marengo 1800

TUSCANY

Toulon

Elba

CORSICA

Rome

Ajaccio

Somosierra
1808

Madrid

KINGDOM
OF SARDINIA

KINGDOM
OF NAPLES

KINGDOM
OF SPAIN

SICILY

M E D I T E R R A N E A N   S E A

Trafalgar
1805

0   300 mi

0   300 km

1813   English novelist Jane Austen publishes *Pride and Prejudice.*

1814   George Stephenson builds first practical steam locomotive. Dutch cede Cape Town to the British.

1815   At New Orleans, Andrew Jackson defeats British under Edward Pakenham.

1819   First British settlement established in Singapore.

1820   The Missouri Compromise allows Missouri to be admitted to the U.S. as a slave state, but slavery is banned from the rest of the Louisiana Purchase north of 36°30' N.

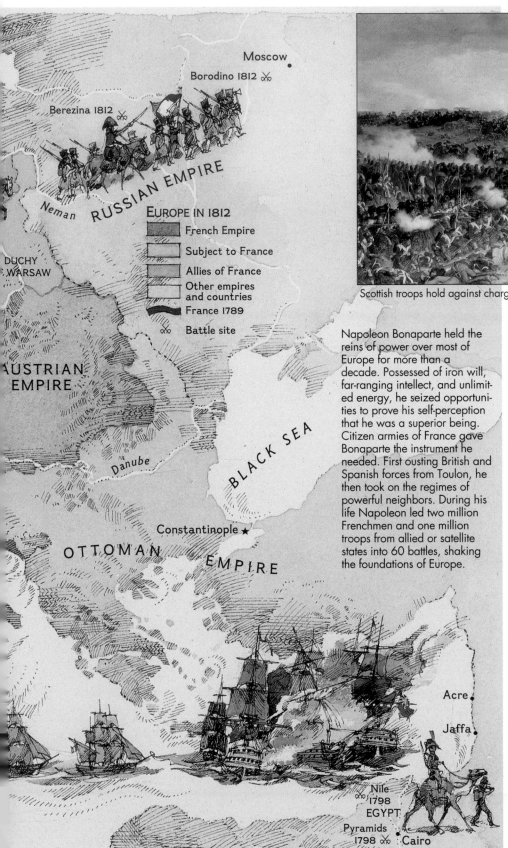

EUROPE IN 1812

French Empire

Subject to France

Allies of France

Other empires and countries

France 1789

Battle site

Scottish troops hold against charging French cavalry in Napoleon's final defeat at Waterloo.

Napoleon Bonaparte held the reins of power over most of Europe for more than a decade. Possessed of iron will, far-ranging intellect, and unlimited energy, he seized opportunities to prove his self-perception that he was a superior being. Citizen armies of France gave Bonaparte the instrument he needed. First ousting British and Spanish forces from Toulon, he then took on the regimes of powerful neighbors. During his life Napoleon led two million Frenchmen and one million troops from allied or satellite states into 60 battles, shaking the foundations of Europe.

forbade any trade ships landing at continental ports to stop at Britain first. Tsar Alexander I defied this dictum, and in 1812 Napoleon invaded Russia. He occupied Moscow, but the Russians burned the city so that his huge army had no shelter.

With winter approaching, the French forces began a long retreat that turned into disaster. Half a million men were lost—some to the Russian army; others, without adequate food and rest, to the elements. Napoleon was defeated and exiled to Elba off the coast of Italy. The boundaries of France were returned to what they had been in 1792.

Escaping dramatically from Elba and returning to France in 1815, Napoleon was welcomed by French forces. In one last great battle he was defeated at Waterloo in the Austrian Netherlands by an allied army led by Britain's Duke of Wellington.

Placed under house arrest on the island of St. Helena, off the coast of Africa, he died there in 1821. ■

● Corn Law is passed in Britain.
1815

● Apothecaries Act prevents unqualified doctors from practicing in Britain.
1815

● Madrid's Prado Museum is founded.
1818

● First professional horse-racing in U.S.
1818

● Egyptians capture Crete.
1824

Conflicts and Rebellions

The French Revolution gave rise to a generation of conflicts based on principles of freedom, equality, and national unity. People long under the thumb of royalty decided that they were more important than the state and that they wanted to have a say about how they were governed.

An almost continuous sputtering of revolutionary movements occurred from 1815 to 1848, while during that time there were no major wars between great powers.

Representatives of the great European nations, in fact, met in Vienna in 1815 to discuss ways of supporting royalty.

In 1820 reformers in Spain forced the Bourbon king Ferdinand VII to accept a liberal constitution.

As word of that revolt spread, reformers in Naples attempted to accomplish the same with their Bourbon king, Ferdinand I. Jumping to the aid of royalty, Austria marched into Naples and restored the monarchy.

France did the same in Spain. But the revolutionary spirit had not yet expired in France. In 1824 Charles X succeeded his brother Louis XVIII to the French throne and moved in the direction of restoring absolute royal authority. French mobs took to the streets again, and Charles abdicated and fled to Britain.

Nationalism became a driving force among people who spoke a common language and who wanted their own nation. For example, in 1821 the Greeks rose against the Ottoman Turks. Thousands were killed in the effort. But Greece won its independence in 1829.

REVOLUTIONARIES OF ANOTHER ILK

The Luddites, organized bands of British textile workers, protested the introduction of machinery like that in this 19th-century textile mill in New England (above). Its use caused the dismissal of handicraftsmen and the lowering of manufacturing quality. Masked and operating at night, Luddites destroyed the machines that took jobs away from people.

In Britain the Chartists demonstrated for "fair wages," but their main petition was for universal suffrage—the right of every adult to vote—which they did not get. Other rebellions sought cheaper food or changes in laws that would allow the common people to own land.

In the year 1848 especially, rebellions and protests broke out all over Europe—in Britain, Poland, Italy, Germany. In France Louis Philippe had agreed to serve as citizen-king, but demonstrators forced him out and declared France a republic once again.

News of the French revolt spread to Austria, after which protesters demanded a constitution and the end to absolutist rule.

In Hungary, part of the Austrian Empire, Magyar nationalists demanded their own constitution and a separate Hungarian parliament. Nationalists in Italy also revolted against Austrian rule.

Revolutions played out for a while after 1848. In that same year Karl Marx published *The Communist Manifesto,* asserting that revolutions by the working class would ultimately destroy capitalism. ∎

1830 Joseph Smith forms the Church of Jesus Christ of Latter-day Saints in the U.S.

1831 Belgium separates from the Netherlands.

1831 British scientist Michael Faraday creates a dynamo, demonstrating how a steady current of electricity could be created mechanically by the rotation of wire around a magnet.

1834 Charles Babbage invents an "analytical engine," a forerunner of the computer.

1844 Five Chinese ports are opened to U.S. ships.

Church spires in Buda face Hungary's neo-Gothic Parliament building across the Danube in Pest, the two halves of the Hungarian capital that rebelled against Austria in 1848.

1701 In England, Jethro Tull invents the horse-drawn seed drill.

1702 Britain's Princess Anne, daughter of James II, becomes Queen of England and Scotland; she is the last of the Stuart sovereigns.

1707 Break up of India's Mogul Empire at death of Aurangzeb.

1710 Mauritius, formerly part of Dutch East Indies, becomes French.

1712 Last execution for witchcraft in England.

American Colonies Grow Apart From Britain

England may have lost its colonies in North America on the battlefields of Europe. Preoccupation with its own affairs and the many wars on the European continent had led the mother country to pay little attention to the thousands of British who had sailed to North America. Meanwhile the colonists were forming their own regional legislatures and learning how to govern themselves.

The British were not greatly enamored of their American colonies. India and the islands of the Caribbean were more profitable. They had a fishing base in Newfoundland and a military outpost against the French in Nova Scotia. To them the eastern seaboard was in some ways simply one more commercial operation to which the rules of efficiency applied.

To the irritation of the colonists, the Navigation Acts of the 1600s limited colonial trade to British and colonial ships and restricted manufacture of woolen and iron goods in the colonies so they wouldn't compete with those made in Britain.

The dangerous antipathy that developed between mother country and colonies grew particularly out of Britain's many wars with France. Between 1689 and 1763 France and Britain battled each other frequently in North America over issues with roots in Europe. The final struggle was the French and Indian War, which Britain won in 1763 and through which it acquired Canada.

Colonists had often fought alongside British troops, but the conflicts

1727 The Spanish lay siege to Gibraltar.

1729 Portugal loses Mombasa to the Arabs.

1734 George Sale translates the Koran into English.

1751 France begins publication of the *Encyclopédie*, considered the leading volume of the Enlightenment.

1756-1763 Seven Years' War, Prussia and Britain defeat France, Spain, Austria, and Russia; France cedes all of Canada and its lands east of the Mississippi to Britain.

1762 Sandwiches are invented in England and named for the Earl of Sandwich.

drained the British treasury. Then, when money was needed in the post-war period, the British tried to make up part of it with tax revenues from the colonies.

The colonists, feeling increasingly estranged from Britain and already chafing at trade policies unfavorable to their own welfare, were not in a mood to help out. By the mid-1700s, generations had been born in America. Hardened by life on the frontier, they did not submit easily to pressure from afar. Tensions were building between the British, who considered the Colonies British territory, and their far-off citizens, who wanted to handle their own affairs. ■

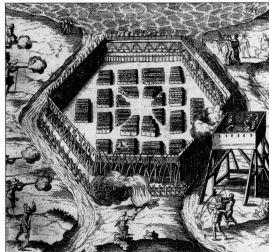

Colonists fought with the British in the French and Indian War. With the British commander Edward Braddock gravely wounded at the Battle of Monongahela (*left*), George Washington, shown here on horseback, led forces—which included the Iroquois—against the French. Iroquois animosity toward the enemy dated from early hostilities such as a siege in 1615 by French and Indian allies against an Iroquois fort (*above*) that protected their longhouses.

1765 Louis Augustus (the future Louis XVI) becomes heir to the French throne upon the death of his father, the Dauphin.

1766 Famine strikes Bengal, India.

1770 Capt. James Cook sails completely around North and South Islands of New Zealand.

1770 Royal Marriage Act is passed in Britain to prevent undesirable royal marriages.

1774 The Shaker sect is founded in U.S. by Ann Lee of Manchester, England, who had emigrated to America with eight followers.

U.S. War of Independence

By 1763 the population of the 13 Colonies lining the east coast of North America was around 1.5 million. Many of the colonists were radicals on the issues of equality, liberty, and universal suffrage. In some cases they were the descendants of people who had fled England over those same principles. The attempts by debt-ridden England to raise revenues struck them as oppressive.

The Stamp Act imposed a tax on commercial uses of paper, such as legal documents, advertisements, and newspapers. The tax on newsprint threw journalists into an editorial rage, which further incited anti-British feeling. Rioters burned the stamps and attacked the issuing agents.

The Stamp Act was repealed, but it was followed by duties on imports of glass, lead, paper, and tea, levied

to pay British officials in America, not to aid in Britain's defense.

Enraged colonists jeered and insulted British troops, and in March 1770 a squad of British soldiers in Boston was pelted with stones and snowballs. A riotous crowd gathered, and nervous British troops opened fire, killing five in what was called the Boston Massacre.

Still, many colonists were reluctant to sever relations with England—reluctant, that is, until passage of the Tea Act. This act let the British East India Company ship tea directly to its agents in America, avoiding import

Several events spurred the American colonists toward a break with England. Engraver Henry Pelham's 1770 sketch of the Boston Massacre *(left)* was spiced with strong anti-British flavor. Paul Revere later copied and embellished this work. Patrick Henry provided a rallying cry when as a Virginia legislator he boomed, "Give me liberty or give me death!" *(above)*. Thomas Jefferson drafted the eagerly sought Declaration of Independence and submitted it to Benjamin Franklin and John Adams for comment *(opposite)*.

1778 La Scala, an opera house, opens in Milan.

1779 Capt. James Cook is murdered by Hawaiian Islanders.

1780 Gervinus invents the circular saw.

1781 Moses Mendelssohn, German philosopher, calls for better treatment of Jewish people.

1782 Josiah Wedgwood develops the pyrometer for checking the temperatures in pottery furnaces.

duties and allowing the agents to undercut the prices of American retailers. When the first cargoes arrived in Boston, radicals disguised as Indians boarded the ships and dumped the tea into the Boston harbor.

In the fall of 1774 colonials called together the First Continental Congress in Philadelphia and drafted a letter to King George III, which they sent to London. This letter called for the right of colonies to make their own laws, although it recognized England's right to regulate trade. Parliament rejected it.

In anticipation of trouble, the colonists began drilling and gathering guns and gunpowder, stockpiling them in Concord, Massachusetts. In the spring of 1775 a British unit in Boston set off to seize them but was met midway, at the town of Lexington, by 70 local militia. Shots were fired, with losses on both sides. A war for independence had begun.

The Second Continental Congress met and named George Washington as the commander-in-chief of the Continental Army.

Most British troops were contemptuous of the fighting abilities of the Colonials who had joined them in the French and Indian War. British general Thomas Gage, commander of British forces, prepared to attack Continentals who were dug in outside Boston and teach the rebels a lesson.

Up Bunker Hill marched his orderly lines toward the colonists, who held their fire until the British were within range of 50 yards, then cut

down the uniformed troops in droves.

It took three attempts by Britain's finest before the colonists gave way. They had proved their courage.

England knew that a protracted struggle might lie ahead.

Meanwhile the Continental Congress appointed a committee to prepare a declaration of independence. Thomas Jefferson of Virginia, a committee member, wrote the first

draft. He was familiar with the work of the 17th-century writer John Locke, who had believed there should be no class distinction in laws; that human beings have a basic right to life, liberty, and property ownership; and that governments exist only to help individuals achieve those rights.

Congress adopted the declaration on July 4, 1776, and Washington read it to his troops to inspire them.

● Famine strikes Japan.
1783

● Bank of Ireland is founded.
1783

● Russians settle the Aleutian Islands.
1785

● French climbers reach the summit of Mont Blanc, the highest peak in the Alps.
1787

● Britain establishes a penal colony in New South Wales, Australia.
1788

The Colonial Army was no match for British forces in the open field, but under Washington's guidance it struck in raids, fought from cover, and eluded unequal confrontations. An attack on Trenton, New Jersey, on Christmas night in 1776 was only a minor military victory, but a great boost to morale. A major defeat was suffered in September 1777 while trying to bar the British from entering the colonial capital of Philadelphia.

An important turning point in the war came at Saratoga, New York, in October when American Colonials fighting in the woods badgered a professional force of some 7,000 British into surrender.

That victory convinced Europeans

Outmatched Colonial troops endured winter cold at Valley Forge, Pennsylvania, in 1777. Gen. George Washington *(above)*, at left, is shown here with the French volunteer Marquis de Lafayette, questioning a sentry. Not many years after the 13 Colonies won independence, the United States fought the British again. In the

War of 1812 the *USS Constitution*, one of the U.S. Navy's first warships, earned the epithet "Old Ironsides" by battering the British frigate *Guerrière* *(right).* The capture of the *Guerrière* stimulated a sense of nationality in the U.S. and marked the end of the new nation's dependence on Europe.

that the Colonies had a chance, and France allied with them in the spring of 1778. Spain followed in 1779.

In August of 1781 American and French forces bottled up Lord Cornwallis's army of 8,000 men at Yorktown, Virginia, while French ships blockaded the coast and prevented resupply. Cornwallis surrendered all his men.

Britain, appalled at the growing cost of this unwanted conflict, granted the rebellious Colonies their independence and concentrated on fighting elsewhere against two other threats, France and Spain.

The new United States first organized as a league of independent states under an agreement called the

Articles of Confederation. This arrangement proved insufficient because it did not cover the essential rights to levy taxes or regulate commerce among the states.

A constitution was then written, setting up a federal system, with power divided between the states and a central government. From the French Enlightenment writer Montesquieu came the idea of dividing the power of the federal government among three main branches—executive, legislative, and judicial.

As final confirmation of the aims of the Revolution, a Bill of Rights was added to the Constitution, guaranteeing citizens the rights to worship and speak freely and to have trial by jury. ∎

1779 First cast-iron bridge is built in England.

1783 The first successful parachute jump is made by Frenchman Louis Lenormand.

1794 The Commune of Paris is abolished.

1796 Napoleon marries Josephine de Beauharnais.

1800 Englishman Richard Trevithick builds a high-pressure steam engine capable of moving passengers in a carriage.

1801 The French astronomer Joseph Lalande publishes a catalogue of 47,390 known stars.

Rebellion in Other Colonies

For more than two centuries after Pizarro defeated the Inca, Native Americans had been forced to work Spanish-run mines and factories in Peru, under deplorable conditions.

In 1780 they revolted. An ill-armed horde, they nevertheless overran the highlands and twice attacked the city of Cuzco. The rebels, in a link to their past, relied on an ancient Inca communication system using knotted ropes.

Their leader was a wealthy Spanish-American named José Gabriel Condorcanqui, who claimed descent from the 16th-century Inca emperor Tupac Amaru. As a sign of his close ties with that former Inca leader, Condorcanqui even took his name. He was captured by Spanish forces in 1781 and tortured to death, but the struggle continued. The rebellion spread to Bolivia where La Paz was twice attacked before the movement was finally crushed in 1782.

In French-owned Haiti, freed mulattoes rebelled in 1791, after being denied the vote that had been guaranteed by the National Assembly that followed the French Revolution. In the ensuing chaos, slaves joined the revolt.

In the bloody uprising, sugar and coffee plantations were burned, and their owners and families were slaughtered. Emerging as an able leader was an educated freed slave who became known as Toussaint L'Ouverture because of his ability to open holes in French lines.

In 1793 Toussaint proclaimed the end of slavery and joined Spanish forces on the Santo Domingo end of the island in their war against France.

The English also joined the Spanish, and the French were close to surrender. But in 1794 Toussaint suddenly changed sides, saying he was pleased that the French had abolished slavery.

Toussaint fought brilliantly against his former allies and in 1798 forced the British to evacuate. In 1801 he declared the entire island independent with himself as ruler.

The French under Napoleon would not stand for it and sent forces to reassert control. After stiff resistance, Toussaint was overcome, arrested, and sent to prison in France. Although he died there in 1803, Haiti became independent. ■

Monument to freedom, the Citadel stands tall as part of Haiti's fight to escape slavery.

THE LOUISIANA PURCHASE

The land sale that doubled the size of the United States in 1803 came as a surprise. U.S. envoys had been negotiating with Napoleon in Paris over the possible sale of New Orleans and western Florida. But Napoleon was disturbed over heavy losses his army had sustained in battling for Santo Domingo in the Caribbean. Suddenly he offered to sell all the prairie lands between the Mississippi River and the Rocky Mountains, the French-held area known as Louisiana. For the sum of 15 million dollars the U.S. gained more than three-quarters of a million square miles.

○ 1805 Lord Nelson defeats the French-Spanish fleets in the Battle of Trafalgar.

○ 1805 Thomas Jefferson begins his second term as U.S. President.

○ 1809 Sweden's King Gustavus IV is deposed; Charles XIII succeeds him. Napoleon divorces Josephine.

○ 1811 Massacre of the Mamelukes at Cairo.

Freedom Movements Throughout the Americas

The successful struggle for independence by the British colonies in North America did not go unnoticed by colonies in other parts of the Americas that had been claimed by various Old World nations. The message was clear: Power could be overthrown from within.

For 300 years Spain and Portugal had ruled Central and South America without serious challenge from the original inhabitants.

The openly stratified society of the Spanish colonies greatly favored those people born in Spain—known

1815   Sumbawa volcano erupts in Indonesia, killing more than 50,000 people. John Macadam, British road surveyor, builds roads of crushed stone.

1820   First American missionaries arrive in the Hawaiian Islands.

1822   London's Royal Academy of Music is founded.

1825   Erie Canal opens, 363 miles long, linking Buffalo, New York, on Lake Erie with Albany on the Hudson.

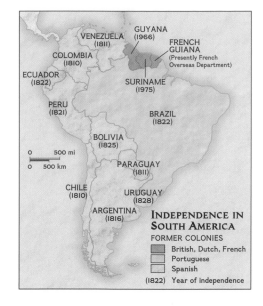

INDEPENDENCE IN SOUTH AMERICA

FORMER COLONIES
- British, Dutch, French
- Portuguese
- Spanish

(1822) Year of independence

as *peninsulares*. Next in line were those of Spanish blood who were born in the colonies—the so-called Creoles; below them in privilege were those of mixed European and Indian or African blood.

The works of Jean-Jacques Rousseau, which espoused justice and equality under the law, were known to many in Spanish America, but while Spain remained strong, there existed little hope for change. When Napoleon invaded Spain in 1808, however, revolutionaries in the Americas saw their chance.

In Mexico two parish priests, Miguel Hidalgo and José María Morelos, tried to lead armies of common people in a revolution for independence and social reforms, but both were caught and executed.

Independence ultimately was achieved not by popular revolution but by the wealthy. With the defeat of Napoleon in Europe, royalists in Mexico feared that a new liberal government would end their privileges,

so they declared their independence from Spain.

Taking a cue from the Mexicans, areas in Central America also declared themselves free. After a civil war in the 1830s they became what are now Guatemala, Costa Rica, El Salvador, Honduras, and Nicaragua.

The man who became known as the liberator of South America was a well-educated Creole named Simón Bolívar. Out of the personal tragedy of the death of his young wife, he became dedicated to the liberation of Venezuela. He and associates declared the colony independent on July 5, 1811, but his forces were defeated in 1812 and again in 1813. He returned in 1817 and, two years later, ended Spanish rule at the crown of South America in the area that now comprises Colombia, Venezuela, Panama, and Ecuador.

On the west coast the struggle for freedom was led by José de San Martín, who had been born in the New World and educated in Spain. After training an army, he joined his men with soldiers led by Bernardo O'Higgins and defeated Spanish forces in Santiago. San Martín took over Lima, Peru, then called on Bolívar for aid.

When the two men did not work well together, San Martín withdrew to live in France. Bolívar won areas that became Peru and Bolivia, completing the expulsion of Spain from South America.

Portuguese-owned Brazil won independence without bloodshed.

When Napoleon invaded Portugal in 1807, the royal family fled to Rio de Janeiro. King João stayed in Brazil after Napoleon was defeated and made it a self-governing kingdom. When liberals took over the government in Lisbon, he returned to save his throne, appointing his son Pedro as regent in Brazil. Pedro declared Brazil independent, and the Lisbon government prepared to invade. But King João, sympathetic to the independence movement, would not let them send troops against his son. ■

Aristocrat turned revolutionary, Simón Bolívar (*above*) led an army of cowboys and colonists to throw off the rule of Spain in several South American countries. Bolívar dreamed of a unified continent, and after victory in hand-to-hand combat at the Battle of Junín (*opposite*) the reality seemed near. But Bolívar's dream included himself as dictator, an imperial notion resisted by others, and his confederation dissolved into separate republics.

1861 — Gold is discovered in New Zealand. Serfs are emancipated in Russia.

1861 — Charles Dickens writes *Great Expectations*. First horse-drawn trams appear in London.

1861 — Passport system introduced in U.S.

1861 — Commercial treaty established between France and Prussia.

1862 — Otto von Bismarck becomes the Prussian prime minister.

The Civil War in America

From the original 13 Colonies along the eastern seaboard, the United States had grown into a large country by the mid-1800s. In 1803 it had doubled in size when Napoleon sold the enormous prairie lands between the Mississippi River and the Rocky Mountains, an exchange called the Louisiana Purchase.

The U.S. nearly doubled again when California and the Southwest were taken in 1848 after the Mexican-American War.

Huge tracts were now open for settlement. New states would be forming. The question over whether they would be free or pro-slavery helped precipitate the young nation's greatest crisis, the Civil War.

In the large cities of the Northeast the economy was based on industry and trade, with droves of unskilled immigrants as a workforce. The South was basically agricultural, with prosperity dependent on money crops, particularly cotton, which it shipped to mills in England. The two regions

● Poland rebels against Russia.
1863

● The French capture Mexico City.
1863

● First salmon cannery opens in U.S. at Washington, California.
1864

● Massacre of the Cheyenne and Arapaho Indians occurs at Sand Creek, Colorado.
1864

● Joseph Lister begins antiseptic surgery.
1865

had different priorities, which led to conflicts in the federal government. Since Southerners sold their cotton in foreign markets and wanted to buy goods in those markets for the return voyage, they wanted to keep tariffs low. Northerners wanted high tariffs to protect the materials and products that they produced.

For Southerners the economic issues involved the reality of slavery, as well, since it was critical, they felt, to the economy of their cotton plantations. For Northerners slavery had become a great moral issue, one that did not resonate well with the nation's ideals about the equality of people.

Many Southerners agreed with presidential candidate Abraham Lincoln that slavery should ultimately be ended. But when Lincoln was elected in 1860, they feared it would happen rapidly, destroying their agrarian economy.

States in the Deep South withdrew from the Union and formed the Confederate States of America. They opened fire on Fort Sumter in South Carolina on April 12, 1861, to prevent its being reprovisioned, and the Civil War began.

By May other southern states had joined the Confederacy, bringing the total to 11. The North had a larger

The heartbreak of slavery, which often separated families sold at auction (*opposite*), helped fire the Civil War. Despite the North's greater numbers, the South had good military leadership, causing a grim President Lincoln to meet with and later replace Gen. George McClellan (*above, right*). Confederates in retreat burned their own capital of Richmond (*above*) to deny Union troops its use, leaving stunned citizens to wander amidst the rubble.

NAT TURNER

The desire for freedom was strong among slaves, but attempts to flee brought severe punishment. A bloody uprising took place in 1831 in Virginia. A slave named Nat Turner became deeply religious and convinced some fellow slaves that he was divinely inspired to lead them against the whites. One night the 31-year-old murdered his master and his master's entire family. Turner also aroused neighboring slaves, who joined in the uprising and killed other white families as well. Captured, Turner was tried, convicted, and hanged.

1865 Napoleon III and Bismarck meet at Biarritz, France.

1865 Wellington becomes New Zealand's capital.

1865 Lewis Carroll publishes *Alice's Adventures in Wonderland.*

1865 The Klu Klux Klan is founded.

1865 War breaks out between Boers of the Orange Free State and the Basutos in South Africa.

Slavery and secession both ended with the Civil War, but serious issues remained. Opinions differed on reconstruction of the ruined South, and freed slaves found they had not gained civil rights. The shadow of the conflict lingered on the national conscience, stark as the silhouettes of Civil War reenactors *(above)*.

population and an industrial infrastructure, as well as a military organization already in place and a communications system to back it up. The South's advantages were a more thoroughly engrained martial spirit and perhaps better generals.

The South under Gen. Robert E. Lee won some of the early battles, but Northern resources and naval blockades to prevent outside help began to turn the tide. Although the United States now stretched all the way to the Pacific, the war was fought almost entirely in the East and South.

Major battles near Washington, D.C., especially at Antietam in 1862 and Gettysburg in 1863, kept vast Southern forces in place defending Richmond, while to the west Union troops controlled the Mississippi Valley by capturing Vicksburg.

In his famous march to the sea, Gen. William Tecumseh Sherman pushed his Union troops from Atlanta to Savannah in five weeks, late in

1864, leaving devastation in his wake and cutting the Confederacy in half. With Union forces to the south and north of him and his own numbers dwindling while enemy troops were growing, General Lee surrendered at Appomattox Courthouse in April 1865.

Confederate officers were not punished, and their troops were allowed to return home. In the bloodiest war on American soil, some 600,000 men had died and some 400,000 had been wounded on both sides of the conflict.

On April 14, 1865, as Lincoln sat in Ford's Theatre in Washington, D.C., he was shot by John Wilkes Booth. He died the next morning. For banning slavery and preserving the Union, Lincoln is an American hero. ■

THE TRAIL OF TEARS

As immigrants flooded to America and spread out to the west and south, they encountered Native Americans who already lived there. In the 1830s the United States government first offered the Cherokees of the South 5.7 million dollars to leave. When most refused, the government forced them to march to reservations in what is now Oklahoma. Many died along the way. The journey is known as the trail of tears.

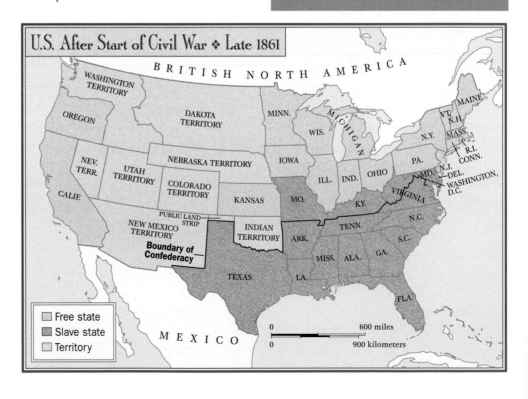

U.S. After Start of Civil War ❖ Late 1861

Free state
Slave state
Territory

1867 ● Dominion of Canada is established.

1869 ● Suez Canal opens, connecting the Mediterranean and the Red Seas and reducing voyages from Britain to India by 4,000 miles.

1887 ● Golden Jubilee of Queen Victoria, celebrating 50 years of her reign.

1889 ● Mark Twain's *A Connecticut Yankee in King Arthur's Court* is published.

1896 ● First modern Olympic Games are held in Athens, Greece.

The U.S. Becomes a Major Power

The mysterious explosion of the battleship *Maine* in Havana's harbor thrust the U.S. into war with Spain in defense of Cuban nationalists and American investments.

By the end of the Civil War, the United States had become an active player in world affairs. Its industrial might provided jobs and prosperity, bringing immigrants from the Old World. With the success of independence movements in South America, the U.S. had also begun to take an interest in inter-American affairs.

In 1823 President James Monroe had issued a warning to European powers not to interfere in the countries of the Western Hemisphere, a policy that came to be known as the Monroe Doctrine.

It was applied in 1895 when Britain disagreed with Venezuela over the boundaries of neighboring British Guiana, now Guyana. The U.S. issued a strong warning to Britain to settle the matter in arbitration; and Britain, with other problems, agreed to a peaceful settlement.

Cuba was still a colony of Spain and seeking independence. When the U.S. battleship *Maine* blew up in the Havana harbor, Spain and the U.S. went to war. Hostilities lasted three months, ending with a U.S. victory. Three former Spanish colonies came under U.S. jurisdiction: Puerto Rico and the Philippines became territories, and Cuba became independent but under U.S. protection.

Now a world power, the U.S. wanted to be able to move ships quickly between oceans. The only possibility was across the Isthmus of Panama, owned by Colombia, which refused to lease the land required to dig a canal. A rebellion broke out in Panama in 1903, and U.S. Marines helped the country win its independence from Colombia. Shortly thereafter, the new nation agreed to a lease that made the canal possible.

American involvement in Latin America was often unwelcome. In the early 1900s President Theodore Roosevelt enforced the payment of some Latin American debts to European creditors who threatened to collect by force. U.S. Marines occupied several countries, including the Dominican Republic, Nicaragua, and Haiti, to keep order and protect the interests of American businesses.

Such actions stirred resentments in countries who felt they were being "colonized" by the U.S. ■

259

● **1850** Australian Colonies Government Act, passed by British Parliament, gives Australian colonies right to form own legislatures, write own constitutions, and fix own

tariffs, all subject to confirmation by the home country.

● **1857** U.S. Supreme Court rules that a slave is not a citizen in Dred Scott decision. Great Mutiny (Sepoy Rebellion) begins in India.

● **1860** Robert O'Hara Burke and William Wills undertake first crossing of wild Australian interior, from Melbourne to Gulf of Carpentaria; only one man survives the return trip.

● **1865** Maria Mitchell is the first woman appointed to a professorship of astronomy, at Vassar College.

China Ends Its Long Isolation

The most destructive civil war in history was the Taiping Rebellion in China, from 1850 to 1864. Hundreds of towns and villages were destroyed, and millions of people died. The revolutionary flame had been fanned by hunger.

After the Manchus, or Qing dynasty, had taken over in the mid-1600s, China enjoyed prosperity for nearly two centuries. Farmers cultivated more land, developed faster-growing varieties of rice, and planted new crops from the Americas, such as sweet potatoes, corn, and peanuts.

As a result of plentiful food, population grew so rapidly that farmlands were subdivided many times. Eventually the small plots would not feed a family in a poor year. Small farmers went into debt, and their farms were taken over by the money lenders, who then became wealthy off the work of hungry peasants.

The first peasant rebellion came in 1774, traced to a secret society known as the White Lotus. More revolts arose in the following decades and were put down, although a White Lotus uprising in northern China in 1796 lasted eight years. It demonstrated the vulnerability of the Manchu troops and the weakening of the Qing dynasty.

So confident had the Qing become in their empire and the

Chinese way of life that they shut off most contact with outsiders. Trade attempts by Europeans were rebuffed. Foreign visitors were received with coldness, required to kneel before the emperor and touch their foreheads to the floor in what was known as the kowtow.

For hundreds of years Chinese civilization had been superior to that of Europe, and the flow of technology had been from East to West—the

wheelbarrow, gunpowder, deep drilling techniques, the compass, mechanical clockwork, and the sternpost ship's rudder. The Chinese saw little to desire in European goods.

For years they demanded silver and gold for their tea, silks, and porcelains. But then the British introduced a product that created its own demand. Forging links with Chinese drug dealers, they began bringing in opium from India to exchange for Chinese goods.

The addictive drug became more and more popular until imports reached 5,000 barrels a year by the 1820s. Silver was now flowing out of China to pay for the shipments. Trade regulations had no effect either on smuggling or on the bribing of officials. In 1839 Chinese officials seized and burned 20,000 chests of opium in British warehouses in Guangzhou. The act set off what became known as the Opium War between Britain and China.

The war demonstrated that China, in its isolation, had missed the industrial revolution that had moved Europeans into technological superiority. British warships sat offshore and demolished age-old Chinese defenses. Provisions of the Treaty of Nanking required the Chinese to open their ports to British trade. The second Opium War (1856-1860) humbled China even more.

U.S. pays 7.2 million dollars to buy Alaska from Russia.
1867

P. T. Barnum opens his circus, billed as "The Greatest Show on Earth," in New York.
1871

Thomas Edison invents the electric light.
1878

Gold is discovered in the Transvaal of Africa.
1884

Adolf Hitler is born.
1889

Hawaii is proclaimed a republic.
1894

Now other countries, sensing China's vulnerability, pushed it into trade concessions that favored the foreigners, and outsiders appeared in the country in large numbers.

European and American traders were not going to let a peasant revolt destroy their newfound source of wealth. So when the bloody Taiping Rebellion broke out in 1850 and lasted 14 years, it was finally put down with aid from foreign powers, and the Qing dynasty was preserved.

European influence now became so pervasive throughout China that many Chinese resented the intrusion. In the late 1800s a group of malcontents secretly formed a group called Society of Harmonious Fists, which became known as the Boxers.

By 1900 the Boxers were burning foreign missions and killing some foreigners and many Chinese Christians. Foreign envoys in Beijing were besieged for two months before troops from Europe, the U.S., and Japan invaded and put an end to the Boxer Rebellion. ■

The demand for opium helped end China's long isolation when British traders introduced it into the Orient as a trade item. When Chinese officials banned the drug and burned British-owned warehouses filled with it, the British attacked, capturing Dinghai in 1840 *(above)*. Angry at growing European influence, a secret Chinese society known as the Boxers *(opposite)* burned foreign missions and killed foreigners and Chinese Christians. Several nations allied to put down the Boxer Rebellion, and China became even more dominated by foreign powers.

○ Florence Nightingale
1855 reforms British military
hospitals during the
Crimean War.

○ U.S. Civil War ends with
1865 Lee's surrender to Grant
at Appomattox
Courthouse.

○ Leo Tolstoy's *War and*
Peace is published.
1869

○ The Chicago Fire results
in 250 deaths and mil-
1871 lions in property damage. Henry Morton
Stanley finds David
Livingstone in Africa.

○ First hydroelectric
power plant is started
1886 at Niagara Falls in
North America.

Japan Learns From the West

Like China, Japan had gone into a period of isolation from the outside world. But when it emerged, it adopted many ways of the West and increased its power.

After years of a total ban on outside contact, restrictions had relaxed, and scholars began reading books about Europeans. Some, seeing that the West was passing the Orient by in certain areas of science, wanted the country to open overseas trade again. But most Japanese still wanted to keep foreigners out.

In 1853 the U.S. pushed the issue when Commodore Matthew Perry sailed into Edo Bay with four modern steam-powered warships and strongly implied that Japan should be more liberal in its trade policies. When Japan vacillated, Perry said he would return within a year for an answer. The threat of power was clear.

Having learned from China's

military humiliation, the Tokugawa shogun then ruling Japan agreed to the Treaty of Kanagawa, which opened up some ports to trade. Similar treaties favoring the outsiders were signed with Russia, the Netherlands, and Great Britain.

The opening of Japan did not sit

Japan in its long isolation fell behind in technology, and Commodore Perry, USN, churned into Tokyo Bay with the first steamship they had ever seen. Seeking peaceful trade, Perry used intimidation as he and an interpreter met with Japanese officials *(above)*. The visit inspired art that depicted the ship as an evil thing with demonized features on the prow *(opposite)*. In a second visit Perry brought more ships and gifts, such as a miniature locomotive, which grew in the mind of a Japanese artist *(top, right)*. Japan later signed treaties allowing U.S. trade.

well with all Japanese, some of whom saw the invasion by foreigners as a threat to their culture.

An opposition group of young samurai overthrew the Tokugawa family and installed a young emperor named Mutsuhito. The decision was made to modernize Japan, but to learn from the West what might be useful while preserving Japanese

COMMODORE MATTHEW PERRY

The commander who sailed into Edo Bay with what amounted to an ultimatum to the Tokugawa shogun was not given to idle threats. Commodore Matthew Perry had been in command of squadrons that captured other coastal cities during earlier hostilities, and he had cooperated in the siege of Veracruz during the Mexican War. Captain of the *Fulton*, one of the first steam-operated warships, he is sometimes referred to as the father of the steam navy. His black warships were the first operated by steam that the Japanese had ever seen.

institutions, a strategy still alive today.

Class divisions were lessened and, in the spirit of the times, all people were declared equal. Samurai privileges were abolished, and these traditional warriors were no longer allowed to wear their swords. Some conservative samurai rebelled in protest in 1877, but the revolt was crushed by the government.

Landlords were ordered to turn their properties over to the government—for which they were later compensated—and feudalism came to an end in Japan. A universal education system was established, and the nation entered the modern world.

Japan learned so well from the West that it became not only modern but expansionist. Its forces were the largest of those that united to put down the Boxer Rebellion in China.

Japan defeated Russia in the Russo-Japanese War in 1904-1905, annexed the Ryukyu Islands, made Korea a Japanese territory, and annexed Taiwan. Japan had attained the status of a world power. ■

| 1811 | Luddites destroy industrial machines in northern England. | 1825 | Brazil's independence is recognized by Portugal. | 1835 | Britain's Municipal Reform Act transfers much of the power of local administration from lawyers and landowners to shopkeepers and tradespeople. | 1836 | Mexican army defeats Texans at the Alamo. Texas gains independence from Mexico later that same year after winning the Battle of San Jacinto. | 1848 | Lucretia Mott and Elizabeth Cady Stanton call the first Women's Rights Convention in Seneca Falls, New York. |

European Powers Influence Asia

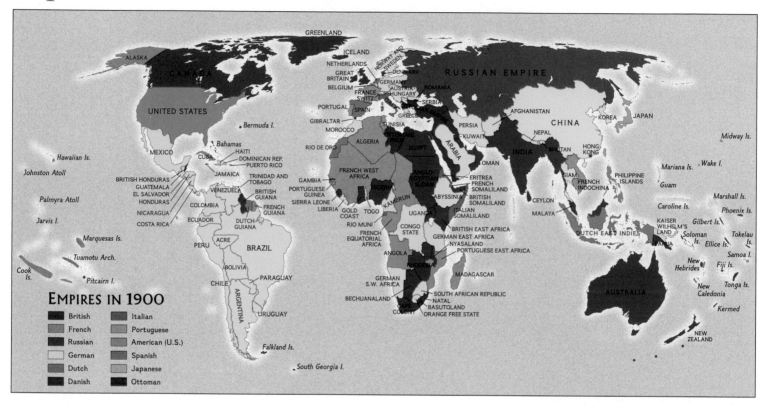

EMPIRES IN 1900

- British
- French
- Russian
- German
- Dutch
- Danish
- Italian
- Portuguese
- American (U.S.)
- Spanish
- Japanese
- Ottoman

The 1800s became known as the period of European expansion and empire building. The Europeans, with a military technical advantage gained from the industrial revolution, swept many Asian countries into their influence. Some of those countries, resenting the imposition of a foreign culture, resisted the intrusions.

Major powers with spheres of influence in Asia included Britain, the Netherlands, Russia, France, and Germany. The Russians, always in search of a year-round, warm-water port, fought the Ottoman Turks for access to the Mediterranean Sea. When that failed, they tried to push into China, Persia, and India. Russia also made incursions into China's

Manchuria and were persuaded to leave only in exchange for large Chinese payments. Meanwhile the Russians completed the conquest of northern Asia, moved across the Bering Strait into Alaska, and built forts on the North American Pacific coast as far south as California.

The British were among the biggest players in Asia. By 1805 they were the single largest European force in India, and within 50 years they controlled the entire subcontinent. British colonialists disrupted much of Indian culture, and for this they were deeply resented and had to deal with frequent rebellions, including the Great Mutiny of 1857.

Burma was conquered as a buffer

between India and the French in Indochina but not without bloody Burmese resistance. Even after British supremacy was established, armed bands of Burmese continued to inflict heavy losses.

Indochina, previously controlled by China at the zenith of its power, included Cambodia, Laos, and what is now Vietnam. The French gradually conquered the area during the 1800s, despite local resistance. In Annam, a part of Vietnam, the emperor Ham Nghi retreated into the mountains and continued fighting in guerrilla warfare until 1888.

The Dutch, from their long association with the Spice Islands, established a colony in the many islands of

Indonesia, which became known as the Dutch East Indies.

The Dutch allowed the Indonesians to retain their own land but required them to pay a tax by growing crops such as sugar and coffee, which the Dutch then exported. So much money poured into the Netherlands through the exploitation

THE SUEZ CANAL

Construction of the Suez Canal, connecting the Mediterranean and Red Seas, reduced a voyage from Britain to India by 4,000 miles. Built by a French company, the canal opened with festivities *(below)* in 1869. It was 101 miles long and 179 feet wide. Initially Egypt had complete control of the canal company, but after financial difficulty it sold a controlling interest in its stock to the British in 1875.

of peasants that the Dutch experienced pangs of guilt. An ethical policy was initiated in which the Dutch made repayments to Indonesia and discouraged westernization of the islands. For a while the policy staved off resistance, but a powerful movement for self-determination came later from Indonesian Muslims. ■

China's Taiping Rebellion is most destructive civil war in history; hundreds of settlements are destroyed, and millions die.

1850-1864

1869 First U.S. transcontinental rail route is completed.

Susan B. Anthony and 15 other women illegally vote in Rochester, New York. Anthony is arrested and prosecuted.

1872

1877 Thomas Edison patents the phonograph.

Austro-Serbian treaty of alliance.

1881

1882 Franklin D. Roosevelt is born.

The British in India

In the 1700s the Moguls who ruled India began to lose their power, and rebellions sprang up in many parts of the subcontinent. Hindu hill people in central India, known as the Marathas, constantly harassed the Moguls. The Sikhs of the Punjab in the northwestern part of the country established their own principality.

Into this political confusion stepped the British, the principal traders in the country. For the protection of their citizens in India, the British established armies composed mostly of locals known as sepoys. Armed and equipped in the fashion of the British Army, they were the most efficient fighters on the subcontinent. When Afghans raided from the north, Indian princes called on British forces for help. After finally quelling the Marathas and defeating the Sikhs in the Punjab, Britain dominated the entire country by 1849. It controlled local rulers and therefore controlled all trade. India became a source of wealth from tea and other goods.

British rule in India was carried out by the East India Company. Many of its employees began living like princes themselves. Their presence was disliked both by the common people and by the aristocracy. Underlying all the complaints was the desire to be free of foreign rule. These undercurrents of resentment boiled over in 1857 in an Indian revolt that was precipitated by the Indian troops under British command.

The Enfield rifles issued to the sepoys used a paper cartridge that

had to be bitten open to expose the powder before it could be fired. Word circulated among the Indian troops that the cartridges were greased with the fat of cows and pigs. This was tantamount to the fat being eaten, offensive to Hindus who held the cow sacred, and to the Muslims who considered the pig unclean. Sepoys revolted, some murdering their British officers, and took over Delhi where they declared a new Mogul empire. Fighting began all over India, with brutal killings on both sides.

THE BLACK HOLE OF CALCUTTA

On June 20, 1756, an Indian prince captured a British garrison in Calcutta for activities contrary to regional laws. A number of prisoners were held overnight in a small cell 18 feet by less than 15 feet, with two small windows. By morning several had died from heat and poor ventilation, an incident that became for the British symbolic of colonial heroism and Indian brutality. A survivor, known for his exaggeration, claimed 141 were jailed and only 23 survived. Later research indicates 15 may have died out of 40.

● **1883** German engineer Gottlieb Daimler creates portable engine that injects vaporized light oil into a cylinder to drive a crankshaft, leading to the age of the automobile.

● **1883** U.S. Congress establishes the Civil Service Commission.

● **1883** Paul Kruger is elected president of Transvaal.

● **1893** France acquires protectorate over Laos.

● **1895** Guglielmo Marconi invents radio telegraphy.

The British eventually put down the rebellion, but the uprisings made the colonial power aware that changes should be made.

The East India Company, which had long served as controller of Indian affairs, was disbanded, and the British instituted direct rule from London. In addition, improvements were made in the Indian economy. The railway system was increased by 30,000 miles, and by 1900 India had more than 50,000 miles of paved roads. Telegraph lines were strung, a postal service was established, and the Indian education system was improved.

Despite these steps to advance the economic and social well-being of the people, anti-British feeling remained because of the Indian resentment of any foreign domination. ■

A revolt in India against foreign rule nearly cost England one of its prize colonies in 1857. To improve conditions, the British built thousands of miles of railroads, at one point ferrying a locomotive across the Indus River on boats with built-in tracks *(above)*. In 1876 Queen Victoria *(left)* became Empress of India, but the nationalistic feelings of her Indian subjects ran high against British rule.

1804 Napoleon crowns himself Emperor of the French, setting himself up as a virtual dictator.

1828 The powerful Zulu King Shaka is assassinated.

1831 Nat Turner leads unsuccessful slave revolt in U.S.

1832 First Reform Act in Britain gives the vote to more middle-class men.

1840 By the Treaty of Waitangi, the British agree to protect Maori property rights, and New Zealand natives recognize the sovereignty of Britain.

The Industrial Revolution

As political rebellions swept the world, a revolution was also taking place in the way things were made and handled. Like the changing of a government, the industrial revolution of the 19th century would alter the way people lived. Improvements in medicines and sanitation lowered the death rate, and therefore caused populations to grow rapidly.

The price of goods dropped, which made them available to more people. Suddenly, it looked as though poverty might be defeated.

Before the 1800s, most people lived in rural areas and worked at home, farming or making individual products as carpenters, blacksmiths, or weavers. London was the largest city in Europe with 750,000 people.

On the continent, 75 percent of the population lived in towns of 200

to 600 people. As industry adopted mechanization and automation, work shifted to large factories, and people moved to cities to be near them.

England had an industrial sector even before the new developments. It had the capital to make major changes, because world trade had created a rich and enterprising mer-

chant class. It also had the requisite natural resources—coal and iron ore.

In the late 1700s the steam engine had appeared on the scene. The earliest models, developed by Englishmen such as Thomas Newcomen and Thomas Savery, were primitive machines used to pump water from mines by the lifting and lowering of a piston. When one was sent to Scot machinist James Watt for repair, his improvements resulted in the modern steam engine, patented in 1769. Watt's engines transferred the up-and-down movement of pistons into rotary motion by a drive shaft, capable of operating machines. Factories making textiles with steam-powered looms soon dominated British industry.

Ironworks came on strong after methods were discovered for

Gearing up for a revolution, Glasgow machinist James Watt studied his steam engine (above), an improvement over the earlier design by Englishman Thomas Newcomen. Working side by side with horsepower (right), Newcomen's simpler engine had pumped floodwater from coal mines but created no rotating motion. The Great Exhibition of 1851 in London's Crystal Palace (top) displayed new inventions of the industrial revolution.

1848 — Mexican-American War ends with U.S. acquiring large new territories, including all or part of California, Arizona, Utah, Nevada, Texas, and New Mexico.

1859 — John Brown raids Harpers Ferry and is later captured and hanged.

1859 — Charles Darwin's *Origin of Species* is published.

1870 — Jules Verne publishes *20,000 Leagues Under the Sea*. French Third Republic is established.

1894-1895 — China is defeated in the Sino-Japanese War.

English inventor James Nasmyth sketched a vertical steam hammer **(below)** in 1839, powerful enough to shape an iron beam, gentle enough to crack an eggshell. Another development in industry: Synthetic dyes were derived from coal tar that collected in the flues of gasworks. Flasks of dyes thereafter tinted woolen fabrics **(top, right)**.

New devices in agriculture and industry increased productivity. With Eli Whitney's cotton gin a field hand could remove seeds 50 times faster than plucking them out by hand **(below)**. The gin made cotton the chief crop of the South. In 1801 Frenchman Joseph-Marie Jacquard invented a punch-card device **(below, right)** that allowed a loom to automatically weave patterns into fabrics. Spring-loaded pins pressed against the card-activated hooks that lifted warp threads when they encountered the impressions.

"puddling" the metal with coal fires so it could be rolled and shaped. It remained brittle and easily broken, however, until it was learned that mixing iron with carbon removed impurities and created more flexible steel. This time-consuming and costly process was replaced when English inventor Henry Bessemer discovered that blasting air through the molten iron burned out any impurities.

Britain became the workshop of the world. The Great Exhibition in London in 1851 celebrated the nation's ascendancy in industry and technology, the first such international exhibition. As industrialization spread across Europe, others began copying British methods, then gradually began innovations of their own.

Frenchman Joseph-Marie Jacquard invented a loom that produced patterns when punch cards were fed through the mechanism.

Without help from England, Alfred Krupp of Germany built up huge ironworks that became the biggest manufacturers of armaments in Europe.

In the United States Eli Whitney invented the cotton gin, a machine that removed the seeds from cotton 50 times faster than it could be done by hand. Equally important, Whitney initiated the system of standardization of parts in a product, which would lead eventually to mass production.

The increased production at the cotton and woolen mills created more demand for the raw products. The mining industry broadened to provide coal and iron for the new factories.

Since raw materials had to come from a distance, the transportation industry expanded—first with canals, then with railroads as the steam engine was harnessed to rails.

Not all the changes were positive. The machines in the factories were noisy and dangerous. Wages were kept low to increase profits, and children were popular as cheaply paid workers of 10-hour days.

In the early 1880s Englishman Arnold Toynbee, first to popularize the phrase "industrial revolution," warned of suffering and social strains as people left the countryside and jammed into cities. ∎

1823 President James Monroe issues awarning to European powers not to interfere in the Western Hemisphere, a policy that would become known as the Monroe Doctrine.

1830 France invades Algeria, using raids by Barbary pirates on the coast as an excuse, and claims the territory after a long and bitter struggle.

1828 The Dutch annex western part of New Guinea.

1833 Slavery is abolished in the British Empire.

1846 Elias Howe patents the sewing machine.

Advances in Health and Sanitation

The industrial revolution lowered the price of goods so that some people experienced increased purchasing power. Perhaps the greatest development of the 18th and 19th centuries, however, was the advancement of health care and sanitation. Discoveries of what caused diseases helped conquer miseries that had plagued humankind throughout time.

The horrors of surgery itself were lessened when American surgeon Crawford W. Long rendered patients unconscious with ether in eight operations between 1842 and 1846. Another American, William Morton, claimed to be the initiator of ether when he gave public demonstrations of its use in 1846.

The medical revolution began in earnest when scientists such as chemist Louis Pasteur of France and medical doctor Robert Koch of Prussia established the germ theory

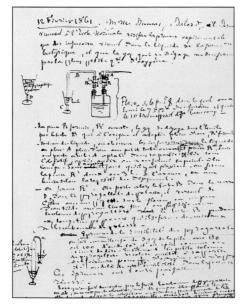

of disease. Pasteur proved in the mid-1800s that bacteria could cause food to spoil. His discovery led to a process for treating food to kill bacteria that might be present, later named "pasteurization," for Pasteur himself.

Pasteur also published a paper that described how bacteria cause disease and refuted previous claims that microorganisms were produced spontaneously.

To advance his germ theory of disease, Pasteur had studied several types of microorganisms. The evidence he turned up encouraged Joseph Lister to eliminate bacteria during operations on patients. He experimented with chemicals that would

1865   Abraham Lincoln is assassinated; Andrew Johnson succeeds him as U.S. President.

1870-71   Franco-Prussian War.

1873   U.S. establishes the gold standard.

1880   Canned fruits and meats first appear in stores.

1881   Tuskegee Institute is founded by Booker T. Washington.

prevent germs from entering a wound. In 1865 he found that carbolic acid, sprayed in operating rooms, disinfected the air. Lister is considered the founder of antiseptic surgery.

In 1882 Koch isolated the bacterium responsible for tuberculosis.

The knowledge that germs cause disease led to widespread immunization—injecting vaccines into the body to create disease-fighting antibodies. More than 20 fatal diseases were soon guarded against in this way, including the cholera that had killed 16,000 people in London in 1849.

The first inoculation is actually credited to an English doctor, Edward Jenner, in 1796, who perforated skin to let scrapings of cowpox into the body as a vaccination against smallpox. More immunizations became possible in the 19th century through the development of precision engineering that allowed the manufacture of slender, hollow injection needles. ■

Science beat back diseases that had long caused misery. In Africa Robert Koch *(left)*, seated third from left, took blood to isolate the microbe that caused sleeping sickness. The reclining man, he found, had been infected by the bite of the tsetse fly *(below)*. Champion disease fighter, Louis Pasteur peers at a flask holding the rabies-infected spinal cord of a rabbit *(opposite)* in studies that led to a rabies vaccine. His notes detail work on anaerobic bacteria *(opposite, below)*.

1720 Tibet becomes a Chinese protectorate.

1755 First publication of Samuel Johnson's *Dictionary.*

1770 British troops open fire, killing five Colonists in Boston Massacre.

1791 Canada is divided by the Constitutions Act, into British- and French-speaking territories.

1796 English physician Edward Jenner pioneers vaccination against smallpox.

Improved Farming Feeds More People

In the early 1700s, few changes had been made in food production for hundreds of years. Crops were grown inefficiently in large, open fields where strips were rented by small farmers from wealthy landowners. The strips were small, unfenced, and so close together that farmers often worked them cooperatively. Land was left idle every three years or more so fertility would return.

Every village had a commons, usually untillable land nearby, where anyone could gather wood or graze their animals. Landless peasants depended on the commons to graze a few sheep or grow a few food crops. Since few animals could be sustained through the long winter, many were slaughtered in fall and the meat stored in ways that did not always prevent spoilage.

Along with the enthusiasm for change that accompanied the industrial revolution came improved techniques in agriculture. As more people lived in towns and did not grow their own food, landowners saw that better production would mean more money in crop sales.

The landowners' first move was to end the open-field system and bring the land under their direct control for more intensive farming. In Britain's Acts of Enclosure in the late 1700s more than seven million acres were enclosed within hedgerows and stone walls. This often displaced small farmers who had depended on the open strips and the commons for their livelihood. The introduction of crop rotation, initiated by the Dutch, kept land in production every year instead of idling one-third or more of it so it could recover. Fields were alternated each growing season among wheat, root crops, barley, and finally clover, which returned fertility by restoring nitrogen to the soil. Turnips, one of the root crops, also served as winter feed for livestock, making fresh meat available year-round.

The potato introduced from America grew well in poor soil and became a common food by the late 1700s. New drainage techniques made marshy areas tillable, increasing the amount of land available for agricultural use.

With their fields enclosed,

Checkerboard fields appeared when open farming yielded to more intensive tracts surrounded by hedgerows. Many remain in England today *(left)*, prized as wildlife havens as well as livestock enclosures. Three curious bovines stare over a lush hedge in Cornwall *(above).* Cyrus McCormick's reaper hastened harvests by cutting and binding the shocks of grain. The later combine *(opposite)* also separated the grain. Compact motorized versions followed.

1801   Engineer Robert Fulton builds the *Nautilus,* his first submarine.

1837   Victoria becomes Queen of Great Britain.

1848   The Second Republic is founded in France with Louis Napoleon as president.

1859   First Great Atlantic and Pacific Tea Company (A&P) chain store opens in New York.

1860   Abraham Lincoln is elected U.S. President.

THE IMAGINATIVE THOMAS JEFFERSON

In step with an age of inquiry and inventiveness, Thomas Jefferson, drafter of the American Declaration of Independence and third President of the U.S., experimented with agriculture and dabbled in gadgets. At his farm in Virginia he tried cover crops of clover and vetch to restore the land, and he developed a streamlined moldboard plow that turned soil more efficiently. A rooftop wind vane could be read for wind direction from inside the house, and a desk with a turntable kept writing supplies nearby. His design of the Virginia Capitol influenced architecture in the early U.S.

landowners began setting aside space for roads so they could more easily move their products to market. With a road system established, they began to sell products farther away, which meant that different regions could specialize in what they grew best instead of growing a wide variety to sell to customers nearby. Specialization produced even better individual crops, as did fertilization.

In 1840 German chemist Justin von Liebig's book, *Chemistry in Its Application to Agriculture,* began a movement toward more scientific crop production. By 1850 fertilizers containing potassium and phosphorus were being produced in the U.S.

New tools also added to efficiency. Seeds had long been sown by hand, a practice that allowed weeds to grow along with the plants.

Around 1701 British agriculturalist Jethro Tull invented a mechanized planter called a seed drill. It dropped seed into the ground in orderly rows and, when the crops grew up, weeding could take place between the rows with a horse-drawn cultivator. Tull also demonstrated the importance of fertilizing the ground with manure and the value of pulverizing the soil before planting. New iron-tipped plowshares helped prepare the ground more quickly for the planting season.

Robert Bakewell had begun to experiment in the mid-1700s with new ideas about the careful breeding of farm animals to produce better livestock. Farmers became interested in selective breeding that created larger sheep, fatter cattle and pigs, and more powerful horses.

In the mid-1800s American Cyrus McCormick developed a mechanical grain-harvesting machine, called the reaper, which cut stalks much faster than a person swinging a scythe.

The mechanization of harvests advanced another step around 1860 with the appearance of the stationary threshing machine, which separated the grain from the severed stalk. No longer did grain have to be beaten loose manually.

Such improvements and efficiencies moved people off the land and into cities, but machines empowered agriculture to meet the demands of a growing population.

Farming became big business. ■

1774 Colonists convene the First Continental Congress, in Philadelphia.

1778 Capt. James Cook discovers Hawaii.

1787 British colony established in Sierra Leone.

1840 First adhesive stamp, called the "penny black" and bearing the image of Queen Victoria, is issued in England, the result of efforts by postal authority Rowland Hill.

1866 Revolts against Turkish rule occur in Crete.

The Coming of Electricity

In the midst of the hurricane changes sweeping the Western world in the industrial revolution of the 18th and 19th centuries, the progress of electrical power was surprisingly slow. As early as the mid-1700s American Benjamin Franklin had made numerous experiments showing the presence of electricity. In his famous kite-flying episode during a thunderstorm, sparks flew off a key tied to the kite's tail, showing that lightning had electrical power. But how could one produce it for human use?

In 1800 Italian physicist Alessandro Volta created the voltaic pile, a crude battery. The electrical unit known as a volt is named in his honor. In 1831 English scientist Michael Faraday created a dynamo that showed how a steady current of electricity could be created mechanically by the rotation of wire around a magnet. But another 40 years passed before big steam-driven dynamos capable of producing large amounts of electricity became reliable.

Electricity was used for specialized purposes such as the electric telegraph and, as of 1876, the electric telephone. The boost needed for worldwide electrical generation came

with the invention of the incandescent light. American Thomas Alva Edison invented the electric light in 1878 and demonstrated it the following year at his laboratory in Menlo Park, New Jersey.

Soon electricity was illuminating streets, factories, and homes around the world. The first electric streetcar began regular operation in Germany in 1881, and within a decade most European and American cities either had or were planning to build electrical street railways.

Edison continued his work with electricity. Among more than a thousand patents granted to him were those for the phonograph, the

microphone, and the kinetoscope, a forerunner of motion pictures.

By 1900 Britain had more than 400 separate electricity-producing stations. Electrical production increased rapidly with the development of the steam turbine in which steam turned a rotary shaft directly instead of running a reciprocal engine that turned the shaft.

Waterpower became an important producer of electricity, especially for countries that had no supply of coal for steam generation. In North America the first hydroelectric power plant was started at Niagara in 1886. Areas with adequate water resources, such as Scandinavia and

North America, built numerous hydroelectric plants, but for most of the world electricity was generated with the steam turbine driven by coal or oil.

As more electrical appliances were developed and powered by small electrical motors—sewing machines, vacuum cleaners, and washing machines—electric lines spread out over the developed nations, and electric power became essential to modern life. ■

Experiments by Ben Franklin (far left) proved the presence of electricity in the mid-1700s. Italian physicist Allesandro Volta made severed frog legs twitch in 1801 with his voltaic pile, at the request of Napoleon Bonaparte, seated second from right (opposite). In his laboratory, Britain's Michael Faraday (above) studied the link between magnetism and electricity, which led to electric motors. American Thomas Edison (left) unlocked power in inventions that included the phonograph and incandescent lights.

1769 Russian troops occupy Moldavia and enter Bucharest.

1773 Boston Tea Party.

1782 Rama I founds new dynasty in Thailand.

1795 British forces occupy Cape of Good Hope.

1815 Allied army led by Britain's Duke of Wellington defeats Napoleon at Waterloo in Netherlands.

Overcoming Distance Brings the World Together

With greater production in the new factories of the 18th and 19th centuries, the faster movement of goods and raw materials became important. In England cargoes were transported to and from factories by wagons mounted on rails and pulled by horses. Canals enjoyed success, especially in England, but materials still moved slowly. Steam provided the first means of traveling faster than could be done by human or animal muscle.

James Watt's improved steam engine of 1769 was too bulky and required too much fuel to move about. It wasn't until 1800 that Englishman Richard Trevithick built a high-pressure steam engine capable of moving passengers in a carriage. In 1804 he built the first locomotive to operate on a rail line, hauling 10 tons of iron, 70 men, and 5 wagons for 9.5 miles at nearly 5 mph.

Fellow Englishman George

Stephenson increased rail speed with his Rocket. Its tubular boiler and smokestack created a draft that increased engine power. On the first modern railroad in 1829, the Rocket pulled a train between Liverpool and Manchester at an average speed of almost 14 mph, proving that steam travel on rails was a workable idea. In 1830 England had 60 miles of railroads. By 1870 all of Europe had 65,000 miles, and the United States had 53,000 miles. By the end of the century steam was propelling ships and horseless carriages also.

Still, a demand existed for smaller, cheaper transportation. The bicycle erupted on the American marketplace in the early 1880s. Bicyclists lobbied for, and got, paved roads in the United States to make their travel safer. But it was the invention of the internal combustion engine that truly revolutionized personal travel.

1824 Three years after declaring independence from Spain, Mexico becomes a republic.

1830 July Revolution in Paris; Louis Philippe is named the "citizen king."

1848 "Year of Revolution" in Europe.

1860 Giuseppe Garibaldi, an Italian patriot who fought against foreign rule, leads rebellion in southern Italy, conquering the kingdom.

1876 Korea becomes an independent nation.

As early as 1805 it was shown in principle that fuel exploding inside a cylinder could drive down the cylinder and create mechanical power. In the 1860s engines burned a mixture of coal gas and air, compressed within the cylinder before being ignited by a spark. In 1883 German engineer Gottlieb Daimler created a portable engine that injected vaporized light oil into a cylinder to drive a crankshaft, and his engine drove a motorcar two years later. The age of the automobile was born.

An engine creating such high compression that fuel oil was ignited without a spark was patented in 1892 by German Rudolf Diesel, and the diesel engine began replacing steam engines in factories and ships.

Speeding the intangible—information itself—was also on the horizon. Throughout history the flow of information had been no faster than

The world sped up in a new age of communication. Horsepower began giving way to steam power at the waterfront of Providence, Rhode Island *(opposite, below)*. Carl Benz's first tricycle cars were coolly received *(opposite, middle)* but ushered in the age of the automobile. By 1887 telephone wires webbed the streets of Manhattan *(above)* but few could afford the local service. Thirty years later two boys called their parents across the United States *(opposite, top)*.

people could travel, although attempts at speed are as old as signal fires from hilltops. In the late 18th century Frenchman Claude Chappe devised a visual system of relaying information that made use of movable arms mounted on towers within sight of each other. An operator would adjust the arms in various positions to send a coded message.

American Samuel F. B. Morse made the electric telegraph successful by inventing the Morse code for transmitting messages with electric signals. In 1844 he sent the first message, "What hath God wrought!" on an experimental line between Washington, D.C., and Baltimore, Maryland.

In 1876 communication took another giant step when American Alexander Graham Bell invented the telephone. Telephone lines soon spread across the U.S. and Europe. ∎

THE SUCCESS OF CANALS

Before railroads, canals moved goods and raw materials across great distances. Canal-building boomed in the late 1700s and early 1800s. In the U.S. the 363-mile-long Erie Canal, linking Buffalo, New York, on Lake Erie with Albany on the Hudson, opened in 1825. In the late 19th century, controversy erupted over the proposed construction of the Panama Canal. An 1899 political cartoon *(left)* showed then U.S. President William McKinley straddling the Gulf of Mexico with pick in hand.

1721 Regular mail service is established between Britain and its North American colonies.

1765 Delegates from the 13 Colonies meet to protest the Stamp Act.

1848 Karl Marx publishes his epic work, *The Communist Manifesto*, asserting that revolutions by the working class would ultimately destroy capitalism.

1868 Last transport of convicts from Britain arrives in Australia.

1871 Otto von Bismarck becomes chancellor of new German Empire.

Revolutions in the Arts

The social changes brought about by both the political and the industrial revolutions had their effects in the world of art as well. And art in return had an effect on the events of the day. Rousseau's appeal to sentiment and emotion as a prime motivator in people's lives played a part in the popular rebellions against monarchical regimes. In Germany Friedrich von Schiller idealized heroic deeds, high ethical principles, and the nobility of the human spirit.

Art, with its frequent changes in mood and emphasis, also reflected the mixed feelings that industrialization and urbanization thrust upon the general public.

A group called the Romantics felt the world was becoming cold, too practical, too machinelike. They believed in a return to nature with its quiet energy and therapeutic beauty.

Poets such as William Wordsworth (an early sympathizer of

the French Revolution), Percy Bysshe Shelley, Samuel Taylor Coleridge, John Keats, and George Gordon Byron emphasized love and individual freedom and believed in the basic goodness of people.

" 'Beauty is truth, truth beauty,'
That is all ye know on earth,
And all ye need to know,"
wrote Keats in "Ode on a Grecian Urn," an apt summary of the Romantic genre.

Such passion and ecstasy in beauty were also reflected in the work of brilliant musicians during the era of change. Romantic music—with works by Germany's Ludwig van Beethoven, Austria's Franz Schubert, France's Hector Berlioz, and Poland's Frédéric Chopin—was widely popular.

Other artists also worked in the

Changes thrust upon society by increasing industrialization spawned genius in the arts as well as science. Composer of more than 600 musical works in many forms, Wolfgang Amadeus Mozart, here playing his opera *Don Giovanni* for a small group *(above)*, still delights listeners. Romantic music by Ludwig van Beethoven *(left, below)* and others also gained popularity. Romantics decried the cold world of industrialization and urged a return to nature. Poets wrote of love, beauty, and the goodness of humanity.

Romantic temper. French novelist Victor Hugo showed compassion toward the sufferings of humanity with *Les Misérables* and *The Hunchback of Notre Dame*.

Scottish writer Sir Walter Scott turned to an idealized past with historical works such as *Ivanhoe* and *The Talisman*.

Painters such as Delacroix and Corot depicted dramatic scenes from history and highly romanticized landscapes, respectively.

1874 ● Benjamin Disraeli becomes British Prime Minister.

1878 ● Microphone is invented by David Hughes.

1896 ● Ethiopia's Emperor Menelik II defeats Italians, discouraging further European moves into his country for nearly 40 years.

1896 ● U.S. Supreme Court hands down historic *Plessy* v *Ferguson* decision, establishing the doctrine of "separate but equal."

1896 ● Alfred Nobel's will establishes annual prizes for peace, science, and literature.

touching stories of people caught in the meshes of the day's social ills—often those that had grown out of the industrial revolution. With his art, Dickens helped speed social reforms.

Similar to the realists, the naturalists wrote and painted of the seamier side of life but with great precision and an almost scientific approach. Naturalists believed in showing life exactly as it was and discussing how it got that way. They not only showed peasants in their misery, but also examined the circumstances of environment, heredity, or misunderstandings that had shaped their lives.

In a reaction to realism and naturalism, the Impressionists painted pictures that evoked emotional responses but avoided many of life's harsh realities. Impressionists appealed to those who wanted art to evoke feelings of pleasure.

Would society be renewed through faith and beauty, by facing unpleasant facts, or by scientific analysis of its shortcomings? Whatever the answer, the changes of the 18th and 19th centuries spurred a flood of major artistic achievements. ■

The altering of society split artists into differing groups. Charles Dickens, relaxing with friends at his home *(left),* wrote of brutal injustice in the slums. Impressionist painter Renoir evoked pleasure with "The Luncheon of the Boating Party" *(below).*

By the mid-1800s artists argued that the world had to be depicted as it "really" was. Instead of idealizing beauty, the realists depicted the character of the new, industrialized society, warts and all. By showing the injustices, they pushed for social reform. Workers were shown with sweat-streaked bodies and peasants were painted in all their misery, not reveling in the joys of a simple life.

In England Charles Dickens wrote of children working in factories and of the brutality of the slums. Often basing his writing on his own experiences, Dickens had the gift of affecting people's consciences with his

1789 Louis XVI calls together the Estates-General, a French legislative body that had not met for some 175 years.

1794 Pennsylvania farmers' objections to liquor taxes lead to the Whiskey Rebellion.

1797-1883 Life of Sojourner Truth, former slave, abolitionist, and women's rights spokesperson.

1856 Tasmania is granted self-government by Britain.

1868 First professional U.S. baseball club, the Cincinnati Red Stockings, is founded.

Moving to the Cities

The industrial revolution with its opportunities for urban employment brought a flood of people to urban areas. Manchester, England, grew from 25,000 in 1772 to 367,000 in 1851. Liverpool expanded more than five times in half a century. In 1785 three British cities had populations over 50,000. By 1860 there were 31 of that size. Other European and American cities also experienced growth, but nowhere was the migration from countryside to city as dramatic as in England. The cities were not ready for the influx of people.

With thousands more seeking urban shelter every year, housing was left to speculative builders who put up maximum housing at minimum cost. Neither city officers nor employers saw care of the new residents as their responsibility. The result was close-clustered housing with no safe water supply and no sanitary toilet facilities. Sewage often ran in open trenches down the middle of unpaved streets. London in the 1850s had 200,000 undrained cesspools; the Thames was a huge flowing sewer.

In addition to the problems of crowded humanity, the factories that attracted workers filled the air with smoke and dangerous gases and piled up their industrial wastes. When railroad fervor struck in the mid-1800s, tracks were built right into the hearts of cities, bringing with them the roar of engines, exhaust fumes, and the rumble of rolling

1871 ● British Columbia joins the Dominion of Canada.

1874 ● Britain annexes the Fiji Islands.

1876 ● At Benjamin Disraeli's suggestion, Queen Victoria becomes Empress of India, a country dominated by the British.

1876 ● Lt. Col. George A. Custer and his men are killed by the Sioux at the Battle of Little Bighorn.

1900 ● Commonwealth of Australia is established.

stock. Diseases such as cholera, typhoid, and tuberculosis ran rampant. Infant mortality was more than one in ten in the years 1838-54.

Ultimately, the horror drove philanthropists and public officials to press for change. Some investment was made in schools, hospitals, and places of leisure. Britain's Municipal Reform Act of 1835 transferred much of the power of local administration from lawyers and landowners to shopkeepers and tradespeople who were more inclined toward improvement. Robert Owen, a Welsh businessman and philanthropist, devoted surplus profits from his cotton mill to worker housing, a school for children, and the abolition of child labor.

Learning from the example of Britain, architects and philosophers of the late 18th century in the U.S. discussed how to build ideal cities. A grid pattern of city blocks developed in place of the irregular, winding streets of older municipalities.

Building materials also changed with the refinement of metalworking. The first cast-iron bridge was built in England in 1779, and flexible steel gave birth to high buildings known as skyscrapers by the end of the 1800s. ■

In the industrial revolution cities became cesspools of crowded living and unhealthy air. Chimneys of mill-workers' houses in Bradford, England (opposite), spit smoke alongside a now dormant factory smokestack. A survivor from an era when quickly built cast-iron bridges were popular stretches across England's Severn River (right). Pierre L'Enfant's grand plan for the new U.S. capital mostly endured (above, right), although George Washington dismissed L'Enfant for demolishing a friend's large house.

1812 — Napoleon invades Russia.

1815-1902 — Life of Elizabeth Cady Stanton, who drafted the Seneca Falls Declaration.

1820-1906 — Life of Susan B. Anthony, women's rights activist who helped women win the vote.

1822 — First photographic image is produced by France's Joseph-Nicéphore Niepce. Liberia is founded as a colony for freed slaves.

1834 — Cyrus McCormick patents the reaper.

New Weapons and Strategies of War

War changed along with technology. Russia lost a naval base in the battle of Sevastopol (*left*) in the Crimean War partly due to poor communication. Exploding artillery shells and rapid-fire small arms greatly increased casualties and drove massed armies into trenches for protection. The dead piled up in the American Civil War (*opposite*), a fact brought home to families by early photography and news reports sent by telegraph from the battlefield.

FLORENCE NIGHTINGALE

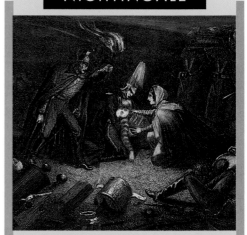

Newspaper reports of the Crimean War gave a boost to nursing when the Englishwoman Florence Nightingale was stirred to help the sick and wounded soldiers (*above*). Born into aristocracy, she became known as the "lady with the lamp," who glided down dark hospital corridors in the Crimea to comfort the injured and dying. Her ministrations sharply reduced the death rate in British army hospitals, and her compassion became known worldwide. The effort ruined her own health, but her continued work of reorganizing hospital administration back in London changed the nursing profession.

A long with the other technological advances of the industrial revolution came advances in weaponry, which eventually would change the ways in which wars were fought. Guns, for all their time-consuming loading procedures, had begun replacing the bow and arrow as early as the 15th century. The use of cannon helped create larger nations. No longer could a small rival faction withstand a long seige by the central government, which could batter down local defenses with heavy artillery.

But strong central governments with heavy artillery did not stop citizen uprisings. The American and French Revolutions and rebellions in South America all demonstrated that unpopular governments could still be thrown off. The success of the French revolutionary army against invading foreign forces proved another important fact, that citizen armies could be effective against professional ones if the participants truly believed in their cause. The revolution helped usher in universal military service. Nations with governments that were backed by a supportive population could raise huge armies that earlier monarchs could not have imagined.

Industrial might and military effectiveness became intertwined. China learned that ignoring the advances of industry could be deadly, as British ships stood offshore in the two Opium Wars of the 1800s and simply battered down age-old defenses. When Japan decided to modernize and

1851   Gold is discovered in southern Australia, bringing a flood of immigrants to the continent.

1853   First railway and telegraph lines in India.

1879   F. W. Woolworth opens first five-and-dime store.

1885   Canadian Pacific railway is completed.

1888   John Boyd Dunlop invents pneumatic tire.

become a major power, high among its priorities was the building of a modern navy. Russia's defeat by the British and French in the Crimean War of 1854 to 1856 revealed how badly it trailed in technology. Russian soldiers lacked up-to-date weapons, and the generals had no efficient way to move troops into battle or maintain battlefield communications. The North won the American Civil War in part because its industries could turn out massive amounts of equipment, its extensive railroad system could move men and equipment to battle areas, and its strong navy could block supplies to the South.

With improvements in metallurgy and explosives, weapons became more devastating, a fact that changed battle strategies. In 1837 France adopted an artillery piece, developed by Henri Joseph Paixhans, that threw an exploding shell, as opposed to a solid cannon ball. Breech-loading artillery came into use in 1845. The French '75, the first quick-loading artillery piece that fired either shrapnel or high explosives, appeared in 1898.

In small arms, the revolving handgun, which could shoot six times rapidly before being reloaded, was patented by American Samuel Colt in 1836. In the same year, Johann Nikolaus von Dreyse of Germany invented the "needle gun," a breech-loading military rifle that could be fired four times for every one shot made by the old muzzle-loaders. The conical projectile developed by

Frenchman Claude Etienne Minié in 1849 improved accuracy. By clustering a number of rifle barrels together that could be fired in rapid succession, American Richard Gatling created the first machine gun in 1862.

Increased firepower brought increased casualties. A devastating example during the Crimean War was made famous by a poem of Alfred Lord Tennyson, "The Charge of the Light Brigade." Due to a misunderstanding in orders, a cavalry unit of 600 men was sent galloping down a narrow valley directly into the fire of Russian artillery, causing a loss of one-third of the unit in the single

charge. In the American Civil War, some 600,000 were killed. High explosives and rapid-firing weapons made the massing of armies in open fields for head-on assaults suicidal. Troops began sheltering themselves in trenches and firing from cover, a prelude to wars that would follow.

Another development would change the way war was regarded by the people. Newspapers began covering conflicts such as the Crimean War and the American Civil War, giving firsthand accounts of suffering and, with early efforts at photography, showing the devastation. War lost something of its glamour. ∎

Improvements in Postal Service

The 17th and 18th centuries brought an increased demand for dependable correspondence by mail. France and several neighboring states made cross-border postal agreements as early as 1601, with letters carried by couriers over short distances and by relays of post horses over longer distances. By 1653 mailboxes and postage stamps were being used in Paris for the first time. In London in 1683 a merchant named William Dockwra set up a penny post system by which letters would be carried anywhere in the metropolis for one penny. In 1721 a regular mail service was established between Britain and its North American colonies.

The desire for rapid mail service spurred a number of postal innovations. Postage stamps first appeared in the mid-1600s, but letters still moved slowly by foot or horseback. Trains sped up delivery, but at first the small number of lines left gaps in the system. England had been using post riders more than a century before the American Pony Express was organized in 1860 to carry mail from the end of the rail line at St. Joseph, Missouri *(opposite)*, to Sacramento, California *(below)*. Instant messaging by telegraph made long-distance horse delivery obsolete.

By 1734 post riders in Britain were carrying mail from town to town, announcing their arrival by a blast on a trumpet. The first adhesive stamp to be affixed to letters was the "penny black," issued in 1840 in England and carrying a portrait of Queen Victoria. The stamp resulted from the efforts of postal authority Rowland Hill, who had printed the pamphlet "Post Office Reform: Its Importance and Practicability." A revolution in postal communication, it allowed letters under half an ounce to be sent to any point in the United Kingdom. Previous charges were exorbitant and varied according to the size, shape, and weight of the letter. The stamp also allowed the sender to pay for delivery, instead of having it paid for upon arrival.

1740 Twenty-three-year-old Maria Theresa inherits the Austrian throne from her father, Charles VI.

1760 Canton becomes the only Chinese port authorized to trade with other countries.

1789 Mob storms the Bastille; word spreads all over France, beginning the French Revolution.

1838 The Medical Missionary Society is formally instituted in China.

1851-52 Harriet Beecher Stowe's *Uncle Tom's Cabin* is published.

The U.S. Post Office issued its first government-sponsored stamps in 1847. To bridge the vast distances in the young United States, the Pony Express was begun in 1860 to carry mail from the end of the rail line at St. Joseph, Missouri, to the Pacific. With relays of fast horses, it cut a letter's travel time to San Francisco from six weeks (by ship and across the Isthmus of Panama) to 10 days. The pony express lasted only 18 months; it became obsolete with the laying of transcontinental telegraph lines.

In 1875 the Universal Postal Union was set up in Bern, Switzerland, providing for an international mail service. ∎

Adopting Standards for Measurement

The ancient Egyptians had determined the height of their pyramids in "cubits," the distance from one's elbow to one's fingertips, about 18 inches (right). Clearly a need existed for some standard of weights and measures.

In the 18th-century Age of Enlightenment, the revolutionary French government approved the use of the metric system. A *mètre* was to be one ten-millionth of the distance from the Equator to the North Pole. To determine this distance, surveyors measured an arc of the meridian from Dunkirk in France to Barcelona in Spain, then extrapolated the total distance from Equator to Pole. The meter was established at 39.37 inches.

To establish volume, the cubing of a tenth of a meter established a liter of liquid. For weight, a liter of water weighed a thousand grams, or a kilogram. Temperature was measured in degrees Celsius, with water freezing at 0 degrees and boiling at 100.

The metric system was quickly adopted by other European nations and eventually spread to most of the world. Today it is used by 95 percent of the world's people, although it is not widely accepted in the United States and a few other countries. ∎

1798 ● Island of Malta surrenders to Napoleon.

1799 ● George Washington dies. Naturalist and explorer Alexander von Humboldt sails for America; he plans to explore Venezuela, Colombia, and Peru.

1816 ● The island of Java is returned to Dutch control.

1821 ● Peru declares its independence from Spain.

1841 ● John Tyler becomes U.S. Vice President and succeeds to presidency, following the death of William Henry Harrison.

The Struggle for South Africa

Long before the Suez Canal was dug, the tip of South Africa was an important stopping place for ships headed from Europe to the trade markets of the East. In 1652 the Dutch had established a supply station for the long voyages at a Cape of Good Hope settlement later called Cape Town. They encouraged Dutch farmers called Boers to settle there and many did, as did a number of religiously persecuted French Huguenots in 1685. The colony grew slowly under Dutch rule for 140 years. The most common European language was Afrikaans, based on Dutch but with local variations.

By the late 1700s the power of the Dutch had diminished because of long wars and new shipping restrictions, while the power of the British was increasing. In 1795 the British occupied Cape Town, and in 1814 the Dutch ceded it to them. Several thousand British joined the Boers and the French Huguenots, and friction grew between the Afrikaners and the English-speaking settlers. British

1845-46 Blight ruins Ireland's potato crop. Some one million citizens starve, and a million others emigrate—mostly to the United States.

1877 Sioux Indians led by Chief Crazy Horse give themselves up to U.S. troops, abandoning claims to Nebraska.

1893 New Zealand becomes the first country to allow women to vote. In the U.S., Colorado votes to grant women the vote.

1900 Sigmund Freud's *The Interpretation of Dreams* is published.

sentiments against slavery were growing, while the Boers kept African slaves to work their farms and practiced what became known as apartheid, a policy that maintained separation of the black and white races.

When the British Parliament abolished slavery in 1833, many Boers felt they could no longer live under British rule. Thousands packed up and began a Great Trek northward into lands occupied by native Africans. There the Afrikaners, also called Trekkers, established two independent republics, the Transvaal and the Orange Free State.

The Boers had long clashed with natives called Xhosa, who also wanted good pastureland for their cattle. Now they began battling the Zulus, who had risen to power in the early 1800s under a powerful chief named Shaka and had conquered most of southeastern Africa. Although Shaka was assassinated in 1828, Zulus under King Dingaan massacred some 60 Trekkers in 1838. In the battle of Blood River, a vengeful force of Boers defeated the Zulus and settled in Natal, founding the city of Pietermaritzburg in 1839.

Three years later, the British, unwilling to let the Boers build independent territories so near their colony, defeated them and occupied Natal. That also put them in conflict with the Zulus. A triangulated conflict unfolded, with the British fighting the Zulus and both British and Zulus fighting the Boers. The Zulus, led by King Cetewayo, defeated the British in a battle at Isandhlwana. Cetewayo was later captured by the British; and the remaining Zulu chiefs, their warriors overwhelmed by superior European weaponry, made peace.

Meanwhile, the discovery of diamonds in the Transvaal and gold in nearby Witwatersrand brought a flood of British to the region. Struggles between the British who wanted a unified South Africa and the Boers who wanted their own independent states continued off and on from the early 1880s until 1902.

The tough, hard-riding Boers, conducting guerrilla warfare, won some of the early battles. Then came the last Anglo-Boer War, partly precipitated by the secret raid led by British administrator Leander Jameson into the Transvaal in 1895. The raid failed, and the invasion raised an outcry in Europe. The German emperor sent a telegram congratulating the Boers for repulsing the British, and the continuing tensions between Britain and Germany contributed to the outbreak of World War I.

The British eventually won the last Boer War in 1902 and later declared a Union of South Africa, with close ties to Britain. In concessions to the Afrikaners, they allowed racial separation to continue and made Afrikaans an official language along with English. ◼

THE DIAMOND RUSH

Children playing on a riverbank in the Transvaal found the first diamond in South Africa. The discovery brought thousands of British people hoping to strike it rich. It also increased tensions between the Boers and British. By 1870 a considerable diamond industry had grown up, with the town of Kimberley as its center. This 1876 photograph *(above)*, taken near Kimberley, shows a diamond mine called the "Big Hole." Within 20 years some six tons of diamonds, worth millions, had been mined. Most of the largest diamonds still come from Africa.

Struggles for South Africa often had complex racial boundaries. Zulu King Shaka *(opposite, above)* subdued other black clans, and Dutch farmers called Boers fought the British over land rights. Zulus resisted Boers moving northward in wagons, as shown in a painting of an attack *(below)*. At a large Zulu *kraal* that housed some 20,000 *(opposite, below)*, King Dingaan hosted Boers for negotiations and killed some 60. Settlers with guns later overran the Zulus, and whites ruled South Africa.

An assassination attempt against Napoleon fails. **1800**

1803 Richard Cleveland and William Shaler introduce horses into the Hawaiian Islands.

1812 The Brothers Grimm publish their volume of *Fairy Tales*.

1820 Reformers in Spain force the country's Bourbon King Ferdinand VII to accept a liberal constitution.

ca 1820-1913 Life of Harriet Tubman, who established the Underground Railroad.

1836 Gen. Sam Houston is sworn in as president of the Republic of Texas.

The Race to Claim Africa

Africa, especially North Africa, had been known to Europeans since ancient times. They penetrated but little, however, into the interior of the continent. Muslims were different, spreading their religion and trading.

In the early 1800s North Africa west of Egypt was made up of several Arab-Berber territories. The Ottoman Turks had conquered Tripoli, Tunis, and Algiers but had little control over them other than demanding allegiance. Morocco, across the Straits of Gibraltar from Spain, was completely independent.

Ultimately the empire-building fervor of the 19th century extended to Africa as well. Industrialization in Europe created demands for new markets and caused new social tensions. Some European politicians saw colonization as an outlet for those tensions and began a race to claim territory in Africa. In 1830 France invaded Algeria, using raids by the Barbary pirates on the coast as an excuse and claiming the territory after a long and bitter struggle.

The Suez Canal was completed in 1869, and the British realized the importance of it as a trade route. When Egypt failed financially, Britain made it a protectorate and pushed southward, seeking to control the Sudan and the entire Nile Valley.

The French also pushed from Algeria all the way to Fashoda in the Sudan and coveted the Nile as well. Conflict over the area seemed imminent. France backed off because of antiwar pressure at home, but the confrontation sent a clear message—that claims to Africa could cause international conflict.

Meanwhile, Italy had established itself in Somaliland at the horn of

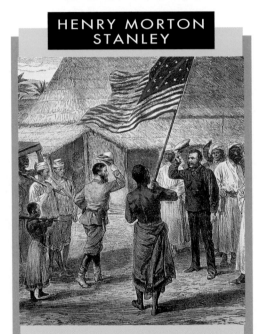

HENRY MORTON STANLEY

Finding David Livingstone in 1871 was only one famous accomplishment in the eventful life of Henry Stanley, seen above doffing his pith helmet to Livingstone. Raised as John Rowlands in a poorhouse in Wales, he ran away at the age of 15 and shipped as a cabin boy to New Orleans. He was adopted by merchant Henry Morton Stanley and took his name. Soldiering in the Confederate Army he was captured at Shiloh, then enlisted in the U.S. Navy and engaged in battle. After the war he was a newspaper correspondent in Europe, Africa, and Asia. He continued his explorations after finding Livingstone, opening up the Congo region and discovering the Ruwenzori—the "Mountains of the Moon." He later returned to England, repatriated, and served in Parliament.

Africa, and Germany made claims on both the east and west coasts. King Leopold, noting Henry Stanley's explorations up the Congo River, authorized him to make claims for Belgium. The Portuguese, long possessors of trading stations in today's Angola, pushed inland and also established themselves on the southeast coast in Mozambique. Spanish ambitions concentrated on the west coast with parts of Morocco, the Canary Islands, and the Rio de Oro coast near the Canaries.

Africans resisted incursions into their territories, but rarely fought together as allies. The slave trade and the Muslim holy wars had fractured social structures, and in their efforts against the Europeans the weapons of native Africans were no match against modern weapons, including the machine gun.

Ethiopia's situation was an exception: Emperor Menelik II foresaw invasion attempts and armed his country with modern weapons. His defeat of the Italians in 1896 discouraged further European moves into his country for nearly 40 years.

With European squabbles over territory reaching a peak, 14 major powers, including the United States, met in Berlin in 1885. With no regard for the traditional territories of many African groups, they drew lines with pencil and ruler and partitioned parts of the continent. No one could enforce the decisions. Many of the rules of conquest were broken, and conflicts would continue for decades. ■

1849 The gold rush begins in California.

1851 Sojourner Truth delivers her famous, "Ain't I a Woman?" speech at a women's rights meeting in Akron, Ohio.

1853 Commodore Matthew Perry sails into Japan's Edo Bay with four modern steam-powered warships, urging Japan to adopt more liberal trade policies with the U.S.

1860 Pony Express is established in the U.S. to carry mail from St. Joseph, Missouri, to Sacramento, California.

1885 The Statue of Liberty arrives in New York from France.

1899 Fighting breaks out between U.S. forces and Philippine rebels, after they proclaim an independent republic.

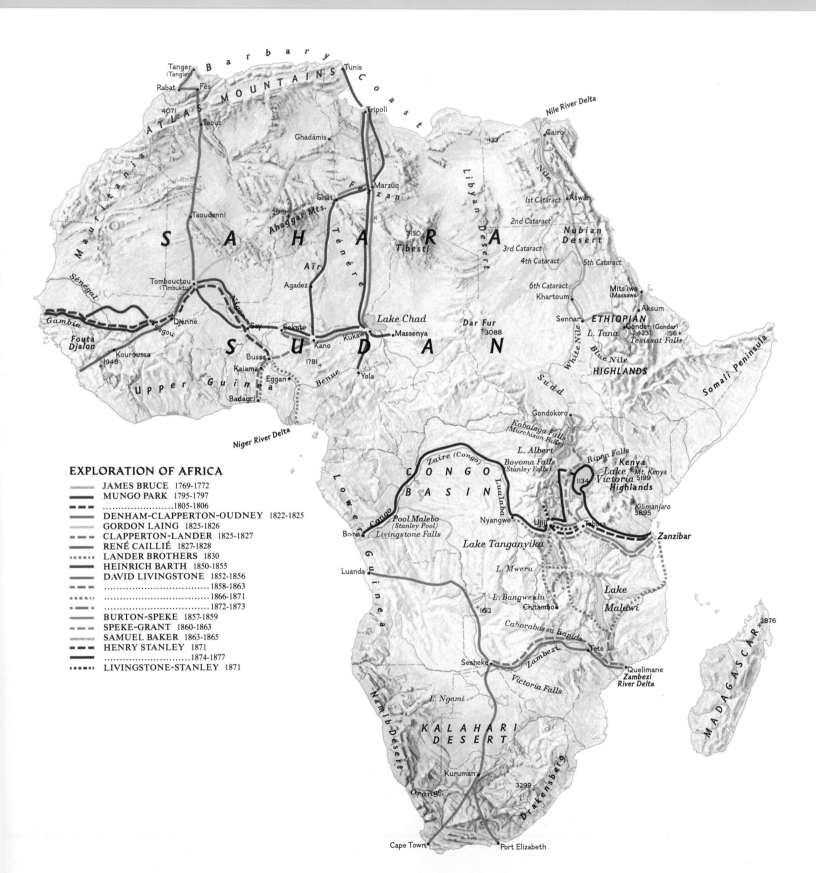

EXPLORATION OF AFRICA

	JAMES BRUCE 1769-1772
	MUNGO PARK 1795-1797
	1805-1806
	DENHAM-CLAPPERTON-OUDNEY 1822-1825
	GORDON LAING 1825-1826
	CLAPPERTON-LANDER 1825-1827
	RENÉ CAILLIÉ 1827-1828
	LANDER BROTHERS 1830
	HEINRICH BARTH 1850-1855
	DAVID LIVINGSTONE 1852-1856
	1858-1863
	1866-1871
	1872-1873
	BURTON-SPEKE 1857-1859
	SPEKE-GRANT 1860-1863
	SAMUEL BAKER 1863-1865
	HENRY STANLEY 1871
	1874-1877
	LIVINGSTONE-STANLEY 1871

● **1768** Wesley Chapel in New York City, the first Methodist church in the Colonies, is dedicated.

● **1774** The physician Franz Mesmer uses hypnotism for therapeutic purposes. The terms "mesmerism" and "mesmerize" are coined.

● **1786** Trade agreement is signed between Britain and France.

● **1794** Robespierre survives two assassination attempts in two days.

● **1800** Philadelphian William Young makes shoes specifically designed for the right and left feet.

Explorers in Unknown Africa

Until colonization began in earnest, most of Africa remained a huge mystery to outsiders, truly a dark continent. As late as 1850 few European countries had established bases at the coastal fringes.

A number of difficulties blocked exploration and development of the interior. Successful agriculture did not seem feasible. Large desert areas such as the Sahara received scant rainfall, while rain forests received such large amounts of moisture that nutrients were leached from the soil when the forest was cleared. Debilitating tropical diseases such as malaria, sleeping sickness, and

yellow fever could strike down Europeans, although Africans had developed some resistance to them. Transportation was also a problem. The high elevations of much of Africa create rapids as rivers flow over rocky scarps on their way to the sea.

Even before Europeans began carving up the continent, some forays into unknown areas had begun in the search for more accurate information.

Scottish explorer James Bruce set out from Alexandria, Egypt, in 1769 and journeyed far up the Nile. Travel was dangerous and sometimes fatal.

Portuguese explorer Francisco de Lacerda went from the east coast to the center of the continent and died in what is now Katanga in 1798. Mungo Park explored the Niger River between 1795 and 1797 and, on a return trip in 1805 and 1806, drowned during a native attack near

● **1821** Greeks rise against Ottoman Turks and thousands are killed.

● **1837** At Lake Okeechobee, Florida, U.S. troops rout Seminole Indians.

● **1844** American Samuel F. B. Morse sends first message by electric telegraph—"What hath God wrought!"—on experimental line between Washington, D.C., and Baltimore, Maryland.

● **1880** German physician Karl Eberth discovers the typhoid bacillus.

● **1898** Spanish-American War.

Bussa. British explorers Richard Burton and John Speke discovered Lakes Victoria and Tanganyika. Meanwhile, concern for one Scottish explorer's safety gave rise to an African drama that captured world attention in the late 1800s.

David Livingstone was a medical missionary whose accounts of exploring the Zambezi River and searching for the source of the Nile were published in European and American newspapers. When the dispatches stopped, Livingstone was feared dead. The New York *Herald* commissioned reporter Henry Morton Stanley to find him. When he did so, his greeting to the explorer at Lake Tanganyika became a household phrase: "Dr. Livingstone, I presume."

The adventure stirred widespread interest in Africa, and further explorations by Stanley and others sped colonization in areas long ignored. ■

Africa claimed Scotsman Mungo Park, whose party perished on the Niger *(above)*. John Speke *(far left)* said he had found the Nile's source in 1858, but other British doubted his claim. First European to see the falls on the Zambezi *(left)*, David Livingstone named them after his queen, Victoria.

● **1790** George Vancouver, British naval officer, explores the Pacific coast of North America.

● **1791** Russia gains Black Sea steppes from Turks.

● **1804** Lewis and Clark begin their exploration of the northwestern U.S.

● **1812** Cylinder printing press invented and is put to use by the *Times of London.*

● **1813** The waltz becomes a popular dance.

Australia Begins as a Penal Colony

The large continent in the South Pacific vaguely referred to as *terra australis* was long ignored by Europeans. Dutch and Portuguese reached the northwest coast in the 17th century, but the native people had nothing that they wanted in trade. Not until Captain James Cook sailed into Botany Bay on the east coast, in 1770, and claimed the coast for Britain did Europeans take an interest in Australia. The unusual plants and animals excited scientists as well as artists.

With the loss of its American colonies a few years later, Britain turned its attention to Australia. Its first use was as a penal colony for convicts, for North America had previously been a way of easing crowded English jails. In 1787 a fleet of 11 ships loaded with 776 prisoners, perhaps a quarter of them women, sailed from England, arriving at Botany Bay in January of 1788.

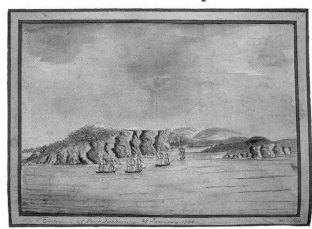

Australia interested England in the late 1700s as a depository for undesirables. A ship's officer painted the arrival of the first fleet of convicts in Sydney Harbour in 1788 *(above)*. In bleak surroundings they fought native people and each other to survive. Hardest cases were sent in chains, often to die, in a grim penitentiary at Tasmania's Port Arthur *(opposite)*, shown here under restoration as an historic reserve. From the vegetative fringe of the continent, English explorer Charles Sturt headed north in 1845 in search of an inland sea and found instead stony wastes and red sand ridges *(below)*.

No land surveys preceded the landing of the fleet. Convicts, who were expected to create a self-sustaining colony, were met by rocky hills and wiry brush in what would later become Sydney. Agriculture was difficult and the Aborigines, while often friendly, occasionally tossed a spear into a newcomer. The convicts were forced to work hard, building roads, churches, and government buildings. Drunkenness, fighting, and stealing were common.

As more prisoners arrived, other colonies were set up along the coast, at Newcastle, Hobart, and Brisbane.

Naval officers charting the coast sighted whales off the southeastern shores, bringing whalers from both Britain and the U.S. Taking the valuable oil provided the colonies with their first economic enterprise.

Convicts who served out their prison terms were given a choice of

1823 Waterproof cloth invented by Scottish chemist Charles Mackintosh.

1829 Greece gains its independence.

1840 German chemist Justus von Liebig's book, *Chemistry in Its Application to Agriculture*, begins a movement toward more scientific crop production.

1852 Victoria and Albert Museum opens in London.

1861 Outbreak of U.S. Civil War.

returning to England on the next available ship or staying in Australia with a land grant of 30 to 50 acres. Discharged soldiers were given 80 to 100 acres and officers even more. Some of the latter became wealthy and began to control trade. Rum was imported into the settlement and became used as currency, with disastrous effects on behavior.

One of the wealthy and influential ex-officers, John Macarthur, began raising sheep, a practice soon copied by others. The rolling hills not far inland provided adequate pasture, and former convicts and soldiers began pushing beyond the mountains that hemmed in Sydney Cove.

The first free settlers, 11 of them, arrived in 1793, just five years after the founding of the penal colony. By 1810 there were 3,000, many involved in raising sheep. Australia became known for something other than a penal colony in the 1820s as

thick, soft wool was shipped back to England. By 1830 free settlers outnumbered convicts, many of whom served out their sentences working for the free farmers and sheep ranchers. Authorities overlooked harsh treatment of them by their masters.

Explorations into the interior began in 1817 with journeys by John Oxley up the Lachlan and Macquarie Rivers. He found more grasslands in the interior, drawing even more settlers. In 1860, Robert O'Hara Burke and William Wills undertook the first crossing of the wild and mostly bone-dry interior from Melbourne in the south to the Gulf of Carpentaria in the north. Only one man, nurtured by Aborigines, survived the return trip.

By mid-century so many free settlers had occupied Australia that they vigorously protested further importation of the criminal element. In 1868 the last of 162,000 convicts transported from England arrived. ■

THE BOUNTY MUTINY

The first free European settlers in the South Pacific were the mutineers of the British ship *Bounty.* In 1789 they overthrew Capt. William Bligh after a voyage to Tahiti. Turning Bligh and loyal crew members loose in an open boat *(above),* nine mutineers sailed east to Pitcairn Island, burned the ship to avoid detection, and settled there. Bligh sailed to safety. By 1808 eight of the mutineers had died of violence or disease.

Aborigines—the First Australians

The native people of Australia, when first contacted by Europeans, had inhabited their island continent for at least 40,000 years. Their ancestors had probably traveled there from Asia on a land bridge when the Ice Age had lowered ocean levels. Then, when the oceans had risen again, the people had been cut off from the rest of the world.

The Aborigines, as the original Australians are called, had developed a culture in close harmony with nature. Seeing themselves as custodi- ans of the land, they gathered plants and hunted but did not cultivate fields, herd animals, or build cities.

The creation of their world and its continuation into the future have been understood by Aborigines for millen- nia through an oral tradition known

Stirring up dust and memories of their storied past, modern Aborigines join in a ceremonial dance that may reenact creator heroes or historical events.

1885   Germany establishes a protectorate over the Tanganyika coast.

1888   National Geographic Society is founded in Washington, D.C. George Eastman develops first box camera.

1888   Jack the Ripper terrorizes London.

1898   Marie and Pierre Curie discover radium and polonium.

1900   Devastating hurricane causes 6,000 deaths in Galveston, Texas.

as the Dreamtime. It has little to do with dreams as outsiders know them. Rather, it refers to the beginnings.

In stories passed down through generations, ancestral beings who took the forms of humans, animals, and plants traveled throughout a

formless world and gave it features such as springs, deserts, and mountains. A female in human form created the land itself and the people on it, and gave them languages.

A crocodile made the rock country; an eagle brought water lilies and planted them in the floodplain. Their work done, the creatures planted themselves in places that could be seen: the eagle as a white rock in a woodland, the crocodile as a rocky outcrop shaped like the reptile's back.

When the ancestral beings were finished, they told the people to take care of the land and never to change it. The Aborigines felt themselves to be part of nature and all things in nature to be part human.

These ancient people and their land had escaped the attention of Europeans for centuries after many other "new" lands had been brought under colonial control.

The Aborigines' isolation was aided by winds and currents. The Portuguese rounding the tip of Africa had their sights set on India and the Spice Islands. The Spaniards rounding Cape Horn had tacked northwest toward China and Japan. The Portuguese possibly encountered the hostile north coast of Australia in the mid-1500s in voyages to the Spice Islands, and the Dutch found it in 1600 when they tried to exploit the prevailing westerly winds for a fast route to the East. But those explorers, finding no trade commodities on the bleak north and west coasts, did not linger there.

In 1770, well past the time of other European explorations, Captain James Cook of England, on a voyage of scientific inquiry, landed on the more hospitable east coast. He found not only extraordinary plants and animals but also the Australian natives. He called them "a timorous and inoffensive race," and his early relations with them were mostly peaceful.

As English colonists eventually spread over the coasts and pushed farther inland, however, the Aborigines were forced into the dry, harsh interior. They offered resistance, often striking from ambush, but their spears were no match for the colonists' rifles.

In less than half a century, the Aboriginal population in all Australia had been reduced by half, and its culture had been scattered. Many of the Aborigines' native institutions have survived only in the center and the extreme north of the continent. ■

CAPT. JAMES COOK

In contrast to many cruel ship captains of his day, the brilliant British navigator and explorer Capt. James Cook took good care of his men and inspired awe and loyalty in them. In three famous Pacific voyages he expanded European knowledge of that vast ocean, taking scientists and artists with him as well as accurately mapping what he found. Ironically, the man who treated native peoples with gentleness was killed by Hawaiian Islanders in a fit of rage.

● **1776** Continental Congress adopts a declaration of independence; George Washington reads it aloud to his troops to inspire them.

● **1824** Charles X succeeds his brother, Louis XVIII, to French throne and tries to restore absolute royal authority; as mobs take to the streets, Charles abdicates and flees to Britain in 1830.

● **1846** Brigham Young leads Mormons on trek to Great Salt Lake.

● **1849** Deadly cholera epidemic kills 16,000 in London.

● **1850** Alfred Krupp, in Germany, produces the first all-steel guns.

The Annexation of New Zealand

The Dutch navigator Abel Tasman, whose name was eventually given to Tasmania, was the first European to encounter New Zealand, in 1642. His stay was brief as he fought with the fierce Maori—Polynesians who had reached the big islands by canoe around A.D. 1000.

Abel Tasman called New Zealand Staten Land, but Dutch authorities later renamed it Nova Zeelandia, meaning "new sea-land."

More than a century later, on the same voyage in which he landed in Australia, Capt. James Cook sailed completely around the North and South Islands of New Zealand in 1770. Hunters seeking whales and seals set up stations in the 1790s. Settlement began in the 1820s and 1830s, mostly by Scots.

The inevitable conflicts between native people and newcomers occurred, with the Maori faring well, living up to their description by Captain Cook as "a brave open warlike people." They incorporated modern firearms readily and fought among themselves but also held off the Europeans.

Weapons they could not combat were European diseases to which they had no resistance, and their numbers dropped from about 200,000 to 100,000 by 1840.

Still, warfare against foreigners on the North Island lasted from 1845 to 1872. In one engagement the British bombarded a Maori fort with

Tattoos and distorted faces greeted the first British in New Zealand. Carvings at fortress gates honored past leaders, including one whose irregular markings tell of his illegitimate birth *(above)*. An artist portrayed men sticking out their tongues to show defiance *(below)*. From the rocky coast projected Cape Reinga *(opposite)*, where Maori believe the spirits of the dead enter the underworld through an old gnarled tree.

artillery, sure the new weapon would terrify the natives. Instead, the Maori devised shell-proof bunkers and rose up to destroy the storming party.

The Maori eventually succumbed to British rule—not for lack of skill or courage. Rather, unlike the British, they lacked an empire to resupply them in war. Maori warriors had to go home to grow their crops.

In the Treaty of Waitangi in 1840 the British agreed to protect Maori property rights, and the natives recognized British sovereignty. The treaty was not fully honored, as more European settlers arrived and often grabbed Maori lands.

Sheep raising supplied the first economy, and discovery of gold in 1861 brought more people. Despite common background (except that no convicts were deposited in New Zealand) and British heritage, the two nations never joined. New Zealand had its own government by 1856 as part of the British Empire.

With the building of the Suez Canal in 1869, improved marine engines, and the advent of refrigerator ships in the 1880s, New Zealand developed a lively economy shipping mutton and dairy products to Britain. New Zealand also became known as a laboratory for social experimentation, with provisions for old-age pensions and an eight-hour working day. It was the first country to allow women to vote (1893) and to provide social security. ■

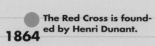

1864 The Red Cross is founded by Henri Dunant.

1876 American Alexander Graham Bell patents the telephone; first commercial telephone exchange is opened in New Haven, Connecticut, two years later.

1889 Panama Canal Company goes bankrupt, stopping work on canal.

1895 German physicist Wilhelm Röntgen discovers X rays.

1898 American battleship *Maine* is destroyed in Havana's harbor.

The Growth of Australia

The discovery of gold in the extreme south of Australia in 1851 brought a flood of immigrants to the continent. Isolated finds had occurred since 1839, but the colonial government played them down, fearing a diversion of labor from the sheep stations.

Large nuggets found at Ballarat, west of Melbourne, however, stirred such excitement that the 1851 population of 400,000 doubled in the next eight years. Campsites became boomtowns. The precious metal, some people said, was so plentiful it could be shaken from the roots of a pulled-up clump of grass.

Britain had little trouble bestowing self-rule on Australia, whether because of its distance from the homeland, the independent nature of

Sheep ranches like this one in New Zealand *(right)* became the basis for Australia's early growth as well. Thick wool shipped to England from both countries kept looms busy in the textile industry. Gold opened Australia's interior. To sift out the precious metal, miners of the 1850s mixed water and earth in a shifting sluice box *(above).*

● **First Kentucky Derby held in U.S.**

1875

● **Game of bingo is developed.**

1880

● **Rubber gloves are used for the first time in surgery at Baltimore's Johns Hopkins Hospital.**

1890

● **First Peace Conference at the Hague.**

1899

the people who went there, or lessons learned in North America.

In 1850 the Australian Colonies Government Act passed by the British parliament gave the colonies the right to form their own legislatures, write their own constitutions, and fix their own tariffs, all subject to confirmation by Britain.

Still, there were acts of rebellion. In August of 1851 a group of miners in the goldfields rebelled over voting rights and representation in the colonial legislature and declared a Republic of Victoria. They were crushed in a single attack by government troops, and 13 of the rebels were tried in Melbourne for treason. All 13 went free, and a number of democratic reforms they sought were soon passed.

By 1855 four separate colonies were scattered around the large country, almost the size of the contiguous U.S. They were New South Wales, Victoria, South Australia, and Tasmania off the south coast. Vast Western Australia became a government in 1893.

Universal voting rights, vote by ballot, and payment of legislators became realities in Australia before they did in the mother country. For a time the five colonies operated in total separation while all recognized Britain as their sovereign. In 1901, with close economic ties and Germany threatening in nearby New Guinea, they formed the Commonwealth of Australia, independent but part of the British realm. ■

1781 American and French forces bottle up Lord Cornwallis's army of 8,000 men at Yorktown, Virginia; Cornwallis surrenders.

1787 U.S. Constitution signed.

1801 Former slave Toussaint L'Ouverture declares island of Haiti independent with himself as ruler.

1803 For 15 million dollars, Napoleon sells all prairie lands between Mississippi River and Rocky Mountains to the U.S. in Louisiana Purchase, doubling U.S. land area.

1824 U.S. House of Representatives elects John Quincy Adams as president when none of the four candidates wins a majority in the national election.

The Race for Pacific Islands

The largest area in which colonies were sought by the European powers was Oceania in the Pacific Ocean. Oceania includes not only the larger islands of Indonesia, Australia, and New Zealand, but also thousands of smaller ones.

In the beginning Britain, France, and the Netherlands led the race. By 1900 they were joined by the United States and Germany. With sea travel and naval power of prime importance, the islands had value not only as trading stations but as strategic points and refueling stops for coal-burning ships.

The Dutch had a long history in Indonesia, having traded in the spice islands since the 16th century. Those interests extended to New Guinea, and in 1828 they annexed the western part of that island. Other nations were also interested in New Guinea, especially the Germans who had become powerful in Europe and were interested in the Pacific. This made

In Liverpool, England, first public bath and **1844** washhouses open.

1851 Great Exhibition held in London, celebrating Britain's ascendancy in industry and technology, is the first such international exhibition.

Switzerland revises its constitution. **1874**

U.S. bans Chinese immigrants for ten years. **1882**

Crete proclaims union with Greece. **1897**

the Australian colonies nervous, and as early as 1873 they asked London to claim the non-Dutch half. When Britain dallied, the Queensland government claimed possession of eastern New Guinea, but Britain disallowed it. By the time England acted, the Germans had already claimed the northeastern part and a nearby archipelago. Britain had to settle for the southeastern corner, today's Papua New Guinea.

Meanwhile, numerous other small islands were being snapped up by the major powers. Although the French were more interested in developing their interests in Indochina at the time, France took over the Marquesas, annexed the Loyalty Islands, and made Tahiti a colony.

The British annexed Fiji north of New Zealand and established protectorates over the Cook Islands, the Gilberts, and the Ellice Islands.

Sometimes joint influence was undertaken to avoid too much concentration under one nation. Britain and France accepted joint sovereignty of the New Hebrides. In 1889 Britain, Germany, and the U.S. arranged for joint supervision over the affairs of Samoa.

European nations competed for the last large area offering colonies, the Pacific islands. The remote Hawaiian Islands saw the end of famed explorer Capt. James Cook, first welcomed and feted by local people *(opposite, above)*, but later killed. Kamehameha *(opposite)* became Hawaii's first king, organizing its government and allowing foreign traders to settle. As the islands became valuable, outside powers struggled to gain ownership.

After Spain lost to the U.S. in the Spanish-American War, it gave up many of its holdings in the Pacific. As part of a treaty, Spain ceded the Philippine Islands and Guam to the United States in 1898, and it sold the Carolines and Marianas to Germany.

The Hawaiian Islands, one of the most remote sets of islands in the world, had an interesting history of human influence. The first people arrived there around A.D. 100, late in the history of world settlement.

THE STATUES OF EASTER ISLAND

Giant stone statues of unknown origin on Easter Island may have been the most surprising and mystifying discovery by Europeans exploring the South Pacific. Dutch navigator Jacob Roggeveen was the first to land on the remote island, easternmost of all Polynesia, on Easter Sunday, 1722. The hundreds of carved statues, quarried from volcanic rock, ranged in height from 10 to 40 feet, and the largest weighed 85 tons. Moving them into place appears to have been a remarkable feat of primitive technology. The statues may have had religious significance for their creators.

Tahitians invaded and won control over them in 1200. The islands were the last discovery of the explorer Capt. James Cook, who was killed by natives when he visited in 1778. The first American missionaries arrived in 1820. In 1824 the Hawaiian king and queen journeyed to London to offer the islands to King George IV, but both died of measles before they could be presented to the monarch.

In 1826 a treaty of friendship and commerce was signed with the U.S., and treaties were also signed with Britain and France. In 1840 a representative government was established, but a number of Americans were appointed by the king to administrative and judicial offices.

Nevertheless, in 1842 the U.S. recognized the independence of the islands, and in 1843 Britain and France did the same and promised not to annex them. When France began making demands on the Hawaiian government eight years later, the U.S. warned the French to keep their hands off.

But the islands had become valuable as producers of sugar and pineapples, and as an important coaling station in the middle of the ocean. When the Hawaiian government was overthrown in a coup d'etat in 1893, American Marines landed. In less than a month the U. S. declared Hawaii a protectorate. A Republic of Hawaii was proclaimed in 1894. But in 1898 the U.S. annexed Hawaii and organized it as a territory of the United States. ■

1900 to the Present

10

7

5

6

4

11

AROUND THE WORLD

1 North America: Once a luxury, the automobile became a necessity when assembly lines brought down the price. Soon farmer or factory worker could afford Henry Ford's Model T.

2 Asia: Foreign powers controlled China by 1900. As dissatisfaction grew, nationalists and communists took over until the latter, led by Mao Zedong, drove out their rivals. For decades, Mao oversaw

China, his portrait here displayed over Peking's Gate of Heavenly Peace.

3 Europe: The Bolsheviks succeeded in taking over the Russian government under the leadership of Vladimir Lenin, founder of Russian Communism. His image on a giant billboard is seen here, towering above Leningrad's Palace Square.

Vanishing Empires, New Challenges

1

3

2

8

9

4 Medicine: Death from infected wounds during World War I propelled the discovery of penicillin. By 1940 huge autoclaves sterilized flasks in the mass production of the drug.

5 Europe: Weight of the Free World on them, Gen. Dwight D. Eisenhower, commander of U.S. forces, and Britain's Prime Minister Winston Churchill review troops before the Allied invasion of Europe.

6 Atomic Energy: The weapon that made full-scale war between the major powers unimaginable, a hydrogen bomb was exploded in 1954 at a Pacific atoll with energy equivalent to ten million tons of TNT.

7 Computer Science: Computers shrink as technology advances. The integrated circuitry of a megabyte chip, easily held in one hand, handles millions of calculations per second.

8 Asia: It's business as usual on the streets of Nazareth as politicians debate the future of Arabs and Israelis on a store-window TV. On-screen, peace accords absorb Egyptian President Hosni Mubarak, second from left; Israeli Foreign Minister Shimon Peres, gesturing; and Palestinian leader Yasser Arafat, with head covering.

9 Africa: New attitudes blend with old in the traditional dress of a Herero woman of Namibia, decorated with animals and the shape of her nation.

10 Space: Two astronauts hover in space in 1985 to repair a communications satellite.

11 North America: A mahogany cutter in Central America continues the felling of tropical rain forests, a prime cause of species extinction.

Vanishing Empires, New Challenges:

There has been no hundred-year period in which life on earth changed as dramatically as in the 20th century. The Ice Age, which sparked human advancements, nevertheless extended over millennia. Discovery of the New World broadened human horizons, but changes in attitudes and terrain were spread over several centuries.

The 20th century, on the other hand—with its leap-frogging technology, its mass communications, and its agents of enormous destruction—changed not only attitudes of people around the earth but also the earth itself. The wars of history have shown that humankind has frequently made enemies of itself. In the 20th century, with weapons capable of wiping out whole cities and domestic activities that threaten to change the climate itself, perhaps for the first time a species in search of enemies could find one in itself.

Man's inventiveness, however, spoke of genius. The groundwork was laid with the industrial revolution, in the previous century, when first coal, then diesel oil and gasoline fueled the engines that replaced human and animal power. The first automobiles chugged across the century mark, but their rapid proliferation began with Henry Ford's assembly line in 1908. Electricity, known for centuries, was harnessed as the workhorse of humanity, and reliance on it spread across the face of the earth. The Wright brothers sputtered aloft in the first powered flight in 1903. Only 66 years later men walked on the moon.

As if inventiveness had sparked independent thought, people grew less tolerant of subjugation. The European colonialism that swept Africa in the 19th century dissolved in the 20th as one group after another fought for self-determination. Freedom, unfortunately, did not always mean peace. Europeans carving up Africa amongst themselves had set boundaries with no regard for ethnic divisions, and tribalism frequently disrupted the unity of new nations.

Racial differences came into tight focus in South Africa, torn early in the century by strife between Dutch and English settlers. When the Boers finally won through the ballot box, they established a system of black and white separateness that became repugnant to the rest of the world. It lasted 42 years before its abolition, and soon after, in free elections, the black majority swept into power.

Everywhere boundaries were being redrawn and new nations were rising on an avalanche of ethnic pride. Arabs, under the boot of foreign powers for centuries, allied with the British to drive out the Ottoman Turks. Egypt later took over the Suez Canal that had been built and owned by Europeans. The shah of Iran moved too fast and too insistently into the future to suit his people, and they rejected him in favor of a religious traditionalist. The Jews, with no nation to call their own since biblical times, carved out a corner in the Middle East and, with approval of the new United Nations organization, formed Israel. The displacement of Palestinian Arabs by the Jewish nation would prove the basis for bitter and often bloody tension between Arab and Jew for the last half of the century.

1900 to the Present

The world had long known regional conflicts, but in the 20th century war went international, with simultaneous battlegrounds around the globe involving many nations on opposite teams. They became known as World Wars I and II—only two decades apart—and they resulted in the deaths of millions.

World War I began as an ethnic quarrel in 1914 when Serb nationalists seeking their own nation killed an Austro-Hungarian prince. World War II was a battle against fascism, a political philosophy whose glorification of raw power threatened to engulf the world. Adolf Hitler, constantly denying his intentions, unleashed his modern army and conquered Europe. Benito Mussolini took advantage of economic chaos to dominate Italy before casting a wider net. Imperial Japan, feeling industrial muscle, moved into China with an eye to enveloping the Far East. Some 20 million people died before the fascist, or Axis, powers were defeated by the Allies, led by Britain, France, the Soviet Union, and the United States.

But another tension was building that would grip the world in a dangerous competition. It was rooted not in ethnic grounds but in ideology. The Bolshevik Revolution in Russia in 1917, feeding off the eternal tension between the haves and the have-nots, espoused universal equality and foresaw a world with neither need nor greed. The vision never became a reality. Leaders of the move toward communal sharing, or communism, found ways to enjoy privilege; and, in forcing their philosophy on others, they squelched freedom and bred resentment.

Although the two opposing economic systems, communism and capitalism, were allied in World War II, the end of the hot war spelled the beginning of the long Cold War between the United States and the Soviet Union. The two superpowers, each possessing devastating nuclear weapons, stood in apocalyptic confrontation for half a century, each struggling to gain more allies to maintain an international balance of power. The Cold War thawed when authoritarian communism finally imploded, bankrupt by its built-in inefficiencies, overthrown by people who wanted to seek their own destinies.

In the midst of this world of tensions, perhaps partly because of it, a series of technological wonders was changing the way people lived. The automobile created a new way of life in America, one more mobile and far-flung. Radio, television, and the movies introduced cultures around the world to each other and flattened out differences. Medical advances defeated many of the biological enemies of humankind but, in so doing, pushed populations to levels that strained the earth's resources.

Concern for humankind evolved into concern for the planet now dominated by the human species. Humans launched themselves into earth orbit and began looking beyond, into deep space. Life on earth, after puttering along little-changed for centuries, had reached new plateaus. ■

Monarchy died in Russia with the killing of the Romanovs—Tsar Nicholas II, his wife Alexandra, and their five children. Historians believe the Bolshevik Lenin ordered their deaths out of fear that the deposed royal family would regain public support.

Overleaf:
A glut of images from 500 screens reflects the number of channels that could be available to viewers of cable TV.

Australia's Evolution

Situated near Asia, settled by convicts, populated mostly by people of European descent, Australia has experienced an unusual history. Its road from colony to independent nation ran more smoothly than that of most nations in the British Empire.

Several factors may have allowed this peaceful transition. No serious economic issues were at stake, as they were in the North American colonies, which were upset over trade policies. Australian wool and mutton found a ready and lucrative market in Britain. There was no native population soured against outsiders and pushing for self-rule, as in India. The native, Aboriginal population had been quickly scattered by the newcomers. Even as the Australian colonies set up their own governments, they remained intensely loyal to Britain. Perhaps the lack of threat or conflict and the extreme distance between mother country and colony combined to make Britain reluctant to carry on the administration of such a faraway land.

Whereas most countries are first a rural population and then an urban one, Australia was the reverse, because of the vast desert interior. By

| 1941 | Intensive atomic research begins in the Manhattan Project. | 1959 | Fidel Castro overthrows the Cuban dictatorship and subsequently sets up a Marxist government allied with the Soviet Union. | 1963 | The first woman to enter space is Valentina Tereshkova, a Russian. | 1991 | The breakup of the Union of Soviet Socialist Republics occurs. | 1996 | Israeli Prime Minister Yitzhak Rabin is assassinated. |
| 1975 | First women ordained as Episcopal priests in the U.S. |

the end of the 19th century, it already held one of the world's most urbanized populations, living on the green perimeter of a continent nearly the size of the contiguous United States. After the separate Australian colonies had formed their own governments, they were reluctant to unite in a federation. In 1901, however, the five mainland colonies and Tasmania, off the southern shore, formed the Commonwealth of Australia.

As its own nation, Australia maintained a unique posture. Its institutions and traditions came from Britain, and—in supporting the mother country's causes—its young men served with distinction in the Boer War and World Wars I and II. More Australians died than Americans in World War I, although the United States was 20 times more populous. The Aussies chose to build a close

relationship with the United States, importing American technology and entertainment and openly seeking U.S. protection in World War II.

Ironically, although a neighbor of Asia, Australia pursued a whites-only immigration policy for years. That policy began to disintegrate in the 1960s, however, and Australia now receives more immigrants from Asia than from Europe. Europeans still dominate the population, but Australia is becoming the Eurasian melting pot that it long tried not to be. ■

From pioneer settlements to powerful cities, Australia moved almost seamlessly into the modern world. In the early 1900s tall forests provided timber for the coach-building Everingham family *(left)*. Today's industries might more likely be in high technology, based in glittering cities like Melbourne *(below)*. Today, outsiders offer many investments such as the skyscraper in the foreground built by the Pacific island nation of Nauru. But Aussies, like this confident 11-year-old girl *(opposite, below)*, still stand on their own.

1913 U.S. Federal Reserve System is established.

1926 First demonstration of transmitting moving pictures through the air with electronic signals is made in London by John Logie Baird, a Scottish engineer.

1933 Nazi Germany opens first concentration camps.

1939 Baseball game is first televised in the U.S.

1947 United Nations agrees to the foundation of independent Jewish and Arab states in Palestine.

Trains and Automobiles Move the Masses

Luxury trains with dining cars and comfortable sleeping compartments became popular in the United States during the Great Depression of the 1930s and lasted until the late 1950s. Steam and diesel locomotives competed for a while until diesel finally won out. Speed records reached

100 mph in 1904 for steam, 144.9 for diesel in 1986, and 319 mph in 1990 for an electric-powered train.

Today electric trains are in considerable use for local commuting and as municipal underground rail systems throughout the world. As a favorite mode of transportation over distance the train has been replaced by the airplane, but the automobile has been the single most significant transportation development of the 20th century.

No other form of travel has so transformed the landscape and the way people live. The automobile is responsible for the growth of suburbs and the decay of inner cities. Hailed as an answer to city pollution caused by horse manure, it has clouded

urban areas with an unhealthful haze known as smog. It has also given people the greatest mobility in history, broken down regional differences, and created a huge industry.

Although the United States has built an entire culture around the automobile, it was not invented there. Gottlieb Daimler's highly portable internal combustion engine came forth in 1885 and 1886. Shortly thereafter Carl Benz began to

First means of mass transportation, trains lapped up passenger miles and shrank the world, powered by steam well into the 20th century. South Africa's plentiful coal kept locomotives lining up at Bloemfontein Station *(left)* as late as 1970, although diesel and electricity took over soon after. In a Paris yard, snakelike electric trains *(below)* sit ready to speed 168 miles in an hour, a distance that horse-drawn coaches not so far back in transportation's past took several days to cover.

manufacture automobiles in Germany. In the latter part of the 19th century inventors from Germany, France, Britain, and the U.S. were turning out motorized wagons.

America's first successful automobile is believed to have rolled out of Charles Duryea's shop in Springfield, Massachusetts. But automobiles remained a plaything of the wealthy until Henry Ford oversaw the creation of an assembly line that lowered the price of a touring car to $850 in 1908. By 1915 Ford alone was building half a million cars annually, and the price had fallen to $290.

Cars came to epitomize the American prosperity that had become evident after World War I. Between the two World Wars a billboard

1955 Rosa Parks's arrest prompts a year-long boycott of Montgomery, Alabama, buses by blacks and brings to prominence civil rights leader Martin Luther King, Jr.

1961 South Africa withdraws from the British Commonwealth and proclaims itself a republic.

1979 Shah of Iran forced to give up his throne; Ayatollah Khomeini proclaims a strict Islamic Republic.

1989 Dissidents seeking freedom face down tanks in Beijing's Tiananmen Square.

1994 U.S. President Bill Clinton ends trade embargo with Vietnam.

appeared that showed a happy family riding in a comfortable sedan. The caption read, "There's no way like the American way, world's highest standard of living."

Within a decade after World War II one in every six U.S. workers held jobs in some way related to cars—working on the assembly lines, building roads, or selling auto insurance.

Kingpins of the car trade, American automakers grew sloppy in their construction methods and ignored warnings that oil prices might rise and make their gas guzzlers outmoded. When the Arabs set up an oil embargo in 1973 to protest U.S. support of Israel, American car buyers discovered that Japanese automobiles were well made and economical to run. In 1980 Japan built more cars than the U.S. Three years later nearly 30 percent of all new American cars sold in the U.S.—7.98 million—were built elsewhere.

The competition resulted in better machines. In the 1990s cars are more reliable, longer lasting, more fuel efficient, and actually cheaper in relation to U.S. median income than they were 30 years before.

The automobile's effects, however, on the environment—pollution, traffic jams, auto salvage yards, and the asphalt paving of farmland for parking lots—is another matter.

With the automobile revolution less than a century old, researchers still look for engines that pollute less, use less fuel, and perhaps even guide themselves. Fuels and methods of operation may change, but as a means of individual conveyance, no rival to the car is in sight. ■

Once a luxury, the automobile became a necessity when assembly lines brought down the price. Soon farmer or factory worker could afford Henry Ford's Model T *(above, left)*, no matter that they all looked alike. Ads for racier versions like the Cord *(right)* pushed snob appeal as carmakers began selling an image as much as a machine. As prices soared and quality slipped, Japan led the way in using robots to weld frames *(below)*, replacing the costly and less consistent human labor.

● Henry Ford establishes
Ford Motor Company.
1903

● **18th Amendment
(Prohibition) is ratified.**
1919

● The electric razor
is patented.
1928

● **The U.S. recognizes
the U.S.S.R.**
1933

● Women's military
services are established
1942 in the U.S.

Slipping the Bonds of Earth

n 1783 two Frenchmen, Joseph-
Michel and Jacques-Etienne
Montgolfier rose skyward in a hot-air
balloon, beginning the era of
manned flight. But lighter-than-air
craft eventually proved to be a dead
end, soon passed by motorized vehicles of greater speed and durability.

The Wright brothers, Wilbur and

Orville, launched the revolution in
travel with their 12-second flight,
powered by a four-cylinder engine,
on December 17, 1903. It was an
inauspicious beginning; only five people showed up to see the demonstration at Kitty Hawk, North Carolina.
Just 11 years later airplanes were flying in battle. And 25 years later

Londoners could book air passage
to India. Three-quarters of a century
after the Wright brothers' first flight,
Christopher Columbus's five-week
journey across the Atlantic could be
accomplished in three hours in a
supersonic passenger plane. Nothing
in the history of travel can match the
speed of that progression.

1944 ● U.S. Congress enacts the GI Bill.

1946 ● The United Nations is established.

1951 ● Julius and Ethel Rosenberg are sentenced to death for passing atomic secrets to the Russians.

1955 ● An East European mutual defense agreement, the Warsaw Pact, is signed.

1975 ● U.S. President Gerald Ford escapes second assassination attempt in 17 days.

Between Kitty Hawk and the Concorde were many aviation heroes and some spectacular advances. Charles Lindbergh was not the first to fly across the Atlantic, but he excited people's imaginations by doing it alone and nonstop. American Amelia Earhart and Englishwoman Amy Johnson further demonstrated the possibilities of long-distance flights, but tragically both disappeared over water.

Throughout the 20th century, aviators and aviation companies have worked to break new ground and create bigger and better machines. In the 1930s it was possible to fly to the Far East in a four-engine float plane that carried 16 passengers. By the 1960s the Boeing 747 jumbo jet could carry 400 passengers 8,400 miles without stopping. The cargo bay of the U.S. military transport, the C-5, is longer than the distance covered in the Wright brothers' first flight. The Soviet-built An-225 is even bigger, the entire aircraft four feet short of a football field in length.

With larger size came larger disasters. The crash of two 747s in 1977 in the Canary Islands took 580 lives, aviation's worst single disaster. Yet flying has become statistically the safest form of travel. ■

A swarm of biplanes buzzed over spectators at an air show early in aviation history (opposite), when the miracle of flight still amazed the public. War brought rapid changes in aviation. Decades later, a Grumman F-14 Navy fighter plane approaching the sound barrier created its own cloud (right) as the sudden changes in pressure and temperature condensed water vapor.

The China Giant

By 1900 China was a huge country with a government that was virtually a puppet to outside powers. After putting down the Boxer Rebellion, had the foreign nations divided up China among themselves, it would have ceased to exist as a country.

To many Chinese, this decline from the greatness their country had possessed made them contemptuous of the Qing (Manchu) dynasty, which

had ruled since the mid-1600s.

Many young Chinese were studying abroad, learning Western ways, and becoming convinced that the Qing should be overthrown. Among them was Sun Yat-sen, who despite

his peasant background, had studied overseas, adopted Christianity, and received a medical degree. He opposed traditional Chinese ways and, from outside China, formed a movement seeking all-out revolution.

The Qing successfully repressed rebellion until 1911, when a number of revolts resulted in provinces' declaring themselves independent. Dr. Sun Yat-sen returned from the United States and was elected president of the Chinese Republic. Still, China was hardly a united nation.

When the powerful general Yuan Shih-Kai moved to rule China from Beijing, Sun Yat-sen stepped down as president and set up the headquarters of his Nationalist Party, the Kuomintang, in Canton. His aim was eventually to defeat the Beijing government and reunify China. He died in 1925 before realizing his goal, and the Kuomintang was taken over by party leader Chiang Kai-shek.

In 1926 Chiang Kai-shek allied with the Chinese Communist Party and defeated powerful warlords who had broken off from the Qing. Then he turned on the communists and drove them out of the Shanghai area. While he could not defeat them completely, he so pressured the forces led by Mao Zedong that the communists were forced to retreat to northwest China. The two sides suspended the civil war in 1937 and for a while presented a united front against invading Japanese forces at the outset of World War II.

Corruption bedeviled the national-

ist government during World War II, and support began to swing to the communists. At war's end Mao refused to surrender northern provinces to the nationalists, and fighting between the two groups was fierce. Eventually the communists drove the nationalists from the mainland, and Chiang Kai-shek and supporters fled to the island of Taiwan, off the southeast China coast.

The United States, in conflict with the communist Soviet Union in the post-war period, refused to recognize the People's Republic of China, as Mao called his nation. The Soviets and their allies declared friendship with the new regime.

Mao reorganized agriculture into a series of communes, where all work and resources were pooled in a common effort. Communal farming and industrialization failed to meet the goals of Mao's program, called the "Great Leap Forward."

Gains were made in other areas, such as industry, public sanitation, and health. But any opposition was brutally suppressed, raising even more opposition. In the first seven years of Communist rule nearly a million "enemies" were executed.

For decades after World War II Mao's China and the U.S. were barely on speaking terms, neither represented by an embassy in the other country. But by the early 1960s Mao had split with the Soviets. The Cultural Revolution that followed was a time of civil disorder and overall confusion throughout China. Then, in

1922 ● Bolsheviks form the Union of Soviet Socialist Republics (U.S.S.R.).

1923 ● Alice Paul writes the equal rights amendment (ERA).

1926 ● A. A. Milne publishes *Winnie the Pooh.*

1933 ● The U.S. Congress votes independence for the Philippines.

1941 ● Lend-Lease Act passed in the U.S.

1972, American President Richard Nixon visited China, and while major differences were not resolved, a dialogue was begun. Following Mao's death in 1973, Den Xiaoping helped to foster China's embrace of capitalism. Cultural and economic exchanges between China and the U.S. continued to increase until 1989, when the Chinese Army crushed pro-democracy demonstrations in Beijing's Tiananmen Square, an act sharply rebuked by the U.S.

In early 1997 U.S. Vice President Albert R. Gore of the Clinton Administration visited China in an effort to restore friendly relations. With its population of slightly over a billion, China is the most populous

Foreign powers controlled China by 1900, and such luxuries as the reception room at the Summer Palace *(opposite)* drained funds as the nation lost the stature it had known for centuries. As dissatisfaction grew, nationalists and communists took over until the latter, led by Mao Zedong, drove out their rivals. For decades, Mao oversaw China, his portrait seen prominently over Peking's Gate of Heavenly Peace *(left).* In 1989 dissidents seeking freedom faced down tanks in Tiananmen Square *(above).*

315

1948 Queen Wilhelmina of the Netherlands abdicates and is succeeded by Juliana.

1951 Libya becomes a constitutional monarchy.

1957 Soviets launch the satellite Sputnik; for the first time a man-made object orbits the earth.

1966 For the first time Michael E. De Bakey implants an artificial heart in a human in Houston, Texas.

1972 U.S. Supreme Court rules that death penalty is unconstitutional.

nation in the world and offers a huge market for international sales.

That large population, however, could have problems feeding itself. China has 20 percent of the world's people but scarcely 7 percent of earth's arable land, necessitating intense cultivation. A famine from 1959 to 1961, greatly exacerbated by disastrous government policies, resulted in the deaths of some 30 million. China increased its grain production, but now the country is rapidly becoming industrialized, which means turning farmland into factories, enlarging cities, and also diverting water from irrigation to other uses. As incomes have risen for many in

China, food consumption and the demand for variety in the starchy diet have risen as well. Increases in the production of pork, beef, poultry, eggs, and milk would create even more demands for grain. Large imports of grain by China could affect world prices.

The economic gains, however, have gone far in restoring the pride that faltered during China's colonial years and during the economic failures of Mao's "Great Leap Forward."

Adding to that pride in 1997 was the return of Hong Kong, which had been ceded to the British in 1842. The enormously successful commercial colony became Chinese again at

midnight on July 1, with celebrations that included fireworks costing 13 million dollars. Hong Kong has a gross domestic product that is 20 percent that of the mainland, with only one-half of one percent of the mainland's population. A new constitution promised to protect Hong Kong's individual freedoms, human rights, and independent judicial system, but the constitution gave China the final say in interpreting it.

The world watched with fascination the marriage of one of the most authoritarian regimes in the world with a small enclave built on a combination of Chinese entrepreneurialism and a Western style of freedom. ∎

Cultures merged in 1997 when Britain turned over Hong Kong to China. A highly regimented nation where workers loyally sing company songs *(left)* began managing a free-wheeling capitalistic center known for its glitter. Although trade between the two areas led to long delays at a customs shed *(opposite),* for years China had raised prickly wire *(above)* to block citizens seeking Hong Kong's bright lights. The world waited to see if two such different systems could blend.

1982 Britain overcomes Argentina in Falklands War.

1983 Menachem Begin resigns as Israel's prime minister; Yitzhak Shamir succeeds him.

1989 Hirohito, Japan's emperor since 1926, dies and is succeeded by Crown Prince Akihito.

1994 South Africa holds first interracial national election.

1995 More than 5,000 die in earthquake that destroys Japanese city of Kobe.

1914 • Panama Canal opens. Chinese National Assembly is dissolved. First traffic lights are installed, in Cleveland, Ohio.

1915 • U.S. Congress establishes the Coast Guard.

1915 • Motorized taxis make first appearance.

1916 • Albert Einstein's General Theory of Relativity is published.

1916 • Bobby Jones makes his debut in U.S. golf.

The War to End All Wars

The continued growth of nationalism early in the 20th century led to the most devastating war ever fought up to that point. Citizens identified strongly with their countries and were proud of their accomplishments. Nationalism had unified Germany and nurtured French pride.

Nationalism had also made the Slavic people of Serbia want to join with those ruled by Austria-Hungary to form a single Southern Slavic nation, or Yugoslavia. That desire would set off the war.

The nervousness about any one nation growing too strong had led to alliances, with countries promising to aid each other in case of attack. Germany, Italy, and Austria-Hungary formed the Triple Alliance. Britain, France, and Russia joined in the Triple Entente.

On June 28, 1914, Archduke Francis Ferdinand, heir to the Austro-Hungarian throne, and his wife were visiting the city of Sarajevo in Bosnia when they were assassinated by a Bosnian-Serb nationalist, seeking the union of his people with Serbia.

In retribution, Austria-Hungary, backed by Germany, declared war on Serbia. Russia, still smarting from its loss of face in the Russo-Japanese War, began mobilizing against Austria-Hungary and Germany. France announced its support for Russia, and when Germany invaded Belgium to reach France, Britain

entered the war. It was a new kind of war, one so destructive and widespread that it was known as the Great War and "the war to end all wars." Later it became known as World War I because of the many countries it involved and the wide area over which it raged.

The fading Ottoman Empire allied with Germany, Austria-Hungary, and Bulgaria, which became known as the Central Powers, so fighting spread to the Middle East. France, Britain, Russia, Serbia, Belgium, and later Japan became the Allied Powers. Italy soon renounced the Triple Alliance and joined the Allies.

The war was often fought along front lines that stretched for hundreds of miles, with agonizingly slow

THE LEAGUE OF NATIONS

At the end of World War I U.S. President Woodrow Wilson insisted that the Treaty of Versailles include a plan for a League of Nations to settle international differences. The League of Nations never gained much prominence, perhaps in part because President Wilson's own Congress refused to approve the U.S.'s joining it, fearing that an attack on a fellow League member would pull the U.S. into another war. Rivalries between the 53 member nations also weakened it, and by the late 1930s the League had little influence. It was replaced by the United Nations in 1946.

● 1916 U.S. purchases the Virgin Islands from Denmark for 25 million dollars.

1916 ● Grigory Rasputin is assassinated.

● 1917 Conscription is introduced in Canada.

1917 ● Literacy test required for all immigrants to the U.S.

● 1918 In Great Britain, all women over age 30 are given the right to vote.

1918 ● Daylight Savings Time is introduced in the U.S.

forward progress measured in yards.

Millions died in artillery barrages against trenches where ground troops huddled. Terrible new weapons were introduced, such as poison gas, flame-throwers, and tanks that were moving fortresses. Airplanes brought death from the skies, bombing and strafing. Submarines lurked under the seas to torpedo ships.

The collapse of Russia, which withdrew after the Bolshevik Revolution, put extra pressure on the Allied Powers. They were aided in 1917 when the United States came into the war, irritated by the loss of

An American gun crew fights in the Argonne Forest *(opposite)* in what many hoped would be the world's last major conflict. Bickering between the victors in European talks over treaty terms blocked efforts by U.S. President Woodrow Wilson, far right *(above)*, to seek a lasting peace.

American lives in the sinking of passenger ships by Germany and alarmed at news of a secret agreement between Germany and Mexico.

Over the next two years the injection of U.S. troops and war matériel helped turn the tide in Europe. In the Middle East the British and Arabs defeated the Turks. Austria-Hungary and Turkey surrendered, and the German Army, although not completely defeated, was without reserves, morale was low, and war-weary Germans began to rebel.

On November 11, 1918, Germany signed an armistice. ■

WORLD WAR I
ALLIANCES AND AREAS OF CONFLICT

- Allied nations and their dependencies
- Central powers and their dependencies
- Neutral nations
- Farthest advances of Central powers
- Trench lines
- Armistice lines
- ✧ Major battles

THE WORLD 1914-1918: Allied Nations & Central Powers

WESTERN FRONT MAJOR BATTLES

● Norway becomes inde-
pendent from Sweden.

1905

● San Francisco earth-
quake and fire; some
500 people are killed.

1906

● Chinese Republic
established after
overthrow of Manchu
dynasty; Sun Yat-sen
named president.

1911

● Ireland's Sinn Fein Party
is established.

1905

● Robert E. Peary and
Matthew Henson reach
North Pole.

1909

● Fire at New York's
Triangle Shirtwaist
Company; 145 die.

1911

The Bolshevik Revolution

B y the end of the 19th century Russia remained behind the rest of Europe in technology and political progress. Its economy still depended on agriculture and the labor of downtrodden people. It had lost the Crimean War, an attempt to gain a warm-water port in the Black Sea.

Tsar Alexander II attempted some reforms, freeing the serfs and improving education. But many discontented people wanted an end to the imperial system, and Alexander II was assassinated. After his successor, Nicholas II, reversed all of Alexander II's reforms,

riots broke out in 1905, but they were brutally crushed by troops.

Nicholas II promised civil rights and fair elections for a national parliament, but the promises were only partly kept. World War I did not pull the Russian people together. Millions of troops were fighting Germans and Austro-Hungarians on the western border, while back home food riots were erupting.

Pressured by revolutionary groups and seeing no way out, Tsar Nicholas II abdicated, and a provisional government took over.

Among those seeking radical reform was a man born Vladimir Ilyich Ulyanov, who took the name Vladimir Lenin.

A believer in the philosophies of Karl Marx, Lenin felt that private property should be abolished and that workers should control industry

Insurgents scatter in Petrograd on July 4, 1917, as soldiers of the provisional government fire on Bolsheviks seeking power *(below)*. Three months later the Bolsheviks succeeded under the leadership of Vladimir Lenin, founder of Russian Communism, whose image on a giant billboard is shown here, towering above Leningrad's Palace Square *(opposite)*. Later, factions battled each other in a civil war. After winning that war, the Reds formed the Union of Soviet Socialist Republics (U.S.S.R.)

1912 ● Capt. Albert Louis makes first parachute drop from an aircraft in the U.S.

1913 ● Henry Ford invents the conveyor belt assembly technique.

1916 ● Margaret Sanger opens first birth control clinic in the U.S.

1919 ● British scientist Ernest Rutherford splits the atom.

1921 ● Forces led by army officer Reza Pahlavi take over the Iranian government; Pahlavi becomes shah.

1922 ● Benito Mussolini takes power in Italy.

and agriculture. The result, he claimed, would be a paradise on earth with no injustice, no inequality, and no private property. Each person would give according to his or her ability, and receive whatever basic essentials were needed.

At the turn of the century Lenin and his followers had joined the Russian Social Democratic Labor Party. It had split in two, and Lenin's branch became known as the Bolsheviks, or "majority."

In October 1917, in the midst of World War I, they overthrew the provisional government in the capital of Petrograd (St. Petersburg) with support from dissident army troops. Shortly after the revolution, elections were held for the constituent assembly, and the Bolsheviks won a minority of seats.

So convinced were the Bolsheviks of the rightness of their way that their soldiers dissolved the assembly when it met in January 1918. To extricate themselves from World War I, they made a separate treaty with the Germans, giving up territories in the Baltic area, Ukraine, and Poland.

But peace did not come to Russia, for many groups disagreed with Lenin's plans for the nation. Royalists wanted a return to the monarchy, middle-class liberals wanted a capitalist democracy, and moderate socialists wanted democracy and a state-controlled economy.

Civil war broke out, with all the non-Bolshevik groups, known as the "Whites," against the Bolsheviks, called the "Reds" because they favored a red flag of revolution. In a cruel and devastating conflict, both sides killed civilians suspected of supporting the opposite cause.

The Reds executed the deposed tsar and his family to avoid a possible return to monarchy. Despite aid from Russia's former European allies and the United States, the Whites were defeated. In 1922 the Bolsheviks formed the Union of Soviet Socialist Republics (U.S.S.R.).

The U.S.S.R. failed Lenin's promise to be an egalitarian, classless society. Although gains were made in industrialization, in electrification, and in literacy, millions died in purges aimed at wiping out dissent against the system.

The Communist Party dominated all levels of government from the top officials to the smallest local council; although elections were held, all the candidates were selected by the party.

Corruption invaded the hierarchy, and while shortages in food and materials occurred, the best went to top party officials. Workers with no hope of personal gain failed to produce top-quality work. ■

THE BLOODY REIGN OF JOSEPH STALIN

The leader of the Soviet Union for some 30 years was a former seminary student from the Republic of Georgia, who later ruled with an iron and bloody fist. Joseph Stalin was Lenin's close associate in the Bolshevik Revolution and his successor at Lenin's death in 1924. His forced collectivization of farms in the 1930s led to widespread famine, which resulted in the loss of some seven million lives. Crushing dissent, he executed many he called "counterrevolutionaries" and sent many more to forced labor camps in Siberia, where at least five million died.

1927 Nicola Sacco and Bartolomeo Vanzetti, Italian-born anarchists convicted of armed robbery and murder, are executed in U.S.

1929 The iron lung is invented.

1932 Charles Lindbergh's infant son is kidnapped; Bruno Hauptmann is convicted of the crime and executed in 1936.

1945 At Yalta, Roosevelt, Churchill, and Stalin plan final defeat of Germany.

1949 Two separate German states—East and West—are established.

The Creation of Saudi Arabia

The Ottoman Empire of the Turks had controlled much of the Middle East since the 16th century. By 1800 the empire was unraveling, weakened by corruption and economic decline. At about the same time, Arabs were regaining pride in their culture; they resented any foreign domination.

In the western part of the Arabian peninsula local leaders increasingly felt little connection to the sultan in Istanbul. An area called the Nejd was taken over by followers of Wahhabism, a philosophy that held to strict observance of Muslim law. This group conquered Mecca and Medina before the Turks reacted forcibly to the challenge. In a seven-year war the many tribes of the Arab forces were widely scattered.

At the beginning of the First World War, the Arabs saw another opportunity to throw off the outsiders. The British, who were fighting the Turks who had allied with the Central Powers of Germany, Bulgaria, and Austria-Hungary, offered independence to Arab leader Ibn Ali Hussein in exchange for Arab help.

The war did not go well for the British and Arabs until British Col. T. E. Lawrence was sent to bring the Arab groups together. Under his leadership they captured the important town of Aqaba on the Red Sea and attacked the railway across the Hejaz in western Arabia, the most important link in Turkish communications.

When the Turks were defeated, however, conflict persisted between the Arabs themselves. Hussein had declared himself king of the Arabs but was opposed by the Wahhabis, led by Ibn Saud, king of the Nejd area. Ibn Saud held much of eastern Arabia and had made his own separate treaty with the British. After a six-year civil war the Hussein family abdicated. Ibn Saud was proclaimed king of the Hejaz and Nejd in 1926.

In 1927 the British recognized the complete independence of the kingdom, which Ibn Saud later renamed Saudi Arabia after his family.

At first the kingdom was poor and undeveloped, with 98 percent of its land either desert or wasteland. In 1933 King Ibn Saud allowed an American oil company to search for petroleum. In 1936 a major discovery was made, and the kingdom became a major oil-producing area. At first most of the oil profits went to the oil corporations, but later the Saudis took control over production.

Today billions of dollars pour into the country annually, allowing Saudi Arabia not only to modernize but also to become a major contributor of foreign aid. It holds a quarter of the world's known oil reserves and supplies the United States with a quarter of its annual oil imports.

Skyscrapers have risen in Saudi Arabia's cities, and jets fly Arab businessmen around the world. Irrigation programs have greened some of the desert. Still, little more than one percent of the soil is cultivated. Recognizing that oil is their future for decades to come, the Saudis limit daily production to prolong the flow. ■

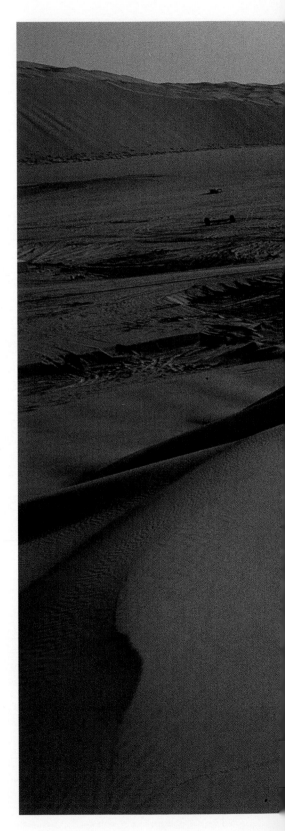

1955 Winston Churchill resigns as British prime minister; Anthony Eden succeeds him.

1959 St. Lawrence Seaway opens, allowing ocean-going ships to reach U.S. Midwest.

1963 U.S. President John F. Kennedy is assassinated.

1969 U.S. astronaut Neil Armstrong becomes the first man to walk on the moon.

1972 PLO extremists take Jewish athletes hostage at the Olympic Games in Munich.

1981 In the U.S. air controllers go on strike.

Amid the salt flats and sand dunes of the vast Empty Quarter a drilling rig probes for more of the oil that has made Saudi Arabia an economic power.

1901 | The Commonwealth of Australia is formed.

1912 | R.M.S. *Titanic* sinks on maiden voyage; some 1,500 people drown.

1915 | Alexander Graham Bell in New York and Dr. Thomas A. Watson in San Francisco hold the first transcontinental telephone conversation.

1918 | Germany signs armistice, ending World War I.

1920 | 19th Amendment (women's suffrage) is ratified in U.S.

Advances in Medicine

Despite 19th-century advances in the understanding of germs, infections, and sanitary measures, some abysmal medical practices were still in place as the 20th century approached. Bloodletting and purging as a means of restoring health continued in both Europe and the United States. U.S. President James Garfield was shot in 1881, and doctors probed for the bullet with unwashed hands and instruments; he died 80 days later, perhaps needlessly. People commonly died of consumption (tuberculosis), pneumonia, measles, typhoid fever, diphtheria, whooping cough, and scarlet fever.

With the dawn of the 20th century, a golden age of medicine was about to begin. In three generations more would be learned about fighting disease and sustaining good health than had been learned in all the previous millennia. Hospitals themselves are a 20th-century phenomenon. In 1800 there were only 2 in all America. By 1992 there were 6,649.

To achieve this progress, science first had to gain credibility. It had long held amateur status, an avocation for people who had the time and money for experimentation. As huge foundations such as those of Rockefeller and Sears offered grants to talented minds, and as permanent academic posts for research were established, science became a profession. Rapid communication by telephone and airplane and the proliferation of academic journals facilitated the exchange of ideas.

In the early decades of this century came the first understanding of how muscles work under stress, how hormones produced by glands trigger certain performances in the body, and how food is metabolized. Understanding these processes helped medical researchers find solutions to specific problems. The discovery of insulin and its function in metabolizing sugar resulted in treatment for diabetes. Study of the thyroid gland led to iodine's use as a treatment for goiter, an enlargement of the gland that becomes visible in the neck. As a side benefit, iodine was identified as a disinfectant.

Sometimes chance led to important discoveries. In 1921 Alexander Fleming sneezed on some bacteria in a culture dish and noticed that the bacteria dissolved, leading to the realization that the enzyme lysozyme in saliva acts as an antibacterial agent. In 1928, while studying molds, the same Dr. Fleming noticed that one particular type of mold in a

1927 *The Jazz Singer,* starring Al Jolson, becomes the first part-talking motion picture.

1932 U.S. protests Japanese aggression in Manchuria.

1948 OAS (Organization of American States) charter is signed at Bogota, Colombia.

1953 Edmund Hillary, of New Zealand, and Tenzing Norgay, of Nepal, reach summit of Mt. Everest.

1954 *Nautilus,* first atomic submarine, is launched.

petrie dish killed all the bacteria around it. Research revealed that the mold was nontoxic to humans. He called the new agent penicillin.

The discovery of viruses triggered a host of vaccinations to prevent disease. Vaccines trick the body into believing it has had a disease so that it marshals forces against its

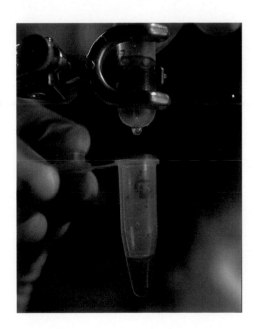

recurrence. Since viruses are living proteins that cannot multiply on their own, they attach to cells in the body and reproduce through them. The body attacks foreign viruses with antibodies, but if the invasion is too great, the antibodies may be overwhelmed and the body may become sick and die. If the body recovers, the immune system now recognizes the signature of the virus and can attack it more readily next time. Injecting a small amount of the virus triggers that recognition without causing the

sickness. Polio with its crippling and sometimes fatal paralysis struck terror until Drs. Salk and Sabin developed the vaccines that conquered it in the 1950s. Vaccines all but eradicated measles and brought under control chicken pox, whooping cough, typhoid, and cholera.

Studies of the body's immune system and advances in surgical methods have resulted in once impossible medical procedures' becoming almost routine. Hearts, kidneys, and livers can be successfully transplanted. Three-dimensional imaging techniques, radioactive tracers, and

other devices let us check the performance of the brain, heart, and other organs. And scientists continue to investigate DNA (deoxyribonucleic acid), each individual's biochemical genetic code, discovered in 1963.

Death from infected wounds in World War I propelled the discovery of penicillin, when a researcher observed mold-killing bacteria. By 1940 sterilized flasks *(opposite),* were used in mass-producing the drug. Electronic tools now pinpoint trouble spots within the body. Images from CAT and MRI scans fill a light box in an operating room *(below),* offering surgeons reference points inside a patient's skull. Uncovering the secrets of life itself, a technician drains excess solution from suspended DNA *(left),* the code that carries an individual's unique genetic signature.

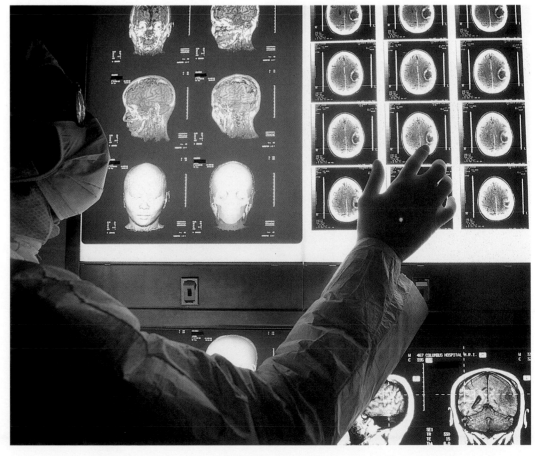

1958 Egypt and Syria merge into United Arab Republic.

1967 Three Apollo astronauts—Virgil Grissom, Edward White, and Roger Chaffee—are killed by fire during a simulated launch.

1968 Martin Luther King, Jr., and Robert F. Kennedy are felled by assassins.

1973 Great Britain, Ireland, and Denmark enter the European Common Market.

1974 U.S. President Richard M. Nixon resigns, following the Watergate scandal; he is succeeded by Gerald Ford.

Slender pipelines for energy, fiber optic cables *(below)* each can transmit the words of 200 books a second, whisking information between computers around the world. Bits of data speed through the needle-thin conduits as electronic pulses. In a medical application optical fiber can carry a laser into cancerous cells in a patient's eye *(right)*, destroying them without harming surrounding tissue. Each use of fiber optics depends on the transmission of energy at tremendous speed.

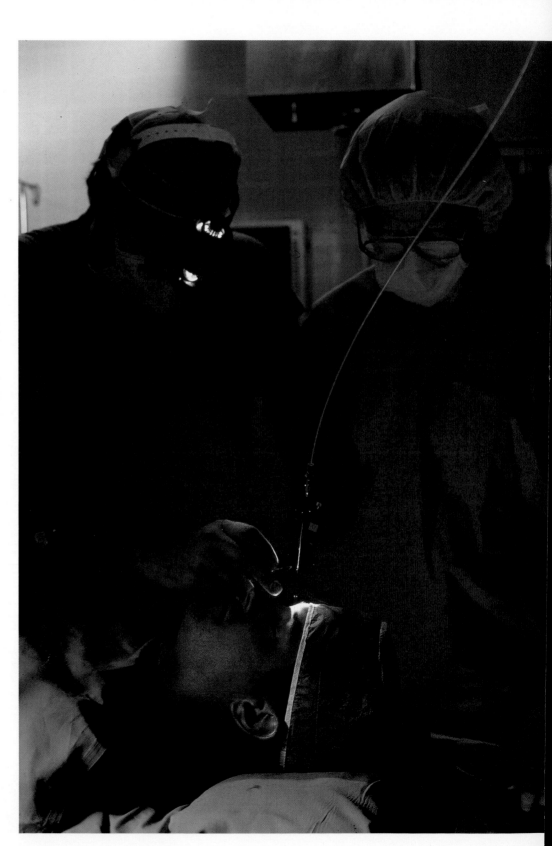

In 1917 Albert Einstein speculated that atoms or molecules might be induced to absorb light or other radiation and then be stimulated to pour forth their borrowed energy. In 1960 Theodore H. Maiman introduced the light from a flash lamp into a rod of synthetic ruby and created a beam of crimson light of incredible intensity. His success inspired other lasers that now perform numerous functions, including reading prices on containers at grocery counters and performing delicate and painless eye surgery.

"Laser" is an acronym meaning "light amplification by stimulated emission of radiation." Lasers operate by harnessing light itself. The visible light we most commonly know is made up of waves of red, orange, yellow, green, blue, and violet, all

1980   John Lennon is killed by a lone gunman outside his apartment building in New York City.

1987   U.S. Supreme Court rules that Rotary Clubs must admit women.

1988   U.S. and Canada reach trade agreement.

1988   In Somalia 22 UN troops are killed.

1994   Thousands die in Rwanda tribal warfare.

jumbled in different wave lengths that appear as white. In laser light the waves are organized and concentrated so they travel in smooth, parallel waves—somewhat as if a jumble of noise were released in a single, pure musical tone. As they move together in unison, the light waves reinforce each other to create great power, a beam capable of reaching the moon and echoing back to earth. At close range, concentrating on a tiny area, they can heat a substance at the rate of a trillion degrees per second.

To create a laser, an outside source of energy is introduced to atoms in a cylindrical container of liquid, gas, or crystal. That outside energy may come from an electrical discharge, a high-intensity light, or from nuclear radiation. The cylindrical container has mirrors at either end, one a total mirror and the other partially silvered. The excited atoms in the cylinder release tiny units of light called photons, which race back and forth between the mirrors in the tube, colliding with other atoms and creating even more photons, all moving together in the same wave length and direction. Within millionths of a second from the time the outside energy was introduced, the photons increase in intensity such that they exit from the partially transparent end of the tube as the powerful beam of a laser.

How powerful? Point your finger at the sun at noon on a clear summer day and perhaps one-tenth of a watt of energy reaches your fingertip. If a piece of steel the size of your finger-

By outlining the known contours of a patient's head in computerized images, surgeons pinpoint the location of a brain tumor *(above)*. Using a 700-pound helmet known as the gamma knife *(below)*, medical specialists beam radiation directly at a tumor without making a single surgical incision.

tip were to be aligned to receive a laser beam, the laser could easily concentrate ten billion watts. In industry, that kind of concentrated power now precisely drills eyes in surgical needles or welds refrigerator doors. In medicine it can weld breaks in the retina of the eye or seal leaking blood vessels by photocoagulation. Other uses, such as quelling cancers and unblocking arteries without open surgery, are still being developed.

The industrial revolution began with the harnessing of steam. Lasers now harness light, another form of energy. Potential benefits to humans haven't yet been fully realized. ■

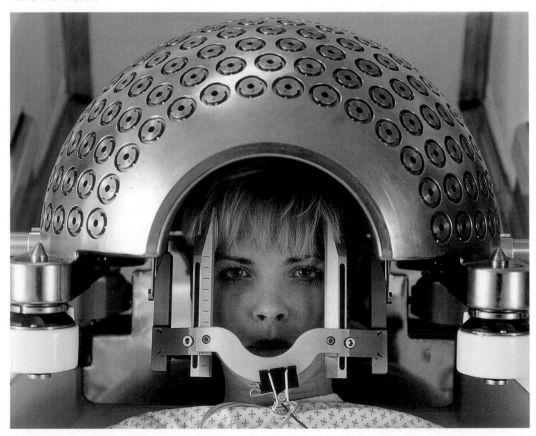

1929 ● Leon Trotsky is expelled
        from the U.S.S.R.

1930 ● Britain, the United
        States, Japan, France,
        and Italy sign a naval
        disarmament treaty.

1931 ● Diamonds are discov-
        ered in Sierra Leone.

1931 ● Spain becomes
        a republic.

1932 ● Iraq proclaims its
        independence.

1932 ● Amelia Earhart becomes
        the first woman to fly
        solo across the Atlantic.

The Great Depression

The end of World War I found the United States in a strong economic position. It had participated in only the final two years of the conflict, and no battles were fought on its own soil. Owing European nations some four billion dollars upon entering the war, the U.S. was owed some ten billion dollars after the Treaty of Versailles.

It was a time of prosperity in America, with proliferating cars, radios, telephones, and other consumer goods—and money to spend on them. People bought things on the installment plan. With industry expanding, they invested in the stock market to make even more money. Some even bought stocks on credit, so confident were they that stock prices would continue to rise and that they could pay for them later.

Such recklessness forced share prices beyond their real value. When that realization hit, investors began selling their stocks rapidly. In October 1929 panic set in, and stock-selling became a flood, with 13 million shares sold on the New York Stock Exchange in a single day.

In what became known as the stock market "crash," stocks fell to nearly half their value. Those who had bought stocks on credit now had to pay for them from previous profits. Many millionaires became penniless. Banks, which had invested the funds of depositors, suddenly did not have funds available when customers wanted their money. Banks closed, and people lost their savings.

Economic problems accelerated. People stopped buying goods, and factories that couldn't sell their products went idle. Loss of jobs created even more nonconsumers. Prices for food crops, such as corn and wheat, dropped disastrously for farmers.

An economy gone sour in the early 1930s put hungry Americans in breadlines, including one in San Francisco *(left)*. The stock market crash of 1929 echoed around the world as people ceased buying goods and factories closed, causing vast unemployment. In "fireside chats" by radio *(opposite, above)* President Franklin Roosevelt tried to rebuild confidence by announcing public works programs that provided jobs for the unemployed.

1934 ● Women's suffrage granted in Turkey.

● 1936 Major oil discovery is made in Saudi Arabia; the kingdom becomes a major oil producer.

1937 ● Nylon is invented.

1938 ● Howard Hughes flies around the world in 3 days, 19 hours, and 17 minutes.

1939 ● Paul Müller invents DDT.

● 1940 U.S. Selective Service Act is signed.

They had not shared in the post-war prosperity because food prices had stayed low while farmers' expenses had gone up; many had been forced to borrow money. Unable to repay those loans, farmers lost their land and moved to the cities or to California in search of new opportunities. A drought hit the Midwest, and lands dried up and blew away as dust. By 1932 a quarter of the U.S. population was out of work.

America's Great Depression reverberated throughout the world. In its boom times America had invested heavily in other countries, but with hard times at home those investments were recalled. Now Europe went into the same downward spiral of factories closing and unemployment. European colonies in other parts of the world suddenly had no market for their raw materials and exports of food, costing them jobs as well.

Economic problems created political unrest. Both Adolf Hitler in Germany and Benito Mussolini in Italy solidified their power at a time when people were dissatisfied and grasping at anything that might lead them out of the morass.

In the United States, Franklin Roosevelt was elected President and initiated a program of recovery, which he called the New Deal.

Banks were more strictly supervised, and deposits were guaranteed by the government. The Securities Exchange Act controlled stock exchanges. The Civilian Conservation Corps was formed to employ idle workers in building bridges, dams, and park facilities, and in reforestation. Farm prices were supported by the government. A system of Social Security for the elderly was begun.

Roosevelt's policies helped put the U.S. economy back on track. He infused it with government money, thereby restoring confidence among lower-income and other people that disaster could be averted. ■

THREATS TO DEMOCRACY

In Italy, Benito Mussolini took over in 1922 with a belief in power and autocratic rule. His followers were known as *fascisti,* or fascists. A youthful elite known as blackshirts squelched all dissent. In Spain in the 1930s the Workers Republic was militarily overthrown by Gen. Francisco Franco, a dictator. In Germany Adolf Hitler, shown here *(left)* at a 1937 rally in Nuremberg, took advantage of a dispirited and depression-wracked Germany to appeal to national pride after World War I. The efficient war machine he oversaw quickly conquered most of Europe in World War II before Germany's eventual defeat.

Electrical Communication Shrinks the World

Trains and cars had already allowed people physically to move great distances in a short time, but the advent of mass communications in the 1920s and 1930s broke down regional barriers and allowed a common culture to spread around the world. The telegraph transmitted thoughts thousands of miles instantaneously. Radio, the movies, and television allowed people to hear and see what life was like in other parts of the world, without being there. Much regional uniqueness was lost, while much universal understanding was gained.

For some 30 years radio was a major source of family home entertainment. From about 1920 until 1950 families huddled around large, cabinet-style radios to listen to news, sports events, music, comedy skits, and dramas. Show-business personalities became household names—Jack Benny, Bob Hope, George Burns, and Gracie Allen.

Political leaders quickly learned to take their ideas directly to the people through radio. President Franklin D. Roosevelt, for example, talked to Americans through his radio series called "fireside chats."

Motion pictures exploded in popularity at about the same time as radio shows, and the golden age of movies arrived in the 1930s. Big Hollywood studios made comedies, dramas, musicals, historical epics, and animated cartoons. Some classics from the '30s are still popular today—*Gone with the Wind, Snow White and the Seven Dwarfs,* and *Top Hat.* Movie

The radio era began in the 1920s when amateur broadcasts paved the way to programming. By 1930 nearly 14 million American homes had radios such as the sleek Echophone *(above).* Talking pictures grew popular in the same decade. Using camera and sound equipment *(below),* movie technicians capture the roar of the MGM lion.

stars attracted tremendous attention from an adoring public. Such personalities as Clark Gable, Greta Garbo, Gary Cooper, Bette Davis, James Cagney, and Katharine Hepburn came under close scrutiny both on the 20-foot screens and in their personal lives. Their glamorous and opulent lifestyles became almost an opiate of the masses during the Great Depression and after.

There were positive effects. Movie heroes were held up as paragons of virtue. John Wayne represented tight-lipped courage; gullible, likable James Stewart demonstrated that a person with principles could stand up to the power elite in *Mr. Smith Goes*

1954 In *Brown v. Board of Education of Topeka,* U.S. Supreme Court unanimously bans racial segregation in public schools.

1960 American U-2 spy plane, piloted by Francis Gary Powers, is shot down over Russia.

1965 U.S. Marines land in Dominican Republic as fighting continues between rebels and the Dominican Army.

1968 North Korea seizes U.S. Navy ship *Pueblo* and holds 83 on board as spies.

1970 Biafra surrenders after a 32-month fight for independence from Nigeria.

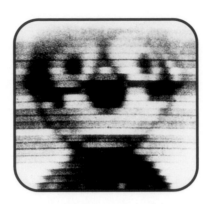

to Washington. The period's strict sexual mores were reflected in the portrayal of cowboys in the movies, who kissed little more than their horses.

Then came a new device whose influence, it was inaccurately predicted, would put an end to movies, radio, and books. The first demonstration of transmitting moving pictures through the air with electronic signals was made in London in 1926 by 38-year-old Scottish engineer John Logie Baird. Baird called his device "television," and the name stuck.

Programming began as a picturized version of radio, with some of the same characters. Some radio stars, such as Jack Benny and Bob

First television star, a Felix the Cat doll spun on a turntable during experimental telecasts in 1928, his blurred image appearing on a screen *(above)*. After a decade of refinements, picture quality had improved enough for a demonstration at the 1939 New York World's Fair. Films have also tried new technologies. Images that seem to appear in three dimensions make kids reach out for a touch at a SONY IMAX movie theater in New York City *(below).* Rapidly blinking liquid crystal headsets synchronized with two film tracks provide the illusion of depth.

Hope made the transition to the television screen. Sports events could be seen as well as heard.

But the real impact of television was felt in the arrival of world events in people's homes. Americans watched the funeral of President John F. Kennedy in 1963 and also witnessed—live on the screen—the murder of his accused assassin. And on the evening news the brutality of war came into homes and helped raise the protests that contributed to America's withdrawal from Vietnam.

With realization of the power of visual impact came the staging of what Daniel J. Boorstin calls "pseudo-events," such as press conferences, marches, and protests presented for the effect they might have on an audience of millions. Politicians soon learned that a good presence on TV lent them vote-getting "star quality." John F. Kennedy had admitted after his election that he might never have won without television exposure.

The important events of history are now seen by nearly everyone. Astronaut Neil Armstrong's first steps on the moon were witnessed as he took them by some 500 million. The Berlin Wall came down in front of television cameras.

The drama, joy, and pathos of the world appears a few feet from us, on both television and movie screens. Little wonder that a generation fed this visual brew of fantasy and reality is frequently heard to say, when dramatic events actually occur in their lives, "It was just like in the movies." ■

● **1938** Douglas Wrong-Way Corrigan flies from New York to Dublin.

● **1938** Forty-hour work week established in the U.S.

● **1939** Britain's King George VI and Queen Elizabeth visit the U.S.

● **1939** First appearance of nylon stockings.

● **1939** The film *Gone With the Wind* opens.

World War II

The Treaty of Versailles, which concluded World War I, demanded that Germany accept blame for the war and pay huge reparations to the Allies for the damage it had caused. The German economy collapsed, and its people were angry and dispirited, looking for a savior. Then the racist, anti-Semitic orator, Adolf Hitler, promised a way out of economic decline. He built a powerful military force, all the time assuring countries such as Britain and the United States that he meant them no harm. In Italy Benito Mussolini was building a dictatorial regime that also reveled in

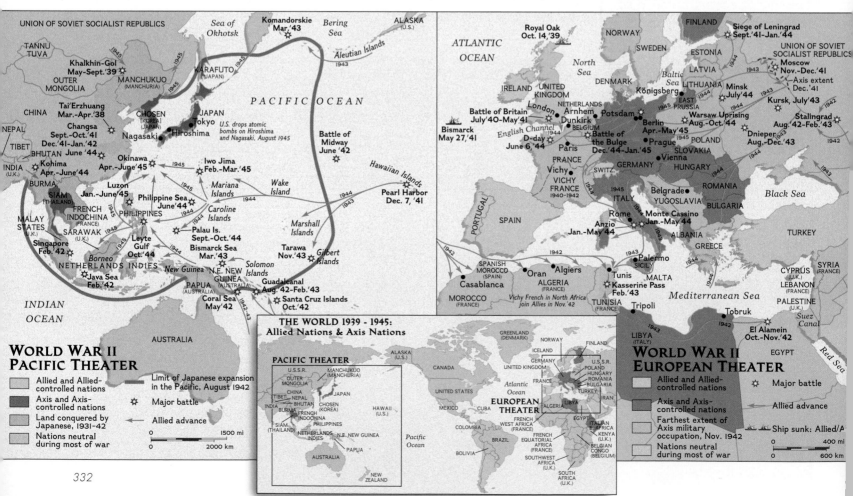

WORLD WAR II PACIFIC THEATER

- Allied and Allied-controlled nations
- Axis and Axis-controlled nations
- Land conquered by Japanese, 1931–42
- Nations neutral during most of war

— Limit of Japanese expansion in the Pacific, August 1942

☆ Major battle

→ Allied advance

0 1500 mi
0 2000 km

THE WORLD 1939 - 1945: Allied Nations & Axis Nations

WORLD WAR II EUROPEAN THEATER

- Allied and Allied-controlled nations
- Axis and Axis-controlled nations
- Farthest extent of Axis military occupation, Nov. 1942
- Nations neutral during most of war

☆ Major battle

— Allied advance

☆ Ship sunk: Allied/A

0 400 mi
0 600 km

1940 — Carl Sandburg wins the Pulitzer Prize in history for *Abraham Lincoln: The War Years.*

1940 — Boxer Joe Dempsey retires from the ring.

1941 — Joe DiMaggio hits safely in 56 consecutive games, establishing a Major League record.

1942 — First all-star bowling tournament held in the U.S.

military power. Japan, now highly industrialized and dominated by military adventurists, sought more territory for the raw materials it needed.

Eventually Germany, Italy, and Japan united as the Axis Powers.

In 1938 Hitler annexed Austria on the premise that all ethnic Germans should be united. The dismemberment of Czechoslovakia began in November of that year, when France and Britain, in a vain attempt at appeasing Hitler's aggression, agreed, at the infamous Munich conference, to German annexation of the Sudetenland. Then in 1939 the rest of the country was dismembered, with Hitler making the present-day Czech

Weight of the Free World on them, Gen. Dwight D. Eisenhower and Prime Minister Churchill review troops before the Allied invasion of Europe. An American cartoon depicted Adolf Hitler's air force chief, Hermann Goering, as a bully dragging along Italy's Mussolini and Japan's Prime Minister Hideki Tojo in chains *(opposite).*

WINSTON CHURCHILL

The prime minister who led the British during World War II was a veteran well acquainted with danger. As a young man Winston Churchill had served with British forces in India, the Sudan, and Khartoum. As a war correspondent in the Boer War in South Africa, he had been captured but had managed to escape. His straightforward, stirring speeches during the aerial Battle of Britain rallied the British people, whose cities were being bombed and who faced a possibly imminent invasion by Nazi Germany.

1943 • Income tax withholding introduced in the U.S.

1943 • The Aqua-Lung is invented.

1943 • Famine strikes Bengal, India.

1944 • First nonstop flight takes place from London to Canada.

1944 • Sunflower oil is first used to make margarine.

Republic a Reich protectorate, Slovakia achieving its independence as a Nazi puppet, and the eastern province of Ruthenia (part of Ukraine today) being annexed by Hungary. In September Hitler invaded Poland— and France and Britain finally declared war.

With his swift, motorized advances aided by aerial attack, which he called *blitzkrieg,* or "lightning war," Hitler took Poland in a matter of weeks. By mid-1940 he had occupied France, Denmark, Norway, Belgium, the Netherlands, and Luxembourg and had driven Britain's troops off the European mainland. The next year, Yugoslavia and Greece would fall, as well.

It was a war involving efforts at wholesale extermination of the Jews, a war against people of color, gypsies, and homosexuals, a war involving immense suffering from starvation and carpet bombing of cities.

Meanwhile, Japan was occupying Indochina. U.S. President Franklin Roosevelt told the Japanese that, if they would withdraw, he would assure them access to the raw materials they needed. While talks were being held in Washington on this subject, the Japanese attacked the U.S. fleet at Pearl Harbor in Honolulu, Hawaii. The U.S. entered the war, allied with Britain and the U.S.S.R.

By late summer of 1942 the war was being fought in Europe, the Mediterranean, Burma, China, and on the Atlantic and Pacific Oceans. The Axis powers won victory after

Stunned American servicemen watch flames rise from the explosion of the destroyer *Shaw* beyond wrecked

● George Orwell
1944 writes *Animal Farm*.

● Women's suffrage
1945 becomes law in France.

● Gen. George S. Patton,
USA, is killed in an
1945 automobile accident.

● Juan Perón becomes
president of Argentina.
1946

aircraft on Ford Island in Hawaii. Japan's surprise attack propelled the U.S. into World War II.

victory on the ground. Germany's troops and fast tanks were initially successful in the North African deserts; the Japanese took Malaya, Singapore, and Burma. Only on the seas did the Allies gain. The U.S. won the Battle of Midway in the Pacific, ending Japan's naval superiority.

With Europe secured, Hitler invaded the U.S.S.R. in 1941, despite a non-aggression pact between the two countries. After the tenacity of the Russian fighters and the severe winter defeated Hitler, he was on the defensive. In 1943 the Allies attacked Europe from the south, invading Italy; and the following June they began landing massive numbers of troops and equipment on the beaches of Normandy in France.

When the Soviets advanced from the east and the British and the Americans closed in from the west and south, Germany surrendered on May 8, 1945. Hitler committed suicide; Mussolini was captured and shot by Italians who opposed him.

Meanwhile the war in the Pacific against the Japanese was being fought island by island. Although the Japanese Navy was devastated, the Japanese refused to surrender.

Rather than invade Japan itself, the Americans used a secret weapon, the atomic bomb. When dropped on Hiroshima, it destroyed more than 60 percent of that Japanese city. After another bomb was dropped three days later, on Nagasaki, Japan surrendered on August 14, 1945, ending World War II. ■

1948 ● State of Israel is created.

● Mao formally proclaims
formation of People's
1949 Republic of China.

1952 ● Elizabeth II becomes
British Queen, following
the death of her father,
George VI.

● Ireland's Eamon de
Valera ends 21 years as
1959 prime minister by taking
up the nonpolitical
position of president.

1961 ● In the first manned
spaceflight, Russian Yuri
Gagarin becomes the
first human to go into
orbit around the earth.

● U.S. begins Medicare
program, which
1965 provides government
medical assistance
for senior citizens.

The Atomic Bomb

Ever since a British scientist, Ernest Rutherford, had split the atom in 1919, many European scientists had been looking into the structure of atoms and speculating on their potential for creating energy. Many of these scientists were living in Germany and Italy. In the 1930s some of them left Europe and went to the United States.

Among them was Italian Enrico Fermi, who had noticed in 1934 that when he bombarded radioactive uranium atoms with neutrons, other radioactive elements seemed to form.

It took five years for scientists to realize that the neutrons were actually splitting a uranium-235 nucleus in two, releasing four times as much radioactive energy as had existed in the single nucleus.

As the nucleus split, it released more neutrons, which split more atoms, releasing more neutrons, and on and on in a chain reaction known as fission. If enough fissionable radioactive material could be gathered, scientists thought, the result might be an immense explosion.

Word of the discovery spread around the worldwide scientific community. A group of scientists in the United States began racing to create an atomic bomb before Germany's Adolf Hitler gained access to one.

In December 1942, with World War II well under way, teams of scientists working with Enrico Fermi in Chicago successfully began a nuclear reaction that created heat before they stopped it. The next step was to

allow it to continue, creating an atomic explosion.

The atomic bomb itself was produced amid high secrecy at Los Alamos, New Mexico. During World War II, when the Japanese appeared ready to fight to the last man to defend their homeland, the bomb was dropped on Hiroshima. So powerful was it that it created a huge fireball 250 yards in diameter. At least 100,000 people were killed either

The weapon that made full-scale war between the major powers unimaginable, a hydrogen bomb exploded in 1954 at a Pacific atoll (above) with energy equivalent to ten million tons of TNT. Atomic blasts that ended World War II held a fraction of that power. Formulas for destruction could also supply energy for peace, although fears of radiation have darkened early dreams of a nuclear age. Attempts at harnessing nuclear fusion as a cheap, safe source of power light up a Particle Beam Fusion Accelerator (right) at Sandia National Laboratory in New Mexico with pulses of electricity aimed at producing a beam of ions.

1967 Thurgood Marshall is sworn in as the first black U.S. Supreme Court Justice.

1977 American entertainer Elvis Presley dies at Graceland, his home in Memphis, Tennessee.

1979 Hurricanes David and Frederick hit southern Florida and Mobile, Alabama, causing damages in the amount of 45 million dollars.

1983 Persistent ethnic and religious riots in Assam, India, result in 5,000 deaths and 300,000 refugees.

1990 Apartheid is abolished in South Africa.

outright by the blast or by the firestorm that followed it. Another bomb was dropped three days later, ending the war.

Other nuclear weapons that were developed after the war proved to be many times more powerful than the first atomic bombs. Countries currently acknowledged to hold nuclear weapons include the U.S., Russia, Britain, France, China, India, and Israel. The potential for other nations to obtain them is fearfully great.

Scientists have also turned to potentially peaceful uses of the atom. Nuclear energy for creating electrical power was believed to be the unlimited energy source of the future. A number of countries built nuclear power plants, including the United States, France, and the Soviet Union.

In April 1986 the partial meltdown of such a nuclear power plant at Chernobyl, in Ukraine, scattered radioactive material over several European countries and raised radioactivity levels even as far away as in California. This incident and the death and illness left in its wake helped raise to consciousness many questions about nuclear power and curbed construction of new plants. ■

ALBERT EINSTEIN

Before he was 40 years of age, Albert Einstein (above) was the most famous scientist in the world. He was born in Germany but renounced his German nationality at the age of 15 and became a Swiss citizen. His theories of relativity, announced at the age of 26, showed that the only absolute, unchangeable thing in nature is the speed of light, and everything else is relative to light's motion. A consequence of the theories, that matter and energy are forms of the same thing and can be converted into each other, laid the basis for the development of the atomic bomb. Moving to the United States in 1933, Einstein became a member of the Institute for Advanced Study at Princeton until his death in 1955.

1918 Worldwide influenza epidemic strikes; nearly 20 million are dead by 1920.

1925 First woman governor is elected in U.S.— Nellie Tayloe Ross of Wyoming.

1928-1930 Richard E. Byrd's expedition to the Antarctic.

1929 U.S. stock market collapses, touching off the Great Depression.

1934 First quintuplets to survive beyond infancy, the Dionne sisters, are born in Canada.

Warfare Becomes Highly Mobile

Earlier centuries had shown that mobility had always been important in warfare. For example, the Japanese had been cowed into treaties with the Americans upon seeing their steam-driven warships. The Russians had lost the Crimean War partly because they lacked the railroads to move men and equipment to the front.

In World War I, trucks with internal combustion engines augmented railroads in transporting troops and matériel, and diesel-powered ships carried equipment swiftly over the seas. Countermeasures against these forms of transportation became important. For example, Arab attacks that cut the Hijaz railroad in Arabia contributed to the defeat of the Ottoman Turks. Germany's use of submarines against supply ships nearly strangled the British war effort.

Perhaps nothing changed war so much as the airplane. At first, in World War I, airplanes were used for observation of the enemy's position and movements. Later, bombs were dropped from them onto the enemy. Whoever dominated the skies had an advantage in bombing, so planes began challenging each other. Outfitting them with machine guns initiated aerial combat or "dogfights."

Between the World Wars the vehicles of combat became much more sophisticated. Lumbering fortress tanks moving at barely a walking pace in World War I became the panzers of Hitler's armored divisions, traveling at speeds of 25 to 30 mph. Airplanes became faster and more specialized: sleek fighters streaking through the skies at 350 mph or heavy bombers carrying tons of explosives speedily to their targets.

During World War II, the weapon in the Battle of Midway that decisively tipped naval power in favor of the Americans was the dive-bomber, which could descend swiftly on rapidly maneuvering Japanese ships. Helicopters made their first appearance in World War II but played their first prominent role in ferrying some 23,000 wounded United Nations soldiers from the front lines to field hospitals during the Korean War. Their value in combat was seen in Vietnam, where they set down U.S. troops anywhere they could land vertically.

In today's armies, the weapons of World War II seem like dinosaurs. Among the technologically advanced nations, unmanned guided missiles deliver high explosives from airplanes, ships, and landcraft. Jet planes flying faster than the speed of sound deliver missiles at targets the pilots may never see. Land-based weapons now have on-board computers, laser range-finders, and night-vision apparatus to help seek and destroy enemies. Helicopters bristle with missiles, rockets, and rapid-fire machine guns.

Space may be the next battleground. Satellites in orbit around the earth suggest that defensive weapons could be placed there to destroy enemy missiles. In fact, hundreds of military satellites are in position for observation, high above the planet. ■

Air power proved its worth in World War II when bombers such as the B-17 *(left)* pounded Germany, seriously crippling Hitler's war machine. To give tomorrow's soldiers an edge, U.S. troops test helmet-mounted video cameras and electronic weapon sights *(opposite)* that offer a clearer picture of combat.

New Materials

A flood of shoppers awaits the premier of nylon stockings in New York City on May 15, 1940. Four million pairs were sold within hours at several locations. Shortages in World War II created the demand for this first man-made fiber.

World War II helped spur the development of man-made materials when international hostilities caused shortages of rubber and silk. Shut off from the rubber plantations of the Far East, scientists made synthetic rubber from minerals. Nylon, a replacement for silk, was fashioned from coal, air, and water. By watching silkworms digest the cellulose in leaves, a French scientist was inspired to grind up old cotton and spruce pulpwood to produce his own cellulose and create silk-like rayon. Many types of plastics became available for use in household goods, electrical equipment, and food packaging. Containing elements of coal and cellulose but mostly petroleum, they rapidly became popular because the heated polymers could be fashioned into objects of any shape—objects that were light, inexpensive, and resistant to corrosion. Now a day cannot pass without our touching plastic in our telephones, computer keys, combs, automobiles, disposable cups, ad infinitum.

Scientists continue to turn out amazing new materials: ceramics in automobile engines that do not melt or break under intense heat, fabrics that stop bullets, glass so clear that you could look through a piece a hundred miles thick without knowing it was there. Tiles of glass ceramic, made of 7 percent solids and 93 percent air, protect the space shuttle from burning up when re-entering the

1983 President Ronald Reagan signs U.S. legislation making Martin Luther King, Jr.'s birthday a national holiday.

1988 Pan American 747 explodes from terrorist bomb and crashes in Lockerbie, Scotland, killing all 259 aboard and 11 on the ground.

1990 Boris Yeltsin resigns from the Soviet Communist Party.

1994 Nelson Mandela is named President of South Africa.

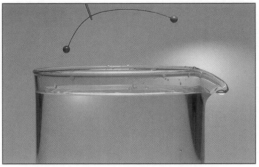

atmosphere. An experimental car with several ceramic engine parts runs so cool it needs no radiator.

An important search now is underway for the perfect superconductor. Superconductivity is the flow of electricity without resistance. Since much electricity is lost in normal conductors such as copper wire, superconductors

could allow superefficient electric motors to perform numerous tasks, calling on electricity that can be stored at will. Trains floating above guided surfaces on supermagnets could zip us to destinations at 300 mph. The possibilities could launch a technological revolution similar to that generated by the computer. ■

Improving materials known for centuries opens doors to new products. Twisted into a spiral, smart wire called Nitinol can be heated *(top, left)*, uncurled and dipped in ice water *(top, center)*, and—when reheated *(top, right)*—return to its spiral shape, a process useful in making springs. A bare hand can hold a glass ceramic cube fresh from the oven *(above)*, displaying a heat resistance vital to engines and spacecraft. Science steals silk from a spider *(right)* to study that polymer's elastic strength and try to synthesize it.

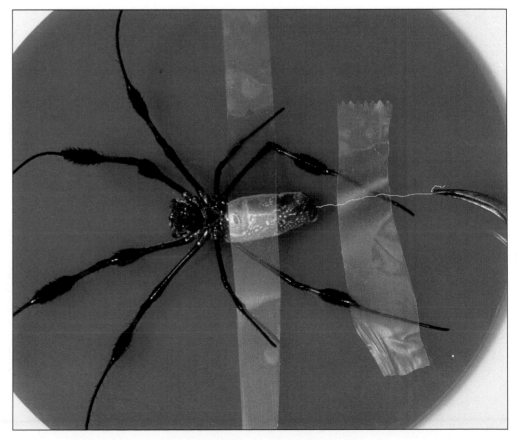

1946 First meeting of UN General Assembly opens in London.

1947 Romanian King Michael abdicates.

1947 The Diary of Anne Frank is published.

1948 Afrikaners sweep into power in South Africa's parliament.

1949 The U.S. completes its withdrawal of forces from South Korea.

Computers and the Information Age

Since the end of World War II the world has been experiencing a technological revolution at the heart of which has been the computer. Capable of storing enormous amounts of data and retrieving it in seconds, computers carry out calculations and process information at amazing speed. The first computer, introduced in 1946, weighed 30 tons and performed 5,000 calculations a second. Today, computers capable of making a million calculations a second can be carried like a small briefcase by one person.

This phenomenal downsizing became possible through the development of the "chip," a wafer of silicon the size of a baby's fingernail and crisscrossed with tiny electronic circuitry. The silicon, most common element on earth after oxygen, is mined from quartz rocks but can be found in common beach sand. Melted down and formed into long, sausage-like crystals, it is sliced into wafers on which individual chips are made, hundreds at a time, before they are separated from the wafer. On each chip, layer upon layer of superthin silicon is laid down and stenciled to leave pathways for metallic circuitry, each layer linked by connecting "windows." The smaller the chip, the less time it takes for the electronic signal to dash from switch to

switch. A microprocessor chip may hold 450,000 of these tiny switches, or transistors, and more than 20 yards of tungsten "wire," deposited in the wafer's pathways in a vapor so no soldered connections exist that might break. So extensive is the circuitry on the tiny chip that an equivalent feat would be mapping every street and freeway of Los Angeles on the head of a pin.

These tiny "brains" allow the computers they operate to be small as well. Specialized computers can be penny-size and planted behind the ear to aid the hearing-impaired. For

Computers shrink as technology advances. The Whirlwind, an electronic, digital machine built at the Massachusetts Institute of Technology in the mid-1940s (below) filled an entire room. Making thousands of calculations per second, it proved useful in air traffic control and used perhaps the earliest versions of video display terminals. Today the integrated circuitry of a megabyte chip (opposite) handles millions of calculations per second and can easily be held in one hand.

people who have lost limbs in accidents, minuscule computers can move electronic arms and legs.

Not surprisingly, computers also allow robots to perform humanlike functions. Robots are now common in industry, used for painting, welding, and assembling new products from automobiles to airplanes, never tiring, never making mistakes. These amazing machines have entered warfare as well, aiming guns, guiding missiles, navigating ships and planes.

They are capable of nurturing human intelligence as well as destroying it. Computers in classrooms give children ready access to selective information with the touch of a few keys. Among the millions with personal computers now in their homes, electronic mail speeds messages across the country instantaneously, giving rise to the computer hacker's term for regular letters sent through the postal service: "snail mail."

Computers now help run automobiles, regulating fuel flow and, on certain models, applying just the right amount of brake pressure no matter how hard the brake pedal is pressed. In much the same way, predict scientists, tiny computers implanted in brains may someday correct mental disorders caused by nerve damage or augment our intelligence. ∎

1956 Soviet troops and tanks crush anticommunist rebellion in Hungary.

1958-1969 Gen. Charles De Gaulle serves as French president.

1972 U.S. government passes the Clean Water Act.

1990 Panamanian General Noriega surrenders to U.S. troops and is arrested on drug-trafficking charges.

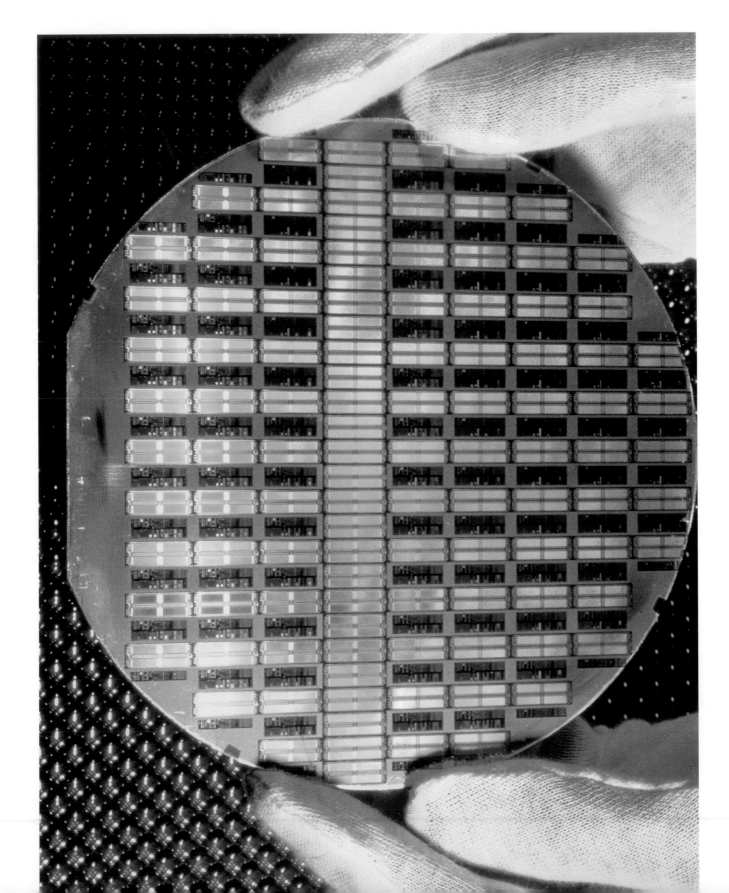

● **National Socialist (Nazi)**
1919 Party is founded
in Germany.

● **Michael Collins forms**
the I.R.A. (Irish
1919 Republican Army).

● **Versailles Treaty signed**
1919 by Allies and Germany.

● **League of Nations**
headquarters estab-
1920 lished in Geneva.

● **Television invented**
1926 by J. L. Baird.

● **British recognize**
complete independence
1927 of what will become
Saudi Arabia.

India Gains Its Independence

ndia, which had gone from more than 250 years of dominance by the Moguls to dominance by the British in the early 19th century, grew tired of outside interference. During World War I the subcontinent loyally assisted Britain in the war against the Germans, but before war's end, rising prices and heavy taxation had stirred unrest.

In response to agitation for self-rule, Britain passed the Rowlatt Acts in 1919, allowing trial by British judges without juries and the imprisonment of agitators without trial.

This action stirred more resentment and brought into the picture an Indian lawyer named Mohandas Gandhi. A believer in passive resistance, Gandhi proposed a day of work stoppage and fasting to protest the Rowlatt Acts, but the Indian people did not fully understand Gandhi's pacifist stance.

At Amritsar in the Punjab rioting took place; five Englishmen were killed, and an Englishwoman was beaten. An English officer there, Gen. Reginald Dyer, decided on forceful retaliation and ordered his Gurkha troops to fire on an unarmed group of protesters trapped in a square with few exits. The fusillade killed 379 Indians, and a horrified Gandhi called off the civil disobedience.

Over the years Gandhi continued his campaign for self-rule through nonviolent action. In 1920 he instigated a noncooperation movement, which involved boycotting foreign goods, schools, law courts, and overseas military service. In 1921, with full authority from the Indian National Congress, he introduced a new campaign for civil disobedience.

Despite his insistence on peaceful protest, in early 1922 Indian insurgents attacked a police station and set it on fire, resulting in 22 policemen burning to death. Held responsible, Gandhi was imprisoned by the British for two years. For the next quarter century he continued to lead

MOHANDAS GANDHI

Born of middle-class parents, **Mohandas Gandhi, at right** *(above),* speaking while in prison with Jawaharlal Nehru, was educated in London and practiced law in South Africa, where he was a leader against racial discrimination. The Indian people called him Mahatma, or "great soul," and his doctrine of nonviolent protest was known as *satyagraha,* or "firmness in truth." He championed the rights of the poor, encouraging villagers to spin their own cloth. Fervently believing in simplicity, Gandhi had few possessions and was against industrialization. Now he is regarded as the father of his country.

India in its quest for independence and was arrested numerous times by the British for his activities.

One of Gandhi's most dramatic acts was leading hundreds of followers on a 200-mile march to the sea, where they made salt out of seawater as a protest against the British Salt

| 1927 | Charles Lindbergh makes first solo crossing of the Atlantic by airplane. | 1929 | St. Valentine's Day gangland massacre occurs in Chicago. | | Radar invented. | | | 1948-49 | Western Allies provide supplies during the Berlin airlift. |

| | 1928 | Italy signs 20-year treaty of friendship with Ethiopia. | 1931 | C. D. Anderson discovers positive electrons. | 1936 | 1938 | Hitler annexes Austria on the premise that all Germans should be united. |

Strings of lights outline Rashtrapati Bhawan, India's White House, as the nation celebrates Republic Day on January 26.

Act that made it illegal to possess salt not bought from the government.

Complicating the move toward independence were differences between Hindus and the minority Muslims in India. In July 1947 the Indian Independence Bill was introduced into the British Parliament, calling for two independent states, a Hindu India and a Muslim Pakistan.

The bill went into effect the following month, and Jawaharlal Nehru, a wealthy intellectual who had been active in independence movements, became prime minister of India.

India admitted Kashmir, a Muslim area, into the Indian Union, setting off an armed conflict with Muslim Pakistan that would continue off and on for years.

Gandhi was assassinated in 1948 by a fanatical Hindu who resented his attempts to bring peace between Hindus and Muslims. ■

1940 — The first successful helicopter flight is made in the U.S.

1946 — First computer is introduced, weighing 30 tons and capable of performing 5,000 calculations per second.

1948 — The transistor is invented.

1948 — Long-playing records are first made.

1949 — Cambodia becomes independent.

1950 — Korean War begins.

The Iron Curtain Divides Europe

The Soviets suffered terribly in World War II, with some 20 million casualties. For a while they bore the brunt of combat against Hitler's German forces on the eastern front, while receiving massive amounts of aid from the U.S. and Britain.

German forces drove into the interior of the Soviet Union, fighting both a stubborn Soviet Army and the Russian winter. A strategic moment

came at the siege of Stalingrad, where the Soviets captured or destroyed 300,000 men; the remaining German forces went into retreat. This pivotal point in the European war put Hitler on the defensive.

In the closing months of the war Soviet troops captured much of Eastern Europe from Nazi Germany while the Allies were attacking from the west. When Germany's defeat became imminent, Soviet guns pounded the German capital of Berlin as Soviet tanks entered the outskirts. Elsewhere in Germany, U.S. and Soviet troops shook hands when they met at the Elbe River.

Near the war's end, American, British, and Russian leaders met to determine occupation of the defeated nation. The meetings were held at Potsdam, west of Berlin, and at Yalta, in the Crimea.

Soviet leader Joseph Stalin convinced western leaders that he needed a broad buffer in Eastern Europe to guarantee no further invasions from the West. U.S. President Franklin Roosevelt and British Prime Minister Winston Churchill agreed to allow the Soviet occupation but only if nations involved, such as Bulgaria, Poland, Hungary, and Romania, were allowed political freedom. Stalin did not accept those terms.

Stalin solidified his hold on Eastern Europe. In 1940 he annexed the small Baltic countries of Estonia, Latvia, and Lithuania. By the post-war period in countries such as Poland, Romania, and Bulgaria, Soviet troops backed governments dominated by communists. Although Germany itself was divided four ways among the wartime allies, the Soviets occupied much of the eastern half.

Berlin, the Nazi capital, lay in the Soviet sector of Germany but was divided between the Soviet Union and the Western Allies. Disagreement over the treatment of defeated Germany became an issue among the major powers. The badly dam-

1951 — Electricity first produced from atomic power, in U.S.

1952 — Beginning of Kenya's Mau Mau rebellion.

1952 — The contraceptive pill is invented.

1958 — The state of Singapore is created.

1959 — Dalai Lama flees to India.

1961 — Russian astronaut Yuri Gagarin becomes first man to travel in space around the earth.

The Berlin airlift by Western Allies *(above)* supplied the noncommunist portion of the isolated and divided city after the Soviet Union shut off ground access in 1948. Concerned by mass migrations to the West, the communists erected a concrete wall at the border in 1961. It included a "death strip" *(opposite)* that held vehicle traps, land mines, electric fences, and floodlights. Ever vigilant against border crossings, patrols walked the perimeter and guards like this one *(far left)* peered over the wall.

aged Soviet Union wanted Germany to pay it ten billion dollars in war reparations, while the West wanted to help Germany recover economically. Differences between communist and noncommunist systems grew.

In mid-1948 the Soviets began interfering with traffic to supply the isolated West Berlin. The Allies responded with the Berlin airlift, flying supplies to the city for a year before the blockade ended. In 1949 two separate German states—East and West—were established.

In 1961, in response to East Germans crossing the border to the West, the Soviet-dominated East German government closed the border, building a cement wall between the two sectors. The Berlin Wall became a symbol of the "iron curtain" from the Baltic Sea to the Mediterranean, dividing the communist from the noncommunist world. ∎

1947 India is granted independence; Jawaharlal Nehru becomes Prime Minister.

1949 The U.S.S.R. tests its first atomic bomb.

1950 U.S. President Truman is advised by Sen. Joseph McCarthy that the State Department is riddled with communists and communist sympathizers, beginning a time of personal attacks, now called McCarthyism.

1952 China's Chou En-lai visits Moscow.

1954 To give warning of approaching aircraft or missiles over the Arctic, the U.S. and Canada agree to build radar stations across northern Canada.

Long Conflict Between Arabs and Israelis

Both Arabs and Jews laid claim to the area known as Palestine on the extreme eastern shore of the Mediterranean Sea. To the Jews, who had no nation of their own, it was the traditional homeland dating to biblical times when the kingdoms of Israel and Judaea were located there.

Several ancient powers occupied Palestine—Egyptian, Persian, Roman—before it was taken over by the Muslims in A.D. 634 and mostly held by them until the early 1900s. Under the Ottoman Empire it was occupied mostly by Arabs. Palestine was also known as the Holy Land because of its religious importance to Arabs, Jews, and Christians.

During World War I Britain, seeking help from both Arabs and Jews against the Ottoman Turks, made promises to both about ownership of Palestine after the conflict. The Arabs had received assurances of eventual independence, which they assumed included all of Palestine. The Jews noted the Balfour Declaration adopted by the British government, which called for "...the establishment in Palestine of a national home for the Jewish people...."

When the war ended, Britain

Both Jew and Arab revere Hebron's Tomb of the Patriarchs, reportedly the burial site of Abraham **(above).** Founder of Judaism, the patriarch also fathered a son Ishmael, from whom Arabs claim descent. Ancestral ties have not prevented bitter conflict between Arab and Jew since creation of the state of Israel in 1948. In the Six-Day War of 1967 an Israeli soldier waves his nation's colors **(opposite)** at the head of a column speeding across the Negev desert.

UN PLAN & 1948-49 WAR

UN Partition Plan of Palestine, 1947
☐ Arab area
▨ Jewish area
— Boundary of State of Israel 1949-1967

LEBANON
SYRIA
Medit. Sea
Haifa
Nazareth
Jordan
Tel Aviv
WEST BANK
Amman
INTERNATIONAL ZONE
Jerusalem
Bethlehem
Gaza
Hebron
Dead Sea
GAZA STRIP
Under Egyptian administration until 1967
ISRAEL
JORDAN
Jordan annexed West Bank in 1950
EGYPT
0   20 mi
0   30 km
Gulf of Aqaba
SAUDI ARABIA

SIX-DAY WAR, 1967 & YOM KIPPUR WAR, 1973

☐ Territory occupied by Israel 1967
▨ Syrian territory held by Israel at cease fire, Oct. '73

LEBANON
GOLAN HEIGHTS (annexed by Israel in 1981)
SYRIA
Medit. Sea
Haifa
Nazareth
Jordan
Tel Aviv-Yafo
WEST BANK
Amman
Jerusalem
Bethlehem
Gaza
Hebron
Dead Sea
GAZA STRIP
ISRAEL
JORDAN
EGYPT (U.A.R.)
Sinai occupied by Israel 1967-1982
0   20 mi
0   30 km
Gulf of Aqaba
SAUDI ARABIA

PRESENT-DAY ISRAEL

▨ Israeli-occupied with current status subject to the Israeli-Palestinian Oslo Interim Agreement *
▨ Israeli Security Zone

LEBANON
SYRIA
GOLAN HEIGHTS
Medit. Sea
Haifa
Nazareth
Jordan
Tel Aviv-Yafo
WEST BANK
Amman
Jerusalem
Bethlehem
Gaza
Hebron
Dead Sea
GAZA STRIP
ISRAEL
JORDAN
*Extent of Israeli withdrawal and permanent status to be determined through further negotiation.
EGYPT
0   20 mi
0   30 km
Gulf of Aqaba
SAUDI ARABIA

1958 First successful U.S. space satellite is launched.

1959 U.S.S.R. launches rocket with two monkeys on board.

1961 Indian forces overrun the Portuguese enclave of Goa.

1962 In Africa, Uganda and Tanganyika become independent.

1963 DNA, each individual's biological code, is discovered.

continued to control the area, but Jews—encouraged by the Balfour Declaration and fearful of growing anti-Semitism in Germany—immigrated until one-third of the population was Jewish. Tensions mounted during the 1930s as Arabs, alarmed at the growing numbers of Jews, attacked their settlements, and Jews fought back against the attacks.

After World War II, when millions of Jews had been killed in the Holocaust in Europe, pressure mounted for a Jewish state. In 1947 the United Nations agreed to the founding of independent Jewish and Arab

states in Palestine. And on May 14, 1948, the Jewish state of Israel was established. Outraged at having a non-Arab nation set up in what they considered Arab land and sanctioned by foreign powers, nearby Arab states attacked the new nation the next day.

Israel defeated them and increased its territory by one-quarter. More than 600,000 Palestinian Arabs lost their homes and fled to refugee camps in Lebanon, Jordan, Gaza, and Syria. Some later formed the Palestinian Liberation Organization (PLO), dedicated to achieving

a homeland, by violence if necessary.

A state of war existed between Israel and Arabs for decades to come, boiling into open conflict several times. In 1956 when Egypt's President Gamel Abdel Nasser took over the Suez Canal, Israel felt threatened and invaded the Sinai Peninsula, aided by France and Britain. Both the United States and the Soviet Union, Cold War adversaries, called for a ceasefire. In 1967 after a military buildup by Egypt, Israel achieved a lightning victory over Egypt and its Arab allies in what was known as the Six-Day War. Israel

1964 Civil rights leader
Martin Luther King, Jr.,
wins the Nobel Prize
for peace.

1969 Two Mariner space
probes send back
pictures of the surface
of Mars.

1972 U.S. President Richard
Nixon makes historic
visit to China.

1975 John N. Mitchell,
H. R. Haldeman, John
D. Ehrlichman, and
Robert C. Mardian
are found guilty
of Watergate cover-up.

1979 Nuclear disaster is
narrowly avoided at
Three Mile Island,
Pennsylvania, where
a reactor building
becomes badly
contaminated.

now occupied even more Arab territories—the West Bank of the Jordan
River, the Sinai desert, and Gaza—
inhabited by more than a million
Palestinians. Between incidents of
open warfare, the PLO performed
acts of terrorism against Israel, attacking school buses and detonating
bombs in cities. Israelis responded by

attacking and bombing suspected
terrorist bases, causing civilian casualties as well. Each side accused the
other of committing atrocities.

In 1973 Arabs and Israelis went
to war for the fourth time, the Arabs
attacking on the Jewish holy day of
Yom Kippur to regain territories they
had lost in 1967. The war had inter-

It's business as usual on
the streets of Nazareth
as politicians debate
the future of Arab and
Israeli on a store-
window TV *(below)*.
On-screen, peace
accords absorb
Egyptian president
Hosni Mubarak, sec-
ond from left; Israeli
Foreign Minister
Shimon Peres, gestur-
ing; and Palestinian
leader Yasser Arafat,

with head covering.
Many Arabs, feeling
unrepresented by any
of the states in the con-
flict, flaunt their radical
bent toward violence. A
mural of masked terror-
ists provides the back-
drop for a band about
to play for a party in
Gaza *(opposite)*.

1980 UN calls for Soviet troop withdrawal from Afghanistan.

1986 Partial meltdown at Soviet nuclear power plant at Chernobyl, in Ukraine.

1987 Terry Waite, envoy for Britain's Archbishop of Canterbury, while seeking the release of Western hostages, is kidnapped in Lebanon.

1989 Hungary proclaims a new constitution to create a multiparty democracy.

1992 North American trade compact announced.

national repercussions as oil-producing Arab countries shut off the flow of petroleum to Western countries in an embargo that protested their support of Israel. The price of oil quadrupled worldwide, and when the embargo ended, the prices did not go down.

The cycle of Arab-Israeli conflict seemed irreconcilable until Egypt's President Anwar Sadat accepted an invitation to visit Israel and address the Israeli legislature, the Knesset, in 1977. Although his gesture displeased other Arab states, Sadat then met with Israeli Prime Minister

TERRORISM AT THE OLYMPIC GAMES

Terrorism in the conflict between Arabs and Jews extended beyond the Middle East in 1972 when PLO extremists took Jewish athletes hostage at the Olympic games in Munich. Two of the athletes were shot dead, and the terrorists threatened to kill others if 200 imprisoned Palestinians were not released. The Israelis refused, and the PLO negotiated a flight by German helicopter with the hostages to a waiting aircraft. Eventually, in an abortive rescue attempt all nine hostages were killed along with four terrorists and one German policeman.

Menachem Begin and U.S. President Jimmy Carter at Camp David near Washington, D.C. The Camp David Agreement set the framework for peace between Egypt and Israel.

Muslim extremists assassinated Sadat in 1981, but progress toward peace continued. In September 1993 PLO chairman Yasser Arafat and Israeli Prime Minister Rabin—also assassinated, in 1996—signed a declaration agreeing in principle to allow Palestinian self-rule in Gaza and Jericho and to cooperate in economic matters. ■

351

The Apartness of South Africa

The Dutch population in South Africa, known as Afrikaners, swept into power in South Africa's Parliament in 1948. Their party platform called for continued apartheid, or apartness, between blacks and whites. Other English-speaking South Africans also played an important part in the development of apartheid. It became the official policy of the South African government.

The policy applied not only to blacks but also to people of mixed ancestry and those from other ethnic backgrounds. Nonwhites were denied civil rights and not regarded as citizens. Small separate homelands were later set up within South Africa where blacks could live and govern themselves.

To accommodate nonwhites working in large cities, separate townships were set up for them at the edges of those cities. At one point the government ordered 100,000 nonwhites to leave their homes in Johannesburg within a year, to make room for whites. Although the races mixed during the workday, they used separate facilities—restaurants, restrooms, and transportation systems. Marriage between them was forbidden.

As world opinion mounted against them, Afrikaners argued that they had a right to their policy. They had occupied the country some 300 years, they pointed out, and in the northward migration of their Great Trek more than a century earlier, they had encountered Zulus moving southward, with no better claim to the land

than they had. They were not denying blacks the right to a better life, they argued, only they must seek it in their own separate areas.

But the system was strongly protested by apartheid's opponents, who pointed to its assaults on human dignity. Whites were paid more than blacks for doing the same jobs, conditions in the townships were often appalling, and dissent against the system was forcibly silenced.

In response to Britain's pressuring

NELSON MANDELA

Nelson Mandela holds the record among modern leaders of nations for the longest time spent in prison. Given a life sentence in 1964 along with seven others for sabotage and subversion in the fight against apartheid, he served 27 years before being released in 1990. His walk to freedom was viewed on television by millions, and with his appeals for reconciliation he became a symbol of hope for South Africa's nonwhite population. Apartheid legislation was dismantled under Afrikaner president F.W. de Klerk, and in 1994 Mandela was elected the first black president. He and de Klerk shared the Nobel Prize in 1993.

South Africa for change, it withdrew from the British Commonwealth in 1961 and proclaimed itself a republic. International pressure increased. In 1963 the United Nations Security Council voted 9-0 to urge members to ban shipments of military equipment to South Africa unless it changed its racial policies. In 1964 the UN general assembly called for international sanctions against the country.

Amidst all the furor around apartheid, South Africa built up the richest, most powerful, and most orderly nation in all Africa, one with bountiful farms, busy factories, and a modern army. Its mineral resources include diamonds and gold.

But behind the scenes lay a tension that would not go away. Outspoken leaders against apartheid were restricted in their movements, imprisoned, or in some cases killed. In June 1976 riots that were fatal to some 500 people exploded in black townships. More riots and killings continued through the years, sometimes black against white, sometimes black against black in disagreements about how to hasten apartheid's end.

Slowly, the Afrikaner government began to moderate its language, and apartheid policies began to relax. In 1985 marriages between blacks and whites became legal.

In 1990 South Africa abolished apartheid. Four years later free elections were held with both blacks and whites voting, and South African lawyer Nelson Mandela was named president. ∎

● **1953** Tito is elected president of Yugoslavia.

● **1955** Dock and railroad strikes occur in Britain.

● **1956** Thousands of Polish youth demonstrate against Russian domination of Poland.

● **1957** Jordan's King Hussein succeeds in facing down an attempted army coup.

● **1958** First parking meters appear in London.

Despair lines faces of the Bakalobeng tribe, forced by South Africa's White Afrikaner government to move from their village of 100 years to an all-black "homeland."

1959 Alaska and Hawaii become the 49th and 50th states in the U.S.

1961 Noted author Ernest Hemingway commits suicide.

1962 Rachel Carson publishes *The Silent Spring,* which focuses attention on the effects of chemical pesticides on the environment.

1965 Malcolm X, Black Muslim leader, is shot and killed.

1968 Vietcong launch massive Tet Offensive against South Vietnam.

The Move Toward Freedom

The colonialism that had carved up Africa in the 19th century began giving way in the 20th as the newly created nations began demanding independence from European masters. The transition to self-government was sometimes peaceful, sometimes bloody, but virtually continent-wide.

At the end of World War II in 1945, only Egypt, Ethiopia, Liberia, and South Africa were sovereign states in Africa; by 1965 there were more than 30. A flood of independence swept the continent in a 12-year period from 1956 to 1968.

Demonstrations of nationalism began stirring in France's African colonies at the end of the 1940s, and they were put down brutally. Libya, controlled by Italy until Axis forces were driven out in World War II, began the independence movement by becoming a constitutional monarchy in 1951.

Next door, the transition went less smoothly. So many French lived in Algeria that France considered it not a colony but a part of the mother country. Moves toward independence were viewed by many French as treason. The war of rebellion there lasted nearly eight years and caused almost a million casualties, but Algeria became its own nation in 1962.

France, sensing the winds of change, offered its other African colonies independence with French

New attitudes blend with old in the traditional dress of a Herero woman *(right)* of Namibia, decorated with animals and the shape of the her nation.

354

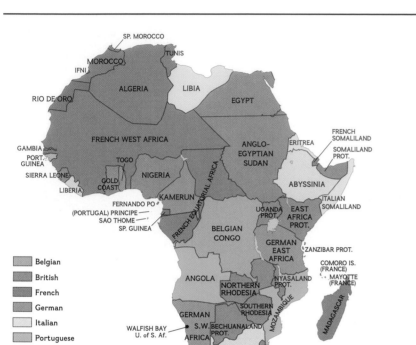

Belgian
British
French
German
Italian
Portuguese
Spanish
Independent

AFRICA
1914

Belgian
British
French
Italian
Portuguese
South African
Spanish
Independent

AFRICA
1939

Belgian
British
Independent member of the British Commonwealth
British Sphere of Influence
French
Portuguese
Spanish
United Nations Trust Territory
Independent

AFRICA
1947

AFRICA
1997

● Death of
Mao Zedong.
1976

● President Sadat of Egypt
visits Israel and
1977 addresses Knesset.

● World's first test-tube
baby is born in England.
1978

● Soviet invasion of
Afghanistan causes
1979 world outcry.

● U.S. hostages are freed
in Iran after 444 days
1981 in captivity.

Playing catch-up in technology, Africans learned skills useful for nationhood at mid-century. In Zimbabwe an instructor teaches welding to an eager learner *(above)*.

Kenyan students mixing chemicals *(right)* attend the Science Teachers College tuition-free, knowing that they, in return, will teach where assigned.

assistance, to prevent them from seeking Soviet help in the post-war competition between communist and non-communist nations.

The offer created the new nations of the Malagasy Republic, Mauritania, the Ivory Coast, Togo, Dahomey, Niger, Upper Volta, and Mali in what had been French West Africa. French Equatorial Africa became Chad, Gabon, the Central African Republic, the Congo Republic, and Cameroon. Last to make the change was French Somaliland on the opposite coast, which became Djibouti in 1977.

Rhodesia (later Zimbabwe) pulled away from South Africa in 1960 while it was still under British control. White settlers remained in charge; but after years of bloody conflict with black nationalists, open elections

were held and black Africans began self-government.

Years of struggle between black residents and the South African government in what had been Southwest Africa resulted in an independent Namibia in 1990.

Some colonial powers attempted to prepare the new nations for self-government. Britain, convinced of Kenya's desire for independence by the persistence of a guerrilla uprising, began preparing the colony for nationhood.

Hoping to avoid the violence of the French in Algeria, Belgium announced a gradual withdrawal from the Congo region over the course of a generation, but the enthusiasm for independence crowded the phase-out into 18 months. Civil war broke out in the aftermath.

THE MAU MAU TERRORIZE KENYA

Among the first African groups to use terrorism to drive out colonials was the secret society in Kenya known as the Mau Mau, which attacked European settlers from 1952-56. Britain declared a state of emergency and sent over a battalion of troops that eventually crushed the rebellion. Fewer than 100 Europeans died compared to 11,500 Africans, but the drive for self-government was still inevitable. When Jomo Kenyatta was released in 1961 after serving nine years as leader of the Mau Mau, he became the first president of the Republic of Kenya.

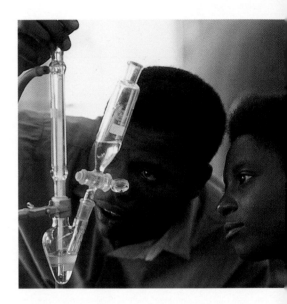

The Portuguese, on the other hand, fought independence movements in Angola and Mozambique until 1975. Finally, they withdrew, leaving virtually no trained African civil servants to run the countries they had vacated.

No matter how careful the preparation, many new countries—whose boundaries had been created arbitrarily by Europe powers—found themselves divided along ethnic lines.

After Nigeria gained independence, civil war broke out between Hausas and Ibos in what became known as the murderous Biafran War. The conflict ended, but a series of military leaders resisted democracy. Throughout Africa, military rule became the norm.

Factions in Angola battled for decades, backed by various foreign powers. The U.S.S.R. supported a Marxist-leaning government, and the U.S. supplied opposing rebels. By the mid-1990s the factions agreed to share responsibility in government. ∎

1982 ● Spain joins NATO.

1983 ● Philippines opposition leader Benigno Aquino is assassinated.

1985 ● Mikhail Gorbachev is elected leader of Soviet Communist Party.

1987 ● Portugal and China agree on the return to China in 1999 of Macao, a Portuguese colony since the 16th century.

1989 ● Mass demonstrations for democracy in Tiananmen Square, Beijing, end in the massacre of participants.

Drought Sweeps Across Africa

Since independence much of Africa has faced precipitous economic decline. One of the major causes has been the Sahel drought.

The continent had long been in a gradual drying process. Signs of ancient civilizations and remains of plants and animals from earlier epochs found in the Sahara indicate periods of much more extensive rainfall than has been experienced in recent times.

But the extreme drought of the 1980s that struck the Sahel, the dividing line between absolute desert and the lush growth of the tropics, was devastating to many young nations.

While much of the drought may be attributable to climate change, it was probably hastened by population pressures on the environment. The Sahel is a semiarid strip of land 200 to 700 miles wide, with poor soil and scant rainfall, perhaps 4 to 24 inches a year. In historical times it had been capable of supporting only a limited number of wandering pastoralists who followed the rains to graze their livestock. A few crops were planted, but fields were often left fallow to allow the soil to recover.

With independence in the 1950s and 1960s, use of the Sahel changed. New African nations constricted the movement of pastoral nomads, which resulted in the overgrazing of areas that had once been used periodically. New commercial crops were introduced so that more land was tilled. Improved medical care contributed to higher population density, which led to denuding the land of trees for fuel and using more land for grazing livestock. The stripping away of vegetation hastened desertification, as topsoil blew away and bare soil fed the dryness.

With the countryside increasingly dry and bare, pastoralists moved to the cities, which resulted in problems of overcrowding and unemployment. ■

Bone-dry land and dust-filled air blend in monochromatic sameness as a girl walks to her home near Timbuktu, Mali, during the devastating drought in Africa's Sahel.

357

● Hitler commits suicide.

1945

● League of Nations
is dissolved.

1946

● More than one million
enroll in college under
America's GI Bill.

1947

● Cortisone is discovered
by Philip Hench.

1949

● Egypt takes control
of the Suez Canal.

1956

The Cold War

World War II ended, as the previous world conflict had, with widespread hopes for a long period of peace. The Allies had defeated the twin threats of Nazi Germany and imperial Japan.

The Soviet concept of a society run by workers bothered U.S. industrialists but seemed to be little threat in a nation bent on buying automobiles and television sets. More disturbing was the boldness with which Soviet leader Joseph Stalin was gaining firm control over huge areas of Eastern Europe—areas the West had hoped

Despite appearances of congeniality *(above)*, Soviet Premier Nikita Khrushchev and U.S. President John Kennedy clashed in Vienna in 1961 over Berlin.

Differences nearly boiled into war in 1962 when Khrushchev placed missiles in Cuba. Today an old Soviet rocket stands there *(below)*.

Stalin would occupy only for a short time and then gradually release to pursue their own directions. Stalin had no such plans. Instead, his brand of totalitarianism—exerting total control over almost every aspect of people's lives—became the leading challenge to democracy in the 20th century. With his economy devastated by the war and with wartime manpower losses of some 20 million, Stalin feared an eventual takeover by his former allies. His defense was an aggressive offense, stacking East European governments with

1965 Blacks riot for six days in Watts section of Los Angeles. The toll is 34 dead, more than 1,000 injured, nearly 4,000 arrested. Fire damage is put at 175 million dollars.

1972 Britain takes over direct rule of Northern Ireland in bid for peace.

1979 Iranian militants seize U.S. Embassy in Tehran and hold hostages.

1984 First female vice presidential candidate, Geraldine Ferraro, selected at Democratic National Convention in San Francisco.

1995 U.S. and North Korea break off talks.

communists allied with the Soviets and making plans to expand.

The U.S., in turn, perceived Soviet expansion as a threat, and the world settled into a period of competition called the Cold War. It was cold because no fighting took place between the two antagonists, although much fighting occurred between smaller states supported by the two superpowers.

It was a dangerous standoff, for by 1949 the Soviets had developed their own nuclear weapons. Nuclear arms became more and more powerful until their potential destruction dwarfed the atomic bombs the U.S. had dropped on Japanese cities.

For nearly half a century, a struggle took place over the worldwide balance of power. Neither side wanted the other to gain too much influence in the world. Both aided and armed small developing countries, trying to win them as allies.

For decades the two powers backed different sides in what the Soviets called "wars of liberation" and the U.S. called a "policy of containment." "Brush fire" wars were fought in Cambodia, Nicaragua, Afghanistan, Angola, and other countries. Meanwhile the two superpowers spent billions arming themselves against possible attack. For decades fear loomed that a small conflict might escalate into a Third World War. Only once did it come close.

In 1959 a young guerrilla fighter named Fidel Castro overthrew a dictatorship in Cuba and subsequent-

FIDEL CASTRO

Architect of the Cuban revolution was the 26-year-old Cuban lawyer, Fidel Castro (above), who began fighting in 1953 with a small force against the dictatorship of Fulgencio Batista. Captured in 1953, he was sentenced to 20 years in prison, but was released after 20 months and fled to Mexico. He returned with 81 men and gained the support of the Cuban people as a freedom fighter. Soon after his takeover, he denied that he was a communist, but his nationalization of American-owned sugar farms and industries irritated the U.S. In 1961 after an attempted invasion by U.S.-backed Cuban refugees, Castro declared himself a Marxist-Leninist. Despite a decades-long U.S. embargo against exports to Cuba, which has caused severe deprivations, Castro remains as the world's longest-standing head of government. Cuba still is a communist state without democracy and civil rights.

ly set up a Marxist government allied with the Soviet Union.

Nervous that communism might spread to other Latin American countries, the U.S. backed a group of non-communist Cubans in an invasion of the island, but it failed. Emboldened by the loss of U.S. prestige, the Soviet leader Nikita Khrushchev in 1962 began building sites in Cuba for missiles that would be capable of carrying nuclear warheads to the U.S. just 90 miles away. President John F. Kennedy declared a blockade on all military shipments to Cuba, demanding that the launch sites be removed.

Soviet ships loaded with more missiles were on their way to Cuba, and American ships were prepared to intercept them. The two leaders, it was said, stood "eyeball to eyeball," while the world waited nervously. Just before the ships met, Khrushchev agreed to dismantle the missile sites if America would promise to lift the blockade and refrain from further invasions of Cuba.

The averting of conflict caused a thaw in relations. Kennedy and Khrushchev set up a "hot line" between Washington and Moscow to allow instant communication with each other. In 1969 representatives of the U.S. and the U.S.S.R. met to discuss the possibility of disarmament. In 1987 they agreed to abolish medium-range nuclear missiles.

The collapse of many communist regimes in the late '80s precipitated the breakup of the U.S.S.R. in the '90s and ended the Cold War. ■

Scattered Conflicts and Wars

After the widespread conflicts of World Wars I and II, a number of smaller, localized wars plagued the world.

Korea, taken from Japan by the Allies, became a divided country after the U.S. and Soviets could not agree on the formation of a government. In June 1950 communist North Korea invaded the noncommunist south to reunify the country by force.

South Korea appealed to the United Nations for help, and UN forces, mostly American, arrived.

After landing behind North Korean lines, UN troops were near victory when Chinese troops reinforced North Korea, driving the UN back. The war ended in a stalemate virtually where it had started, at the 38th parallel.

At the end of World War II, Vietnamese nationalists who had battled the Japanese declared their country independent under their leader Ho Chi Minh, who espoused communist ideology. The French fought to keep their former colony, but they were defeated by the Vietnamese at the fortress of Dien Bien Phu in 1954.

As had been the case with Korea, international negotiators divided the country into communist and noncommunist sectors. A national vote was supposed to determine who would head a reunified government, but South Vietnam's President Ngo Dinh Diem refused to allow the referendum. When in 1961 communist guerrillas known as Vietcong appeared to be gaining against the

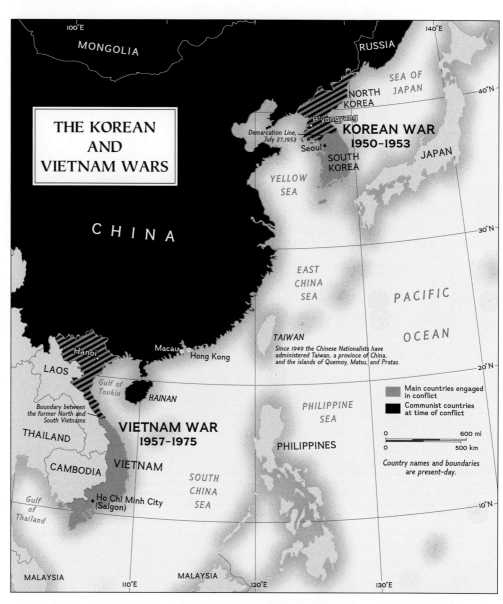

THE KOREAN AND VIETNAM WARS

KOREAN WAR 1950–1953

VIETNAM WAR 1957–1975

Demarcation Line, July 27, 1953

P'yongyang

Seoul

TAIWAN Since 1949 the Chinese Nationalists have administered Taiwan, a province of China, and the islands of Quemoy, Matsu, and Pratas.

Boundary between the former North and South Vietnams

Ho Chi Minh City (Saigon)

Main countries engaged in conflict
Communist countries at time of conflict

0   600 mi
0   500 km

Country names and boundaries are present-day.

South Vietnamese, the U.S. started helping the south to avoid what it saw as a communist takeover. During the decade, U.S. involvement escalated to the point of committing hundreds of thousands of soldiers.

Despite their huge resources and heavy weaponry, U.S. forces were unable to pin down and defeat the

Innocent in a war that tore their country and their lives apart in the early 1950s, Korean children wear helmets in the trenches with U.S. Marines *(opposite)*. The conflict ended in a truce after China sent troops to aid North Korea, causing United Nations forces to retreat below Seoul, South Korea's capital. The cease-fire line at the 38th parallel became the new border dividing the two parts of Korea.

1962 American actress Marilyn Monroe is found dead in her home of suicide.

1964 U.S. Civil Rights Act bans racial discrimination in federal funding and employment.

1969 First test flight of the Concorde.

1970 China puts its first satellite into space.

1971 American tennis player Billie Jean King is the first female athlete to earn $100,000 a year.

● Ceylon becomes a
1972 republic and changes
its name to Sri Lanka.

● Patricia Hearst, the 19-
1974 year-old daughter of
newspaper publisher
Randolph Hearst,
is kidnapped by
the Symbionese
Liberation Army.

● Calcutta's Mother
1979 Teresa is awarded
the Nobel Prize
for peace.

● World's first space
1981 shuttle, *Columbia,*
is launched in U.S.

● Sally Ride becomes the
1983 first U.S. female
astronaut in space.

In the 1980s British combat troops seeking information about terrorists in Belfast, Ireland, played an uneasy role as peacekeepers. Here, as one soldier cradled a baby, another kept watch around the corner for snipers. Lasting peace is yet to come.

elusive Vietnamese forces. Back home U.S. citizens held massive protests against U.S. involvement. In 1975, after 14 years of fighting, the U.S. pulled its forces out, and Vietnam was united as one communist nation.

In 1990 the U.S. and troops of the United Nations landed in Saudi Arabia after Iraq invaded Kuwait, threatening the West's oil supplies. The militaristic Iraqi leader Saddam Hussein had built up an impressive,

modern army, and UN forces spent months in buildup to assure they had an adequate force to oppose it.

When the UN struck with high-technology weaponry in late February of 1991, they drove the Iraqis out of Kuwait in less than a hundred hours, killing large numbers of Iraqi troops.

A local conflict of long standing has been the struggle between Irish Catholics and Protestants in Northern

Ireland. In answer to Irish calls for independence after World War I, the British kept six counties in the north-eastern part of Britain and granted independence to the remainder of the country. By the 1960s the Protestant majority controlled the Northern Irish

1984 — New Zealand is declared a nuclear-free zone.

1988 — Benazir Bhutto, first Islamic female prime minister, is chosen to lead Pakistan's government.

1990 — Nelson Mandela is freed from prison in South Africa.

1990 — Lech Walesa is elected president of Poland.

1995 — USFDA moves to regulate tobacco.

parliament. Meanwhile, the Catholic minority began a movement for civil rights. Some members of the minority wanted Northern Ireland to join the Catholic southern Republic of Ireland. Both Protestants and Catholics have committed acts of terrorism, such as bombings in Ireland and England. ■

In comradeship born of battle, a wounded Marine reaches out to a fallen friend in Vietnam *(below)*. The presence of U.S. troops in that Southeast Asian conflict proved unpopular with citizens at home, who remained unconvinced by arguments that communism had to be contained. Protests led to confrontations with soldiers. Arguing for peace, not war, a demonstrator *(left)* stuffs flowers into the guns of military police.

1956 ● Hungary is put under martial law by the Soviets.

1957 ● Eisenhower Doctrine calls for aid to Mideast countries that resist armed aggression from communist nations.

1965 ● India and Pakistan at war over Kashmir.

1969 ● The Stonewall Uprising marks the beginning of the Gay Rights Movement.

Social Problems in the U.S.

Despite the emancipation of slaves after the American Civil War, social segregation continued, which kept blacks from participating equally and fairly in the mainstream of national life. In the South, blacks attended separate schools, ate in separate restaurants, and rode in separate public buses or were asked to take seats in the back.

Seeking more opportunity, millions of blacks moved to northern and western cities during and after World War II. There, also, they found that social customs accorded more privilege to whites.

In the 1940s and '50s blacks began a movement toward civil rights, aided by whites and other groups, and achieved some progress.

In the decision *Brown v. Board of Education of Topeka,* the U.S. Supreme Court ruled that separate schools for blacks and whites was illegal. President Dwight Eisenhower enforced the decision with U.S. marshals, who escorted black children to schools past crowds of jeering whites. The civil rights of blacks became the leading domestic issue in the U.S.

On December 5, 1955, a 43-year-old black woman named Rosa Parks sat down in a front seat of a bus in Montgomery, Alabama, and refused to give up her seat to a white man. She was arrested for that act, but the incident prompted a year-long boycott of city buses by other black women in Montgomery and brought to prominence civil rights leader Martin Luther King, Jr.

King continued peaceful protests against discrimination in housing, public facilities, and voting, and drew nationwide attention to injustices. In 1963 he called for a march on Washington, D.C., and on the steps of the Lincoln Memorial before

Racial disharmony in the U.S. flared into the open in the 1950s with the integration of schools. Whites taunted blacks who enrolled in Central High School in Little Rock, Arkansas *(below),* but troops sent by President Eisenhower enforced their right to attend.

Similar scenes erupted across the South and in northern cities with large black populations. Thirty years later 56 percent of the student body at Central High were black.

○ **1971** Idi Amin seizes power in Uganda.

1979 ○ U.S. President Jimmy Carter, Israeli Premier Menachem Begin, and Egyptian President Anwar Sadat settle on the Camp David peace agreement.

1981 ○ Attempt to assassinate Pope John Paul II in Rome is unsuccessful.

1982 ○ Israel invades southern Lebanon.

1984 ○ South African Bishop Desmond Tutu receives the Nobel Prize for his work against apartheid.

an audience of some 200,000, he delivered a stirring speech about his dream for America—an America where whites and blacks could live in equality and peace.

President John F. Kennedy urged the Congress to enact civil rights legislation, and after his assassination in 1963 his successor, Lyndon Johnson, persuaded Congress to pass the laws. The legal basis for ending the discrimination was established.

Women had also experienced discrimination in the workplace, being passed over for important positions in favor of men and receiving less pay than their male counterparts. Encouraged by the success of blacks,

they began voicing their dissatisfaction, campaigning for equal pay, equal job opportunities, and the right to have abortions.

By 1970, 47 percent of women were employed. But most held positions below those of men, and pay remained unequal. In the 1970s an attempt to pass an amendment to the U.S. Constitution guaranteeing equal rights for women failed to win ratification in a majority of states.

Other groups began to campaign for legal protection. In 1987 half a million gays and lesbians rallied in Washington, D.C., to protest discrimination against them that is based on their sexual orientation. ■

MARTIN LUTHER KING, JR.

Pictured on a fan held by two protesters (above), **Martin Luther King, Jr., was America's most famous civil rights leader and winner of the Nobel Peace Prize in 1964. Born in Atlanta, Georgia, King admired India's Mohandas Gandhi for his nonviolent protests against social injustice. King persuaded American blacks to demonstrate for their rights peacefully, even though in the South they were at times treated roughly by police. He participated personally in the protests and was jailed 16 times, winning the admiration of blacks and whites alike. In 1968 King's assassination in Memphis, Tennessee, touched off riots, some involving property destruction, across the U.S.**

1957 ● Studies implicate smoking in the development of cancer.

1960 ● U.S. property is seized in Cuba.

1962 ● France transfers sovereignty to new republic of Algeria.

1964 ● Northern Rhodesia becomes independent as Zambia.

1969 ● Woodstock music festival is held in U.S., attracting some 300,000 fans.

Satellites: Eyes on the World

On October 4, 1957, the Soviet Union used a rocket to hurl into space a 184-pound ball bristling with antennas. High above the earth the rocket arched in a trajectory that sent the beeping sphere around the planet, near enough to be tugged slightly by earth's gravity, but fast enough that its centrifugal force kept it from falling immediately back toward the ground. For the first time ever, a man-made object was in orbit around the earth.

Forty years later more than 15,000 satellites had been launched into space by several countries. Most either failed in their orbit attempt or gradually fell back into earth's atmosphere and burned from the intense friction. Hundreds remain, serving as communications antennas, spying on potential enemies, sending back overviews of our planet's condition, and turning outward to explore the far reaches of the universe.

Early communications satellites had certain limitations. They could relay and enhance messages to earth only when their orbits carried them directly above the recipients.

The solution to this limitation had been suggested by science fiction writer Arthur C. Clarke as early as 1945: If a satellite traveled 22,300 miles above the Equator and completed an orbit every 24 hours, it would stay in the same place relative to a point on the earth. Geostationary orbits, as they are called, allow satellites to be in position for round-the-clock transmission of electronic signals to earth. These might be the signals for telephone calls, for overview images of earth's surface, and for television programming, to name a few applications.

The progression of satellite service has been steady over the decades. In 1960 Tiros I took 22,952 images of earth's weather and transmitted them to ground-based meteorologists for interpretation. In 1962 Telstar was the first communications satellite to transmit TV programs overseas. In 1971 Intelsat IV began relaying phone calls and television programs

for nations that were members of the International Telecommunications Satellite Organization, or Intelsat—a remarkable example of international cooperation.

In 1974 Applications Technology Satellite brought TV to isolated communities. In 1976 geologists began plotting the movement of tectonic plates by bouncing laser beams off a satellite. In 1982 Landsat began sending back to earth images of the planet's surface to aid agriculture, geology, bathymetry, and land use.

Satellites can either be sent up on their own or be carried aloft in manned vehicles such as a space shuttle and then released. Some have also been retrieved and repaired in a shuttle by human technicians capable of leaving their spacecraft while traveling at thousands of miles an hour in the weightlessness of space.

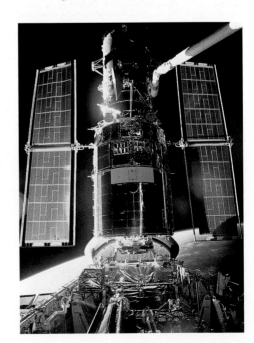

Mock-up of a Telstar communications satellite undergoes final testing *(left)* in the early 1960s before the real thing rocketed into space. Toothy plastic walls absorb all but direct signals to the Telstar antenna. Numerous orbiters now relay telephone and television signals instantaneously around the globe. Preparing for clear visions into outer space, the Hubble telescope docks with the U.S. space shuttle *Endeavor (right)* for repairs to blurry lenses.

● **1974** Revolution in Ethiopia leads to downfall of Emperor Haile Selassie.

● **1979** Sandinistas seize power in Nicaragua.

● **1981** Egyptian President Anwar Sadat is assassinated.

● **1983** U.S. and Caribbean allied troops invade Grenada.

● **1984** Indian Prime Minister Indira Gandhi is assassinated by Sikhs.

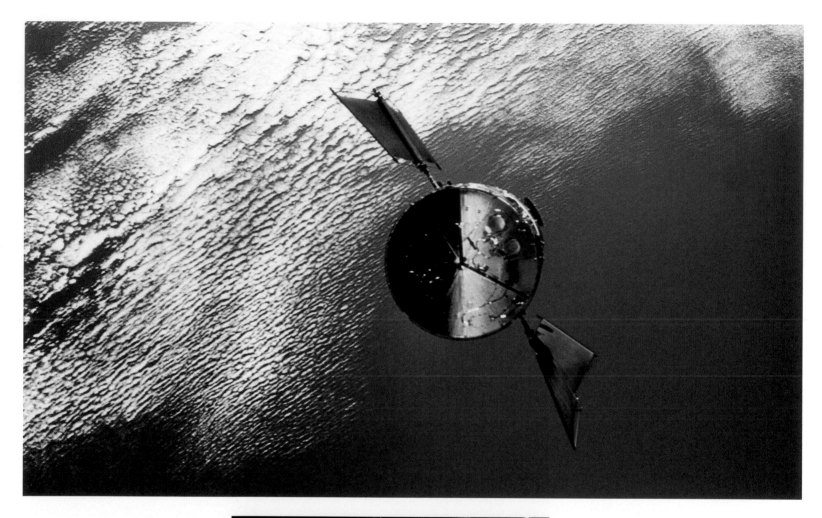

Orbiting humans—satellites themselves, whether in or out of a spacecraft—have experienced physiological changes. The reflexes and sensory perceptions of astronauts are monitored and tested for changes caused by sustained weightlessness. Some have shown altered heart rhythms. Some have lost red blood cells.

One of the most famous repair jobs was done on the Hubble Space Telescope. Boosted into orbit in April 1990, today it cruises 370 miles above earth to give us clear

In the clear vacuum above the earth's atmosphere the orbiting Hubble telescope *(top)* peers into corners of space never before seen. Pointed at a seemingly empty portion of sky, it sends back images of stars and galaxies without end *(above)*.

views of space never before seen. The Hubble gave us a ringside seat for a comet's collision with Jupiter and has shown us explosions of distant dying stars.

Aimed at one empty-looking piece of sky the size of a grain of sand held at arm's length, the telescope has sent back images of galaxies so distant that the light from them takes 11 billion years to reach earth.

Whether scanning our own planet or peering into the far universe, satellites have become our highly sensitive eyes, seeing the way to new worlds. ■

1961 Russian ballet star Rudolf Nureyev defects to the U.S. from the Soviet Union.

1965 Capital punishment is abolished in Great Britain.

1967 Cuban leader Che Guevara is killed in Bolivia.

1971 Communist China joins the United Nations.

1972 Eight members of an Arab terrorist group invade Olympic Village and kill 11 Israeli athletes at the Olympic Games in Munich.

Traveling in Space

On April 12, 1961, Russian Yuri Gagarin rose in a rocket and became the first human to leave earth's environment, speeding above its atmosphere to go into orbit around the planet. On his return, Gagarin ejected at 22,000 feet and parachuted to safety, so officially he did not complete the flight. The point was lost in the world's excitement that a person had traveled in space.

Gagarin's voyage had its roots in the theories of another Russian almost a century earlier. In 1857 a Russian engineer, Konstantin Tsiolkowski, wrote an article suggesting that travel in space might be accomplished by rockets propelled by liquid fuels, with several stages that could drop away as their fuel was expended. Russia continued its interest in space travel by forming a research institute for studying jet propulsion in 1932.

But it was Adolf Hitler's V-2 rockets in World War II, which reached heights of 50 miles before dropping on London, that made scientists see that space travel was within reach. Both the Soviet Union and the United States recruited German rocket specialists after World War II.

On October 4, 1957, at the height of the Cold War, the Soviets shocked the world and particularly the U.S. by placing a 184-pound satellite called Sputnik into orbit. The two superpowers began a race to place the first man in space, which the Soviets won with Gagarin. A month later, before the U.S. had even placed a person in orbit, President

John F. Kennedy announced plans for sending people to the surface of the moon and back before the end of the decade. The goal was reached eight years later.

Even in retrospect, the feat seems almost impossible. A vehicle had to reach an orbit around earth, then break free of that orbit and head toward the moon. Once in orbit around the moon, a separate vehicle had to be detached that could descend to the moon's surface, land, and then take off to reunite with the orbiting vehicle for the flight home.

The U.S. National Aeronautics

1975 ● Great Britain's Conservative Party elects Margaret Thatcher as its first female leader.

1976 ● U.S. celebrates its Bicentennial.

1981 ● Sandra Day O'Connor appointed as first woman justice on U.S. Supreme Court.

1986 ● After ruling the Philippines for 20 years, President Marcos flees as newly elected Corazon Aquino succeeds him.

1989 ● Tanker Exxon *Valdez* spills 11 million gallons of crude oil into Alaska's Prince William Sound after foundering and rupturing.

and Space Agency (NASA) accomplished the moon landing in a series of steps. They experimented in earth orbit with the detaching and docking of two vehicles in space. Unmanned spacecraft with cameras were landed on the moon to see if the surface was solid and level. In three missions astronauts rode the powerful Saturn 5 rocket into orbit around the moon, separating and docking the two vehicles for practice.

In July 1969 Neil Armstrong, Edwin (Buzz) Aldrin, and Michael Collins went into lunar orbit. Then Armstrong and Aldrin entered a module and descended to the moon's surface. On July 20 some 500 million TV-viewers watched as Armstrong stepped onto the moon saying, "That's one small step for a man, one giant leap for mankind."

Several more missions were undertaken to the moon before scientists began concentrating on long-term voyages in earth orbit in space laboratories, in preparation for journeys to other planets. With the Cold War ended, Russians and Americans have cooperated in ventures, sharing space stations and conducting experiments that cannot be duplicated on earth.

Like most pioneering developments, space travel was not accomplished without fatalities. A Russian cosmonaut burned up while conducting experiments in a rocket still on the ground. Three American astronauts

In 1997 *Pathfinder* landed on Mars *(above)*. Beyond parts of the lander and air bags, loom Martian peaks and floodplain. In 1969 Edwin "Buzz" Aldrin stood on the moon, his visor reflecting the landing vehicle and fellow astronaut Neil Armstrong *(below)*. Two astronauts hovered in space *(opposite)* in 1985 to repair a communications satellite.

died when their cockpit burst into flames while the craft was on the launch pad. On January 28, 1986, the American space shuttle *Challenger* exploded 74 seconds after launch, killing seven astronauts. The benefits of space exploration include the developing of improved materials, the carrying out of experiments that could not be duplicated on earth, and opening the way to exploration of other planets. ■

1914 — Archduke Ferdinand, heir to the Austro-Hungarian throne, is assassinated in Sarajevo by a Bosnian-Serb nationalist, touching off events that lead to World War I.

1922 — Mussolini marches on Rome.

1926 — Gertrude Ederle of the U.S. becomes the first woman to swim the English Channel.

1933 — Adolph Hitler is appointed German chancellor, and the Nazi nightmare begins.

1947 — The Truman Doctrine is proposed—the first significant attempt by the U.S to contain communist expansion.

Turbulence in Iran and Iraq

At the beginning of the 20th century, two cultures with rich histories dating to ancient times found themselves entering a period of turmoil. One was Iraq, in ancient times known as Mesopotamia. The other was Iran, the seat of the once powerful Persian Empire. In World War I they were battlegrounds for opposing forces.

In 1914 Iran, still called Persia, proclaimed its neutrality in the coming hostilities of World War I but had no power to enforce it. Russian troops battled the Turks, and the British fought Persian tribes organized by the Germans. In Iraq the British fought the remnants of the Ottoman Empire and drove them out of Baghdad.

The end of the war brought a surge of nationalistic feeling as both countries found themselves divided among the victors. Iraq, created out of the remnants of the old Ottoman Empire, was transferred to Britain in a League of Nations mandate. Riots and bloodshed resulted as Iraqis

demanded self-government. The country was proclaimed independent in 1932, although under close treaty arrangement with Britain.

In 1958, with Arab nationalism running at fever pitch with the ascent of Egypt's President Nasser, Iraqi nationalists assassinated three members of a regime set up by the British and took over the government. Other revolutions followed until the government came under the firm control of the Arab Ba'ath Socialist Party, headed by Saddam Hussein.

At the end of World War I Iran was occupied by Britain and Soviet Russia. The two powers signed agreements that gave Iran independence, but Iranian nationalists still felt they were not in control of their own destinies. In 1921 forces led by army

Once battlegrounds for foreign powers, fiercely independent Iran and Iraq went to war in 1980. Under the stern gaze of the Ayatollah Khomeini, Iranian women send young men off to fight *(opposite)*. Painted flags of other perceived threats—Israel, the U.S., and the Soviet Union—allow citizens to "walk on their enemies" *(below)*.

The Gulf War broke out in 1990, when Iraq invaded Kuwait. UN forces quickly acted and stopped Iraq. As Iraqi troops retreated, they set oil fields burning, blackening the area with smoke.

officer Reza Pahlavi took over the government. As shah of Iran, he began extensive modernization, a program continued by his 22-year-old son Mohammed Reza Pahlavi, when he assumed the throne in 1941.

For decades the younger Reza Pahlavi tried to modernize the country, but his autocratic methods and rapid changes offended many Iranians, especially strict Muslims. Opposition grew so strong that in 1979 he was forced to give up his throne, and the religious leader Ayatollah Khomeini proclaimed a strict Islamic Republic.

Plentiful oil had been discovered in both Iran and Iraq. In the name of Middle East unity several treaties had been concluded between the two countries. But differences between Iran's strict religious government and Iraq's secularist regime, plus Iraq's concern about the growing power of its neighbor, boiled into war in 1980.

Hundreds of thousands died in the eight-year conflict that drained the oil-rich treasuries of the two nations. ∎

1958 Khrushchev becomes Premier of the Soviet Union.

1961 Bay of Pigs invasion by some 1,200 U.S.-aided anti-Castro exiles is crushed.

1962 Lt. Col. John Glenn becomes first American to orbit the earth.

1964 UN General Assembly calls for international sanctions against South Africa.

1997 Mother Teresa dies in India at age 87.

● 1980 Eruption of Washington State's Mount St. Helens.

● 1983 Explosion set by terrorists kills 237 U.S. Marines in Beirut.

● 1984 Discovery of virus that causes AIDS is announced.

● 1986 U.S. space shuttle *Challenger* explodes shortly after launch, killing all on board.

● 1987 Monsoon in Bangladesh leaves 24 million people homeless.

Breakup of the Soviet Union

n 1961 in Moscow the Communist Party predicted that within 20 years the Soviet Union would have the world's highest standard of living.

In 1980, the year the economic system was supposed to surpass that of the United States, workers struck the Lenin Shipyards at Gdansk, Poland, protesting depressed wages and increases in food prices. Worldwide attention was focused on the birth of the Solidarity Union, led by electrician Lech Walesa, which challenged the Communist Party. A year later martial law was declared and Walesa and others were interned, but the long-barred door to freedom had been cracked.

In the 1980s Soviet President Mikhail Gorbachev began a program of *glasnost,* or openness, that allowed citizens to speak freely, and the Soviet system began to unravel. Suddenly a Soviet leader was a driving force in the movement toward economic change. In 1989 in East Germany, Bulgaria, and Czechoslovakia demonstrators took to the streets and brought down their governments. In

The final brush-off to communism came with astounding suddenness. At Vilnius, in Lithuania, a factory worker prepares a prone, paint-stained statue of Joseph Stalin for storage *(above).* West Berliners begin knocking holes in the Berlin Wall *(below)* after a more open-minded East German leadership allowed people to cross freely into West Berlin.

Hungary, as well, communism fell. In Romania the conflict grew bloody, as secret police fired on demonstrators, killing hundreds. Military units in revolt seized their heavy-handed dictator Nicolae Ceausescu and his wife Elena, both of whom had lived in luxury as their people stood in breadlines, and executed them both.

But nothing so demonstrated the failures of communism as the toppling of the Berlin Wall. Since its construction 28 years earlier, 81 people had died trying to climb it to escape a repressive society.

Before November 1989 when the hard-line communist leadership fell, hundreds of thousands of East Germans fled to the West, especially across the newly opened Hungarian-Austrian border, and large-scale demonstrations took place. Then the new, more open-minded leadership declared that people could start crossing freely to West Berlin. With this new freedom, West Berliners began chipping away at the wall.

Everywhere in Europe the pillars of communism toppled. After a failed coup attempt by hard-line communists in 1991, Gorbachev resigned. Not long

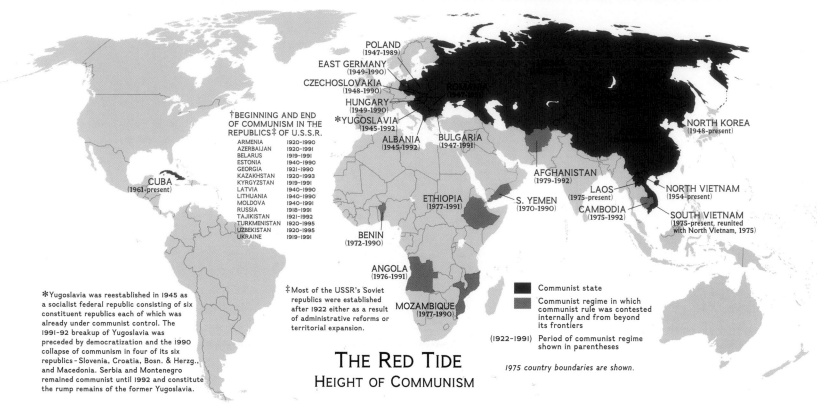

POLAND
(1947-1989)

EAST GERMANY
(1949-1990)

CZECHOSLOVAKIA
(1948-1990)

HUNGARY
(1949-1990)

*YUGOSLAVIA
(1945-1992)

ALBANIA
(1945-1992)

BULGARIA
(1947-1991)

ROMANIA
(1947-1990)

NORTH KOREA
(1948-present)

†BEGINNING AND END
OF COMMUNISM IN THE
REPUBLICS‡ OF U.S.S.R.

ARMENIA	1920-1990
AZERBAIJAN	1920-1991
BELARUS	1919-1991
ESTONIA	1940-1990
GEORGIA	1921-1990
KAZAKHSTAN	1920-1993
KYRGYZSTAN	1919-1991
LATVIA	1940-1990
LITHUANIA	1940-1990
MOLDOVA	1940-1991
RUSSIA	1918-1991
TAJIKISTAN	1921-1992
TURKMENISTAN	1920-1995
UZBEKISTAN	1920-1995
UKRAINE	1919-1991

CUBA
(1961-present)

AFGHANISTAN
(1979-1992)

LAOS
(1975-present)

NORTH VIETNAM
(1954-present)

CAMBODIA
(1975-1992)

SOUTH VIETNAM
(1975-present, reunited
with North Vietnam, 1975)

ETHIOPIA
(1977-1991)

S. YEMEN
(1970-1990)

BENIN
(1972-1990)

ANGOLA
(1976-1991)

MOZAMBIQUE
(1977-1990)

*Yugoslavia was reestablished in 1945 as a socialist federal republic consisting of six constituent republics each of which was already under communist control. The 1991-92 breakup of Yugoslavia was preceded by democratization and the 1990 collapse of communism in four of its six republics – Slovenia, Croatia, Bosn. & Herzg., and Macedonia. Serbia and Montenegro remained communist until 1992 and constitute the rump remains of the former Yugoslavia.

‡Most of the USSR's Soviet republics were established after 1922 either as a result of administrative reforms or territorial expansion.

■ Communist state

■ Communist regime in which communist rule was contested internally and from beyond its frontiers

(1922-1991) Period of communist regime shown in parentheses

1975 country boundaries are shown.

THE RED TIDE
HEIGHT OF COMMUNISM

(St. Petersburg) Petrograd

BOLSHEVIK REVOLUTION
November 1917

Moscow

BIRTH OF COMMUNISM
1917

NORTH
KOREA

CUBA

LAOS

VIETNAM

PRESENT-DAY COMMUNISM

after, Russian President Boris Yeltsin temporarily banned the Communist Party, and the Bolshevik Revolution was over.

Constituent Republics of the Soviet Union began declaring their independence, and the Union of Soviet Socialist Republics fell into disarray. However, the end to East-West tensions did not bring world peace. With police states gone, ethnic

conflicts that had been simmering for decades erupted into bloody rivalries.

The Republic of Chechnya declared itself independent of the Russian Federation, and Russian troops attempted, unsuccessfully, to oppose the move.

In Yugoslavia fighting erupted between Serbs, Croats, and Muslims after the breakup of the Federal Republic in 1991. Atrocities were

common in conflicts over enduring ethnic resentments and battles for borders defining the new nations.

In many countries, the transition from a communist system to a market economy was not an easy one. It brought new wealth for some, new hardship for others, and onslaughts of crime as people long controlled by the state struggled with the responsibilities of self-determination. ■

1956 Israel launches attack on Egypt's Sinai Peninsula and drives toward Suez Canal.

1957 The British colony of the Gold Coast becomes the independent nation of Ghana.

1959 Seven non-Common Market countries, including Sweden, Britain, and Portugal, form the European Free Trade Association.

1960 Millions watch the first televised debate between presidential candidates, as Richard M. Nixon and John F. Kennedy match wits.

1961 The Berlin Wall is erected.

World Refugees

At no time in history have so many people been uprooted from their homes as now to live lives as drifting refugees, with few opportunities to acquire food, shelter, or protection.

As recently as 1960, fewer than three million people qualified as refugees, people forced to flee their homelands to escape persecution. By 1995 the number had climbed to 23 million.

Armed conflicts are the single biggest cause of official refugees. Modern weapons have made wars not only more devastating to those who fight them, but also to those who innocently get in the way.

While soldiers have always faced each other in battle and have

sustained the largest number of casualties, the number of civilian casualties has grown with the advent of weapons of mass destruction, dropped on or hurled at enemy cities.

As recently as the 1950s, only half of all war-related deaths were civilian. By the 1980s, civilian deaths amounted to three-quarters, and now in the 1990s, some 90 percent of all people killed in wars are civilians. Little wonder so many people become refugees when fighting breaks out.

In general the scale of warfare has grown smaller since 1945, but wars have become more frequent. At any one time in the 1950s, wars causing more than 1,000 casualties numbered about 11.

By the mid-1990s the number of conflicts occurring simultaneously

1965 Canada's distinctive maple-leaf flag is raised for the first time.

1967 Six-Day War between Arabs and Israelis.

1971 26th Amendment lowers U.S. voting age to 18.

1988 Australia unveils the most powerful radio telescope in the Southern Hemisphere.

1993 U.S. House of Representatives approves North American Free Trade Agreement. The Senate follows.

1997 Diana, Britain's Princess of Wales, dies in Paris automobile accident at age 36.

numbered 34. The total number of people killed since 1945, either directly from the fighting or in war-related famine or illness, approaches 50 million.

Most modern wars are internal conflicts, making it difficult for civilians to remain uninvolved or to seek places of safety within their own countries. In 1995 Afghanistan produced the biggest single number of refugees—nearly three million. Rwanda was second, due to conflicts and massacres that took place there.

Europe in the 1990s became not only a sanctuary for refugees from other countries, but also for the first time since the 1940s, a creator of refugees as people were uprooted by fighting among Serbs, Bosnians, and Croats.

Besides the official refugees, millions more flee their homes for reasons other than persecution. Famine and failure to find the means to care for their families force some to seek relief or opportunity elsewhere. As illegal immigrants, their numbers cannot be known definitely but are believed to total some 10 million.

In some ways illegal immigrants are worse off than the official refugees because no international machinery exists to care for them. Sometimes international aid agencies do feed illegal immigrants who are actually starving from crop failure.

Even worse-off may be those uprooted who stay within their own countries, for international agencies cannot operate freely there because of issues of sovereign control.

The "internally displaced" in places such as Bosnia-Herzegovina, Azerbaijan, Rwanda, and others may total 27 million, with very little help likely to be forthcoming from their own governments. ∎

IMMIGRATION

In the dawn of the 20th century a veritable flood of humanity seeking work and a better life in America gazed on the beckoning torch of the Statue of Liberty as the immigrants passed through Ellis Island into the United States. In the biggest mass movement in history, a million immigrants came to the U.S. in 1905, and more than a million and a quarter arrived in 1907. Expansive America's great demand for unskilled and semi-skilled labor drew immigrant workers, most of whom clustered in industrial areas, finding jobs in the burgeoning cities where muscle and manual dexterity counted more than the ability to speak English. In fact, many immigrants lived quite isolated from mainstream America, surrounded by their fellow countrymen and leaving it to the next generation to learn English and feel truly at home.

Kurds uprooted by hostile neighbors at the border between Iran and Iraq huddle around an open fire *(left)*. The tears of a Serbian woman *(opposite, above)*, who fled the shelling of her Bosnian village, reflect the sorrow felt by all refugees. Many desperate "boat people" like these Vietnamese, apprehended by Hong Kong police *(opposite, below)*, ended up in detention camps after fleeing a communist regime.

1970 U.S. planes heavily bomb the Ho Chi Minh Trail in Laos.

1971 Lt. William Calley is found guilty of murdering Vietnamese civilians at Mylai in 1968.

1973 Egyptian and Syrian forces attack Israel as Jews mark Yom Kippur, holiest of their holidays. The war is the fourth and largest Arab-Israeli conflict to date.

1975 The American merchant ship *Mayaguez*, seized by Cambodian forces, is rescued by U.S. Navy and Marines, 38 of whom are killed.

1976 Argentina's President Isabel Perón is deposed in a bloodless coup.

Legacy for the Future

First coal, then petroleum came into prominent use as fuels for the modern age. The early supply of inexpensive fossil fuels fed a gluttonous habit that the modern world has found hard to break. Both coal and petroleum are fossil fuels because they derive from formerly living plants and animals that, through heat and pressure, were

slowly transformed into concentrated, highly combustible material.

In the last quarter of the 20th century, the cost of using fossil fuels began to rise, environmentally and monetarily. Sulfur from both coal and oil can raise the acidity of rainfall, believed harmful to many living organisms. Combustion releases

1977 U.S. President Jimmy Carter pardons Vietnam War draft evaders.

1979 Vietnam, along with the Cambodian insurgents it backs, announces the fall of Phnom Penh, the Cambodian capital, and the collapse of the Pol Pot regime.

1980 Nicaragua's deposed President Somoza is assassinated.

1982 Monaco's Princess Grace dies in an automobile accident.

carbon dioxide, and an increase of that gas in the atmosphere can raise global temperatures.

The burning of gasoline in automobile engines releases nitrous oxides, principal contributors to the brownish haze of atmospheric ozone that hangs close to the land and can cause respiratory problems as well as crop damage.

The problems and limitations of nonrenewable fossil fuels have launched a search for alternate sources of energy. Sunlight can produce electricity through photovoltaic cells, but the cost of making the cells remains high.

The oceans are a vast storage tank of solar energy, absorbing nearly 75 percent of the sun's heat that strikes the earth. Harnessing the temperature differences between warm surface water and cold ocean depths can produce electricity, but, again, it

A geothermal power plant in Iceland warms homes and bathers in a runoff pond *(above)*. A California "wind farm" generates clean electric power *(below)*. Both bypass the effluent of fossil fuels, mingling with clouds on a murky day near Vancouver, Canada *(opposite)*. Jet noise intolerable to humans saved the habitat of the deaf and endangered El Segundo blue butterfly *(opposite, above)*.

remains more costly than that produced by conventional means.

Turbines turned by the wind have been tried in areas that are frequently breezy. The problem is that wind is not constant. Because of wind-free days, California's 15,000 wind turbines deliver only a quarter of the power they are capable of.

Deep within the earth lies another source of power, geothermal heat resulting from the radioactive decay of rocks. Homes in volcanic Iceland already are warmed by earth's inner heat, but elsewhere technical difficulties hold up progress.

Some landfills are now being mined for methane gas formed by yesteryear's garbage. The process of decay produces a combustible gas called methane, capable of being burned as fuel.

1983 After 19 months, martial law is lifted in Poland.

1986 Twelve people die in confrontations between demonstrators and police in Soweto, South Africa.

1987 U.S.A. and U.S.S.R. agree to ban medium-range nuclear weapons.

1988 Carbon-dating tests at Oxford reveal the Turin Shroud to be a medieval fake.

1989 After 28 years, Berlin Wall opens to the West.

More and more garbage, filling more and bigger landfills, is just one of the effects of an exploding human population. Another is the direct impact the population has on the surface of the earth. The grass-covered plains of the American Midwest, for example, have been almost completely reconfigured into cropland. In fact, American farmland is being overrun by suburban sprawl at the rate of 50 acres an hour, but nationwide, the shift is barely noticeable.

The alteration of the landscape from natural vegetation to agriculture, from farmlands to widespread cities, has seemed so gradual as to raise few alarms. It took life-threatening smog to trigger efforts to clean up the air. A river catching fire in Cleveland, Ohio, in 1969 prompted the Clean Water Act in the U.S. in 1972.

At the beginning of the industrial revolution the flight from the countryside to the cities triggered new social problems of poor sanitation, crime, and lack of recreation. Today, people

1990 ● Haiti elects leftist priest as president in its first democratic election.

1991 ● A military junta headed by Gen. Sunthron Kongsompong takes power in Thailand.

1992 ● Rebels occupy the Afghan capital of Kabul.

1994 ● The English Channel Tunnel between England and France is formally opened.

1995 ● Scores are killed as the Alfred P. Murrah Federal Building in Oklahoma City is destroyed by a terrorist bomb.

1997 ● Hong Kong is peacefully returned to China after more than a century of British domination.

WORLD TROPICAL RAIN FOREST
■ Tropical rain forest

A mahogany cutter in Costa Rica *(above)* continues the felling of world forests, a prime cause of species extinction. One solution for ruined habitat, a manmade fish ladder *(below)* aids a single spawning salmon on California's American River, once crowded with such sojourners. Around the globe, as in this West Coast suburb *(opposite),* an expanding human population adds an ever increasing burden of pollutants to earth, air, and water.

still flock to the cities and encounter problems of crime, traffic jams, pollution, and the lack of a sense of community. Some might find emotional renewal in pleasant parks and natural lands, but the disadvantaged cannot afford to reach them. For those who can, the recreational areas themselves are increasingly crowded.

Perhaps nothing has so dramatized the alteration of earth's surface by human use as the destruction of tropical forests. They once covered about four billion acres of Africa, Asia, and South and Central America. Today perhaps half of that amount remains.

A serious side-effect of the destruction of natural habitats to make way for more people is the loss of species that could potentially hold great value for humankind. A quarter of our prescription drugs are derived from, or contain, plant extracts, and only a relative handful of species has been tested for pharmaceutical use.

Rain forests are important not only because they are home to indigenous peoples and numerous animal and plant species—many endangered—but also because their lush vegetation takes in carbon dioxide (CO_2) and gives off oxygen.

Worldwide, the percentage of CO_2 in the atmosphere is on the increase, possibly speeding the rate of global warming, which could drastically alter life on earth.

Not the least benefit of good land use is the retention of natural beauty and its positive effects on humankind. Poets and painters have extolled the wonders of natural beauty for centuries, while little has been expressed about the joys of tenements and parking lots.

For centuries land was exploited for personal profit. By the end of the 20th century conservation-minded citizens were increasing their pressure on government to develop high-density areas more attractively and to preserve large natural areas for human renewal through recreation. ■

379

Birth of
New Worlds

As dwellers on a single planet in the universe contemplate what seems a long history, whole new stars take shape far beyond unassisted human sight. Looking deep into space, the orbiting Hubble Space Telescope reveals in the Eagle Nebula pillars of dense, cool gas and dust, the tallest measuring three light years in height.

Deep inside the pillars, molecular hydrogen and dust condense into lumps that contract and ignite under their own gravity to become stars, even as ultraviolet light from other stars evaporates their outer layers. New worlds are being born, while our own world struggles to understand itself.

Appendix

Highlights of Chinese History

Yuanmou Man	1.6 million years ago	Western Jin	265–316
Lantian Man, Peking Man	700,000–500,000 years ago	Southern and Northern Dynasties	317–581
Upper Cave Man	18,000 years ago	Sui Dynasty	581–618
Yangshao culture	5000 B.C.	Tang Dynasty	618-907
Longshan culture	2500 B.C.	Five Dynasties (north) and Ten Kingdoms (south)	907–960
Three Rulers and Five Emperors	ca 2852–2205 B.C	Song Dynasty	960–1279
Xia Dynasty	ca 2205–1766 B.C.	Yuan Dynasty (Mongol)	1279–1368
Shang Dynasty	ca 1766–1122 B.C.	Ming Dynasty	1368–1644
Zhou Dynasty	ca 1122–256 B.C.	Qing Dynasty (Manchu)	1644–1911
Qin Dynasty	221–206 B.C.	Republic of China	1911–1949
Han Dynasty	206 B.C.–A.D. 220	People's Republic of China	1949–present
Three Kingdoms	220–280		

Roman Rulers

The Kingdom

B.C.

753	Romulus (Quirinus)
716	Numa Pompilius
673	Tullus Hostilius
640	Ancus Marcius
616	L.Tarquinius Priscus
578	Servius Tullius
534	L.Tarquinius Superbus

The Republic

509	Consulate established
509	Quaestorship instituted
498	Dictatorship introduced
494	Plebeian Tribunate created
494	Plebeian Aedileship created
444	Consular Tribunate organized
435	Censorship instituted
366	Praetorship established
366	Curule Aedileship created
362	Military Tribunate elected
326	Proconsulate introduced
311	Naval Duumvirate elected
217	Dictatorship of Fabius Maximus
133	Tribunate of Tiberius Gracchus
123	Tribunate of Gaius Gracchus
82	Dictatorship of Sulla
60	First Triumvirate formed (Caesar, Pompeius, Crassus)
46	Dictatorship of Caesar
43	Second Triumvirate formed (Octavianus, Antonius, Lepidus)

The Empire

27	Augustus (Gaius Julius Caesar Octavianus)

A.D.

14	Tiberius I
37	Gaius Caesar (Caligula)
41	Claudius I
54	Nero
68	Galba
69	Galba; Otho, Vitellius
69	Vespasianus
79	Titus
81	Domitianus
96	Nerva
98	Trajanus
117	Hadrianus
138	Antoninus Pius
161	Marcus Aurelius and Lucius Verus
169	Marcus Aurelius (alone)
180	Commodus
193	Pertinax; Julianus I
193	Septimius Severus
211	Caracalla and Geta
212	Caracalla (alone)
217	Macrinus
218	Elagabalus (Heliogabalus)
222	Alexander Severus
235	Maximinus I (the Thracian)
238	Gordianus I and Gordianus II; Pupienus and Balbinus
238	Gordianus III
244	Philippus (the Arabian)
249	Decius
251	Gallus and Volusianus
253	Aemilianus
253	Valerianus and Gallienus
258	Gallienus (alone)
268	Claudius Gothicus
270	Quintillus
270	Aurelianus
275	Tacitus
276	Florianus
276	Probus
282	Carus
283	Carinus and Numerianus
284	Diocletianus
286	Diocletianus and Maximianus
305	Galerius and Constantius I
306	Galerius, Maximinus II, Severus I
307	Galerius, Maximinus II, Constantinus I, Licinius, Maxentius
311	Maximinus II, Constantinus I, Licinius, Maxentius
314	Maximinus II, Constantinus I, Licinius
314	Constantinus I and Licinius
324	Constantinus I (the Great)

(Continued on next page)

Roman Rulers *(continued)*

337 Constantinus II, Constans I, Constantius II
340 Constantius II and Constans I
350 Constantius II
361 Julianus II (the Apostate)
363 Jovianus

West (Rome) and East (Constantinople)

364 Valentinianus I (West) and Valens (East)
367 Valentinianus I with Gratianus (West) and Valens (East)
375 Gratianus with Valentinianus II (West) and Valens (East)
378 Gratianus with Valentinianus II (West) Theodosius I (East)
383 Valentinianus II (West) and Theodosius I (East)
394 Theodosius I (the Great)
395 Honorius (West) and Arcadius (East)
408 Honorius (West) and Theodosius II (East)
423 Valentinianus III (West) and Theodosius II East)
450 Valentinianus III (West) and Marcianus (East)
455 Maximus (West), Avitus (West); Marcianus (East)
456 Avitus (West), Marcianus (East)
457 Majorianus (West), Leo I (East)
461 Severus II (West), Leo I (East)
467 Anthemius (West), Leo I (East)
472 Olybrius (West), Leo I (East)
473 Glycerius (West), Leo I (East)
474 Julius Nepos (West), Leo II (East)
475 Romulus Augustulus (West) and Zeno (East)
476 End of Empire in West; Odovacar, King, drops title of Emperor; murdered by King Theodoric of Ostrogoths A.D. 493

Historical Periods of Japan

Yamato	ca 300–592	Kamakura	1192–1333	Edo	1603–1867
Asuka	592–710	Namboku	1334–1392	Meiji	1868–1912
Nara	710–794	Ashikaga	1338–1573	Taisho	1912–1926
Heian	794–1192	Muromachi	1392–1573	Showa	1926–1989
Fujiwara	858–1160	Sengoku	1467–1600	Heisei	1989–
Taira	1160–1185	Momoyama	1573–1603		

Major Wars

Date	Name of war	Date	Name of war	Date	Name of war
ca 1250 B.C.	Trojan wars	1700	Great Northern War	1861–1865	U.S. Civil War
431–404 B.C.	Peloponnesian War	1701–1713	War of Spanish Succession	1866	Austro-Prussian War
264–241 B.C.	First Punic War			1870	Franco-Prussian War
218–101 B.C.	Second Punic War	1730–1738	War of Polish Succession	1894–1895	Chinese-Japanese War
149–146 B.C.	Third Punic War	1740–1748	War of Austrian Succession	1899–1902	Boer War
1096–1099	First Crusade			1904–1905	Russo-Japanese War
1147–1149	Second Crusade	1756–1763	Seven Years' War	1914–1918	World War I
1189–1192	Third Crusade	1775–1783	Revolutionary War (American)	1918–1921	Russian Civil War
1202–1204	Fourth Crusade			1931–1933	Chinese-Japanese War
1337–1453	Hundred Years War	1793–1815	Napoleonic wars	1936–1939	Spanish Civil War
1455–1485	Wars of the Roses	1821–1829	Greek War of Independence	1939–1945	World War II
1562–1598	French Wars of Religion			1967	Six Day War
1642–1648	English Civil War	1846–1848	Mexican-American War	1950–1953	Korean War
1618–1648	Thirty Years' War	1854–1856	Crimean War	1964–1973	Vietnam War
1689–1697	War of League of Augsburg	1859	War for Italian Independence	1980–1988	Iran-Iraq War

Appendix

The Popes

St. Peter (d. ca 64)
St. Linus (ca 66–78)
St. Anacletus (ca 79–91)
St. Clement I (ca 91–101)
St. Evaristus (ca 100–109)
St. Alexander I (ca 109–116)
St. Sixtus I (ca 116–125)
St. Telesphorus (ca 125–136)
St. Hyginus (ca 138–142)
St. Pius I (ca 142–155)
St. Anicetus (ca 155–166)
St. Soter (ca 166–174)
St. Eleutherius, or Eleutherus (ca 174–89)
St. Victor I (189–98)
St. Zephyrinus (198/9–217)
St. Callistus I (often Calixtus) (217–22)
St. Urban I (222–30)
St. Pontian (21 July 230–28 Sept. 235)
St. Anterus (21 Nov. 235–3 Jan. 236)
St. Fabian (10 Jan. 236–20 Jan 250)
St. Cornelius Mar. 251–June 253)
St. Lucius I (25 June 253–5 Mar. 254)
St. Stephen I (12 May 254–2 Aug. 257)
St. Sixtus II (Aug. 257–6 Aug. 258)
St. Dionysius (22 July 260–26 Dec. 268)
St. Felix I (3 Jan. 269–30 Dec. 274)
St. Eutychian (4 Jan. 275–7 Dec. 283)
St. Gaius, or Caius (17 Dec. 283–22 Apr. 296)
St. Marcellinus (30 June 296–ca 304; d. 25 Oct. 304)
St. Marcellus I (Nov./Dec. 306–16 Jan. 308)
St. Eusebius (18 Apr.–21 Oct. 310)
St. Miltiades, or Melchiades (2 July 311–10 Jan. 314)
St. Silvester I (31 Jan. 314–31 Dec. 335)
St. Mark (18 Jan.–7 Oct. 336)
St. Julius I (6 Feb. 337–12 Apr. 352)
Liberius (17 May 352–24 Sept. 366)
St. Damasus I (1 Oct. 366–11 Dec. 384)
St. Siricius (Dec. 384–26 Nov. 399)
St. Anastasius I (27 Nov. 399–19 Dec. 401)
St. Innocent I (21 Dec. 401–12 Mar. 417)
St. Zosimus (18 Mar. 417–26 Dec. 418)
St. Boniface I (28 Dec. 418–4 Sept. 422)
St. Celestine I (10 Sept. 422–27 July 432)
St. Sixtus, or Xystus III (31 July 432–19 Aug. 440)
St. Leo I (Aug/Sept. 440–10 Nov. 461)
St. Hilarus (19 Nov. 461–29 Feb. 468)
St. Simplicius (3 Mar. 468–10 Mar. 483)
St. Felix III (II) (13 Mar. 483–1 Mar. 492)
St. Gelasius I (1 Mar. 492–21 Nov. 496)
Anastasius II (24 Nov. 496–19 Nov. 498)
St. Symmachus (22 Nov. 498–19 July 514)
St. Hormisdas (20 July 514–6 Aug. 523)
St. John I (13 Aug. 523–18 May 526)
St. Felix IV (III) (12 July 526–22 Sept. 530)
Boniface II (22 Sept. 530–17 Oct. 532)
John II (2 Jan. 533–8 May 535)
St. Agapitus I (13 May 535–22 April 536)
St. Silverius (8 June 536–11 Nov. 537: d. 2 Dec. 537)
Vigilius (29 Mar. 537–7 June 555)
Pelagius I (16 Apr. 556–3 Mar. 561)
John III (17 July 561–13 July 574)
Benedict I (2 June 575–30 July 579)
Pelagius II (26 Nov. 579–7 Feb. 590)
St. Gregory I (3 Sept. 590–12 Mar. 604)
Sabinian (13 Sept. 604–22 Feb. 606)
Boniface III (19 Feb.–12 Nov. 607)
St. Boniface IV (15 Sept. 608–8 May 615)

St. Deusdedit (later Adeodatus I) (19 Oct. 615–8 Nov. 618)
Boniface V (23 Dec. 619–25 Oct. 625)
Honorius I (27 Oct. 625–12 Oct. 638)
Severinus (28 May–2 Aug. 640)
John IV (24 Dec. 640–12 Oct. 642)
Theodore I (24 Nov. 642–14 May 649)
St. Martin I (5 July 649–l7 June 653: d. 16 Sept. 655)
St. Eugene I (10 Aug. 654–2 June 657)
St. Vitalian (30 July 657–27 Jan 672)
Adeodatus II (11 Apr. 672–17 June 676)
Donus (2 Nov. 676–11 Apr. 678)
St. Agatho (27 June 678–10 Jan. 681)
St. Leo II (17 Aug. 682–3 July 683)
St. Benedict II (26 June 684–8 May 685)
John V (23 July 685–2 Aug. 686)
Conon (21 Oct. 686–21 Sept. 687)
St. Sergius I (15 Dec. 687–9 Sept. 701)
John VI (30 Oct. 701–11 Jan. 705)
John VII (1 Mar. 705–18 Oct. 707)
Sisinnius (15 Jan.–4 Feb. 708)
Constantine (25 Mar. 708–9 Apr. 715)
St. Gregory II (19 May 715–11 Feb. 731)
St. Gregory III (18 Mar. 731–28 Nov. 741)
St. Zacharias (3 Dec. 741–15 Mar. 752)
Stephen (II) (22 or 23–25 or 26 Mar. 752)
Stephen II (III) (26 Mar. 752–26 Apr. 757)
St. Paul I (29 May 757–28 June 767)
Stephen III (IV) (7 Aug. 768–24 Jan. 772)
Hadrian I (1 Feb. 772–25 Dec. 795)
St. Leo III (26 Dec. 795–12 June 816)
Stephen IV (V) (22 June 816–24 Jan. 817)
St. Paschal I (24 Jan. 817–11 Feb. 824)
Eugene II (ca 5 June 824–27 Aug. 827)
Valentine (Aug.–Sept. 827)
Gregory IV (late 827–25 Jan. 844)
Sergius II (Jan. 844–27 Jan. 847)
St. Leo IV (l0 Apr. 847–17 July 855)
Benedict III (29 Sept. 855–17 Apr. 858)
St. Nicholas I (24 Apr. 858–13 Nov. 867)
Hadrian II (14 Dec. 867–Nov. or Dec. 872)
John VIII (14 Dec. 872–16 Dec. 882)
Marinus I (16 Dec. 882–15 May 884)
St. Hadrian III (17 May 884–mid-Sept. 885)
Stephen V (VI) (Sept. 885–14 Sept. 891)
Formosus (6 Oct. 891–4 Apr. 896)
Boniface VI (Apr. 896)
Stephen VI (VII) (May 896–Aug. 897)
Romanus (Aug.–Nov. 897: d. ?)
Theodore II (Nov. 897)
John IX (Jan. 898–Jan. 900)
Benedict IV (May/June 900–Aug. 903)
Leo V (Aug.–Sept. 903: d. early 904)
Sergius III (29 Jan. 904–14 Apr. 911)
Anastasius III (c. June 911–c. Aug. 913)
Lando (c. Aug. 913–c. Mar. 914)
John X (Mar./Apr. 914–deposed May 928:d. 929)
Leo VI (May–Dec. 928)
Stephen VII (VIII) (Dec. 928–Feb. 931)
John XI (Feb. or Mar. 931–Dec. 935 or Jan. 936)
Leo VII (3 Jan. 936–13 July 939)
Stephen VIII (IX) (14 July 939–late Oct. 942)
Marinus II (30 Oct. 942–early May 946)
Agapitus II (10 May 946–Dec. 955)
John XII (16 Dec. 955–14 May 964)
Leo VIII (4 Dec. 963–1 Mar. 965)
Benedict V (22 May–deposed 23 June 964: d. 4 July 966)
John XIII (1 Oct. 965–6 Sept. 972)

Benedict VI (19 Jan. 973–July 974)
Benedict VII (Oct. 974–10 July 983)
John XIV (Dec. 983–20 Aug. 984)
John XV (mid-Aug. 985–Mar. 996)
Gregory V (3 May 996–18 Feb. 999)
Sylvester II (2 Apr. 999–12 May 1003)
John XVII (16 May–6 Nov. 1003)
John XVIII (25 Dec. 1003–June or July 1009)
Sergius IV (31 July 1009–12 May 1012)
Benedict VIII (17 May 1012–9 Apr. 1024)
John XIX (19 Apr. 1024–20 Oct. 1032)
Benedict IX (21 Oct. 1032–Sept. 1044; 10 Mar.–1 May 1045; 8 Nov. 1047–16 July 1048: d. 1055/6)
Silvester III (20 Jan.–10 Mar. 1045: d. 1063)
Gregory VI (1 May 1045–20 Dec. 1046: d. late 1047)
Clement II (24 Dec. 1046–9 Oct. 1047)
Damasus II (17 July–9 Aug. 1048)
St. Leo IX (12 Feb. 1049–19 Apr. 1054)
Victor II (13 Apr. 1055–28 July 1057)
Stephen IX (X) (2 Aug. 1057–29 Mar. 1058)
Nicholas II (6 Dec. 1058–19 or 26 July 1061)
Alexander II (30 Sept. 1061–21 April 1073)
St. Gregory VII (22 Apr. 1073–25 May 1085)
Bl. Victor III (24 May 1086; 9 May–16 Sept 1087)
Bl. Urban II (12 Mar. 1088–29 July 1099)
Paschal II (13 Aug. 1099–21 Jan. 1118)
Gelasius II (24 Jan. 1118–29 Jan. 1119)
Callistus II (2 Feb. 1119–14 Dec. 1124)
Honorius II (21 Dec. 1124–13 Feb. 1130)
Celestine (II) (15/16 Dec. 1124: d. 1125/6)
Innocent II (14 Feb. 1130–24 Sept. 1143)
Celestine II (26 Sept. 1143–8 Mar. 1144)
Lucius II (12 Mar. 1144–15 Feb. 1145)
Bl. Eugene III (15 Feb. 1145–8 July 1153)
Anastasius IV (8 July 1153–3 Dec. 1154)
Hadrian IV (4 Dec. 1154–1 Sept. 1159)
Alexander III (7 Sept. 1159–30 Aug. 1181)
Lucius III (1 Sept. 1181–25 Nov. 1185)
Urban III (25 Nov. 1185–19/20 Oct. 1187)
Gregory VIII (21 Oct.–17 Dec. 1187)
Clement III (19 Dec. 1187–late Mar. 1191)
Celestine III (Mar./Apr. 1191–8 Jan. 1198)
Innocent III (8 Jan. 1198–16 July 1216)
Honorius III (18 July 1216–18 Mar. 1227)
Gregory IX (19 Mar. 1227–22 Aug. 1241)
Celestine IV (25 Oct.–10 Nov. 1241)
Innocent IV (25 June 1243–7 Dec. 1254)
Alexander IV (12 Dec. 1254–25 May 1261)
Urban IV (29 Aug. 1261–2 Oct. 1264)
Clement IV (5 Feb. 1265–29 Nov. 1268)
Bl. Gregory X (1 Sept. 1271–10 Jan. 1276)
Bl. Innocent V (21 Jan.–22 June 1276)
Hadrian V (11 July–18 Aug. 1276)
John XXI (8 Sept. 1276–20 May 1277)
Nicholas III (25 Nov. 1277–22 Aug. 1280)
Martin IV (22 Feb. 1281–28 Mar. 1285)
Honorius IV (2 Apr. 1285–3 Apr. 1287)
Nicholas IV (22 Feb. 1288–4 Apr. 1292)
St. Peter Celestine V (5 July–13 Dec. 1294: d. 19 May 1296)
Boniface VIII (24 Dec. 1294–11 Oct. 1303)
Bl. Benedict XI (22 Oct. 1303–7 July 1304)
Clement V (5 June 1305–20 Apr. 1314)
John XXII (7 Aug. 1316–4 Dec. 1334)
Benedict XII (20 Dec. 1334–25 Apr. 1342)
Clement VI (7 May 1342–6 Dec. 1352)
Innocent VI (18 Dec. 1352–12 Sept. 1362)
Bl. Urban V (28 Sept. 1362–19 Dec. 1370)

(Continued on next page)

The Popes (continued)

Gregory XI (30 Dec. 1370-27 Mar. 1378)
Urban VI (8 Apr. 1378-15 Oct. 1389)
Boniface IX (2 Nov. 1389-1 Oct. 1404)
Innocent VII (17 Oct. 1404-6 Nov. 1406)
Gregory XII (30 Nov. 1406-4 July 1415: d. 18 Oct. 1417)
Martin V (11 Nov. 1417-20 Feb. 1431)
Eugene IV (3 Mar. 1431-23 Feb. 1447)
Nicholas V (6 Mar. 1447-24 Mar. 1455)
Callistus III (8 Apr. 1455-6 Aug. 1458)
Pius II (19 Aug. 1458-15 Aug. 1464)
Paul II (30 Aug. 1464-26 July 1471)
Sixtus IV (9 Aug. 1471-12 Aug. 1484)
Innocent VIII (29 Aug. 1484-25 July 1492)
Alexander VI (11 Aug. 1492-18 Aug. 1503)
Pius III (22 Sept.-18 Oct 1503)
Julius II (1 Nov. 1503-21 Feb. 1513)
Leo X (11 Mar. 1513-1 Dec. 1521)
Hadrian VI (9 Jan. 1522-14 Sept 1523)
Clement VII (19 Nov. 1523-25 Sept. 1534)
Paul III (13 Oct. 1534-10 Nov. 1549)
Julius III (8 Feb. 1550-23 Mar. 1555)
Marcellus II (9 Apr.-1 May 1555)

Paul IV (23 May 1555-18 Aug. 1559)
Pius IV (25 Dec. 1559-9 Dec. 1565)
St. Pius V (7 Jan. 1566-1 May 1572)
Gregory XIII (14 May 1572-10 Apr. 1585)
Sixtus V (24 Apr. 1585-27 Aug. 1590)
Urban VII (15-27 Sept. 1590)
Gregory XIV (5 Dec. 1590-16 Oct. 1591)
Innocent IX (29 Oct.-30 Dec. 1591)
Clement VIII (30 Jan. 1592-5 Mar. 1605)
Leo XI (1-27 Apr. 1605)
Paul V (16 May 1605-28 Jan. 1621)
Gregory XV (9 Feb. 1621-8 July 1623)
Urban VIII (6 Aug. 1623-29 July 1644)
Innocent X (15 Sept. 1644-1 Jan. 1655)
Alexander VII (7 Apr. 1655-22 May 1667)
Clement IX (20 June 1667-9 Dec. 1669)
Clement X (29 Apr. 1670-22 July 1676)
Bl. Innocent XI (21 Sept. 1676-12 Aug. 1689)
Alexander VIII (6 Oct. 1689-1 Feb. 1691)
Innocent XII (12 July 1691-27 Sept. 1700)
Clement XI (23 Nov. 1700-19 Mar. 1721)
Innocent XIII (8 May 1721-7 Mar. 1724)

Benedict XIII (29 May 1724-21 Feb. 1730)
Clement XII (12 July 1730-6 Feb. 1740)
Benedict XIV (17 Aug. 1740-3 May 1758)
Clement XIII (6 July 1758-2 Feb. 1769)
Clement XIV (19 May 1769-22 Sept. 1774)
Pius VI (15 Feb. 1775-29 Aug. 1799)
Pius VII (14 Mar. 1800-20 July 1823)
Leo XII (28 Sept. 1823-10 Feb. 1829)
Pius VIII (31 Mar. 1829-30 Nov. 1830)
Gregory XVI (2 Feb. 1831-1 June 1846)
Pius IX (16 June 1846-7 Feb. 1878)
Leo XIII (20 Feb. 1878-20 July 1903)
St. Pius X (4 Aug. 1903-20 Aug. 1914)
Benedict XV (3 Sept. 1914-22 Jan. 1922)
Pius XI (6 Feb. 1922-10 Feb. 1939)
Pius XII (2 Mar. 1939-9 Oct. 1958)
John XXIII (28 Oct. 1958-3 June 1963)
Paul VI (21 June 1963-6 Aug. 1978)
John Paul I (26 Aug.-28 Sept. 1978)
John Paul II (16 Oct. 1978-   )

Rulers of England and Great Britain

	Reign Began	Died		Reign Began	Died		Reign Began	Died
Saxons and Danes			*House of Blois*			*House of Tudor*		
Egbert	829	839	Stephen	1135	1154	Henry VII	1485	1509
Ethelwulf	839	858				Henry VIII	1509	1547
Ethelbald	858	860	*House of Plantagenet*			Edward VI	1547	1553
Ethelbert	860	866				Mary I	1553	1558
Ethelred I	866	871	Henry II	1154	1189	Elizabeth I	1558	1603
Alfred	871	899	Richard I	1189	1199			
Edward	899	924	John	1199	1216	*House of Stuart*		
Athelstan	924	940	Henry III	1216	1272			
Edmund I	940	946	Edward I	1272	1307	James I	1603	1625
Edred	946	955	Edward II	1307	1327	Charles I	1625	1649
Edwy	955	959	Edward III	1327	1377			
Edgar	959	975	Richard II	1377	1400	*Commonwealth*	1649-1660	
Edward	975	978						
Ethelred II	978	1016				*Council of State*	1649	
Edmund II	1016	1016	*House of Lancaster*					
Canute	1016	1035				*Protectorate*	1653	
Harold I	1035	1040	Henry IV	1399	1413			
Hardecanute	1040	1042	Henry V	1413	1422	Oliver Cromwell	1653	1658
Edward	1042	1066	Henry VI	1422	1471	Richard Cromwell	1658	1712
Harold II	1066	1066						
			House of York			*House of Stuart* (Restored)		
House of Normandy			Edward IV	1461	1483	Charles II	1660	1685
William I	1066	1087	Edward V	1483	1483	James II	1685	1701
William II	1087	1100	Richard III	1483	1485	William III	1689	1702
Henry I	1100	1135				and Mary		1694
						Anne	1702	1714

(Continued on next page)

Rulers of England and Great Britain (continued)

	Reign Began	Died		Reign Began	Died		Reign Began	Died
House of Hanover			*House of Saxe-Coburg and Gotha*			*House of Windsor* Name Adopted July 17, 1917		
George I	1714	1727	Edward VII	1901	1910			
George II	1727	1760				George V	1910	1936
George III	1760	1820				Edward VIII	1936	1972
George IV	1820	1830				George VI	1936	1952
William IV	1830	1837				Elizabeth II	1952	
Victoria	1837	1901						

Rulers of France

The Carolingians
A.D.
- 843 Charles I *(the Bald)*
- 877 Louis II (the Stammerer)
- 879 Louis III *(died 882)* and Carloman, brothers
- 885 Charles II *(the Fat)*
- 888 Eudes *(Odo)*
- 898 Charles III *(the Simple)*
- 922 Robert
- 923 Rudolph *(Raoul)*
- 936 Louis IV
- 954 Lothair
- 986 Louis V *(the Sluggard)*

The Capets
A.D.
- 987 Hugh Capet
- 996 Robert II *(the Wise)*
- 1031 Henry I
- 1060 Philip I *(the Fair)*
- 1108 Louis VI *(the Fat)*
- 1137 Louis VII *(the Younger)*
- 1180 Philip II *(Augustus)*
- 1223 Louis VIII *(the Lion)*
- 1226 Louis IX
- 1270 Philip III *(the Hardy)*
- 1285 Philip IV *(the Fair)*
- 1314 Louis X *(the Headstrong)*
- 1316 Philip V *(the Tall)*
- 1322 Charles IV *(the Fair)*

House of Valois
A.D.
- 1328 Philip VI *(of Valois)*
- 1350 John II *(the Good)*
- 1364 Charles V *(the Wise)*
- 1380 Charles VI *(the Beloved)*
- 1422 Charles VII *(the Victorious)*
- 1461 Louis XI *(the Cruel)*
- 1483 Charles VIII *(the Affable)*

- 1498 Louis XII
- 1515 Francis I
- 1547 Henry II
- 1559 Francis II
- 1560 Charles IX
- 1574 Henry III

House of Bourbon
A.D.
- 1589 Henry IV
- 1610 Louis XIII *(the Just)*
- 1643 Louis XIV *(The Grand Monarch)*
- 1715 Louis XV
- 1774 Louis XVI

First Republic
A.D.
- 1792 National Convention of the French Revolution
- 1795 Directory, under Barras and others
- 1799 Consulate, Napoleon Bonaparte, first consul. Elected consul for life, 1802.

First Empire
A.D.
- 1804 Napoleon I

Bourbons Restored
A.D.
- 1814 Louis XVIII
- 1824 Charles X

House of Orleans
A.D.
- 1830 Louis-Philippe

Second Republic
A.D.
- 1848 Louis Napoleon Bonaparte

Second Empire
A.D.
- 1852 Napoleon III

Third Republic—Presidents
A.D.
- 1871 Thiers, Louis Adolphe
- 1873 MacMahon, Marshal Patrice M. de
- 1879 Grevy, Paul J.
- 1887 Sadi-Carnot, M.
- 1894 Casimir-Perier, Jean P. P.
- 1895 Faure, Francois Felix
- 1899 Loubet, Emile
- 1906 Fallieres, C. Armand
- 1913 Poincare, Raymond
- 1920 Deschanel, Paul
- 1920 Millerand, Alexandre
- 1924 Doumergue, Gaston
- 1931 Doumer, Paul
- 1932 Lebrun, Albert
- 1940 Vichy govt. under German armistice: Henri Philippe Petain, Chief of State, 1940-1944. Provisional govt. after liberation: Charles de Gaulle Oct. 1944-Jan. 21, 1946; Felix Gouin Jan. 23, 1946; Georges Bidault June 24, 1946.

Fourth Republic—Presidents
A.D.
- 1947 Auriol, Vincent
- 1954 Coty, Rene

Fifth Republic—Presidents
A.D.
- 1959 de Gaulle, Charles Andre J. M.
- 1969 Pompidou, Georges
- 1974 Giscard d'Estaing, Valery
- 1981 Mitterrand, Francois
- 1995 Chirac, Jacques

Rulers of Russia Since 1533

Ivan IV the Terrible	1533-1584
Theodore I	1584-1598
Boris Godunov	1598-1605
Theodore II	1605-1605
Demetrius I	1605-1606
Basil IV Shuiski	1606-1610
"Time of Troubles"	1610-1613
Michael Romanov	1613-1645
Alexis I	1645-1676
Theodore III	1676-1682
Ivan V	1682-1689
Peter I the Great	1682-1725
Catherine I	1725-1727
Peter II	1727-1730
Anna	1730-1740
Ivan VI	1740-1741

Elizabeth	1741-1762
Peter III	1762-1762
Catherine II the Great	1762-1796
Paul I	1796-1801
Alexander I	1801-1825
Nicholas I	1825-1855
Alexander II	1855-1881
Alexander III	1881-1894
Nicholas II	1894-1917

Provisional Government (Premiers)

Prince Georgi Lvov	1917-1917
Alexander Kerensky	1917-1917

Political Leaders of U.S.S.R.

N. Lenin	1917-1924
Aleksei Rykov	1924-1930
Vyacheslav Molotov	1930-1941
Joseph Stalin	1924-1953
Georgi M. Malenkov	1953-1955
Nikolai A. Bulganin	1955-1958
Nikita S. Khrushchev	1958-1964
Leonid I. Brezhnev	1964-1982
Yuri V. Andropov	1982-1984
Konstantin U. Chernenko	1984-1985
Mikhail Gorbachev	1985-1991

President of Russia

Boris Yeltsin	1991-

Prime Ministers of Great Britain

Sir Robert Walpole (W)	1721-1742
Earl of Wilmington (W)	1742-1743
Henry Pelham (W)	1743-1754
Duke of Newcastle (W)	1754-1756
Duke of Devonshire (W)	1756-1757
Duke of Newcastle (W)	1757-1762
Earl of Bute (T)	1762-1763
George Grenville (W)	1763-1765
Marquess of Rockingham (W)	1765-1766
William Pitt the Elder (Earl of Chatham) (W)	1766-1768
Duke of Grafton (W)	1768-1770
Frederick North (Lord North) (T)	1770-1782
Marquess of Rockingham (W)	1782
Earl of Shelburne (W)	1782-1783
Duke of Portland (Cl)	1783
William Pitt the Younger (T)	1783-1801
Henry Addington (T)	1801-1804

William Pitt the Younger (T)	1804-1806
Baron Grenville (W) (Sir William Wyndham Grenville)	1806-1807
Duke of Portland (T)	1807-1809
Spencer Perceval (T)	1809-1812
Earl of Liverpool (T)	1812-1827
George Canning (T)	1827
Viscount Goderich (T)	1827-1828
Duke of Wellington (T)	1828-1830
Earl Grey (W)	1830-1834
Viscount Melbourne (W)	1834
Sir Robert Peel (T)	1834-1835
Viscount Melbourne (W)	1835-1841
Sir Robert Peel (T)	1841-1846
Lord John Russell (later Earl) (W)	1846-1852
Earl of Derby (T)	852
Earl of Aberdeen (P)	1852-1855
Viscount Palmerston (L)	1855-1858

Earl of Derby (C)	1858-1859
Viscount Palmerston (L)	1859-1865
Earl Russell (L)	1865-1866
Earl of Derby (C)	1866-1868
Benjamin Disraeli (C)	1868
William E. Gladstone (L)	1868-1874
Benjamin Disraeli (C)	1874-1880
William E. Gladstone (L)	1880-1885
Marquess of Salisbury (C)	1885-1886
William E. Gladstone (L)	1886
Marquess of Salisbury (C)	1886-1892
William E. Gladstone (L)	1892-1894
Earl of Rosebery (L)	1894-1895
Marquess of Salisbury (C)	1895-1902
Arthur J. Balfour (C)	1902-1905
Sir Henry Campbell-Bannerman (L)	1905-1908
Herbert H. Asquith (L)	1908-1915

(Continued on next page)

Prime Ministers of Great Britain *(continued)*

Herbert H. Asquith	1915-1916	Neville Chamberlain **(Cl)**	1937-1940	Edward Heath **(C)**	1970-1974
David Lloyd George **(Cl)**	1916-1922	Winston Churchill **(Cl)**	1940-1945	Harold Wilson **(La)**	1974-1976
Andrew Bonar Law **(C)**	1922-1923	Winston Churchill **(C)**	1945	James Callaghan **(La)**	1976-1979
Stanley Baldwin **(C)**	1923-1924	Clement Attlee **(La)**	1945-1951	Margaret Thatcher **(C)**	1979-1990
James Ramsay MacDonald **(La)**	1924	Sir Winston Churchill **(C)**	1951-1955	John Major **(C)**	1990-1997
Stanley Baldwin **(C)**	1924-1929	Sir Anthony Eden **(C)**	1955-1957	Tony Blair **(La)**	1997-
James Ramsay MacDonald **(La)**	1929-1931	Harold Macmillan **(C)**	1957-1963		
James Ramsay MacDonald **(Cl)**	1931-1935	Sir Alec Douglas-Home **(C)**	1963-1964	**(W**=Whig; **T**=Tory; **Cl**=Coalition; **P**=Peelite;	
Stanley Baldwin **(Cl)**	1935-1937	Harold Wilson **(La)**	1964-1970	**L**=Liberal; **C**=Conservative; **La**=Labour)	

Presidents of the U.S.

George Washington	1789-1797	James A. Garfield	March 4, 1881- September 19, 1881
John Adams	1797-1801	Chester A. Arthur	1881-1885
Thomas Jefferson	1801-1805, 1805-1809	Grover Cleveland	1885-1889
James Madison	1809-1813, 1813-1817	Benjamin Harrison	1889-1893
James Monroe	1817-1825	Grover Cleveland	1893-1897
John Quincy Adams	1825-1829	William McKinley	1897-1901, March 4, 1901- September 14, 1901
Andrew Jackson	1829-1833, 1833-1837	Theodore Roosevelt	1901-1905, 1905-1909
Martin Van Buren	1837-1841	William H. Taft	1909-1913
William Henry Harrison	March 4, 1841- April 4, 1841	Woodrow Wilson	1913-1921
John Tyler	1841-1845	Warren G. Harding	1921-1923
James K. Polk	1845-1849	Calvin Coolidge	1923-1925, 1925-1929
Zachary Taylor	1849-1850	Herbert C. Hoover	1929-1933
Millard Fillmore	1850-1853	Franklin D. Roosevelt	1933-1941,1941-1945, January 20, 1945-April 12,1945
Franklin Pierce	1853-1857		
James Buchanan	1857-1861	Harry S. Truman	1945-1949, 1949-1953
Abraham Lincoln	1861-1865, March 4, 1865- April 15, 1865	Dwight D. Eisenhower	1953-1961
		John F. Kennedy	1961-1963
Andrew Johnson	1865-1869	Lyndon B. Johnson	1963-1965, 1965-1969
Ulysses S. Grant	1869-1873, 1873-1877	Richard M. Nixon	1969-1973, 1973-1974
Rutherford B. Hayes	1877-1881		

(Continued on next page)

Presidents of the U.S. *(continued)*

Gerald R. Ford	1974-1977
Jimmy (James Earl) Carter	1977-1981
Ronald Reagan	1981-1985, 1985-1989
George Bush	1989-1993
Bill Clinton	1993-1997, 1997-

Prime Ministers of Canada

Sir John A. MacDonald	1867-1873, 1878-1891
Alexander Mackenzie	1873-1878
Sir John J. C. Abbott	1891-1892
Sir John S. D. Thompson	1892-1894
Sir Mackenzie Bowell	1894-1896
Sir Charles Tupper	1896
Sir Wilfrid Laurier	1896-1911
Sir Robert L. Borden	1911-1920
Arthur Meighen	1920-1921
W. L. Mackenzie King	1921-1930, 1935-1948
R. B. Bennett	1930-1935
Louis St. Laurent	1948-1957
John G. Diefenbaker	1957-1963
Lester B. Pearson	1963-1968
Pierre Elliott Trudeau	1968-1979, 1980-1984
Joe Clark	1979-1980
John Turner	1984
Brian Mulroney	1984-1993
Kim Campbell	1993
Jean Chrétien	1993-

Additional Reading

The reader may wish to consult the *National Geographic Index* for related books and articles. The following books may be of special interest.

Barraclough, Geoffrey, ed. *The Times Atlas of World History*

Farah, Mounir, et al. *The Human Experience*

Grun, Bernard. *The Timetables of History*

The Kingfisher Illustrated History of the World

McNeill, William H. *A World History*

Parker, Geoffrey, ed. *The Times Illustrated History of the World*

Somerset Fry, Plantagenet. *The Dorling Kindersley History of the World*

Wright, Esmond and Kenneth M. Stampp, eds. *The Times Illustrated History of the World*

Consultant's Note

Chief consultant for this book, David A. Bell holds an associate professorship in the Johns Hopkins University Department of History, in Baltimore, Maryland. After completing his A.B. in History and Literature *magna cum laude* at Harvard University, Bell earned his M.A. and Ph.D. at Princeton University in history and taught at Yale University before assuming his post at Johns Hopkins.

In 1995 Bell was awarded the Pinkney Prize by the Society for French Historical Studies for the best book of 1994 in French history–*Lawyers and Citizens: The Making of a Political Elite in Old Regime France,* published by Oxford University Press. In addition, Bell has authored other books and numerous academic articles.

Illustrations Credits

Abbreviations
NG = National Geographic
NGP = National Geographic Photographer
NGS = National Geographic Staff

DUST JACKET "Map of Discovery of the Eastern Hemisphere", mural painted by N. C. Wyeth for Society headquarters in 1927. Autochrome by Charles Martin.

COVER STAMPING and page 1. Drawing of a compass rose, ca A.D. 1375: from cartographic archives of the Society.

INTRODUCTION
2-3 Kenneth Garrett. 4-5 Michael S. Yamashita. 6-7 Sisse Brimberg. 8 Aldus Archive. 9 Original NASA photograph printed from digital image, c. Corbis. 10-11 "Journey of the Magi" 1459 by Benozzo Gozzoli from a fresco in the Medici-Riccardi Palace, Florence: SCALA/ART RESOURCE, N.Y.

CHAPTER I. THE ANCIENT WORLD
12 (upper left) David Brill. 12 (upper center) Chris Johns, NGP. 12 (upper right) Antony Edwards/THE IMAGE BANK. 12 (lower left) Gordon Donkin, National Library of Australia. 12 (lower center) Kenneth Garrett. 12 (lower right) Vatican Museums. 13 (upper left) Georg Gerster. 13 (upper right) Metropolitan Museum of Art, on loan from the Shaanxi Provincial Museum, People's Republic of China: Victor R. Boswell, Jr. 13 (lower left) O. Louis Mazzatenta. 13 (lower right) detail from "Conquest of Kaliya," ca1760, Metropolitan Museum of Art, New York. 15-17 Jean-Marie Chauvet/SYGMA. 18 Kenneth Garrett. 18-19 Jay H. Matternes. 19 Gordon Donkin, National Library of Australia. 20 David Brill. 21 (left) Musée des Antiquités Nationales, Saint-Germain-En-Laye, France: Erich Lessing/MAGNUM. 21 (right) from Malta, Siberia, at the Hermitage Museum: Sisse Brimberg. 22 Columbia University, New York: Lee Boltin. 22-23 Jack Unruh. 23 Musée des Antiquités Nationales, Saint-Germain-En-Laye, France: Victor R. Boswell, Jr. 24 James P. Blair. 25 Sisse Brimberg. 26-27 Kenneth Garrett. 28 Steve McCurry. 28-29 NG Maps. 29 Georg Gerster. 30 Lynn Abercrombie. 31 British Museum: Victor R. Boswell, Jr. 32-33 Antony Edwards/THE IMAGE BANK. 34 (left) Egyptian Museum, Cairo: Victor R. Boswell, Jr. 34 (right) E. Streichan/SUPERSTOCK. 35 (upper) David Sailors/THE STOCK MARKET. 35 (lower left) O. Louis Mazzatenta. 35 (right) C.F. Payne. 36 (upper) Museo Nacional de Antropologia, Mexico City: David Brill. 36 (lower) and 37 (upper) Kenneth Garrett. 37 (lower) Chris Johns, NGP. 38-39 "Conquest of Kaliyah", ca 1760, Metropolitan Museum of Art, New York. 39 Henry Wilson. 40 (left) John C. Trever. 40 (right) National Museum, Israel. 41 Fred Anderegg. 42 (upper) Metropolitan Museum of Art, New York, on loan from the Shaanxi Provincial Museum, People's Republic of China: Victor R. Boswell, Jr. 42 (lower) Art Institute of Chicago: Fred Ward/BLACK STAR. 43 (upper left) Academic Sinica, Taipei, Taiwan: Wan-Go H.C. Weng. 43 (lower left) Nelson-Atkins Museum of Art, Nelson Fund, Kansas City, Missouri: Fred Ward/BLACK STAR. 43 (right) Metropolitan Museum of Art, New York, on loan from the Historical Museum, Beijing, People's Republic of China: Victor R. Boswell, Jr. 44 (left) Ukraine Historic Treasures Museum, Kiev: Sisse Brimberg. 44 (right) NG Maps. 45 (left) Museum of Fine Arts, Boston: Enrico Ferorelli. 45 (right) Enrico Ferorelli. 46 (upper) Ekdotike Athenon S.A. National Archaeological Museum, Athens. 46 (lower left) National Archaeological Museum, Athens: Gordon W. Gahan. 46-47 Kevin Fleming. 47 Vatican Museums. 48 Antikenmuseum, Staatliche Museen Preussischer Kulturbesitz, Berlin, Germany: Victor R. Boswell Jr. 48-49 Ekdotike Athenon S.A., National Archaeological Museum, Athens. 49 Musée du Louvre, Paris: Kevin Fleming.

CHAPTER II. THE CLASSICAL AGE
50 (upper left) Richard Alexander Cooke III. 50 (upper right) Musée du Louvre, Paris: Jonathan Blair. 50 (center left) Martha Cooper/PETER ARNOLD, INC. 50 (center right) British Museum London: Werner Forman Archive. 50 (lower) Metropolitan Museum of Art, N.Y.: Nathan Benn. 51 (upper left) Museo Nazionale, Naples: American Heritage. 51 (upper right) D.E. Cox/TONY STONE IMAGES. 51 (lower left) Nicolas Thibaut/EXPLORER. 51 (lower center) H.Kanus/SUPERSTOCK. 51 (lower right) Horyuji, Nara/Shogakukan. 53 Archaeological Museum, Syracuse: Sisse Brimberg. 54-55 Sisse Brimberg. 56 (left) Letrone Papyrus, Musée du Louvre, Paris: Victor R. Bowell, Jr. 56 (right) The National Museum, Athens: Philip Harrington. 57 James P. Blair. 58-59 NG Maps. 60-61 James M. Gurney. 62 Brian Brake/PHOTO RESEARCHERS, INC. 63 (upper) Musée du Louvre, Paris: Jonathan Blair. 63 (lower) Blaine Harrington. 64 (upper) NG Maps. 64 (inset) from Pompeii, National Archaeological Museum: O. Louis Mazzatenta. 64-65 Museum of Antiquities in Tripoli, Libya: Pierre Belzeaux/RAPHO. 65 Alan Becker/THE IMAGE BANK. 66-67 Andre Durenceau. 68 Roland and Sabrina Michaud. 68-69 Georg Gerster/PHOTO RESEARCHERS, INC. 71 Museo Nazionale, Naples: American Heritage. 72 British Museum, London: Werner Forman Archive. 73 (upper) Spyros Tsavdaroglou, Archaeological Museum of Thessaloniki Greece, permission of Dr. Manolis Andronicos. 73 (lower) Leonid Bogdanov and Vladimir Terebenin. 74 (left and right) O. Louis Mazzatenta. 75 (upper) NG Maps. 75 (lower) Reza. 76-77 D.E. Cox/TONY STONE IMAGES. 77 Horyuji,Nara/Shogakukan. 78 James P. Blair. 78-79 H.Kanus/SUPERSTOCK. 79 Archaeological Museum, Sarnath, India: Kodansha, Ltd. 80-81 Reza. 82-83 Richard Alexander Cooke III. 83 Peabody Museum, Harvard University: Hillel Burger. 84 (left) Loren McIntyre. 84 (right) Loren McIntyre/WOODFIN CAMP AND ASSOCIATES. 85 Metropolitan Museum of Art, N.Y.: Nathan Benn. 86 Enrico Ferorelli. 87 David Alan Harvey. 88 NG Maps. 89 Martha Cooper/PETER ARNOLD, INC. 90 James L. Stanfield. 91 Nicolas Thibaut/EXPLORER. 92 Andre Held/Sonia Halliday Photographs. 92-93 Mosaic from Hippo Regius, 3rd cent. A.D., Archaeological Museum of Hippo, Bône, Algeria: Pierre Belzeaux/RAPHO.

CHAPTER III. ISOLATED REALMS
94 (upper left) painting by Issho Yada, Mongolian Invasion Memorial Museum, Japan: Koji Nakamura. 94 (upper center) Tor Eigeland. 94 (upper right) Aldus Archive. 94 (lower left) "The Alliance of Cortés" by Desiderio Hernandez Xochitiotzin: Guillermo Aldana E. 94 (lower right) Bibliothèque Centrale de la Musée Nationale d'Histoire Naturelle: Jacques L'Hoir. 95 (top left) 14th cent. French miniature in Musée Goya, Castres, France: GIRAUDON/ART RESOURCE, N.Y. 95 (upper right) "Emperor Ming-Huang's Journey to Shu," Tang Dynasty, National Palace Museum, Taipei, Taiwan. 95 (center left) Österreichische Nationalbibliothek, Vienna. 95 (center right) National Palace Museum, Taiwan: Wan-Go H.C. Weng. 95 (lower left) James L. Stanfield. 95 (lower right) Bruno Barbey/MAGNUM. 97 Bibliothèque Nationale, Paris. 98-99 Peter Essick. 100-101 James L. Stanfield. 102-103 NG Maps. 104 Bibliotheca Nacional, Madrid. 105 Jean-Leon Huens. 106 Sonia Halliday Photographs. 107 Mehmet Biber. 108 (upper) Bob Sacha. 108 (lower) James L. Stanfield. 109 (left) Tor Eigeland. 109 (right) Annie Griffiths Belt. 110 Bruno Barbey/MAGNUM. 111 (left) Diagrams by Susan Sanford and Beth Collins. 111 (right) Thomas J. Abercrombie. 112 NG Maps. 112-113 Musée Guimet, Paris. 114 NG Maps. 115 (upper) "Emperor Ming-Huang's Journey to Shu," Tang Dynasty, National Palace Museum, Taipei, Taiwan. 115 (lower) Norman Kerr. 116 (upper) Qing Dynasty, 17th cent. Museum of Fine Arts, Boston, Charles B. Hoyt Collection. 116 (lower) NG Maps. 117 Qing Dynasty. 17th cent. watercolor on silk, Bibliothèque Nationale, Paris: GIRAUDON/ART RESOURCE,N.Y. 118 Bruno Barbey/MAGNUM. 119 (upper) Victor R. Boswell, Jr. 119 (lower) Georg Gerster. 120 Bibliothèque Centrale de la Musée Nationale d'Histoire Naturelle: Jacques L'Hoir. 121 James L. Stanfield. 122 National Palace Museum, Taiwan: Wan-Go H.C. Weng. 123 (upper) Illustration from an Indian manuscript ca 1600, India Office Library, British Library. 123 (lower) James L. Stanfield. 124 National Museum of Mongolian History, Ulaan Baatar: James L. Stanfield. 124-125 NG Maps. 125 National Palace Museum, Taiwan. 126 (upper left) Bibliothèque Nationale, Paris. 126 (upper right) Bodleian Library, Oxford. 126 (lower) and 127 Paintings by Issho Yada, Mongolian Invasion Memorial Museum, Japan: Koji Nakamura. 128 Aldus Archive. 129 By special permission of the City of Bayeux: Milton A. Ford and Victor R. Boswell, Jr. 130 (upper) 14th cent. French miniature in Musée Goya, Castres, France: GIRAUDON/ART RESOURCE, N.Y. 130 (lower) Bibliothèque Nationale, Paris. 131 (left) From Flemish calendar, British Museum. 131 (right) Bayerische Staatsbibliothek, Munich: Max Hirmer. 132 "Le Livre de la Chasse," 15th cent. Bibliothèque Nationale, Paris. 133 The labors of October from "Les Très Riches Heures:" James L. Stanfield. 134 (upper) British Library, London. 134 (lower left and right) Istituto Rizzoli, Bologna: Albert Moldvay. 134-135 NG Maps. 135 15th cent. French illumination from "Renaud de Montauban," Bibliothèque de L'Arsenal, Paris: Philippe Brosse. 136 Tom Lovell. 138 Bibliothèque Nationale, Paris. 138-139 Österreichische Nationalbibliothek, Vienna. 140 Peter Essick. 141 Bibliothèque Nationale, Paris. 142 15th cent. miniature, Bibliothèque Nationale, Paris. 142-143 15th cent. miniature from Froissart's "Chronicles," Bibliothèque Nationale, Paris. 143 15th cent. Flemish miniature, British Museum. 144 (left) British Museum: Lee Boltin. 144 (right) Bodleian Library. 145 Stuart Franklin. 146 16th century Aztec Codex Tudela: Tor Eigeland. 147 "The Alliance of Cortés" by Desiderio Hernandez Xochitiotzin: Guillermo Aldana E.

CHAPTER IV. NEW LINKS AND CONTACTS
148 (upper left) Fukui Asahid Co. Ltd. 148 (upper center) National Gallery of Canada, Ottawa. 149 (upper right) Richard Schlecht. 148 (lower left) David Doubilet. 148 (lower center) Musée de l'Homme, Paris. 148 (lower right) Bob Sacha. 149 (upper) Cary Wolinsky. 149 (center left) the "Ermine Portrait" by Nicholas Hilliard, courtesy the Marquess of Salisbury. 149 (center) Magyar Nemzeti Müzeum, Budapest. 149 (center right) Marc Riboud. 149 (lower left) miniature from 14th cent. edition of Marco Polo's "Les Livres des Merveilles," Bibliothèque Nationale, Paris. 149 (lower right) Metropolitan Museum of Art, N.Y., gift of Mrs. Albert Blum. 151 ca 1530, Harrach Collection, Schloss Rohrau, Austria. 152-153 "Birth of Venus" by Sandro Botticelli: SCALA/ART RESOURCE, N.Y. 154-155 By Ambrogio Lorenzetti, 1338, in Siena's Palazzo Publico: SCALA/ART RESOURCE, N.Y. 156 (upper) NG Maps. 156 (lower) Detail from "Works of Mercy," school of Domenico Ghirlandaio, ca 1480 in San Martino degli Buonuomini, Florence: SCALA/ART RESOURCE, N.Y. 157 Detail from "Carta della Catena" by an unknown artist ca 1490 in the Museo Dell' Opera del Duomo, Florence: SCALA/ART RESOURCE, N.Y. 158 (upper) National Gallery, London. 158 (lower) Corbis-Bettmann. 159 (left) Royal Library, Windsor. 159 (right) Biblioteca Nazionale, Florence: SCALA/ART RESOURCE, N.Y. 160 (all) Bibliothèque Nationale, Paris. 161 (upper) "The Last Judgement": Victor R. Boswell, Jr. 161 (lower) "Carrousel for Queen Christina" by Filippo Lauri and Filippo Gagliardi, in the Museo di Roma: Robert Emmett Bright/RAPHO. 162 Detail from a Pinturicchio painting, Vatican Museums. 163 Allen Carroll, NGS. 164 (upper) "A l'Egide de Minerve", Musée des Beaux Arts, Dijon, France: Erich Lessing/ART RESOURCE, N.Y. 164 (lower) The Granger Collection, N.Y. 166 (upper) Metropolitan Museum of Art, N.Y. 166 (lower) Bob Sacha. 167 Adam Woolfitt. 168 (upper left) Detail of portrait, artist unknown, Museo de Arte Moderno, Madrid: Bruce Dale. 168 (upper right) Adam Woolfitt. 168 (lower) Björn Landström. 169 National Gallery of Canada, Ottawa. 170 "Discovery of the Hudson by Hendrick Hudson" by Albert Bierstadt: Architect of the U.S. Capitol. 171 (upper) Nuttall Codex: George E. Stuart, NGS. 171 (lower) "Ships Trading in the East," by H.C. Vroom, 1614: National Maritime Museum. 172 (upper) Gold Museum, Bogotá: Adam Woolfitt. 172 (lower left) Metropolitan Museum of Art, N.Y., gift of Mrs. Albert Blum. 172 (lower right) British Museum. 173 (upper) Miniature from 14th cent. edition of Marco Polo's "Les Livres des Merveilles": Bibliothèque Nationale, Paris. 173 (lower) David Doubilet. 174 Musée Conde, Chantilly: GIRAUDON/ART RESOURCE, N.Y. 175 (left) Corbis-Bettman. 175 (right) Jean-Leon Huens. 176-177 "The Defeat of the Armada" by P. J. de Loutherbourg, 1796, on loan to the Royal Hospital School Suffolk, National Martime Museum, Greenwich, England. 177 The Granger Collection, N.Y. 178 (upper) detail, Bibliothèque Nationale, Paris. 178 (lower) James L. Stanfield. 178-179 NG Maps. 179 (left) Museum für Kunst und Gewerbe Hamburg, photographed on exhibit at the National Gallery of Art, Washington, D.C.: James L. Stanfield. 179 (right) James L. Stanfield. 180 (upper) Bibliothèque de l'Histoire du Protestantisme, Paris: GIRAUDON/ART RESOURCE, N.Y. 180 (lower left) The Granger Collection, N.Y. 180 (lower right) Adam Woolfitt. 181 GIRAUDON/ART RESOURCE, N.Y. 182 (left) British Museum. 182 (upper right and lower right) National Portrait Gallery, London. 183 British Museum. 184 (left) by Hans Holbein the Younger: SCALA/ART RESOURCE, N.Y. 184 (center) The Folger

Nicholas Hilliard, courtesy Marquess of Salibury. 185 Galleria d'Arte Moderna, Florence: ART RESOURCE, N.Y. 187 copyright reserved. Reproduced by gracious permission of Her Majesty Queen Elizabeth II. 188-189 (all) The Granger Collection, N.Y. 190 (left) The Granger Collection, N.Y. 190 (right) Musée des Beaux Arts, Lille, France: GIRAUDON/ART RESOURCE, N.Y. 190-191 by Andrea Vincentino ca 1585, in the Palazzo Ducale, Venice: SCALA/ART RESOURCE, N.Y. 191 Attributed to Titian: GIRAUDON/ART RESOURCE, N.Y. 192 Archive Photos. 193 Etching by J. Mulder, ca1690, Nederlands Scheepvaart Museum, Amsterdam. 194 (upper) "The Lace-Maker" by Jan Vermeer: The Granger Collection, N.Y. 194 (lower) Sisse Brimberg. 195 "The Painter and His Model as Klio" by Jan Vermeer, Kunsthistorisches Museum, Gemaeldegalerie, Vienna, Austria: Erich Lessing/ART RESOURCE, N.Y. 196-197 NG Maps. 197 (all) Details from miniatures: Roland and Sabrina Michaud. 198 (left) National Museum, New Delhi. 198 (right) Roland Michaud. 199 (left) The Granger Collection, N.Y. 199 (right) Pete Turner/THE IMAGE BANK. 200 Roland Michaud. 201 BRIDGEMAN/ART RESOURCE, N.Y. 202 (left) Magyar Nemzeti Mùzeum, Budapest. 202 (right) Topkapi Palace Museum: James L. Stanfield. 203 NG Maps. 204 Historisches Museum der Stadt Wien, Austria: James L. Stanfield. 205 (upper) Topkapi Palace Museum: James L. Stanfield. 205 (lower) James L. Stanfield. 206-207 Marc Riboud. 208 Victoria and Albert Museum, London. 209 J.C. Revy and P.H. Bourseiller, Le Figaro. 210 Metropolitan Museum of Art, N.Y. 211 Galen Rowell/Mountain Light. 212 Fukui Asahido Co. Ltd. 212-213 Christopher Knight. 214 (upper) The Granger Collection, N.Y. 214 (lower) A fresco detail at Cuernavaca Cathedral in Mexico: Sisse Brimberg. 215 (left) The Granger Collection, N.Y. 215 (right) George F. Mobley. 216-217 Scott Rutherford. 217 George F. Mobley. 218 and 219 (upper) Stuart Franklin/MAGNUM. 219 (lower) Musée de l'Homme, Paris. 220 (upper) Richard Schlecht. 220 (lower) NG Maps. 221 NG Maps. 222 "The Cossacks of Zaporozje" by Ilya Repin, Russian State Museum, St. Petersburg: SCALA/ART RESOURCE, N.Y. 223 "Ivan the Terrible with the Body of His Son" by Ilya Repin, Galleria Statale Tret 'Jakov, Moscow: ART RESOURCE, N.Y. 224 (both) Cary Wolinsky/STOCK BOSTON. 225 (left) Gordon W. Gahan. 225 (right) Cary Wolinsky. 226 Steve Raymer.

CHAPTER V. QUICKENING CHANGE

228 (upper left) Detail from hand colored engraving by Samuel Middiman and John Hall after Webber, "An Offering before Capt. Cook, in the Sandwich Islands," Mitchell Library, Sydney. 228 (upper center) L.W. Harris. 228 (upper right) American Antiquarian Society. 228 (lower left) Mitchell Library, Sydney. 228 (lower right) Herbert Tauss. 229 (upper left) Science Museum, London. 229 (upper right) National Army Museum, London. 229 (center) from "The Inauguration of the Suez Canal" by Marius Fontaine, illustration by M. Riou: Jonathan Blair. 229 (lower left) from Nathaniel Isaac's "Travels and Adventures in Eastern Africa," 1836, South African Library. 229 (lower center) Hulton Getty Picture Collection/TONY STONE IMAGES. 229 (lower right) Auckland Institute and Museum: Brian Brake/PHOTO RESEARCHERS, INC. 231 Bibliothèque Nationale, Paris. 232-233 by William Walcutt, 1864, collection of Gilbert Darlington: Leo Choplin/BLACK STAR. 234 Heeresgeschichtliches Museum, Vienna, Austria: Erich Lessing/ART RESOURCE, N.Y. 235 Archive Photos. 236 "Le Serment du Jeu de Paume," attributed to Jacques-Louis David, Musée National du Château de Versailles: Photo Bulloz. 237 The Granger Collection, N.Y. 238 Bibliothèque Nationale, Paris: GIRAUDON/ART RESOURCE, N.Y. 239 (upper) Archive Photos. 239 (lower) Archive Photos/Illustrated London News. 240 "The Last Farewells of Louis XVI to His Family," by Jean-Jacques Hauer, Musée Carnavalet, Paris: James L. Stanfield. 240-241 "Capture of the Bastille," Musée Carnavalet, Paris: James L. Stanfield. 242 Bibliothèque Nationale, Paris. 243 (upper) Painting by Paul Delaroche, Musée de l'Armée, Paris. 243 (lower) From the book "Description de L'Egypt," France, Commission des Monuments d'Egypt, Paris, 1809-1828, vol.V, plate 8. 244-245 NG Maps. 245 Felix Philippoteaux, Victoria and Albert Museum, London. 246 Progress of Cotton No.4, Carding, Yale University Art Gallery, Mabel Brady Garvan Collection. 247 Blaine Harrington. 248-249 The Granger Collection, N.Y. 249 Engraving from Champlain's "Voyages and Discoveries, 1615-1618," New York Public Library. 250 (left) American Antiquarian Society. 250 (right) Virginia Historical Society: George Cook. 251 Painting "Drafting of the Declaration of Independence" by J.L.G. Ferris, Smithsonian Institution. 252 (upper) Detail of painting by John Ward Dunsmore, courtesy, Sons of the Revolution, Fraunces Tavern, N. Y. 252 (lower) Painting by Thomas Birch, U.S. Naval Academy Museum. 253 James P. Blair. 254 Herbert Tauss. 255 Watercolor portrait of Bolívar by José María Espinosa ca 1828, Museo Nacional, Bogotá, Colombia. 256 Chicago Historical Society: Eyre Crowe. 257 (left and right) Library of Congress. 258 (left) Joel Sartore. 258 (right) painting by Robert Lindneux, 1942, Woolaroc Museum, Bartlesville, Oklahoma. 259-260 The Granger Collection, N.Y. 261 National Army Museum, London. 262 Private Collection. 263 (left) "Commodore Matthew C. Perry's First Landing in Japan at Kurihama in 1853" by Gessan Ogata, ca 1950, U.S. Naval Academy Museum, Annapolis, Md. 263 (right) Yochikazu Ichikowa, ca 1853, Library of Congress. 265 from "The Inauguration of the Suez Canal" by Marius Fontaine, illustration by M. Riou: Jonathan Blair. 266-267 Illustrated London News Picture Library. 267 Hulton Getty Picture Collection/TONY STONE IMAGES. 268 (left) Courtesy Mrs. Dorothy Henry, Institution of British Engineers, London. 268 (upper right) Corbis-Bettmann. 268 (lower right) Detail, National Museums and Galleries on Merseyside, Walker Art Gallery. 269 (upper left) Science Museum, London. 269 (upper right) Analytical Laboratory, Smithsonian: Breton Littlehales. 269 (lower left) The Granger Collection, N.Y. 269 (lower right) National Museum of American History: Bill Ballenberg. 270 (left) Roger-Viollet, Paris. 270 (right) "Pasteur dans son Laboratoire," by Albert Edelfelt, 1884, Musée Pasteur, Institut Pasteur. 271 (left) Brown Brothers. 271 (right) Georg Gerster. 272 (both) Sam Abell, NGP. 273 Corbis-Bettmann. 274 (left) Painting by John Trumbull, Yale University Art Gallery, John Hill Morgan Fund: Linda Bartlett. 274 (right) The Bakken, Minneapolis. 275 (upper) Watercolor by Harriet Moore, 1852, The Royal Institution, London. 275 (lower) U.S. Department of the Interior, National Park Service, Edison National Historic Site. 276 (upper) L.W. Harris. 276 (center) Mercedes-Benz of North America. 276 (lower) Herman Decker, Museum of Art, Rhode Island School of Design. 277 (upper) Morris Rosenfeld, Library of Congress. 277 (lower) Judge, 1899, Library of Congress. 278 (left) Beethoven House, Bonn, Germany: Erich Lessing/ART RESOURCE, N.Y. 278 (right) The Granger Collection, N.Y. 279

(left) Trustess of the Dickens House. 279 (right) The Phillips Collection, Washington, D.C. 280 Ian Berry/MAGNUM. 281 (upper) "Plan of the City of Washington," as adapted by Andrew Ellicott, based on Samuel Hill engraving, 1792, Library of Congress and Geography and Map Division: Pat Lanza Field. 281 (lower) Michael Holford. 282 (left) "Battle of Sebastopol," Tryptich, left panel, by Jean Charles Langlois, after 1855, Musée des Beaux-Arts, Caen, France: GIRAUDON/ART RESOURCE, N.Y. 282 (right) The Granger Collection, N.Y. 283 Chicago Historical Society. 284-285 Paintings by George S. Gaadt, calligraphy by Paul M. Breeden, compiled by John R. Treiber, National Geographic Art Division. 285 Donald A. Mackay. 286 (upper) from Nathaniel Isaac's "Travels and Adventures in Eastern Africa," 1836, South African Library. 286 (lower) Volkmar Wentzel. 287 (left) Detail, Blaauwkrantz, by Thomas Baines, ca 1854, Africana Museum, Johannesburg. 287 (right) Sam Wagstaff. 288 The Granger Collection, N.Y. 289 NG Maps. 290 Royal Geographical Society. 290-291 Kevin Schafer/PETER ARNOLD INC. 291 British Library. 292 (upper) Mitchell Library, Sydney. 292 (lower) Grenville Turner/WILDLIGHT. 293 (upper) Jean-Paul Ferrero/AUSCAPE. 293 (lower) Aquatint after R. Dodd, ca 1790, National Martime Museum, Greenwich, England. 294-295 Belinda Wright. 296 (upper) Auckland Institute and Museum: Brian Brake/PHOTO RESEARCHERS. 296 (lower) Alexander Turnbull Library, Wellington. 297 Warren Jacobs. 298 Radio Times Hulton Picture Library. 298-299 Terry Hann/COMMUNICATE NEW ZEALAND. 300 (upper) Engraving, hand colored, by Samuel Middiman and John Hall after Webber, "An Offering Before Capt. Cook, in the Sandwich Islands," Mitchell Library, Sydney. 300 (lower) Bernice P. Bishop Museum. 301 Bob Sacha.

CHAPTER VI. VANISHING EMPIRES, NEW CHALLENGES

302 (upper left) M. Simpson/FPG INTERNATIONAL. 302 (upper center) NASA. 302 (upper right) UPI/Corbis-Bettmann. 302 (lower left) BLACK STAR. 302 (lower center) U.S. Air Force/Defense Nuclear Agency. 302 (lower right) Michael Melford. 303 (upper left) Henry Ford Museum and Greenfield Village. 303 (upper right) Dick Durrance II. 303 (lower left) Jim Brandenburg. 303 (lower center) Joel Sartore. 303 (lower right) Jodi Cobb, NGP. 305 Historical Pictures/Stock Montage. 306-307 Televisions and VCRs used for this multiple exposure are courtesy of Mitsubishi Electric America: Louis Psihoyos. 308-309 Courtesy Glen Ryce. 308 Michael O'Brien. 309 Philip Quirk/WILDLIGHT PHOTO AGENCY. 310 (left) C.P. Lewis. 310 (right) French National Railroad. 311 (upper left) Henry Ford Museum and Greenfield Village. 311 (upper right) From May 1937 Esquire Magazine, Library of Congress: Victor R. Boswell, Jr. 311 (lower) George Steinmetz. 312 Archive Photos. 313 Paul A. Ludwig. 314 Dean Conger. 315 (left) Jodi Cobb, NGP. 315 (right) Charlie Cole/SIPA PRESS. 316-317 (all) Michael S. Yamashita. 318 National Archives. 319 Corbis-Bettmann. 320 Lenin Museum Archive, Moscow. 321 (left) Dick Durrance II. 321 (right) Lenin Museum Archive. 322-323 Robert Azzi, WOODFIN CAMP AND ASSOCIATES. 324 BLACK STAR. 325 (left) Peter Menzel. 325 (right) Roger H. Ressmeyer. 326 (left) Dominique Sarraute/THE IMAGE BANK. 326 (right) Charles O'Rear/WEST LIGHT. 327 (upper) Thomas Mayer/BLACK STAR. 327 (lower) Roger H. Ressmeyer. 328 Dorothea Lang, The Oakland Museum. 329 (upper) UPI/Corbis-Bettmann. 329 (lower) Associated Press, London. 330 (upper) National Museum of American History: Bill Ballenberg. 330 (lower) MGM/Kobal Collection. 331 (upper) RCA. 331 (lower) Louie Psihoyos. 332 Arthur Szyk for Esquire Magazine February 1942, Esquire Associates. 333 UPI/Corbis-Bettmann. 334-335 U.S. Navy from National Archives. 336 U.S. Air Force/Defense Nuclear Agency. 337 (left) Danny Lehman. 337 (right) UPI/Corbis-Bettmann. 338 91st Bomb Group (H) Memorial Association, Inc. 339 Louie Psihoyos. 340 The Hagley Museum and Library. 341 (upper left, center, and right) Hank Morgan/PHOTO RESEARCHERS. 341 (lower left) James L. Amos. 341 (lower right) Dan McCoy, Rainbow. 342 The Computer Museum. 343 M. Simpson/FPG INTERNATIONAL. 344 Hulton Getty Picture Collection/TONY STONE IMAGES. 344-345 Sarah Leen. 346 (left) Emory Kristof. 346 (right) Cotton Coulson. 347 Walter Sanders/LIFE Magazine, Time, Inc. 348 Joanna B. Pinneo. 349 Charles Harbutt/MAGNUM. 350 Joel Sartore. 351 Alexandra Avakian. 352 James Nachtwey. 353 James P. Blair. 354 Jim Brandenburg. 356 (left) Leroy Woodson, Jr. 356 (right) Bruce Dale. 357 Steve McCurry/MAGNUM. 358 (upper) Cornell Capa/MAGNUM. 358 (lower) Jose Azel. 359 Fred Ward/BLACK STAR. 361 David Douglas Duncan. 362 Cary Wolinsky/STOCK BOSTON. 363 (upper) Bernie Boston. 363 (lower) Larry Burrows/LIFE Magazine, Time, Inc. 364 UPI/Corbis-Bettmann. 365 Louie Psihoyos. 366 (left) Robert B. Goodman. 366 (right) NASA. 367 (upper) NASA. 367 (lower) Robert Williams and the Hubble Deep Field Team and NASA. 368-369 (all) NASA. 370 (left) Michael Coyne/THE IMAGE BANK. 370 (right) Steve McCurry/MAGNUM. 371 Mohsen Shandiz/SYGMA. 372 (upper) Larry C. Price. 372 (lower) Anthony Suau/BLACK STAR. 374 (upper) Joanna B. Pinneo. 374 (lower) Jodi Cobb, NGP. 375 Ed Kashi. 376 (upper) Joel Sartore. 376 (lower) Grant V. Faint/THE IMAGE BANK. 377 (upper) Bob Krist. 377 (lower) Ron Sanford/BLACK STAR. 378 Joel Sartore. 379 (upper) Michael Melford. 379 (lower) Rick Rickman. 380-381 Paul Scowen and NASA.

Picture credits for back of dust jacket. Credits run from left to right.

1. L.W. Harris. 2. National Gallery of Art, Ottawa. 3. Musée du Louvre, Paris: Jonathan Blair. 4. National Palace Museum, Taipei, Taiwan. 5. Richard Schlecht. 6. UPI/Corbis-Bettmann. 7. BLACK STAR. 8. D.E. Cox/TONY STONE IMAGES. 9. M.Simpson/FPG International. 10. Auckland Institute and Museum: Brian Brake/PHOTO RESEARCHERS. 11. "The Alliance of Cortés" by Desiderio Hernandez Xochitiotzin: Guillermo Aldana E. 12. Michael Melford. 13 Jim Brandenburg. 14. O. Louis Mazzatenta. 15. Detail from "The Conquest of Kaliya," Metropolitan Museum of Art, N.Y. 16. Herbert Tauss. 17. NASA. 18. Gordon Donkin, National Library of Australia.

Index

Credits

Published by
The National Geographic Society

Reg Murphy
President and Chief Executive Officer
Gilbert M. Grosvenor
Chairman of the Board
Nina D. Hoffman
Senior Vice President

Prepared by the Book Division
William R. Gray
Vice President and Director
Charles Kogod
Assistant Director
Barbara A. Payne
Editorial Director and Managing Editor

Staff for this book
Martha Crawford Christian
Editor

Greta Arnold
Illustrations Editor

Cinda Rose
Art Director

Victoria Garrett Jones
Researcher

Carl Mehler
Senior Map Editor

Patti H. Cass
Illustrations Researcher

Joseph F. Ochlak
Principal Map Researcher
Paul W. F. Bothwell, Margaret Bowen,
Anthony Di Iorio, Mickey Edwards,
Thomas L. Gray, National Geographic
Maps, Tracey M. Wood
Map Research

Jehan Aziz; John S. Ballay;
Mapping Specialists, LTD;
National Geographic Maps;
North Park Studios; Michelle H. Picard;
Martin S. Walz; Louis J. Spirito, *assistant*
Map Production

Carolinda E. Hill
Consulting Editor

Kevin G. Craig
Dale-Marie Herring
Editorial Assistants

Jennifer L. Burke
Illustrations Assistant

Peggy Candore
Staff Assistant

Richard S. Wain
Production Project Manager
Lewis R. Bassford
Production

Manufacturing and Quality Management
George V. White
Director
John T. Dunn
Associate Director
Vincent P. Ryan
Manager
Polly P. Tompkins
Executive Assistant

Deborah E. Patton
Indexer

Acknowledgments

The Book Division wishes to thank the many individuals, groups, and organizations who assisted with this book. In addition, we are especially grateful to the following: Dr. David A. Bell, Johns Hopkins University; Anthony Di Iorio; Professor F. Clark Howell, University of California, Berkeley; and the National Geographic Society Administrative Services, the National Geographic Society Image Collection, the National Geographic Society Indexing Division, and the National Geographic Society Library.

Author's Note

Noel Grove, a member of the National Geographic staff for 25 years, authored 28 bylined articles for the NATIONAL GEOGRAPHIC magazine and contributed chapters to five National Geographic books. He is the author of *Wild Lands for Wildlife: America's National Refuges*. Outside the Geographic, Grove has authored *Preserving Eden* (Abrams) and *Birds of North America* (Hugh Lauter Levin).

Journalism has taken the author to all 50 states in the United States and to more than 60 foreign countries. Grove now freelances out of his home near Middleburg, Virginia, and is editor of *SEJournal*, a quarterly publication for environmental writers.

Library of Congress Cataloging-in-Publication ☐ Data
Grove, Noel.
    National Geographic atlas of world history / by Noel Grove ;
   prepared by the Book Division, National Geographic Society.
        p.   cm.
    Includes bibliographical references and index.
    ISBN 0-7922-7048-7. —ISBN 0-7922-7023-1
   (deluxe ed.). Book
   Division. II. Title. III. Title: Atlas of world history.
   D20.G76 1997

   909—DC21
                             97-28731

                             ☐

Composition for this book by the National Geographic Society Book Division. Printed and bound by R. R. Donnelley & Sons, Willard, Ohio. Color separations by Digital Color Image, Pennsauken, New Jersey. Dust jacket printed by Miken, Inc., Cheektowaga, New York. Paper by Consolidated/Alling & Cory, Willow Grove, Pennsylvania.

Visit the Society's Web site at
www.nationalgeographic.com